THE SEVENTH MUSE

To Elayne –
A fellow Demon and a
good friend.

Bill

THE SEVENTH MUSE

✦

William V. Muse

A MEMOIR

iUniverse, Inc.
New YorkBloomington

The Seventh Muse
A Memoir

iUniverse books may be ordered through booksellers or by contacting:

iUniverse
1663 Liberty Drive
Bloomington, IN 47403
www.iuniverse.com
1-800-Authors (1-800-288-4677)

ISBN: 978-0-595-52864-6 (pbk)
ISBN: 978-0-595-62919-0 (ebk)

Printed in the United States of America

iUniverse rev date: 11/26/08

CONTENTS

The Muse Family Tree

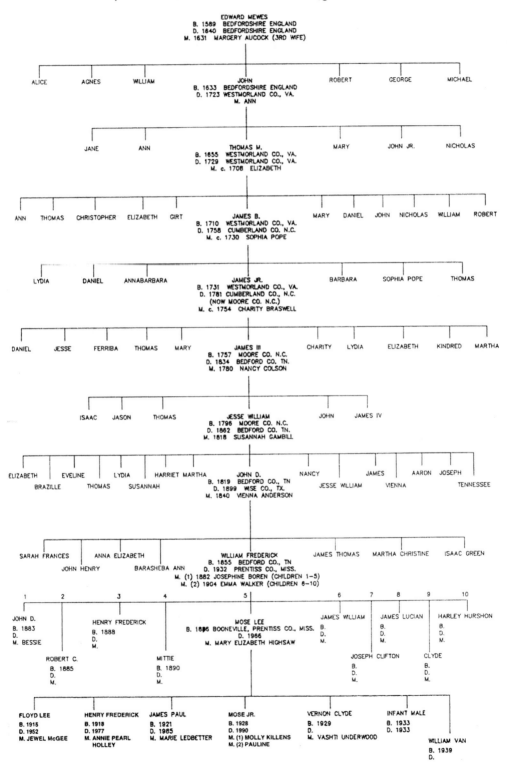

PREFACE

I was born on April 7, 1939, the seventh son of a Pentecostal preacher in rural Mississippi. As a seventh son born on a seventh, I have always felt lucky and have certainly been blessed to have had a long and interesting life, loving parents, a wonderful family, the opportunity to advance to the top of my chosen profession, and great friends from coast to coast.

Sometimes I marvel at how improbable my career achievements must seem. Although I was born into a low income community and educated in schools that are considered inferior by today's standards, I was able to earn a Ph.D. and advance to become President or Chancellor of three major public universities -- the University of Akron, Auburn University, and East Carolina University -- for a period of nearly twenty years. Few of my classmates at the elementary level even made it through high school.

The credit for the strong sense of self-worth and desire for success that I developed rests primarily with my Mother who kept telling me that, "if I was a good boy, worked hard, and did well in school, I would be SOMEBODY." She never explained who "somebody" was, or when I would get there, but I knew it was something that she wanted, so that was enough for me.

Did I ever reach that goal? I am certainly not "somebody" of national stature who has instant name recognition. But I am proud of what I have been able to accomplish in all the communities where I have lived, in the organizations in which I have worked, and in the various dimensions of my life, recognizing that all achievements have resulted from the support and assistance of family, friends, and co-workers.

So this is my story -- and the story of my family. The perceptions and views are my own, but I am grateful to my brother, Clyde, for his help in describing the lives of our father and mother and in verifying other information about our family, especially events that occurred before I was born. Special thanks also goes to my wife, Marlene, and our children—Amy, Ellen, and Van—for reading chapters as they were written and for providing additions and corrections. Additionally, three colleagues who are distinguished authors assisted by reviewing specific chapters: Dr. Wayne Flynt, Distinguished Professor of History at Auburn University; Dr. George Knepper, Distinguished Professor of History at the University of Akron; and Dr. Elizabeth Neeld, author and former Professor of English, Texas A & M University. Dr. John Tallmadge of Cincinnati provided valuable editorial assistance, helping to organize the material and to make the text more readable.

Gratitude is also extended to Dr. David Mathews and Dr. John Dedrick of the Kettering Foundation for their support in allowing me to use some of my time as a Lombard Fellow at the foundation in 2007 to complete this manuscript.

I have written this book so that members of my family, especially my children and grandchildren, will have a better understanding of their roots and the ancestors who preceded them, and so that friends with whom I have worked or interacted at different stages of my life might know the full story. My life has been significantly shaped and deeply enhanced by my family and friends.

William V. Muse
Cincinnati, Ohio
December 2008

CHAPTER 1:
FROM MEWES TO MUSE

I have always liked my name. "Muse" is a four-letter word, easy to spell and easy to pronounce -- or at least I thought so. I have been surprised, however, at the times I have been called "Muss", "Mu-sea", or "Moose". In fact, I had a high school football coach who called me "Moose" so much that my teammates started calling me "Bull Moose", rather than Bill Muse.

I didn't learn about the Muses of Greek mythology until I was in college, but was quite impressed with that sort of "heritage" even though I did not inherit any of their creative talents. That lineage seems to have skipped a generation to my children.

Ancestry was not a topic of great interest or discussion while I was growing up. I never met my Grandfather Muse who died about seven years before I was born. By the time I was born, we had moved away from the community where my Daddy grew up, so I had very little contact with his brothers and sisters. The most impressive thing I remember being told about my ancestors was that my great-grandfather had been a Confederate soldier and had fought in the Battle of Shiloh.

I was in my late 40's before I began to explore my family roots. While I was President of the University of Akron, Roger Ryan was one of my vice-presidents and I discovered that he and his wife, Carolyn, were into genealogical research in a heavy way. Carolyn had a Muse somewhere in her ancestral line, was intrigued as to whether we might be "kin", and offered to do some research for me. I eagerly agreed.

Having left home to attend college and then to pursue a career that took me away from family and the area where I grew up, I was anxious to fill that void with information about my origins. But I wasn't much help; I couldn't even remember my grandfather's name! I did remember that my Daddy had a brother named J.D and a sister named Mittie, both of whom we had visited when I was very young. I also knew that Daddy had a half-brother, Harley, who was still alive, but I had not talked to him in years. Finally, after searching through some family documents, I discovered that my grandfather's name was William Frederick and that he had died in Prentiss County, Mississippi, in 1932.

With those meager clues, the Ryans began research in various libraries with extensive genealogical records. A few weeks later, Carolyn reported that they had traced my line back to Bedford County, Tennessee before the trail went cold. Fortunately, a breakthrough occurred a few weeks later. While they were doing research at a library in Virginia, they met a George Muse of Johnson City, Tennessee, who shared with them information he had on the Muse family tree and told them about the Muse Reunion Association in North Carolina. This group hosted a reunion each year and maintained extensive genealogical data on the Muses. With this linkage, the Ryans were able to trace my ancestry all the way back to Bedfordshire, England.

The Muse Reunion Association publishes a newsletter twice annually and has been the source for much valuable information. I have attended the reunion, which is held on the first Sunday in October in Moore County, North Carolina, on two occasions and was the guest speaker on one occasion. My brother, Clyde, was also the speaker one year. The reunion is usually held in the town of Southern Pines.

The Muse family tree begins with Edward Mewes in Bedfordshire, England, a county about 70 miles north of London. Although the line cannot be clearly established beyond this point because of inadequate records, the English tradition of names that describe one's occupation (e.g., carpenter, sawyer, etc.) suggests that the Mewes may have been caretakers of horse carriages, since the carriage house was often called the Mewes.

Edward Mewes was born in Bedfordshire in 1589 and died there in 1640. He had two daughters and four sons. One of his sons, John, traveled to the English Colonies in 1668 and settled in the northern neck of Virginia in what is now Westmoreland County. The land that he purchased there adjoins the birthplace of George Washington, and has been in continuous possession of someone in the Muse family since September 16, 1668. In 1986, the Muse Reunion Association erected a permanent monument on this site.

Upon arriving in Virginia, John used the Muse spelling, rather than Mewes. The reason for this change is unknown, though it may have been to avoid being typecast as the "caretaker of the carriages." Or, it could have been for clearer spelling or pronunciation. In any case, the spelling "M-u-s-e" has been used ever since.

John was accompanied on his journey to Virginia by two of his brothers, one of whom returned to England a year or so later while the other never married. So, all of the Muse family in America can be traced back to John Muse who raised a family of three girls and three boys and died in Virginia in 1723 at the age of 90.

One of John's sons, Thomas M., spent his entire life in Westmoreland County, Virginia, raising a family of 12. But one of Thomas' sons, James B., migrated to what is now Moore County in central North Carolina, beginning a presence of the Muse family in that area that has continued until this day. One of James' sons, James, Jr., became quite prominent in Moore County (then called Cumberland County), reportedly being one of the leaders in the Battle of Alamance during the Revolutionary War.

His son, James III, moved with his family around 1800 to Tennessee, settling in Bedford County, near the town of Shelbyville, where he died in 1834. My great-great-grandfather, Jesse William, moved with the family and lived in Bedford County until 1862.

In the late 1980's, I had an occasion to visit Bedford County. The University of Akron was playing the University of Tennessee in football and my wife, Marlene, and I traveled with the Ryans down to the game, going a couple of days early so we could do some genealogical work. Through county records in Shelbyville, we were able to locate a farm that had been owned by Jesse William Muse, about three miles west of the town. The property was then vacant and was listed for sale. We discovered a graveyard upon a small knoll under a tree that was over-grown with weeds and looked deserted. Roger and I uncovered the tombstone of Jesse William, which had broken off its base and was partially buried. We dug it out and loaded it into my car. I was not sure how I would explain the tombstone, if the police ever stopped me, but I was not going to leave such a family treasure behind. I also traveled to the real estate office and got all the information about the farm, including the price. It was a beautiful piece of land, surrounded by rolling hills and horse farms, complete with a house and barn.. I thought about buying it, but since we lived so far away, I did not. I have often regretted that I missed this opportunity to preserve a little piece of family history.

Having the tombstone with me may not have been a good omen, since UT "buried" Akron, 52-0, in the football game. But when we got back to Akron, Roger had it cleaned and we discovered that the stone contained quite a bit of script. We learned that it also marked the grave of one of Jesse's sons, Aaron, who had died during the Battle of Shelbyville, fighting for the Union Army. Although a number of other residents in this area had joined the Union troops, other members of Jesse's family were strong supporters of the Confederate cause. Apparently, the split in the family was more than Jesse could handle as he died in 1862, according to his tombstone, of a "broken heart."

Another one of Jesse's sons, John D. (my great-grandfather) left Bedford County in 1860 and moved to Tishomingo County, Mississippi, bringing with him his family which included my grandfather, William Frederick, who had been born in 1855 in Bedford County. John D. was a strong Confederate supporter, becoming a lieutenant in the Confederate Army in Mississippi and was involved in the Battle of Shiloh. John D. moved to Wise County, Texas in 1885 where he died in 1899. William Frederick settled in Prentiss County and it is there that my father, Mose Lee, was born.

I remember well the story that Daddy related to me as I was growing up about my great- grandfather. He owned a big red mare that he brought into battle with him. At this point in the war, many of the Confederate soldiers had to supply their own uniforms, weapons, and other materials. On one march, the troops had to cross a river. John D. rode his horse across and, when arriving on the opposite shore, found that two other soldiers were clinging to her tail!

Several years ago, my brother, Clyde, and I visited the Shiloh National Park, just over the Mississippi border in Tennessee, and drove all around the battleground. It was an eerie feeling. At the Visitor's Center I looked up names of soldiers who had fought in the battle. There was a number of Muses listed, including a John D., which I assumed was my great-grandfather.

In the summer of 1998, while president of Auburn University, I was invited to present a paper at an international conference on Total Quality Management in Sheffield, England. I took all members of my family with me, including spouses. After spending a few days in London, we split up to see different parts of the country, agreeing to meet in Sheffield later. I rented a car and drove up to Bedfordshire, with my wife and oldest daughter, Amy, going with me.

The county seat of Bedfordshire is the beautiful and historic town of Bedford. It is best known as the birthplace of John Bunyon, a revolutionary preacher who led a fight against the Church of England and spent many years in prison where he wrote Pilgrim's Progress. There is a statute of Bunyon in the town centre and a restaurant named "Pilgrim's Progress".

With the help of the local Visitor's Center, we were able to get a map that indicated the village of Soldrup, a suburb of Bedford where Edward Mewes had lived and died. Soldrup consists of 25-30 houses, a small store and tavern, and a beautiful little church. We walked around the graveyard, but the oldest tombstones we found were from the early 1700's.

The most intriguing aspect of the visit to Bedfordshire for me was finding the connection to John Bunyon. My father had spent much of his life as a minister and was quite fond of the Pilgrim's Progress. I often saw a copy sitting next to <u>The Bible</u> on his desk. But I doubt that he knew that John Bunyon was from the town of his ancestors.

In my journey through the past, I have had the good fortune to visit the birthplace of my ancestors in Bedfordshire, England; the area where they lived in Moore County, North Carolina; the actual farm that they owned in Bedford County, Tennessee; and the area in Prentiss County, Mississippi where my grandfather died and my father was born. I have not visited the place where John Muse settled in Westmoreland County, Virginia, but I hope to do that someday.

Having learned about the lineage of my ancestors, I was now ready to explore more fully the lives of my parents who significantly influenced my character and the kind of person I had become. In the chapters that follow, what I discovered and what I remember about my parents is described, followed by the story of my life. I believe such introspection is valuable in helping one understand themselves and in conveying to others the insights that are gained.

CHAPTER 2:
BROTHER MUSE

I wish that I had known my father, known him as I imagined father and sons would, sharing the insights of their experiences and the feelings of their hearts. That did not occur, however, for at least a couple of reasons.

The first is gender. Sadly, men don't talk, at least not to each other; and certainly, not about the things that matter. The second is timing. When I was growing up, my conversations with my father were usually short and specific, instructional or disciplinary in nature, and one way. Then I left home at seventeen to go to college and returned only during school vacations or for a couple of summers during which I worked full-time to earn money for my college expenses. Then it was graduate school, marriage, and the beginnings of career. Then he was gone, dead at the age of 69 when I was only 27.

I regret that we never had those "man-to-man" talks that I imagined other fathers and sons having. What I know about my father, whom my brothers and I always called "Daddy", comes from observation and from information that has been shared with me by others. Nevertheless, while the mature discussions I craved were missing, I had numerous opportunities to watch and learn valuable lessons that have served me well.

Mose Lee Muse was born on June 13, 1896 in Prentiss County, Mississippi, near the town of Baldwyn, in the northeastern part of the state. He was the fifth and youngest child of William Frederick Muse and Josephine Boyer. When Josephine died, William married Emma Walker and they had five additional children. In the late 1990's, I traveled to the cemetery where my grandfather was buried. It is in a desolate area that I would never have found (and probably could not to find again), without the help of my Uncle Harley, the youngest child of grandfather's second family, and my brother, Clyde. The interesting thing that I observed was that William, who died in

1932, was buried between his two wives, perhaps a symbol of the closeness of the two families.

In 1914, Mose married Mary Elizabeth Hisaw who lived nearby. At the time, Mose was eighteen and had finished the eighth grade while Mary Elizabeth or "Lizzy" was fifteen and had gone through the sixth grade. The eighth grade was as high as their schools went. They eloped or, as my Momma would later describe it, they just "run off and got married." Grandfather Hisaw was quite angry as he felt Lizzy was too young to marry. Grandfather Hisaw was a large man with rough-hewn features, a shaggy mustache and a mean disposition. I only met him once, when I was a small child, and he frightened me greatly. But Daddy was able to survive his wrath.

Momma and Daddy made a life together in the hard scrabble Mississippi of the 20's and 30's. They had seven sons: Floyd (1915), Henry (1918), Paul (1921), Mose, Jr. (1928), Clyde (1929), a male infant who died shortly after birth (1933), and me (1939).

With hungry mouths to feed and few opportunities to earn money, they survived by hard work and ingenuity. There is no record that they ever owned any land, so I suspect they worked as tenant farmers and supported themselves through a variety of skills that Daddy learned.

Running a sawmill was one of the valuable skills that Daddy developed. He learned how to guide the saw as logs were conveyed to it and converted into lumber. He was eventually able to acquire a portable "Peckerwood" sawmill that could be hauled into a forest. The trees, as they were cut, would then being dragged to the mill by mules.

He also learned how to operate a sugar cane mill where farmers would bring their crop to be converted into syrup. Daddy's special skill was boiling down the juice. I suspect that his compensation was only a share of the output, but it served the family well. The "Ribbon-Cane Syrup" that he brought home directly from the mill, when combined with butter and put inside Momma's hot biscuits, made for a "sopping-good" breakfast!

By the time he had reached his late 30's, during the middle of the Great Depression in one of the most poverty-stricken areas of the country, Daddy had worked himself into an enviable position. He had become the manager of a large farm in Benton County between the towns of Hickory Flat and Potts Camp. The farm was known as the "Riley Place" because a Mrs. Riley, a widow, owned it. She had provided the family a nice house on the property and depended on Daddy for the complete operation of the farm. Since Mrs. Riley was elderly and had no children, everyone expected that she would leave the farm to Daddy when she died.

But in early 1936 a major change took place in the life of Mose Lee Muse and his family. A traveling preacher came through and persuaded Daddy to help him set up a "brush arbor" on the Riley Place and to give him permission to conduct a revival there. In those days, installing several tree trunks in the ground and then covering the top with the branches to protect against the sun or rain constructed a brush arbor. People who attended the services sat on logs in the arbor. It was in this location and at this revival that Daddy dedicated his life to God and felt that he had been called to preach.

This decision must have shocked the rest of the family. Daddy and Momma had been raised as Methodists, but had joined the Church of God in 1921. Over the subsequent years, Daddy served as a clerk and as a deacon of the church but had shown no inclination toward the ministry. Once that decision had been made, however, he had the challenge to fulfill that calling. With an eighth grade education, and a large family to support, going to a seminary was not an option. Fortunately, he learned that the Church of God, headquartered in Cleveland, Tennessee, had correspondence courses that he could take to be licensed to preach. The Church of God was one of the larger Pentecostal denominations that flourished in the rural South during this time.

Daddy began holding prayer meetings at home while taking the courses that were required. He received his license in early 1937 and was "rewarded" with an assignment to establish a new church in a rural area about six miles from the town of Marks in Quitman County. The move from the Riley place was made in two wagons, pulled by mules. The 60- mile trip took two full days and occurred in November 1937.

When they arrived, all they found was a plat of land that a farmer had donated for the new church. Furthermore, since this was in the Mississippi Delta, the site was swampy and consisted of "new ground" -- i.e., covered by virgin timber. Daddy leased 40 acres nearby on what was called the "Cook Place" cleared some land and built a house. Then he began the process of establishing a church by constructing a brush arbor. It was here that Daddy began his ministry, preaching and bringing people into the church. With the help of the new members and with the full participation of the family, they began clearing the ground and constructing a church and parsonage. One of my favorite photographs from this era shows the entire family standing in a section of "new ground" that had been cleared, including Momma with my pending arrival prominently announced by her protruding belly!

Carpentry, one of Daddy's other skills, was put to good use during this time. With the help of others, he constructed the church and the parsonage where we would live, thereby building up the church both physically and spiritually. Daddy would use his sawmill and his carpentry skills often to earn money by constructing structures for others. By 1941, Daddy had met all the requirements and was ordained as a minister, the Goodwill Church of God was officially established, and we moved into the new parsonage.

All of my recollections of Daddy are of him as a minister of the gospel. From his ordination until his retirement in 1959, he served the Church of God as a pastor in Mississippi or Louisiana. All of his churches, except for one two-year assignment in Meridian, were located in rural areas, serving low-income farm families. In the Church of God, all members, including the pastor -- were called "Brother" or "Sister". Therefore, my Daddy and Momma were "Brother and Sister Muse" to everyone we knew. Because the State Overseer made church assignments every two years, we moved a lot, but two locations were particularly meaningful to me.

The first was Goodwill Church of God, not only because it is where I was born, but also because we moved back there when I was beginning high school. I completed the ninth and tenth grades at Marks High School and have many memories of those formative years in my life. Daddy's initial work here spanned six years, probably due to his role as the founding pastor. Combined with the second assignment, his leadership of this congregation spanned eight years.

In 1999, while President of Auburn University, I served as the Chairman of a Southern Association (SACS) Re-accreditation Team at the University of Mississippi. On one of my trips to Oxford, I was traveling through Marks on a Sunday morning and decided to stop by Goodwill Church for the service. Since it had been about 45 years since I had been there, I wasn't sure I could find it, but I did. The dirt roads had been paved and the white wood frame church and parsonage had been replaced by new brick structures. But the site was familiar and brought back a lot of memories.

The service had already begun so I tried to move quietly into one the back pews. But the crowd was sparse that morning and all heads turned as I walked in. All during the service, a little white-haired lady kept looking back at me every few minutes. As soon as the benediction was given, she made a beeline for me and asked, "What's your name?" When I told her, she exclaimed, "I knew it! You look just like your Daddy." She said that she had joined the church while Daddy was the pastor and told me what a great man he had been, and how much he had influenced her life. Several other individuals joined the discussion and reinforced those sentiments. For Daddy to be remembered that way, fifty years or so later, proved what a powerful impact he had on the lives of others.

The second location of special importance to me was Rocky Hill Church of God in the far southwest corner of Neshoba County, near the town of Sebastopol. The church sits majestically upon a hill and can be seen from perhaps a mile away as one traverses the county road leading to it. We moved there when I was four years old and I began my formal education at a little rural schoolhouse called Dixie. I completed much of my elementary schooling here, as Daddy came back to Rocky Hill for a second assignment years later. This site is also meaningful because both of my parents are buried in the little cemetery beside the church.

Brother Muse was a formidable force in these two churches and in every other location where he pastored. His ministry was so important to families trying to survive in an inhospitable world. In many cases, what kept them going was the hope for a better life in Heaven; understandably, the church occupied a central role in their lives. Daddy was widely respected in the communities where he lived, by both those in the church and those outside of it.

Daddy's compensation came from a percentage of the tithes that were paid by the members of the church and by any offerings he received. Since the church members were mostly poor, hardly any of Daddy's churches provided enough income to support the family. But we survived. We always had a big garden and raised chickens. When a church member would kill a hog, he would bring us a ham or pork chops. So we always had plenty to eat. As for clothing, Momma would sew many of my shirts from flour or seed sacks but that was true for most others in the community as well.

In addition to preaching on Sunday and at Wednesday night Prayer Meeting, visiting the sick, and ministering to the other needs of the congregation, Daddy almost always worked at some other job to support the family. Sometimes he worked as a carpenter, sawmill operator, or sugar cane cooker. And he developed additional skills, particularly as a salesman. Daddy would find a product that he liked and would decide that everyone else needed one, too.

For example, after buying a pair of Mason shoes from the mail-order house in Chippawea Falls, Wisconsin, he signed on to represent the company. I don't know how many shoes he sold, but I always had a nice pair of shoes during that time. Next, he sold WearEver Cookware, a line of aluminum pots and pans. Daddy liked to cook, often preparing special dishes he had sampled somewhere. WearEver was sold at a "party" where the host would invite her neighbors and Daddy would prepare the meal with the featured pots and pans.

When we were living in Meridian, he sold used cars. I guess the owner figured that people would trust a preacher to tell them the truth. One day he brought home a motorbike that had been received in a trade-in and let me ride it for several weeks. I was twelve or thirteen at the time and enjoyed tooling around town on my bike.

My brother, Clyde, remembers that Daddy also sold Watkins products (flavoring, spices, etc.), when I was a child. How Daddy balanced the need for income with the demands of the church -- preparing sermons, attending to the needs of the congregation -- is unclear. There never seemed to be a time when he was not working.

While Daddy and I didn't have the man-to-man conversations I would have valued, I had many opportunities to hear him talk -- every Sunday and on Wednesday nights. He was not a fiery preacher, certainly not the sort that I recall from traveling evangelists who preached in the church or a tent for several nights in a row. What he lacked in animation, however, he made up for in conviction. Daddy would spend long hours reading his Bible, interpreting it into language that the common people could understand and explaining how they could implement it in their daily lives. He poured all his energies into his sermons, often using personal examples that would bring tears to his eyes. His shirt was often soaked with sweat after a sermon, given the effort he exerted and the fact that the church buildings were not air-conditioned.

Daddy was particular about his appearance, always wearing a suit with a white shirt and tie to church, even though he would often remove his jacket when it was very hot. He only owned a few suits, but he kept them clean and always shined his shoes. Even during the week, except when he was working on a dirty job, he wore a long sleeved white shirt. As a minister, he felt he had an image to uphold.

Daddy was slightly built, perhaps 5' 9" and weighed 160 pounds, although he put on a little extra weight during his later years. By the time I came along, he was nearly bald, wore false teeth, and small wire-rimmed glasses. But he had a peaceful disposition and a quiet confidence that engendered trust from others. He would look directly at a person with his clear brown eyes and would listen carefully to what they had to say.

Beyond the sermons and the day-to-day interactions that I observed, there are several incidents that illustrate the compassion, courage, and character that Daddy exhibited throughout his life. The first occurred before I was born. While the family was living at the Riley Place, Daddy and Momma found out that a young girl in the community had been disowned by her family and did not have a place to live. She attended prayer meetings at our house and Momma invited her to stay with us. The girl, Lula Belle Stanton, came to live with the family and stayed with them until she married, moving with them from Benton to Quitman County. Taking on another mouth to feed during the middle of the Depression was challenging, but I suspect Lula Belle represented the daughter that Momma had always wanted. While we were at Goodwill, Lula Belle met and married Randolph Jones and had a family of her own. But she was always regarded as a member of the Muse family.

The second incident occurred in the fall of 1947. Daddy had been assigned to a rural church between Indianola and Shaw in Sunflower County in the middle of the Mississippi Delta. I was eight at the time and attended a little school where several grades were crammed into the same classroom and not much teaching or learning took place. One evening after supper, Daddy invited me to go with him and I happily responded, as I loved to go with Daddy on his trips to the store or to visit people in the church. This time, though, we drove down a dirt road to a run-down church in the corner of a cotton field. Our car was the only vehicle there. But when we opened the door, we saw that the place was filled with black people. This didn't frighten me because blacks were everywhere out working in the fields and made up a majority of the population in the Delta. But society was totally segregated at this time, particularly in the Delta.

Shortly after we arrived the service began. Daddy and I were sitting on the front row, the only white faces in the building. The singing was spellbinding, with everyone standing, swaying, and clapping. They had an old beat-up piano with missing keys, a guitar with three strings, and a "tambourine" made out of bottle caps nailed on a board. The whole building seemed to be moving with the music. Then, Daddy was introduced and asked to preach. And preach he did, pouring all his energy into a message about Jesus' love. He quoted scripture that said, "Man looked on the outward appearance but that God look on the heart" and that all people were equal in the eyes of God. Resounding "Amens" and shouts from every sector of the building seemed to go on forever.

On the way home, I was in awe of what I had seen and felt. But Daddy didn't say anything to me about the incident then or later. Within a few days, however, several deacons from the church and other men I had not seen before came to see Daddy. They met in the front yard; I heard some loud voices but could not understand what was being said. Then Momma and Daddy went to their bedroom for a long time and I heard them praying.

Within a day or two, Momma started packing our things. When I asked her where we were going, she told me that we were moving back to Rocky Hill. While I was pleased to be going back to the place where I had begun my education and where I knew people, I was mystified by the sudden turn of events. Daddy explained to me later that the men advised us to leave for our safety; so he had contacted the State Overseer and that Rocky Hill, looking for a pastor, had welcomed him back.

In the years since this event, I have often wondered why Daddy preached to the black church; surely he understood the tremendous risk he was taking. I suspect he talked with some black people working on one of the farms, was invited to preach to them, and he did what he felt Jesus would have done -- he ministered to them. Daddy tried to exemplify Jesus' example at a time and in a place where those feelings were rarely felt and seldom or never acted upon.

The third incident happened a year or so later. We were living in the parsonage at Rocky Hill when some men banged on the front door late one night. We were all in bed, but Daddy went to the porch and talked with them; he shortly came back in the house, put on his shoes and additional clothing, and left with the men. He returned hours later. It was only through other boys at school and through men in the church that I learned about the traumatic events that unfolded that night.

A tenant farmer had come home after a night of drinking bootleg whiskey. Drunk and despondent, he began to beat his wife with a stick of stove wood and, then, turned on his three children. One young boy escaped to a neighboring farmhouse and told them what happened. Someone went to find the sheriff who lived on the other side of the county while some other men went to get Daddy, asking him to go into the house and talk to the drunken husband. Daddy arrived at the house, finding several men holding shotguns but no one willing to go into the house. But Daddy walked up on the front porch, announced his name, and said that he was coming in to pray with the man. When Daddy opened the door, he found the wife and two children dead and the husband in a corner crying. The whiskey had worn off and the realization of what he had done now weighed on him. Daddy stayed and prayed with the man until the sheriff came and took him away to jail.

After spending all of his life in Mississippi, Daddy took two pastoral assignments in Louisiana. The first was in Dunn, a small community about five miles from Delhi, in northeastern part of the state. This is where I graduated from high school. His last church was Sharps Chapel Church of God in a rural area near Covington in southeastern Louisiana during the time I was away at college.

While we were at Dunn I remember an incident that illustrated Daddy's sense of humor and ability to keep things in perspective. I was playing high school sports and my body was well muscled from all the workouts. I had just come home one Saturday morning from baseball practice, taken a shower, and put on a tee shirt and shorts. I was in the living room reading the paper when I overhead two men talking to Daddy on the front porch.

It was two deacons in the church, including a guy that I thought was quite pompous. He would sit in the front pew and look back over the congregation; I felt he was checking to see if I was asleep or misbehaving. Soon I realized that the deacons were criticizing Daddy for a number of things. The pompous deacon jumped on Daddy for mispronouncing the word "compromise" in the previous Sunday's sermon. Daddy had called it "com-promise." (I doubted if any of the congregation knew the difference!)

After hearing all I could stand, I picked up my baseball bat, walked out on the porch and sat down on the railing across from the two deacons. Conversation immediately stopped, the pompous deacon glanced at his watch and announced he had another appointment, and they beat a hasty retreat to their car.

After they were gone, Daddy let out a huge laugh -- one of the heartiest I can remember -- and said, "Well, I guess that ended that!" And it did. The deacons never came to offer Daddy their" advice" again.

By the time he retired, Daddy had served the Church of God for forty-four years, including twenty-three as a minister. He organized six new churches and held thirteen pastoral assignments. He also served for a time as a District Overseer. In retirement, Daddy and Momma lived in a house on a dairy farm that was owned by my brothers, Paul and Henry. He worked in his garden and woodworking shop, and often served as a guest preacher at churches around the area of Union in east central Mississippi.

On May 10, 1966, Daddy got up early to work in the garden as he often did before the temperature got too hot. When Momma got up later, she looked out and saw him lying on his back. She rushed to his side only to discover that he was dead. All indications were that his death was a peaceful one, either from a stroke or a heart attack, and he passed away looking toward Heaven.

It is useful, I believe, to view Daddy's life in two distinct stages. Up until he was almost forty, he struggled to make a living for himself and his family during a time and in an environment where that was not easy. But he was a hard worker and was willing to learn new skills. He had arrived at a job where he may have been able to achieve some security. Had he inherited the Riley Place, it is possible that he could have become a rich man, given his skills and the economic growth that was to occur after World War II.

But, instead, he chose to use his life helping all those he encountered during his ministry. He never owned any property more valuable than an automobile and frequently worked at two jobs to make ends meet. But few individuals were richer in the admiration and love they received from others. His ministry affected thousands of people, giving them hope by exemplifying the teachings of Jesus wherever he went.

Most of all, Daddy's example was a powerful one for me. He exemplified resourcefulness, generosity, dignity, and racial tolerance, while practicing considerable courage and compassion. His life spoke more clearly than any conversation could have.

CHAPTER 3:
SISTER MUSE AND THE BOYS

Momma was Daddy's constant companion and ardent supporter. Almost any reference to their ministry was phrased as "Brother and Sister Muse." She was his "rock," always at his side. She was also my "beacon", setting high aspirations and reminding me that I could be somebody. Unlike Daddy, who I came to know primarily by observation, Momma provided frequent oral feedback, letting me know what she expected and how she evaluated my performance. I was the beneficiary of her undivided attention as the last child and the only one at home during my elementary and high school years. But Momma's messages were always encouraging.

"Lizzy" Hisaw was born on October 10, 1899 and married Daddy when she was very young.She loved him her entire life and was totally devoted to her family. Momma rarely read anything except the Bible or Church of God publications. She never watched television until late in life when I bought a TV set for her after Daddy retired. She didn't belong to any organizations except the church. Her focus was totally on her family and the church.

From sun up to sundown, Momma worked with hardly any rest between. She cooked, cleaned house, washed and ironed clothes, or labored in the fields. My brothers told me that, before Daddy became a minister, Momma worked on the farm picking cotton or helping to clear land, only stopping long enough to go to prepare dinner (what we called the noon meal) for the family and whomever else was working with them.

Momma was a great cook. I remember waking up in the morning to the smell of hot biscuits. Virtually every morning we would have a big breakfast of fried eggs and some kind of meat, but the big meal of the day was dinner. The table would groan with bowls of fresh vegetables -- butter beans, green beans, peas, corn, okra, squash, cucumbers, and sliced tomatoes. Maybe there'd be some fried chicken or pork, lots of iced tea and cornbread on the side. Supper, the evening meal, usually consisted of leftovers from noon, warmed up and served with a fresh batch of cornbread, topped off with pie or cake.

Living in the country, we always had a big garden and grew most of the food we ate. Daddy would plow the soil and assist with the other tasks like "stringing the beans," or "sticking the tomatoes", but Momma and the boys did most of the watering, weeding, and picking. As I got older, I took over part of that work, including the shelling of the peas and beans, which I did not particularly enjoy. One job I really hated was gathering the okra. The prickly and sticky plant really irritated my arms until I finally learned to wear long sleeves and gloves.

We also grew sweet potatoes and white potatoes (which we called "Irish" potatoes), as well as cabbage and onions. Plants I had to be "encouraged" to eat were carrots, radishes, peppers, and turnips, although I did like the turnip greens. Perhaps my favorite meal was Momma's butter beans, which she would pick young and cook with pieces of ham or "fatback." Combined with sliced tomatoes and a piece of fried chicken, that made for a delicious meal.

In addition to preparing fresh vegetables for meals, Momma was also constantly canning them for the winter. This was before the advent of home freezers. All we had was an "ice-box", a cabinet into which a block of ice was placed, to keep food cool. As a result, food was prepared largely on a day-to-day basis. I loved eating the watermelons and cantaloupes we grew, having the cantaloupes for breakfast and the melons for dinner or supper, after cooling them in a tub of water. Sometimes, we would make ice cream in a hand-turned freezer.

We always raised chickens for eggs and meat and when members of the church killed a hog, they would share the meat with us. My brothers would go hunting and bring back rabbits or squirrels, sometimes even a deer. If one or more families in the church had dairy cows, they would supply us with milk. I don't recall us having much "store-bought" food, except for flour and condiments.

Although preparing the food seemed like a full-time job, Momma had many other tasks. She swept the house and dusted the furniture: since we had no lawn, she even swept the yard using a "brush broom" of smaller tree limbs tied together. Sweeping was a task I was often recruited to assume. Washing, ironing, and mending clothes was also hard work, particularly without modern-day appliances. Momma washed clothes by hand, using a "rub-board" with a grooved surface over which wet soapy clothes were rubbed to loosen the dirt. When we got our first electric washing machine, complete with a wringer, it was a great day for Momma. She also had a Singer sewing machine and made a lot of her own dresses, as well as most of my shirts.

The most enjoyable times for Momma, other than church meetings, were when her older sister, Rosa, would visit. Aunt Rosa would stay three or four weeks with us each winter and she and Momma would quilt. They would hang a frame from the ceiling to hold the quilt, spending the day quilting and talking until they completed the bed covering. Almost all of the quilts I remember from my youth were made by Momma and Aunt Rosa.

In addition to all the work of maintaining a household, Momma was always available to assist with the work of the church. She attended every service, sitting in the front pew, participating and offering her support. In the early years of their ministry, Brother and Sister Muse sang duets at many services. And Sister Muse often went with Daddy when he visited the sick or performed other ministerial duties.

I don't ever recall seeing a picture of Momma as a child or young woman; I suspect no one in the family had a camera in those days. But I imagine she was very attractive. By the time I came along, she was the pastor's wife and always under scrutiny by the women in the church. The Church of God in those days had strict rules about a woman's appearance -- no lipstick or rouge, no jewelry of any kind, and no cutting of the hair. Momma's hair hung down to her hips; so she platted it into two strands and then pinned them up around her head. She never cut her hair, nor used any cosmetics except for face powder or lotion, but she was always clean and neatly dressed. Whether it was a dress she made or the occasional one she would buy (probably from Sears Roebuck), Momma took pride in her appearance and was always appropriate attired. In her later years, she wore false teeth but had a beautiful smile and donned glasses which accented her deep brown eyes.

After Daddy died in 1966, Momma seemed to be in a deep depression. Her life had been geared to support Daddy. She had not learned to drive a car and had no interests other than her house, her family, and her church. Clyde taught her to drive after Daddy's death, but I don't think she used those skills very often. She was happiest when Aunt Rosa visited and they could spend the whole day quilting and talking. Momma paid little attention to the television I gave her until Aunt Rosa introduced her to "As The World Turns", a daytime soap opera, they would watch together.

When Paul and Henry sold the dairy farm where she and Daddy had lived in retirement, she moved with Paul and Marie into Union. They bought a mobile home that was moved onto their property and that became Momma's residence. She lived there until she needed constant attention, whereupon she moved into a nursing home in Union. Living far from Mississippi during those years, I only saw Momma a couple of times annually, always feeling good to see her but sad to leave. Momma lived there until she died on July 16, 1979 at age 80.

Mary Elizabeth Hisaw Muse was a devoted wife and a wonderful mother. She never complained about the work she had to do or her station in life. As Sister Muse, she was the model minister's wife -- always active in the church, supporting Brother Muse's ministry, and living her life by the principles that he preached. But, perhaps, her greatest legacy was the boys to whom she gave birth and raised to responsible adulthood.

I will now discuss and describe each of the boys from my perspective.

FLOYD LEE

Floyd Lee, the first child, was born October 14, 1915 in Prentiss County. He was an outstanding athlete in both basketball and boxing at Hickory Flat High School in Benton County where the family had moved in the mid 1920's. He was good enough in boxing to win a regional Golden Gloves Championship in Memphis, Tennessee. Floyd served in the U.S. Army after graduating from high school and married Jewel Gee, also from Benton County. They had three daughters: Shirley Mae, Floyd Jeanne, and Mary Elizabeth. Floyd was a strikingly handsome man; many of his pictures that I have seen remind me of Clark Gable. And Jewel was a beautiful woman with jet-black hair, olive complexion and sparkling dark eyes. Even until her death at age 75, she retained her beauty. All three daughters inherited their mother's good looks.

Floyd worked at a number of jobs as he tried to support his family. One job was that of an "iceman", delivering blocks of ice to homes to put in their iceboxes. He subsequently went to work in retail for the B.F. Goodrich Company, managing stores in Oxford and Pontotoc, Mississippi. By the time he was 37 he was running the Goodrich store in Jackson, Tennessee, but a tragic accident cut short his promising career. He was delivering a TV set and had to install an antenna on the roof of the house. During the process, the antenna broke loose and fell onto a power line, electrocuting both Floyd and his assistant. Losing Floyd in the prime of his life, with a wife and three young daughters left behind, was a tremendous shock to the whole family. Jewel moved to Little Rock, Arkansas, where she had relatives and raised her daughters there, remarrying years later.

I was only thirteen when Floyd died and felt his loss keenly. He was dashing, confident, handsome and energetic - all the qualities that a young boy would admire. But my suffering was minor, compared to that of his wife and three daughters who lost a husband and father that they loved very much. Floyd died on May 29, 1952 and was buried in Benton County at the Ebenezer cemetery, near the Methodist church he attended as a child.

HENRY FREDERICK

The second son, Henry Frederick, was born on June 19, 1918 in Prentiss County. Like Floyd, he graduated from Hickory Flat High School but joined the U .S. Navy soon afterward in 1937. He served on the aircraft carrier, U.S.S. Enterprise, before and during World War II.

The U.S.S. Enterprise was scheduled to arrive at Pearl Harbor on December 7, 1941 when the Japanese attack occurred, but its journey had been delayed by a storm. Early reports indicated that the ship had been destroyed and all those on board killed. The family thought that Henry was dead. While Daddy was stoic, Momma was very emotional in grieving about the news. She and Daddy prayed every day hoping that it was not true. One day, they even received a message that his body would arrive on the evening train, but that did not occur. Finally about six weeks later, a post card arrived that said "I am well" with Henry's signature on it. But no official confirmation from the U.S. Government could be obtained. Momma and Daddy even heard that Henry was alive, but that he had lost an arm. Finally, on June 1, 1943, a letter from Henry arrived, verifying that he was alive and was not wounded.

The U.S.S. Enterprise was one of the most distinguished ships during the battles of the seas during W.W.II, fighting in both the Battle of Midway and the Battle of Guadalcanal. Overall, it was credited with sinking 36 Japanese warships and destroying 140 Japanese warplanes in combat. The ship was at sea for 27 months before touching land. It is amazing that Henry survived. I still remember how we all rejoiced when he came home at the end of the war.

After the war, Henry married Annie Pearl Holley, a native of Newton County. They had three boys - Larry, John, and Allen and a daughter, Patsy. Henry and Paul bought a farm between Union and Decatur in Newton County and began to operate a dairy - milking cows and growing much of the feed they needed. They both built houses on the farm. After a number of years, Henry turned over most of the operation of the farm to Paul and accepted a full-time job as a supervisor at a shirt factory in the town of Newton.

Henry was very quiet and reserved. He rarely raised his voice or lost his temper. He seldom talked about the war and, when persuaded to do so, only in the briefest of terms. In fact, he seemed to talk about any subject only when asked, but always had a thoughtful response. He was widely respected by those who knew him and served for several years as a member of the Board of Education in Union. He died on June 23, 1977 at the age of 59 from complications arising from heart surgery and was buried in the Union cemetery.

JAMES PAUL

Paul was born on June 22,1921 while the family still lived in Prentiss County, moving with them a few years later to Benton County and then on to Quitman County when he was about sixteen. Paul graduated from Crowder High School where he was an excellent basketball player. Towards the end of his senior year, he married Marie Ledbetter, a fellow student at Crowder. Their first child, Rotha Nell, lived only about five weeks, but they, subsequently, had three girls - Paula, Ruthie, and Sylvia and one son, James Delaine.

Paul spent several years in the Navy and the Naval Reserves before he and Henry bought the dairy farm near Union. He was the primary operator of the farm until it was sold in his later years. He and Marie then moved into a house on the edge of Union where Paul raised and showed horses, one of which, a big Palomino, won numerous prizes. Paul was well known around Union, serving for a time as a Deacon in the First Baptist Church.

A very energetic and personable man, Paul rarely met a stranger. He was volatile, capable of quick anger but also great compassion. He worked hard, rising at 4 a.m. each morning (seven days a week) to milk the cows and laboring the rest of the day at various farm chores until the evening milking session. And he expected those around him to work just as hard. I remember helping Paul to bring in the hay in the heat of summer, one of the least enjoyable tasks I ever undertook.

Paul had nicknames for almost everyone. He called me "Quill" for some unknown reason. Maybe it was a takeoff on Bill or maybe he foresaw that I would be a writer. He called his son "Duck", a name that has stuck with him, and his oldest daughter was "Wuss". The youngest daughter, Sylvia, was called "Tibby." Junior was "Prock" and Clyde was "Dusty". I'm sure there were others who had nicknames as well.

Paul died on May 8, 1985 at the age of 63 from coronary disease and is also buried in the Union cemetery.

MOSE JUNIOR

Mose Junior, was born on March 14, 1928 in Benton County. Within the family he was always called "Junior". He attended schools in Benton and

Quitman Counties before graduating from high school in Sebastopol in Scott County where he played on the basketball team. After high school, he joined the U.S. Army and began a twenty-four year career in the military. He married Mollie Killens of Sebastopol and they had two sons, Randy and Cecil.

Junior served in both the Korean War and the Vietnam War, where his specialty was the maintenance and piloting of helicopters. He flew several missions under fire in Vietnam and had assignments in many other locations, including two years in Germany, retiring with the rank of Warrant Officer.

When Junior and Mollie divorced after about 20 years of marriage, she moved back to Mississippi and he, subsequently, married Pauline Pickrell, a widow from Danville, Virginia, where he lived after his retirement. Junior worked for several civilian companies doing aircraft maintenance and died on October 14, 1990 from congestive heart failure.

It is ironic that Junior was named for my Daddy since he was the least like him in appearance and personality. Junior, like Paul, had blonde hair and blue eyes, while Daddy and all the other boys had brown hair and brown eyes. Junior had a quick temper and could be described as "high strung", perhaps because of his military experience. He loved to hunt and fish and often brought home meat for the table. He seemed to be the happiest when he was out doors.

In retirement, Junior enrolled in Averett College in Danville and completed the requirements for a degree in business administration. His funeral was with military honors provided by the U.S. Honor Guard from Fort Lee, Virginia at the Highland Burial Park in Danville.

Vernon Clyde

Clyde was born on December 25, 1929 in Benton County. Because there was only a year and nine months difference in age betweem him and Junior, my parents decided to hold Junior back a year so that he and Clyde would go through school together. Many people thought they were twins, although the two of them differed in both appearance and personality.

Clyde was tall and lanky and developed into an outstanding basketball player at Sebastopol High School, winning a scholarship to attend East Central Junior College in Decatur. He was the first member of our family to attend college. At 6'3", Clyde was tall enough (in those days) to be the center on the basketball team and had a great career at ECJC. He was recruited to play at Southwestern Louisiana, but decided after one semester that he wanted to come back to Mississippi. Delta State Teacher's College in Cleveland, Mississippi, offered him a scholarship and he was an outstanding member of an excellent team there for the next two years, graduating with a degree in physical education and science. One of my greatest thrills was getting to see Clyde play basketball in a game between Delta State and Mississippi Southern.

At Delta State, Clyde met a lovely young coed, Vashti Underwood from Leland, and they were married shortly after his graduation. They had two daughters - Julia and Susan, and a son, Vernon Clyde, Jr.

Clyde began his career as a biology teacher and basketball and track coach at Canton High School. After being successful there, Starkville recruited him to be the basketball and track coach where he won a state championship in 1961. He eventually became Principal of Starkville High School and then Assistant Superintendent. While in Starkville, Clyde enrolled in Mississippi State University and earned a Master's degree in education and an Ed.D. in educational administration.He then moved to Jackson where he served as Superintendent of Schools in Hinds County during a very difficult period of the integration of public schools in Mississippi.

His next post was that of Superintendent of Schools in Meridian, the second largest city in Mississippi. He had a distinguished tenure in that capacity for a period of seven years serving until being chosen to be the President of Hinds Junior College in Raymond. Clyde has provided remarkable leadership for Hinds, now Hinds Community College with campuses in Raymond, Jackson, Vicksburg, Rankin, and Utica, over a period of over 30 years. The college has grown in enrollment and programs and Clyde has become widely respected by his colleagues and the Mississippi Legislature as one of the outstanding leaders of the state.

Clyde has always been very humble about his achievements. He is passionate about his work and compassionate in his response to the needs of others. Being the closest in age among the brothers and working in the same profession, Clyde and I have always felt a strong bond between us.He has always been a very positive role model for me.

Momma and Daddy had another son, an infant born in 1933, but he died within hours of birth and was not named. One would have expected this to be their last child since both Momma and Daddy were in the mid 30's. But, for whatever reason (it could have been an accident or, as Momma often said, she kept trying to eventually have a daughter), I arrived in 1939. Daddy was 42 at that time and Momma was 40, hardly the ideal ages for raising a young child. But they were wonderful parents to me and I am grateful that they brought me to life.

Many close observers of our family have commented that the boys seemed to come in "pairs", i.e. that there were three groups that were very similar in appearance and personality.

Among the boys, Floyd and Clyde were much alike -- both tall and slim with dark wavy hair and very outgoing with excellent leadership skills. Paul and Junior had blonde hair and blue eyes and similar personalities and temperaments. Henry and I possessed personality traits that were alike and many folks said that the two of us looked the most like Daddy.

While each of my brothers had distinct personalities, I loved each of them very much and they loved me. Floyd, Henry, and Paul were more like surrogate fathers while I was growing up because of the differences in our ages. But, fortunately, I got to spend considerable time with both Henry and Paul as an adult. Because Junior married right after high school and then began a military career, my relationship with him was limited until his years in retirement. Clyde is the brother with whom I most engaged growing up and then as an adult. His guidance was critical in sparking my interest in athletics and in my selection of a career field. All of my sisters-in-law were very supportive and their children—my nieces and nephews—were often like siblings to me. I am so appreciative of all members of my family who helped shape my life that will be described in the chapters that follow.

CHAPTER 4:

GROWING UP: THE PRE-SCHOOL AND ELEMENTARY YEARS

My arrival on this earth occurred on April 7, 1939 in the Marks Hospital, the only medical facility in a town of about 2,000 residents, about six miles from where we lived in Quitman County. My family was then residing on the Cook Place and Daddy was operating a sawmill while building the Goodwill Church of God. I was named William Van, with William coming from my grandfather and Van from a family friend, but was called Billy until adulthood and beyond, by some family members. And, in the true Southern tradition, I was often called Billy Van.

As the preacher's new baby, I quickly become the center of attention in the church community. There are many stories that are told about me. While I do not remember the events myself, members of my family confirm them, so I'll accept their word.

The first concerns my drinking preferences. After Momma weaned me, I refused to drink from a bottle. She then added some sugar to the milk and I found it satisfactory. I called this mixture "giggie" and would reject the bottle unless the milk was sweetened. I may have been trying to say "gimme some of that good stuff!" but they couldn't understand me.

The second story concerns one of my playmates. Momma had a black lady to help part-time with the washing and ironing. This lady had a son about my age that she would bring with her to work. He and I would play together and, when he and his mom left, I would cry to go home with them. Momma wouldn't let me, but one day I took matters into my own hands and followed them home to a little "shotgun" house on a nearby farm. When

Momma discovered my absence, she walked down there and found us playing away, oblivious to any possibility that this might not be socially acceptable practice during those days.

I remember several other episodes from early childhood, two that were painful and one joyous. When I was nearing age four, a doctor recommended that I have a tonsillectomy. I was scared, but Momma and Daddy promised me that, if I had my tonsils removed, they would buy me all the ice cream I could eat. That sounded like a great deal, so I readily agreed. What I did not realize was that my throat would be so sore after the operation that I could hardly eat anything for days. But Momma and Daddy kept their promise and gave me my ice cream later.

The second painful memory involved an encounter with a broken bottle. In my fourth year, I begged my parents to let me ride on a "ground-slide" with my brother, Paul. A ground slide is a wooden platform with two 2-x- 4s' serving as "runners" on the underside and a trace on the front so it could be hooked to a horse or mule. It was used to transport sacks of seed or fertilizer from the barn into the fields by sliding along the ground.

Paul was taking the mule and the ground-slide back to David Parish, the owner of the farm next to the church property. Paul rode on the ground-slide by standing on the platform, while holding onto the reins of the mule. I was fascinated by the contraption and wanted to ride with Paul as he took it back to Mr. Parish's house. I got my way, unfortunately, and held unto one of Paul's legs as we slid along to our destination.

When we arrived, eager to brag to about my adventure, I jumped off the slide and landed on the jagged edge of the broken bottle -- in my bare feet! The glass almost sliced off my left heel. Paul wrapped it in towels to contain the blood flow and Daddy drove to the hospital in Marks where fifteen stitches were needed to close the wound. I carried away from this experience a permanent scar and an important lesson: Look before you leap!

The other episode was the joyous occasion when Henry came home from the Navy after we had thought he had been killed or seriously injured. He arrived without notice, riding the train to Marks and being provided a ride to our house. I remember him standing on the front porch in his white uniform with Momma and Daddy hugging him, crying, and praising the Lord. Soon the good news had spread throughout the community and church members began to show up with food for the celebration. I had never witnessed so much love and joy; it was a vivid lesson on the importance of love and support in a family, church, and community.

I spent many hours in the church. During services, Momma would either hold me in her arms during the services or lay me on a pallet at her feet. I remember people dancing or "shouting" around the area near my pallet as they let the Holy Spirit take control of their bodies. Such behavior occurred often in Pentecostal services at that time. When I was about four, I told others that I wanted to be a preacher when I grew up, just like my Daddy. That pronouncement pleased Daddy immensely and he would talk about it from the pulpit. The preacher was the most important person in the world that I knew at that time; so my choice of careers could be easily understood.

ROCKY HILL

In the fall of 1943, we moved from Goodwill to Rocky Hill. The move from the "delta" to the "hills" provided a contrast between the two major cultures in Mississippi at that time. Situated on the edge of the delta region, Marks and Goodwill were located on flat fertile land that was almost black. Vast cotton farms and plantations covered the region, and blacks comprised a major share of the population. There was a significant concentration of wealth in the delta among a few white families.

Rocky Hill was located in the extreme southwest corner of Neshoba County, only a few miles from the borders of Newton, Leake and Scott Counties. The country was made up of rolling hills and red clay soil, populated by small subsistence farms. The people were predominantly white. Wealth was more evenly distributed; everyone was poor.

It was at Rocky Hill that I first became aware of the church as a community. Rocky Hill was a well-established congregation, with a handsome brick building that sat on the hill and a parsonage resting at the bottom away from the road. Its membership consisted mostly of farmers and day laborers, one of whom, Kelly Comans, also owned a small country store and seemed to be the most well to do man in the congregation.

But I most remember the Bassetts, who owned a farm immediately across the dirt road from where we lived. Brother Oscar and Sister Nellie were pillars of the church, there every time the doors were open. They had twelve children who worked to keep the farm going. The Bassetts had cows, mules, hogs and chickens and they raised cotton and corn. Brother Oscar went into the fields by sunrise and worked until after dark. I remember hearing him praising the Lord and praying as he plowed the fields with a mule. Sister Nellie had her hands full with all the children. I remember two boys, Dorman and Stancil, who were a few years older than me, and a girl, Dorothy, who was my age. Dorothy, who was called "E-Dot", and I played together a lot. There was a baby boy named Henry (who owns and operates the Bassett farm today).

There were several times when I happened to be at the Bassetts at suppertime, and I was invited to eat with them. Supper would consist of leftovers from dinner, served with a fresh pan of cornbread. I remember all the Bassetts sitting around a big table, bowing their heads while Brother Oscar "offered the blessing" in a loud voice; then they would dig into the cornbread, crumbling it up into a big glass of milk. I loved this dish, to the delight of Sister Nellie; she would remind me of this when she saw me many years later.

E-Dot and I would also make our way nearly everyday to Sister Tildy's house, just up the road. Walking up or across the road was no risk for us because the only traffic consisted of farmers with their wagons or an occasional slow moving car. Sister Tildy Wolverton always had a batch of delicious "tea cakes" ready for us.

The parsonage at Rocky Hill, like the one at Goodwill, had no plumbing, central heating, or air conditioning, but we did have electricity, thanks to REA. The "outhouse" was located some distance away; so we had a container called a "slop jar" that we used at night, if we had to go. A fireplace in the living room was the primary source of heat. So on cold nights, Momma would warm blankets and bring them to my bed. There were several large trees that kept the house reasonably cool during the hot summers.

In the spring of our first year at Rocky Hill, when I was five years old, Daddy took me to Dixie School to talk to the teachers about enrolling in the Primary grade that fall. Primary was the equivalent of today's kindergarten. The teacher asked Daddy to bring me to the class for a week so she could evaluate me to see if I was ready for school. She concluded that I was too advanced for the primary level and should start in first grade that fall. Apparently, I could already read and had mastered many of the intellectual skills they were teaching. I'm not sure how I learned to read; Momma must have read to me.

I entered the first grade at age five with Ms. Mary McBeth, a wonderful teacher. I don't remember what she taught me, but I recall the encouragement and nurturing she provided. I loved going to school and doing all the exercises she assigned. By the end of that year, Ms. McBeth had determined that I should skip the second grade and move on to the third grade the next fall. So at age six I entered the third grade.

My teacher was Ms. Ruby Germany, another wonderful teacher who gave me personal attention and encouragement. She also provided extra books for me to read. I don't know if either Ms. McBeth or Ms. Germany were married; they seemed to me to be angels who lived at the school and had no other earthly existence!

Dixie School was a wood-frame structure on top of a red clay hill. One of the biggest challenges each day was for the school bus to make it up the hill, especially after it had rained. By all objective standards - quality of facilities, quantity of resources, credentials of the faculty, etc., - I suspect that Dixie would have been classified as an "inferior" school; but it gave me an excellent start on my intellectual journey - largely because of the caring teachers who worked there.

THORN

In the late summer of 1946, we moved to Thorn - a rural community about five miles west of Houston, Mississippi, in Chickasaw County. The roads here were graveled, a step up from the dirt roads around Rocky Hill. Thorn consisted of a crossroads at which a school and a general store, which included a small post office, were located. The Thorn Church of God, to which Daddy had been assigned as Pastor, was about a half mile east.

The church was situated on a flat piece of land just off the road, with the parsonage right next door. I don't remember much about the membership or activities of the church since my attention was focused primarily upon the new school I was attending.

The Thorn School was a wood frame building organized into three classrooms. In the first classroom were pupils enrolled in the primary, first and second grades. The second was for grades 3, 4, and 5 and the third room was for students in the 6th, 7th and 8th grades. There were three teachers, one for each classroom. I don't remember my teacher's name, or much of what we learned. She gave out assignments that we completed at our desks, meeting occasionally with us individually. It seemed to me that most of her time was spent trying to maintain order in the classroom.

The things I remember most about my experiences at Thorn schools were the problems I encountered outside the classroom. Since I lived about one-half mile from the school, I was not eligible to ride the school bus. So Daddy bought me my first bicycle. I was so proud of the bike and rode it to school each day. Since it was new and one of the few bikes around, many of the older boys kept taking it for a ride at recess. Fearful that they would damage it, I got Daddy to buy me a lock and chain so I could secure the bike to a tree. Needless to say, this didn't go over well with those kids who wanted a "joy ride."

The school did not have any food service so Momma would prepare a sack lunch for me each day, usually consisting of a biscuit with ham or sausage, a piece of cake or cookies, and a container of milk. Each student had a lift-top desk with a compartment in which we stored our books and lunches. One day, when I opened the desk, my lunch was gone. That day I did not say anything about it then, but the next day the same thing happened. I told the teacher and she said she would watch the next day and try to catch the culprit. And she did. When all the kids were outside for recess, one young boy came back to the classroom and tried to eat my lunch. The teacher did not tell me who he was, but assured me that it would not happen again.

There were few organized activities at recess. I spent the time trying to avoid the bullies who were angry because they couldn't ride my bike, trying to keep an eye on my lunch, and finding a time to use the outdoor toilets when the big boys were not around. This wasn't my most joyful year at school.

The times that I remember most fondly were the visits to my brother Floyd, who lived with his wife, Jewel, and their girls in Pontotoc, a town about 25-30 miles north.It was a great thrill for me to play with the girls. Shirley was about two years older than me, Jeanne was the same age, and Elizabeth was a couple of years younger. We would have such a good time that I would cry when it was time to go home!

SUNFLOWER COUNTY

After one year at Thorn, Daddy was asked to take over a church in a rural area of Sunflower County between Shaw and Indianola. I don't remember the name of the church, nor much about the parsonage. The most memorable event that occurred was when Daddy took me with him to the black church, as described in Chapter 2.

There were, however, two other incidents that I particularly remember. The school that I attended was an old wood-frame building with no indoor plumbing. I don't remember my teacher's name, nor even if the fifth grade had its own teacher. But I do recall that, if you needed to go to the toilet, you had to get the teacher's permission to go during class. What I didn't realize was that kids were using this ruse to get out of class; so the school stationed a man in the outhouse to catch the offenders. When I saw him there looking at me, my urge to pee went away and I couldn't perform. He, therefore, took me back to the teacher and told her I was one of the transgressors. Greatly embarrassed, I never asked to go to the outhouse again, but held my bladder until I could make a dash at recess.

My greatest triumph occurred early that fall. The boys were going to play baseball and "choose up sides" to determine the teams. Since I was a new kid that no one knew, I was the last player chosen. Even though I had never played baseball before, a very lucky thing happened when I came to bat that first time. I hit a pitch right on the nose and the ball landed on the roof of the school. It was not that far away but it certainly impressed the other students. For the rest of that fall, when we chose up sides, I was the first person selected. This sparked my interest in baseball and was the beginning of what would eventually become a passion.

ROCKY HILL - PART II

After only a few months in Sunflower County, we moved back to Rocky Hill, prompted by Daddy preaching at the black church. To my great joy, I learned that we were going back to Rocky Hill. Daddy and Momma were welcomed back by the congregation and I returned to Dixie School to finish the fifth grade, which I was overjoyed to learn, was being taught by Mrs. Germany.

The second tour at Rocky Hill was a great time for me. I was reconnected with old friends and began to venture around the community on my own. In addition, to the Bassett kids across the road, Melvin Loper lived nearby and we played together, sometimes fishing in a little creek not far from the church. I also hung out with the Pierce boys, James and Burma, who lived on another road that I could get to by walking through the woods behind the parsonage.

But my best friend was Hubert Killens. My brother, Junior, would often go hunting with Hubert's older brother, Rupert, and subsequently, married their sister, Mollie. Junior would take me over to the Killens' house when he went, and I would play with Hubert. He was a good athlete; so we would play basketball in his backyard or go hit fly balls to each other out in the cow pasture. Hubert's family fascinated me. They didn't go to church and would smoke, play cards, cuss, and probably drink a little beer. I had never met any folks like that. The parents, Alex and Lona, were hard-working people who struggled to make a living but were always generous to others.

Clyde bought me a basketball and installed a hoop on a tree in our yard. I spent many hours playing alone and with other boys when they came over. I, also, got Daddy to order me a baseball glove from Sears Roebuck at a cost of about $3.95. With that prized possession, I would pitch and catch with anyone who would play with me. When Clyde was home, he would always take the time to shoot a few baskets or toss the baseball with me.

Although I would sometimes go fishing by myself in a nearby creek or in a pond that was located on the diary farm owned by Paul and Henry, I did not really care that much about fishing. I didn't like sitting around, waiting for the fish to bite. Nor did I have any interest in hunting, unlike most boys who were raised in the country. I didn't like guns and never owned one. But Junior decided that I needed to know how to hunt. He took me with him and some other men to hunt squirrels in a wooded area near our house. I went along with them, trying to be enthusiastic. Finally, the dogs treed a squirrel and Junior handed me a shotgun, telling me how to aim. With the gun nestled against my right shoulder, I pulled the trigger. I heard a deafening blast in my right ear and felt a powerful kick against my shoulder that sent me falling backward. I don't know what happened to the squirrel.

All I remember is how hard all the men were laughing. That was my only shot of the day and my only hunting experience!

There were several boys my age in the community who would go down to swim in a wide place in the creek called the "wash-hole." We wore no bathing suits, of course. One day several older boys came down with some girls who stood on the bank, pointing and laughing. Fortunately the water was so muddy that they could not see through it; so we crouched down and waited until they finally left. But that did not stop us from going to the wash-hole, or from swimming in the nude.

While at Rocky Hill, I was very active in the church, going to all the services and to Sunday School. On Sunday nights, we would have YPE (Young People's Endeavor), the youth program. We would sing and, on special occasions, put on a play. YPE was followed by the Sunday night service, which usually consisted of singing. There was no choir, per se; instead the entire congregation joined in with Daddy or someone else leading. I still remember the old spirituals like "Amazing Grace"; "The Old Rugged Cross"; and "I'll Fly Away", with the church resounding as people sang at the top of their lungs. "I'll Fly Away" would often motivate someone to dance or run up and down the aisles, moved by the Holy Spirit.

It was during this time that Daddy decided I needed to learn how to play the piano. So he hired Mary Grace Comans, a girl several years older who played in church, to teach me. She would come to the church, giving me lessons and showing exercises that I was supposed to do. But shooting baskets, tossing a ball, or any other activity was more interesting than practice. After much frustration, Mary Grace finally gave up.

The Wednesday night prayer meetings were typically smaller and less structured than the Sunday service. There would be some singing and Daddy would read some scripture and have a brief message, but no sermon. Most of the meeting involved members giving their testimonies. Almost everyone would speak, describing the trials they had encountered that week or declaring their love for the Lord and their confidence in His care. Brother Oscar Bassett was always the first to testify and often concluded by speaking in tongues. He sat in the same pew at every service, with the men sitting on the right side of the church and the women on the left. The women were often very emotional in their testimonies, ending by either crying or breaking into a shout.

On Sunday, everyone dressed in their "Sunday best" which, for some of the farmers, consisted of a clean pair of overalls. There were no separate rooms for the Sunday School classes; each group would simply meet in a corner of the sanctuary. Then came the main service where Daddy would deliver his longest sermon of the week. But what I enjoyed the most was what followed

- good food! We would often go to someone's house for Sunday dinner or, on special occasions, there would be "dinner on the ground." The members of the church would bring dishes of food that would be spread on tables under the trees where my basketball goal was. The food would be delicious and plentiful -- fried chicken, all sorts of vegetables, and great desserts, like banana pudding. All the women in the church would want to make sure I tasted their favorite dishes and I readily complied.

It was during the second tour at Rocky Hill that I felt closest to Daddy. He would often take me with him when he went to town on Saturday or when he went to visit someone during the summer. I loved to ride in the car and loved to be with him. We would always stop at one of the country stores and he would buy me a "cold drink." While he would often get a Coke, I didn't think you got enough for your money (5¢) with a 6 oz. Coke, so I would buy a 12 oz. Double-Cola or a Nehi orange. On the occasions when Momma would go with us, she would get a Grapette. I couldn't understand how she would spend 5¢ on such a small drink! Almost everywhere we went, people would remark about how much I looked like my Daddy. That always pleased me -- and him too.

Physically, I was a little skinny kid until I reached 8 or 9. I was usually smaller and younger than the other boys in my classes. But I began to gain weight, probably from too many dinners-on-the-ground, and became a little fat. Momma always told me that I was just a little "chunky" or "fleshly". But that did not keep some boys at school from taunting me by calling me 'fatty'. I usually just smiled and walked away, trying to disguise the hurt that I felt. But one day on the school bus, a kid started taunting me and I struck back with a solid punch to his nose. Everyone on the bus stood up and started screaming, as they always did when a fight broke out. The kid grabbed me and we started wrestling in the aisle. By then the bus driver had stopped and come back to break up the fight. The kid's nose had started to bleed and he began to cry. The fight was over and so were the taunts. Neither this kid, nor the others, bothered me after that. This taught me a lesson: "At some point, you have to stand up for yourself."

At home I helped Momma with the work around the house. Each day I would feed the chickens and gather the eggs. There was a small building not far from the parsonage that contained a chicken coop and a storage area where we kept 10-20 chickens at a time. I became quite attached to the hens and even gave them names; they would all come running when I went out to feed them each evening. But when Momma wanted to have chicken for dinner, I would have to help her catch one and then watch as she wrung its neck. This made me sad, but I had usually recovered by the time she set fried chicken on the table. I also helped her in the garden, gathering and preparing vegetables along with many other tasks.

Our outhouse at Rocky Hill was located fifty yards past the chicken house, positioned over a drainage ditch. One summer day, as I was on my way to take care of business, I stepped on a snake that was sunning itself in the path. Barefooted, as I usually was all summer, I don't know who was more frightened, the snake or me! I jumped high in the air and it slithered off. But I got a hoe from the garden and leaned it against the hen house and carefully watched my steps on future trips to the outhouse. One day the snake was back; so I eased back to the hen house, got the hoe and killed it with several whacks. This was an important lesson that I should have learned: "if you find a snake in the grass, kill it!"

Momma had the task of disciplining me. I was not an unruly child but I sometimes just got distracted. Shooting baskets or reading a book was more interesting than shelling peas! Therefore, I often had my "head stuck in a book" rather than completing the job I was assigned. When she became exasperated, Momma would yell at me, "Go cut me a switch!" A switch is a thin limb from a tree or bush that is used to administer a whipping. Why she thought I would secure the weapon to be used for my own punishment, I don't know. But the threat was enough to make me get back to what I was supposed to be doing.

Daddy was involved in discipline on only one occasion but it was sufficient to ensure no future transgressions of that type occurred. One Saturday morning I got up and was ready to go to a boy's house to play, as I had been promised I could. But it was rainy and cold that day and Daddy decided it was not a good day to go out. In my disappointment, I began to "throw a fit", yelling and throwing my clothes around. Daddy grabbed his belt and proceeded to "wear me out", as the old timers would say, leaving my backside sore for days. I quickly concluded that "fits" were not a good way to express my disappointments.

During this period, I got an introduction to politics. Neshoba County was divided into "Beats" of which each had an elected supervisor whose primary responsibility was to take care of the roads. In the rural section where we lived, that meant using a grader to smooth the ruts and clean out the ditches. The beat supervisor got paid a small salary and had access to the equipment and materials he needed. One year a well-to-do farmer decided he wanted the job and came to ask Daddy for support. He had brought along a Shetland pony that he let me ride, saying that if he was elected that he might give that pony to me. I was overjoyed and pictured myself riding around the community. I expected Daddy to tell people from the pulpit to vote for this farmer, but he did not. In fact, I didn't see anything that he did to promote his candidacy. So I told Daddy one day how badly I wanted the farmer to win so I could have a pony. He reminded me that the farmer said he <u>might</u> give me the pony if elected and said that farmer probably promised that pony to every kid in the area. I still didn't believe him and waited anxiously for Election Day. When the results came in, the farmer did not win. This was probably good; otherwise I suspect I would have gotten my first bitter taste of empty campaign promises.

I don't recall much about the sixth grade at Dixie School. By that time I suspect that we had several subject matter teachers, rather than one, and I don't remember anyone's name. I read a lot of books that the teachers gave me. Dixie, to my knowledge, did not have a library; but the teachers had books they would loan kids who liked to read. I read every book I could get about sports. Two that I still remember clearly were <u>The Kid Who Never Struck Out</u>, about a boy who kept fouling off pitches until the pitcher finally walked him and <u>Highpockets</u>, about a kid who had long legs.

MERIDIAN

In the fall of 1950, Daddy was assigned a new church in Meridian, the second largest city in Mississippi. The church was located just a few blocks from the center of town. I had never lived in the city, had never lived on a paved road, and had never lived in a house with indoor plumbing. The school that I attended, Kate Griffin Junior High, provided an even more striking contrast. It served the whole city, contained only grades 7 and 8, and was huge in size. These changes should have been traumatic for me. Here I was eleven years old, going into the seventh grade, in a strange environment. But, remarkably, I adjusted to these major changes in my life.

Kate Griffin was on a large plot of land, the front part green space that included a football field, baseball diamond, tennis courts, and outdoor basketball court. The building itself was a red brick two- story building that covered a whole block with an indoor gym in the rear. I had classes in different rooms every hour and was often lost until a hall monitor helped me locate my room. The only teacher that I remember was Mrs. Stennis who taught me English. She was a good teacher, but I most recall her talking about her brother, John, who was a U.S. Senator who became one of the most influential political leaders in the nation.

At Kate Griffin, I had my first physical education class. We basically just did exercises and played basketball, the first time I had done so inside. I found that the ball bounced a lot better on the gym floor than on the dirt courts at Dixie. Moreover, Clyde had given me some beautiful green and white basketball shorts from Delta State where he was playing then.I took them to school to wear during P.E, but one day when I opened my locker, my shorts were gone. I was in a total panic, as I loved those shorts and because Clyde had given them to me. To my surprise, I looked out on the court and there was a kid wearing my shorts! (How stupid can you get? You steal a kid's shorts and wear them right out on the court!) Since the kid was considerably bigger, I found the teacher and told him what happened, figuring that the kid would deny it and it would be my word against his. But he admitted it, came back to the locker room and changed and gave the shorts to me. After that day, I took the shorts home and brought something less attractive to wear in P.E. the rest of the semester.

Up until this time, I had never taken a shower. We had a bathtub at home, which was novel enough for me. We were supposed to take a shower after PE but I did not because I did not know how it worked. After a week or so, by watching the other boys, I figured things out and began to shower, but usually waited until the others were finished.

Although I am sure that I had excellent teachers at Kate Griffin, the only two classes that I remember distinctly, other than English and gym, are Art and Shop. Judging from the teacher's reaction, I don't believe I ever evidenced any talent as an artist, although I enjoyed trying to draw and paint. In shop, we worked in sheet metal. I made a container of some sort, but it would not hold water so I decided I didn't have much of a future in this field, either.

The church in Meridian was on Sixth Street, which was at a higher elevation than Fifth Street, which ran parallel to it. The building was on a corner and there was an unpaved street that ran beside it down to 5th from the front on 6th. The parsonage was underneath, with the entrance off a dirt backyard at the rear. The lower floor, which comprised the foundation, was made of concrete block while the upper floor was a white wooden frame. Our living quarters consisted of a kitchen, dining room, living room, three bedrooms and a bath. There were also several rooms that served as Sunday School rooms for classes on Sunday. There were stairs at the rear of our living quarters that led up to the sanctuary. Across the unpaved street from the church was a large cemetery that was overgrown with weeds. I do not know who owned the cemetery, nor do I remember it ever being cleaned up.

In the summer of 1950, prior to our move to Meridian, my interest in baseball had intensified and I enjoyed listening to the games I could pick up on the radio. In Meridian, I didn't have anyone to play with, so I devised a way to play by myself and develop my skills. The backyard at the church was a large dirt parking lot where Daddy parked our car and where some other cars often parked on Sundays. But when the cars were gone, it became my baseball diamond. The back wall of our "house" was built out of concrete block and served as my backstop against which I would throw a baseball and then field it as it bounced back to me. I would do this for hours, everyday after school, throwing the ball at various angles so that I would have to really hustle. I would play a whole imaginary game this way and became increasingly proficient in fielding grounders. As I think back, I must have driven Momma crazy with the constant "thump', "thump" against the wall, but she never made me quit.

Likewise, I would practice my hitting by putting a baseball inside a sock, tying it with a piece of heavy twine, and hanging it from the clothesline where Momma hung our clothes to dry. I would swing the ball around the clothesline and hit it with my bat. This would work fine until the sock began to wear out; then the ball would sometimes burst out of the sock. Fortunately I never broke any windows although I came close a time or two. Finally, to practice my pitching, I would go over into the graveyard where I had beaten a path through the weeds. I would put a can on top of a tombstone and throw rocks at it. But I never ventured into the cemetery at night.

By the summer of 1951, I was fairly skilled at baseball although I had never played in a real game. That summer I got Clyde to take me to a tryout for a youth league in Meridian. I was selected for a team called the Meridian Stars and was subsequently chosen as the team captain. All those hours of practice by myself had paid off. We won the city championship that summer and my baseball "career" was underway.

The Meridian Star, the daily newspaper, sponsored the Stars; so our team got its picture in the paper and there was often a story about our game. Up until this time, I had never read a newspaper, but I got Daddy to subscribe, beginning a lifelong practice of reading a paper everyday.

Because of our team's success, the newspaper sponsored a trip to Pensacola, Florida at the end of the season. Several adults drove us down there in their cars and we stayed overnight in a motel on the beach. This was my first encounter with the ocean and I was frightened by the waves. The sea was a lot different from the wash hole! But I finally ventured into the water and had a great time.

Clyde also erected a basketball goal for me on a tree next to the sidewalk in our backyard, just as he had at Rocky Hill. Whenever I took a break from baseball, I would shoot baskets. The risk, however, was that the basketball would often hit one of the roots of the tree and take off down the unpaved street toward a culvert leading to the sewer underneath. I would have to run at breakneck speed to catch the ball before it disappeared.

After that summer with the Meridian Stars, one of my teammates and I became friends. Jimmy lived on 10th street, several blocks away, in a well-to-do section of town. I would ride my bike over to his house, a white two-story colonial with columns in front, where he taught me how to play Monopoly.

Jimmy would get us a couple of soft drinks from their refrigerator and we would play for hours. .

One evening, I had gone to a little store about two blocks from the church to pick up something for Momma. Near the entrance to the cemetery, I was confronted by a group of boys blocking my way. There was one kid about my size and three larger boys. The smaller kid was real cocky, demanding to know "what I was doing in East End". I explained that I lived just on the other side of the cemetery. He said he didn't believe me because he had never seen me in East End. One of the other boys, eventually, confirmed that he had seen me on the school bus and verified that I did live in the neighborhood. So they let me pass. I later learned that this was one of the neighborhood gangs and did not venture out much at night.

I also remember taking a couple of trips during our time in Meridian. The first was to Hattiesburg to see a basketball game between Mississippi Southern (now the University of Southern Mississippi) and Delta State, where Clyde was a senior and a starter on the team. DSTC had a great team that year and the rivalry with Southern was intense. Paul and Henry drove down to the game and took me with them. It was a tremendous thrill for me to see Clyde play for the first time in such a big game. He played well, although Southern won the game in a close contest.

The second trip was to Fort Benning, Georgia to visit Junior and Mollie, while he was stationed there. Henry and Paul drove me and Hubert Killens there where we stayed for a week before Junior and Molly drove us back. This was my first trip away from home for more than a night. Hubert and I had a great time there.

Momma, Daddy and I often visited Paul and Henry and their families on the dairy farm. I always enjoyed playing with my nieces and nephews, being close in age to many of them. But I also learned that, if you stayed very long, Paul would put you to work!

It was while we were living in Meridian that my brother, Floyd, died. Although I had been to funerals before, as Daddy often preached at funerals in our church, this was the first time I had experienced the death of a member of our family. Momma and Daddy were shocked and overcome with grief, as was I. It seemed like we couldn't stop the tears. I still remember how sad Jewel and the girls were. Floyd's loss is still felt, even today.

I don't remember that much about the church in Meridian or its members. I was not as involved as I had been at Rocky Hill. My schoolwork was much more challenging but I still managed to get good grades. And there were always the baseball skills to work on.

REFLECTIONS

My childhood involved considerable change -- living in five different communities and going to four different schools -- including a significant transition from a rural setting to a city. And the schools I attended, with the exception of the junior high in Meridian, were poorly funded and ill equipped. One might think that such experiences left me ill prepared to face the future.

In retrospect, I believe the changes I had to deal with -- new schools, new neighborhoods -- helped me to develop the ability and confidence to adapt to new surroundings and to the challenges that I was to confront later. As an adult, I frequently went into new organizations and communities in a leadership role; I always found those challenges exciting, rather than intimidating, and looked forward to them.

My early education at Dixie School helped spark in me a life-long love of learning because of the nurturing I received from the teachers there. By the time I got to Thorn and to the school in Sunflower County, I was capable of learning on my own, a necessity because of the limited instruction. I always did my assignments, motivated by the positive feedback I got from my teachers and my parents. And I read all the time, studying not only the textbook but also any other books the teachers would give me. That is probably why I made a relatively easy transition to a city and a much larger school when we moved to Meridian.

The most important factor in my life was my parents. They provided stability, always there even though other things were changing. I never had to wonder whether I was loved, nor worry about being cared for. Momma and Daddy, both mild-mannered and even-tempered, worked hard and were widely respected by others. They always seemed proud of me, praising my good grades in school and other things I would do. They were wonderful role models in their attitudes about life and their concern for others. The church was also a powerful influence, as I witnessed the sincere beliefs that people possessed and the efforts they made to live by those beliefs.

One of the disadvantages of moving as often as we did was that I had very few close friends. I would have playmates wherever we lived, but no one with whom I "grew up". The only person from my elementary years with whom I have maintained any contact is Hubert Killens, probably due to our relationship from the marriage of Junior and Mollie. But moving often, in my estimation, had a positive element to it as well. I learned how to play by myself, as evidenced by the hours I spent shooting baskets or throwing a baseball against the wall. And, of course, I spent a lot of time reading. This made me, I believe, more self-reliant and less dependent on others --able to entertain and care for myself.

As mentioned earlier, my family had very few material goods. The only time I lived with indoor plumbing was our two years in Meridian. We never owned a television set, although we did have a radio that I could use to listen to baseball games. But I never felt deprived. We always had food, clothing and a nice place to live. Above all, I had wonderful parents, a great family, and friends who helped me get a good start in life. I felt fully prepared for the next stage in my life, the high school years.

CHAPTER 5:
GROWING UP: THE HIGH SCHOOL YEARS

In the late summer of 1952, Daddy announced that we were moving back to Goodwill, the church he had founded. This pleased both Momma and Daddy, as they would be reunited with many old friends they had brought into the church. Whether Daddy requested this assignment or the congregation at Goodwill asked for him back, it seemed to me that everyone was happy. And so was I.

The physical environment at Goodwill had changed little in the time we had been away. The parsonage and the church sported a new coat of white paint and the road by the church was now gravel but the parsonage still did not have indoor plumbing. We still had to use an outhouse, draw water from a pump in the back year and take baths in a washtub on the back porch. In the summer we filled the tub with water and left it to warm in the sun. In the winter, Momma heated water on the stove. Needless to say, during the winter we took fewer baths!

One of the great benefits of moving back to Goodwill was reuniting with James Ray Jones, the oldest son of Lula Belle (Momma's "adopted daughter"). He was one year behind me in school but we were close to the same age. During the next two years, James and I were almost inseparable, particularly during the summers. We played ball or just hung out, either at his house or at mine. We devised a game of baseball that we played in the front yard of the church. Goodwill faced the road and there were no windows in the front (which was the rear entrance); so we used one-half of the wall as a backstop to "home plate". The batter would stand there while the other one pitched. Depending on where the ball landed, it would be an out or a base hit; if it flew across the road into a cotton patch, that was a home run. We often played a nine-inning game each day, but our season was interrupted when some members of the church complained about the marks left on the wall where the ball had struck.

James and I also played ball with some other kids in that neighborhood, which was called Locke Station. There was a boy nearby named "Jam-Up" who had a cow pasture behind his barn that we sometimes used or we would go up to Lake Carrier Elementary School to use the playground. Since neither James nor I had a car, walking was our primary means of transportation. Jam-Up's family owned one of the few televisions in the community, so I would often walk over to his house on Monday nights to watch "The Cisco Kid", followed by wrestling, broadcast live from Memphis.

We often spent the night together at James' house, where we listened to the radio in bed, keeping it under the covers so his mother would not hear. First, we tuned in the Memphis Chicks, a minor league baseball team that broadcast its games in this area, or the St. Louis Cardinals, the only major league team we could pick up. Next came WDIA, a Memphis station that played the records of the black "rhythm and blues" singers late at night. It was my first introduction to the "Delta Blues" and great artists like Jimmy Reed, Muddy Waters, B.B. King, ' Howlin' Wolf, and Big Joe Turner. None of the white or mainline radio stations would play the black artists.

James lived in two different houses during this time; the first was within easy walking distance but the second was about two miles away, so Daddy had to drop me off there. James' father, Randolph, worked at a steel mill in Joliet, Illinois, and came home only for a few days each month. There were few jobs, other than farm labor, in Mississippi at this time. With the advent of the mechanical cotton picker, many blacks had lost their jobs and fled to Chicago and Detroit for employment. Many white workers were similarly affected.

I attended Marks High School for the ninth and tenth grades, riding the bus six miles each way. The high school was an attractive brick building about three blocks from the center of town. I made good grades (all A's and B's) and have positive memories of my teachers, but no one stands out. The things I remember most clearly, however, are those that happened outside of class.

On the main street of Marks was a pool hall. Some of the boys would go up there during lunch hour to shoot pool and they sometimes invited me to go along. At the pool hall grill a hamburger and a soft drink cost 30 cents, which is what I had for lunch money. At first I would just eat my hamburger and watch the other boys play. But before long I was lured into a game. The rules required the loser to pay for the game, a cost of 15 cents. At the beginning I lost every time, but if I stopped after one game, I would still have 15 cents to buy an R.C. Cola and some "Nabs" (cheese crackers). But, more often than not, my competitive spirit would get the best of me and I would challenge the winner to another game. If I lost the second game, all my money would be gone -- and my lunch, too! I went hungry several days until my skills (or my choice of opponents) improved enough that I could enjoy a game and lunch as well.

The town of Marks was located about 40 miles east of the Mississippi River on Highway 6, a major east-west road from Oxford to Clarksdale. The commercial district occupied about three blocks of stores with a railroad track and a depot separating the east side of town from the west. On a side street leading to the high school was a movie theater and several stores. On Saturdays the town would be filled with blacks, but they would be concentrated on the western end of the main street where a few stores catering to blacks were located. It was rumored that one of the stores would sell bootleg whiskey late on Saturday night, leading to many fights. I was instructed to stay away from that end of town.

In the spring of my freshman year at Marks, I tried out for the baseball team. I made the team, not as a starter but played quite a bit at either second or third base. By my sophomore year I was the regular third baseman and was developing into a decent player.

I also played baseball each summer for a Locke Station team. At that time, almost every community had a baseball team that played on Sunday afternoons. Herman Flemmons, who owned one of the two stores in Locke Station, sponsored our team and our home field was a cow pasture behind his store. The other teams we played often had their games on a high school diamond. I was the youngest player on the team, with many of the players being grizzled veterans in their twenties and thirties -- with scraggly beards and tobacco juice dripping down their chins!

In my sophomore year I tried out for the basketball team and was one of ten players chosen. Being both short and slow, I didn't have the skills to be an outstanding player. But I was scrappy and, because of the hours of practice, had an excellent shot. The minutes I played were often in the last quarter, after the result was decided. But I once scored six points, my highest total, and played in enough games to get a letter -- a mark of excellence in those days! I also went out for football during spring practice in my sophomore year preparing to play the next fall. The team had a lot of good athletes, perhaps the best being the Collins boys. Gary was a senior and the star quarterback. His younger brother, Cloray, was only a freshman but was destined to become a great player in later years.

My best friend in my class, Sonny Tedford, a stocky freckled-faced kid, was also on the baseball team. I went home with Sonny once or twice and we hung out together. One day in P.E. class, the teacher brought out boxing gloves and paired me up with Sonny. I had never boxed before but I was willing to try.Clearly Sonny was more skilled and got in several good licks. When the round was over, I decided that I liked Sonny better as a friend than as an opponent! Sonny went on to become a member of the Mississippi House of Representatives in later years.

One of my most pleasant memories involved spending a week with Clyde and Vashti during the summer. The head basketball coach at Canton by then, Clyde would take me to the gym to work out with some of his basketball players. I swam in the pool at the Canton Recreation Center, jumping for the first time off a high diving board.One afternoon I watched a baseball game between Canton and Yazoo City. From reading Willie Morris' books, I think he was playing centerfield for Yazoo City that day.

Our return to Goodwill also introduced me to the world of work via the hard labor of picking cotton. Harvest time drew almost everyone to the fields and the schools would even close for a week so the students could help. Only the very largest farmers had mechanical cotton-pickers; the others needed plenty of "hands". I was intrigued that many employers in those days called their employees "hands", implying that they were hiring their hands and not their heads!I picked cotton all day on Saturdays and when school was out. It was hard work, dragging a sack and bending over to pluck the cotton from the prickly bolls. Farmers paid $3 per hundred pounds, about the best I could do in a day. But, since I had no allowance, this was my only way to get some spending money. The majority of the pickers would be local black people, many of who could pick 200 or more pounds per day. I didn't have to pick cotton, but it was about the only way to earn any spending money. But I decided very early that there had to be a better way to make a living, one that relied more on the brains than the hands!

It was during this time, too, that I discovered the opposite sex. I remember the first time I kissed a girl, a slightly older female who was visiting.I do not remember her name, but I certainly recall the experience. She asked me if I had ever kissed a girl and I admitted that I had not.So she leaned over and kissed me on the mouth. I felt dizzy and walked around in a haze for most of the afternoon, contemplating this new world I had suddenly discovered. I was immediately in love with her, but she left town the next day!

My first "girlfriend" was Frances, one of three daughters of David Parish, a farmer who lived a short distance from Goodwill. Two of her sisters were older than me, while Frances was one grade behind. I don't think we ever had a "date", since I was not old enough to drive, but I used to hang around her house whenever possible. The Parishes had a television so I would go to their house to watch baseball games. When Frances entered the ninth grade, she and I would sit together on the school bus.

The Parishes did not attend Goodwill Church, so I did not see Frances there. This allowed me to become increasingly aware of the girls in the church. James Jones had an attractive sister, Jean. And there were the Pritchetts -- Louise, Betty, and Etta Faye. My attention to the service frequently waned, as watching the girls became an enticing alternative.

James Pritchett, the brother to the Pritchett girls, was a couple of years older than me but was short and slight of build. He had a car, which made him a valuable friend, and he took me with him as he drove around. James could play the guitar and sing. He ended up dropping out of school, going to Memphis where he joined a rock and roll band, calling himself "Little Jimmy Pritchett".

While at Goodwill, I persuaded Daddy to subscribe to <u>The Commercial Appeal</u>, the main daily newspaper in Memphis. We would receive it in the mail a day late, but that did not matter to me. I would pore over the sports page including the box scores for all the baseball games. Some boys at Marks High would kid me, saying I knew the batting average of every player in the major leagues. That was not true, but I could come close! James Ray and I also found some guys in the community at Locke Station who attended games of the Memphis Chicks on Sunday and persuaded them to take us with them on a couple of occasions.

Although I had been a little "chunky" in elementary and junior high, I had slimmed down to about 5'6" and 150 lbs by the time I got to high school. I guess all the days playing ball and walking a lot produced that result. But in the spring of my sophomore year, I finally turned fifteen and got a driving license. I still didn't have a car, but Daddy would let me borrow his occasionally. As with every teenager, that was a glorious moment!

As I mentioned earlier, I was often distracted in church during these years. Sometimes on Sunday nights, I would sneak out the back and go to the house to listen to the radio. Lying on the couch in the dark, I would listen to "The Lone Ranger", "The Green Hornet", and, my favorite, "The Shadow". And on some Saturdays when I could get a ride into Marks, I would go to the "picture show". This was the first time I had ever seen a movie. On Saturdays, the theater would show a double feature (usually two Westerns) with a serial in between that would leave you in suspense from one week to the next, wondering how the star could possibly escape from the danger he faced at the end of the episode.

I don't know for sure if Daddy knew I was going to the movies, but, if he did, he was tolerant of my "misbehavior" since the church believed that going to the movies was a sin. But I still participated actively in church, attending virtually all the services.

THE MOVE TO LOUISIANA

In late summer, 1954, Daddy was sent to Louisiana to pastor the Dunn Church of God. Dunn was located on Highway 80, the main east-west road from Vicksburg to Shreveport and on to Dallas. It consisted of a service station, a café, and a post-office, and was about five miles from Delhi, a larger town where I would attend high school.

Even though it meant leaving good friends like James, I was excited about the move to Louisiana. I had spent all my 15 years in Mississippi, with only brief trips outside the state. This move would take us away from our family in Mississippi, as well as Aunt Rosa who was now living in Memphis with her daughter, Quay. She and her husband, Gene, lived in a nice neighborhood near Memphis State University. I always enjoyed those visits because Quay was very friendly and a good cook!

From what I had read about Louisiana, it sounded like an exotic place -- filled with alligators, bayous, and people called Cajuns! But, in fact, the area into which we moved was not much different from Mississippi in terms of terrain and in how the people looked and sounded. As I found later, northern Louisiana is very similar to Mississippi culturally, but southern Louisiana is a whole different world.

Delhi was a town of about 5,000, a little larger than Marks. The center of town was bisected by railroad tracks that ran parallel to Highway 80. There were numerous stores but the teenagers liked to hang out in Hopson's Drug Store, the Saljobar Café, or the pool hall. The high school was located about one-half mile north of downtown. It was a handsome brick building on a large lot, with an attached gym and a football stadium out back. I learned quickly that football was important at Delhi. Delhi was classified as a Class B school, which meant there were fewer than 100 boys in grades 9-12; the male enrollment at the school in 1954 was nearly 100 and Delhi was reclassified as Class A one year or so after I graduated. In 1954, the Delhi Bears were a dominant force in Class B football.

Shortly after moving into the parsonage at Dunn, a visitor representing the football boosters at Delhi came calling. He told me they had heard I had played football in Mississippi. I told him I had not played but only participated in spring practice. He told me they wanted me to try out for the team and took me to see Coach Raymond Richards who invited me to come out for fall practice, which started in a few days -- about the middle of August.

Coach Richards was a proponent of "hard-nose" football. He struck fear in the hearts of every boy on the team and was determined to "make men" out of them. I was not fully prepared for Coach Richards, the intensity of football at Delhi, or the August heat in Louisiana. The next two weeks were the toughest I had ever spent in my life. Every day, it was running, blocking, and tackling until you dropped. You learned not to eat anytime close to practice, lest you deposit your lunch on the field! And the coaches would not let the players drink any water during practice. The practices were total torture but, stubborn and determined, I stuck with it. I realized that playing football was a test of "manhood" in that culture. As a new kid in school, if I quit, I would never be accepted or fit in.

Coach put me at guard. Guards were kids too small to play tackle, too short to play end, and too slow to be running backs. All you had to do was run into people as often and as hard as you could. I won a position on the second team. But when the season started, Coach Richards told me I was not eligible to play because Delhi had not received my birth certificate from Mississippi. This was a great disappointment, but I came to practice every day and worked hard. The season was about half over before I got into a game, but I played enough to earn a letter.

Delhi had a great team in 1954 with George (Sonny) Sumlin as the star running back and Clyde Thompson as the quarterback. We lost only one game during the regular season, won the district playoffs and the North Louisiana Championship. The Bears then played Donaldsonville, the South Louisiana champ, for the State Class B Championship. The game was in Delhi and, unfortunately, we lost in a close game. But it was a thrill, being part of the team.

By the time my senior year rolled around, better prepared and more skilled, I began to like football more than I did at first. Still small at about 155 pounds, I learned to block by hitting my opponent low and knocking him off his feet. I was the starting right guard on another great team. Larry Bonner was the left guard, Jimmy Britt and Dickie Thompson played tackle, with Garland Kyle the center. Eugene Gilley and George "Sappy Dog" Brown were the ends, Buster Harrell the quarterback, and Tommy Mathieu, Roy O'Neal, and Bobby Leach the running backs.

Coach Richards had brought in a new assistant, Cecil Burchfield, a good contrast to the head coach. While Coach Richards ruled by intimidation, Coach Burchfield motivated by encouragement and positive reinforcement. I reacted much more positively to Coach Burchfield and enjoyed him as a coach.

We again went through the regular season with only one loss and won the district and the North Louisiana championships. In the district championship game, I pulled out and got a key block on a linebacker that sprung our halfback for the winning touchdown. For the State Championship, Delhi played a Catholic school in New Orleans (St. Mary's of Holy Name).A new school that had been classified as B, St. Mary's eventually moved up to Class AA because of the size of its student body. We played in New Orleans and were badly outmatched, losing 33-7. But playing on such a good team represented a good experience for me. And at the end of the season, I was named to the All-District team as the second team right guard. I was proud of the progress that I made in this sport.

I also played basketball for two years, with my performance similar to that at Marks. In my senior year, I did start a few games but my highest scoring game was six points. Coach Burchfield led the basketball team during my senior year and I enjoyed playing for him. Even though I was not a star player, he made me feel like I was an important part of the team.

But what I enjoyed most about basketball was the away games where we would travel by bus with the girls' team. On the return trip, we would pair off and I would often sit with Fannie Mae Hutchinson, the star of the girls' team. A group of us would often start to sing. Once I sang a solo of "Only You" by the Platters while others on the bus provided harmony. I was able to do such a bold thing because it was dark and no one could see me!

The sport at which I excelled at Delhi was baseball, playing second base both seasons with some occasional games at shortstop. We had a great baseball field with a covered grandstand.Located across town from the high school at the county fairgrounds, it must have been built to serve other teams, in addition to high school. I don't remember our won-lost records, but we had a good team each year. One of my favorite memories is hitting a triple with the bases loaded in one game. My best friend on the baseball team was Richard Dearman, a skinny kid who played neither football nor basketball, but was a terrific baseball player. He lived out in the country and we would often get together to practice. Richard would pick me up to go to the ballpark where we would hit fly balls and grounders to each other for hours.

For two summers, I also played American Legion baseball. The American Legion in Delhi would sponsor a team, consisting of players not only from Delhi but also from other nearby towns. American Legion baseball was quite popular then with a high caliber of play. In the summer of my senior year, we won the district championship and advanced to the state tournament before losing. As a reward for our success, the team received a trip to St. Louis to see a four-game series between the Cardinals and the Dodgers. This was my first time to see a major league game. And, on top of that, we got to meet Stan Musial, one of St. Louis' greatest players ever.

The academic program at Delhi was excellent. The Principal, Mr. Carlton Johnson, was a very positive person and I had some excellent teachers: Mrs. Wiggers in English, Mrs. Stout in History, Mr. Hazlitt in Science, and Mrs. Bell in Math. Mrs. Bell was probably the most influential teacher I had in terms of my decision to go to college. She always praised the work I did in math and told me I ought to become an engineer. I also took a course in Agriculture under Mr. Gaharan and joined the FFA -- when the last thing I wanted to be was a Future Farmer! But I liked him and he was a good recruiter.

I didn't have a steady girlfriend at Delhi and, in fact, hardly dated at all. I was too busy playing ball! The two prettiest girls in my class were Sally Sumlin and Carolyn Dark, but I didn't have the courage to ask them for a date. I even had a "crush" on a little cheerleader, Suzy Bradley, two grades behind me, but I think I only spoke to her once. Thankfully, Bertha Lou Travis invited me to the Senior Prom and I went out a couple of times with Frances Hunter.

In my senior year, I tried out for and won the male lead in the senior play, "Seventeenth Summer".Evelyn Green, a quiet girl who seemed to blossom out on the stage, won the female lead.Many of our classmates said we would be a "perfect match", since we were both shy.So we went out a couple of times, but the magic we experienced on stage wasn't there in real life.I was thrilled that Momma and Daddy came to see me perform in the senior play. They never came to see me play any sports at Marks or Delhi. The church did not support involvement in such "worldly" activities; therefore, Momma and Daddy felt that members of the church would criticize them if they attended. But, fortunately, the play was determined to be acceptable.

In Dunn, the parsonage was a nice old house, with indoor plumbing, about a quarter mile from the church. We had a big garden and I did my share of work there. And I picked cotton in the fall and chopped cotton in the spring to earn spending money. I participated in activities at the church but would have to admit that my life was pretty full with schoolwork and play. A classmate at Delhi, Bobbie Nell Sheppard, lived nearby in Dunn and taught me how to dance, particularly the "jitter-bug", an important skill in high school.

I rode the school bus from Dunn to Delhi each morning but, because I played sports and had to practice after school, I would miss the bus home in the afternoon. To get home in the evening, I worked out a deal with a barber who was a member of our church and lived near us in Dunn. He worked at a shop on Main Street in Delhi that closed at six o'clock each evening. So I would walk down to his shop after practice and wait for him to finish. If practice ended early, I would stop by the pool hall and shoot a few games until six o'clock. But one day I got on a winning streak and didn't watch the clock carefully; when I got to the shop, the barber was gone. So I had to walk the five miles home. I was too embarrassed to call Daddy -- or to blame the barber. But I didn't miss my ride any time after that! When we had a game at night, Daddy would let me borrow the car.

All during my senior year, I thought about going to college. Since my grades were excellent, my teachers were urging me to do so. I wanted to go because Clyde had gone, but knew that Daddy did not have the resources to pay for it. Clyde had won a basketball scholarship, but I didn't feel I was good enough to earn such an athletic grant-in-aid. I did drive over to Southwest Mississippi Junior College and talked to the football coach about going there. He invited me to come and try out but could not offer me a scholarship; I thought that was too much of a risk. I believed I was good enough to play baseball in college but schools gave very few, if any, scholarships in baseball.

Mrs. Bell, my Math teacher, urged me to apply for a T.H. Harris Legislative Scholarship, awarded annually to outstanding high school graduates across the state by the Louisiana legislature. I didn't know if I could win but, since Mrs. Bell had gotten the application forms, I filled them out and mailed them in, indicating that I could go either to Louisiana Tech, Northeast, or Northwestern, all state colleges. I was too intimidated to think about going to LSU because of its size. But I did apply for admission to the three schools listed and was accepted to each.

Louisiana Tech was my first choice because of Mrs. Bell's influence, and I was thinking about majoring in electrical engineering. While waiting to hear about the scholarship, Daddy drove me over to Ruston one Saturday early in the summer. In notifying me I had been accepted, Tech had indicated that all their dorms were full. Daddy and I got a list of off-campus rooming houses, but everywhere we went the rooms had already been rented. I returned home very disappointed.

I didn't want to go to Northeast in Monroe, even though several of my classmates at Delhi were planning to go there. And I didn't know much about Northwestern, never having visited their campus. So I felt kind of left out. Later that summer, Daddy met with a representative of Draughon's Business College in Monroe and made a $100 deposit on a course in bookkeeping. It was a six-week course that cost $300. I'm sure that Daddy thought he was doing the right thing for me, but I was not enthusiastic. I felt capable of going to college and hoped that something would develop. I think Daddy felt I was making a mistake in not taking the bookkeeping course, but he let me pursue my dream and I vowed to pay him back for the deposit.

Finally, in late July, I received a letter from Northwestern State College in Natchitoches, informing me that I had been awarded a Harris scholarship and that they had a dorm room for me. So I got ready to become a Demon. Although I had never visited the campus, I was excited. Thankfully, I had somewhere to go to college and most of my expenses would be paid by the scholarship.

Before taking that big step, however, we had another move to make. Daddy had been appointed as pastor of the Sharp's Chapel Church of God near Covington in south Louisiana. I moved there with Momma and Daddy just a week or so before I had to be at Northwestern for the fall semester, 1956.

REFLECTIONS

Overall, I would rate my high school experiences very positive. This was in spite of the fact that I was an "outsider" in each school, i.e. I came from the outside, instead of having grown up in the community, and I lived outside of town, in the country. But through my participation in athletics (particularly in Delhi), I was able to bridge the gap and have relationships with many other students. Playing competitive sports helped to develop my drive and desire to succeed, as well as demonstrate the benefits of being part of a team. I suspect that I spent more time with athletics than I did with academics in high school, but I was still very conscientious with my studies. I paid attention in class, did my homework, and made good grades. Therefore, I felt prepared for college.

As I mentioned earlier, Momma and Daddy were not able to come to see me play any of the sports in which I participated. That was a little strange as the parents of many of the other players came to the games. But I don't believe I ever resented their absence because I understood why they felt they could not attend. I appreciated them letting me play when some members of the church may have criticized them for doing so. I was pleased that they did attend my graduation ceremonies at Delhi, as well as the Senior Play.

My parents seemed to be proud of the high grades I earned, but I never felt any pressure from them to excel academically. I believe that they would have loved me just as much had I earned C's rather than A's. The drive to excel both -- academically and athletically -- was largely "inner-directed". I was always my own worst critic and drove myself to succeed. But the role model that Clyde provided was clearly a source of positive motivation.

I am grateful for the caring teachers that I had. Mrs. Bell, my math teacher, wrote me a note in the yearbook my senior year at Delhi that I still treasure. She said, "You have the wonderful combination of a more than pleasing personality combined with intelligence. This is rare indeed and I'm expecting big things from you." With encouragement like that, I could not fail.

I left Delhi in 1956 never to return there to live and only to visit on rare occasions. I did attend the 48th and 50th anniversaries of my graduating class at Biloxi, Mississippi, and Monroe, respectively. As with most such ceremonies, I recognized very few of my former classmates but enjoyed getting to know them again and to learning what had happened in their lives.

But the challenge that faced me in 1956 involved entering a whole new environment at a place I had never been and with people that I did not know.

CHAPTER 6:

DEMON DAYS AND THE SUITCASE HANDLE

I first saw the Northwestern campus when Daddy drove me up there from Covington. Northwestern is located in the town of Natchitoches, about halfway between Alexandria and Shreveport. Distinguished by being the oldest settlement in the Louisiana Purchase, Natchitoches traces it's founding to 1714. The Cane River runs along a bricked main street past many beautiful old homes surrounded by trees, draped with Spanish moss.

The Northwestern campus lies on the western side of the community about a mile from the center of the town. Known as Northwestern State College (NSC) when I enrolled in the fall of 1956, it had been a "normal" school established to train teachers, but over the years its curriculum had expanded to include non-teaching degree programs. At the time I entered, the college enrolled about 2,400 students, certainly much larger than the high schools I had attended but small enough to feel very comfortable.

The attractive campus, beautifully manicured and filled with both pine and hardwood trees had a mixture of French and Colonial architecture. One of the landmarks of the campus was "The Columns", the remnants of the Bullard Mansion that had been built in 1832. They sat in a quadrangle in front of the main administration building, Caldwell Hall.

Because my decision to attend NSC occurred late in the summer, I received one of the last available dormitory assignments. The acceptance letter instructed me to report to D-Frame dorm. After some searching, Daddy and I finally found it on the far northwestern edge of the campus. To respond to its growing enrollment, the college had purchased four old Army barracks and had converted them into dormitories for men. They were astutely named -- A, B, C and D-Frame -- with A-Frame being the closest to the campus and

D-Frame the furthest away. There was nothing beyond D-Frame except a cow pasture and the road to Many, a small town west of Natchitoches.

We found the dormitory monitor and got the keys to my room, which was furnished with two desks, two straight chairs, and bunk beds. Daddy helped me unload the car of my clothes and other things and then took off to drive back to south Louisiana, leaving me alone -- away from home for the first time except for short trips with family or friends. My roommate, Billy Miller, a skinny redhead from Pitkin, Louisiana, soon arrived. He was very quiet, planned to major in business (the same major I had selected), and appeared to be as frightened as I was, so we got along fine.

I had no idea what to expect when I went to college nor what to do, beyond going to class, of course. Clyde was the only member of my family who had gone to college and he had not told me much about his experiences other than playing basketball. I learned very quickly, however, that freshmen's hazing was a major part of campus life at that time.

FRESHMAN HAZING

Early the next morning, my roommate and I were instructed that all freshmen boys were to report to the Student Center for a haircut. Sure enough, the Center (called the "Field House") had several barber stations where we each got a "military style" haircut almost to the skin. Then we had to buy a small purple beanie with an "N" on the front and were told to wear it at all times. Furthermore, the upperclassmen explained that all freshmen were "dogs" and that, when they called us, we were to respond and carry out whatever commands we received. These conditions would continue until the Louisiana Tech-Northwestern football game in late October. If NSC won the game, the beanies came off; if they lost, we had to wear them until Christmas break.

A few days later I was walking through the Student Center between classes when an upperclassman called "Dog!" and motioned for me to come over. I saw then that the ballroom of the center was filled with upperclassmen and that they had a small rooster in a cage. They let the rooster out and demanded that I catch it. I chased the rooster all over the ballroom to no avail, but to the great merriment of the upperclassmen. Finally getting away, I resolved to avoid the Student Center whenever possible. The student mailboxes were in one end of the center but I would sneak in the side entrance early in the morning to check my box and avoid the upperclassmen (who, I hoped, all slept late!)

Hazing was not relegated only to the Student Center, but was conducted in the dorms also. D-Frame residents included about half freshmen and half upperclassmen, with many of the upperclassmen quite older, including some veterans of the Korean War. An event occurred there in D-Frame that left me with a nickname that I carried throughout my four years at Northwestern.

THE SUITCASE HANDLE

Toward the end of the first week in school, the upperclassmen in D-Frame told all the freshmen to be in their room by 9:00 PM that night. Shortly after that time, an upperclassman came to my room, ordered me to strip down to my underwear, and to come with him. I followed him to the lounge in the dorm where all the upperclassmen were gathered. In the middle of the room was a desk. I was ordered to stand on the desk and to remove my underpants. Then, one end of a string was tied around my penis and the other end was tied to the handle of a suitcase.

I was handed the suitcase and found it to be quite heavy. I instructed was to hold the suitcase with both hands out in front of me and, on the count of "three", drop the suitcase. My task, if I wanted to "save myself" was to beat the suitcase to the floor! Needless to say, at this stage of my life, I had become quite fond of my penis and did not want to lose it. So I began to ponder what I could do.

In the meantime, all the upperclassmen were hollering, "Dog this and Dog that" with threats as to what was in store for me if I did not comply with their instructions. One upperclassman suggested that my eyes be covered so I wouldn't have to witness the destruction if I didn't beat the suitcase to the floor. So a blindfold was put on me.

By the time they began the countdown, I had decided on my strategy. When the count reached three, I threw the suitcase upward and dove off the desk to the floor, skinning my knees and elbows in the process. I think I may have actually beaten the suitcase to the floor! But what I didn't realize was that, during the time after the blindfold was secured, someone cut the string but kept tension on the end tied to my penis.

By the time I hit the floor, the whole room had erupted in laughter. Apparently, the upperclassmen had not had so much fun in years! From that point on, the upperclassmen in D-Frame called me "Suitcase". With all the "dogs" having their heads shaved and beanie caps on, I guess we all looked alike. But everyone recognized me! Pretty soon, other men on campus began to call me "Suitcase" and I kept the nickname my whole time there, running for student government office on that identifier and writing a column in the student newspaper with that by-line. So almost everyone knew me as "Suitcase". Even though only a very few individuals knew how I got that handle!

At some time during my years at Northwestern, I overheard a conversation between two guys who were speculating about the origin of my nickname. One said that, during my freshman year I always had my suitcase packed and went home every weekend. Little did they know! During my first year and throughout my four years at NSC, I hardly went home at all except for summers and when the university was closed.

THE FRESHMAN YEAR

For the remainder of that fall semester, I concentrated my time in three places: in the classrooms for my classes, in the cafeteria for my meals, and in my room studying. The NSC-Tech game in late October ended in a tie. No one seemed to know what that meant as regards freshman hazing; so virtually all the freshmen quit wearing their beanies. Since our hair had grown out by then, an upperclassman that did not know you personally would not know for sure that you were a freshman. The hazing ended, thankfully.

The cafeteria, called the "chow hall" by everyone, served the entire campus. Located at the end of a quadrangle of women's dorms, it was not only the place to eat but also a good place to meet girls. But I didn't have much time for that as a freshman as I was determined to do well academically. My scholarship required that I maintain a "B" average and I did not want to take any chances.

The cost of attending Northwestern in 1956 was $250 per semester for tuition, room and board, and books. My scholarship paid for half of that; so I got Daddy to loan me the remaining money, with a promise that I would pay him back. I was also determined to reimburse him for the down payment on the bookkeeping course in Monroe.

Not having a car at college, I did not go home for Thanksgiving break but spent the holidays with my roommate, Billy Miller, in Pitkin. I enjoyed the time with his parents. For Christmas break, Daddy drove up and brought me home for the holidays.

Over the course of the freshman year, I got to know the campus by walking all over it for classes and other activities. And I also walked downtown to the movie theater. I don't remember having any dates my freshman year, although I attended several campus events. There was a freshman dance where I spent the evening standing in the corner with other freshmen -- too shy to ask anyone to dance! There were three girls from my graduating class at Delhi who came NSC -- Delma Donahoe, Lorraine Hosea, and Bertha Lou Travis -- but we had no classes together and I hardly ever saw them on campus.

In the spring I tried out for the baseball team and became the regular second baseman on the freshman team. We practiced with the varsity and played several games with freshmen teams from other colleges and with teams from Junior Colleges. NSC had a great team that year, being co-champs of the Gulf States Conference.

MY ACADEMIC WORK

My choice of a major in business administration was primarily a decision by default. NSC did not have an engineering school; so that alternative was eliminated. I had thought at various junctures about majoring in physical education and becoming a coach. I like sports and that was the route Clyde had taken. But by then I knew I would not be playing any sports in college except baseball and thought that perhaps some other major would suit me better.

I didn't know anything about business, having never worked anywhere except the cotton fields. And I didn't know any "businessmen" except owners of neighborhood stores. But I figured my aptitude for mathematics might serve me well in this field and that this major might be the best bet to insure myself a job upon graduation.

As it turned out, I really enjoyed my classes in business. Noble B. Morrison headed the department in the School of Applied Arts and Sciences. There were some terrific teachers in the business department. I was particularly fond of Joe Johnson, Allan Steele, and Kenneth Durr. They were all good instructors and were available to students outside of class. Mr. Johnson advised me throughout my undergraduate years and became a great friend. By the beginning of my junior year, I decided to move into the specialized major in accounting.

By the end of my freshman year my academic record was in fine shape -- A's and B's in all my courses. But I was ready to go home for the summer.

SUMMER, 1957

My first objective was to get a job so that I could repay Daddy and save funds for the next school year. One of the members of Daddy's church, Otha Fussell, worked at a shipyard and had told him that I might be able to get a job there. During my first week at home, Daddy took me there to make an application.

The Equitable Equipment Company built and repaired barges and tugboats at a large shipyard on the banks of Lake Pontchatrain in the town of Madisonville. They needed workers and I was hired on as a tacker, working with a ship fitter to weld pieces of steel in place. Then skilled welders would finish the job, making sure the seams were watertight. I wore a shield or hood over my face, with a small tinted-glass window, to protect my eyes from the welding arc.

My shift began at 4:30 PM and ended at 2:00 AM. For the first three days I worked in the shop where a guy taught me to weld. Then I was assigned to a ship fitter, a big fat guy named Mack. I don't remember his last name; everyone just called him "Fat Mack". He was not a likable guy, working me hard and never letting up the entire shift. I was still learning the process of welding. When I had to tack together two beams or pieces of deck steel overhead, the sparks would land on my back and sometimes burn a hole in my shirt and create blisters on my arms and back. For the first couple of weeks, Momma would get up when I got home early in the morning and put salve on my wounds. Finally I got the knack and things went a little smoother for the rest of the summer. But working for "Fat Mack" was not a pleasant experience.

One night Mack and I were working on the deck of a barge, fitting deck plate. Mack told me to bend over the side of the barge to weld a place there. I did so, but blood must have rushed to my head. When I rose up, I got dizzy and lost my balance, falling about ten feet to the ground headfirst. Fortunately, I flipped in the air and landed on my butt, sore but not injured. Some other ship fitters saw what happened and told the shift supervisor. He criticized Mack severely for putting me in an unsafe situation. Mack "cut me a little slack" after that but was still a hard man to work for.

The best part of the job included riding to and from work with Otha Fussell and Arthur Ragusa, another employee who lived near our house. The three of us rode in the cab of Arthur's old pickup and the trip took about 30-45 minutes. Fussell (pronounced FUS-SELL) and Ragusa were authentic Cajuns who regaled me with stories everyday. It took me awhile to understand their accents, but then the stories were truly funny -- although I was never certain whether they were true or not. On the ride home, Otha and Arthur liked to stop at an all-night tavern for a beer or coffee. I would have a soft drink. We would get home about 3:00 or 3:30 AM. I would sleep until noon or later and then get ready to go to work again.

Madisonville and the shipyard sponsored a semi-pro baseball team that played on Sundays against other towns in southeastern Louisiana. The manager of the team gave me a tryout and I ended up playing third base for the club that summer. A scout for the St. Louis Cardinals saw our team play and invited me to come to a tryout camp in Ponchatoula, along with a left-handed pitcher on our team. The camp was on a Monday and Tuesday; so I played baseball from 9:00 AM to 3:00 PM on Monday, before leaving for my job and working until 2:00 AM. The scout did not invite either of us back for the second day, which was just as well because I don't think I could have managed it physically. I'll talk about this experience more in chapter 15.

Since I needed a car to travel to my baseball games on Sundays, as well as drive to work when I wasn't able to ride with Otha and Arthur, I persuaded Daddy to loan me the money to buy a car. For $400, we purchased a tan 1948 Ford that wasn't much to look at but provided reliable transportation. Working and playing ball took up most of my time that summer, so I saved almost all of my paycheck. As a result, I was able to pay Daddy back the money he provided me for school, the car, and the down payment on the bookkeeping course. I set up a "set of books" and recorded the amount I paid him each payday. And I had even saved the money that I would need for Northwestern that fall.

THE SOPHOMORE YEAR

Most of the courses that I took during my freshman year were to satisfy the general education requirements, with only a couple of business courses included. But the sophomore year curriculum thrust me into the core courses in business, particularly accounting. Accounting intimidated many of the students but I took to it "like a duck to water". I found myself frequently being asked by classmates to work problems and explain the theory to them. This "teaching experience" actually benefited me as well, giving me a deeper understanding of the subject matter. And I came to enjoy the courses and the process of learning.

For my sophomore year, I had applied for a dormitory room close to the center of the campus in East Caspari Hall, the "jock dorm" where most of the athletes lived. It was located between the football stadium and the gymnasium. My roommate was Kenneth Ivy, a tall, thin guy who had been a basketball star at Sarepta; his friends called him "Lum" because he liked to sleep so much. A physical education major who wanted to be a coach, Ken was a serious but easy-going student; so we had an excellent relationship. Ken went on to become an outstanding high school basketball and football coach in Shreveport.

As was the case during my freshman year, I went to all the home football and basketball games each year I was at Northwestern and rooted hard for the Demons. Student attendance at athletic events was excellent and the gym, particularly, would be packed when NSC played a conference opponent. Northwestern was in the Gulf States Conference which consisted of all Louisiana schools -- the "directional" colleges (Northwestern, Northeast, Southwestern, and Southeastern), plus La. Tech, McNeese, and La. College. The Demons almost always contended for the GSC Championship, with

Tech being the biggest rival. The football game with Tech each year was held during the State Fair in Shreveport. The stadium at the fairgrounds, now used for the Independence Bowl, served as the site for the contest and was usually filled. I went to the game on two occasions, once sleeping in my car at an all-night restaurant after the game.

Northwestern had some great football players during the 1956-60 era. Two in particular were Charlie Tolar and Charlie Hennigan, both of whom later starred with the Houston Oilers in the AFL. Tolar was a short stocky fullback, nicknamed "The Tank" in college and called the "Human Bowling Ball" in the pros, while Hennigan played wide receiver and set pass-catching records. Another great player was Jackie Smith, an end who went on to an All-Pro career with the St. Louis Cardinals.

In the spring semester, I became interested in campus politics and ran for the Junior Class Representative. I used my nickname as an advantage and printed up handbills asking students to vote for me, using the slogan "Carry on with the Case". I posted these on bulletin boards in the dorm and around campus. But I didn't do what a good politician should do -- ask people personally to vote for me. So, as a result, on Election Day I finished third in a five-person race, falling one vote short of being in a runoff. I was very disappointed by the defeat but even more so when I learned so many of my friends "forgot" to go vote.

But an even better opportunity emerged later that spring. A classmate in the business school, Ray Sawyer, approached me about becoming the business manager for The Current Sauce, the student newspaper. Ray had held the position for two years and would be graduating at the end of the next fall semester and wanted to recruit someone to succeed him, beginning in fall, 1958. The business manager had the responsibility of selling advertising for the weekly newspaper, creating the ad copy, collecting from advertisers, keeping the accounting records, and paying the bills -- and it paid a one-half time scholarship! With this job and my T.H. Harris Scholarship, I would have all my college expenses covered. I accepted the offer and began to work with Ray to learn the job.

I played baseball again that spring on the varsity, but only as a reserve. For many years, I had harbored the dream of being a major league baseball player. But, after the unsuccessful tryout with the Cardinals, some realism began to settle in and I did not approach baseball with the same devotion as before. I still loved the sport but realized that I was going to have to make a living in some other way.

SUMMER, 1958

Summer this year was very different in one respect -- I did not have to work! I had my college expenses for the next year covered. So I took a week or so to just hang around the house with Momma and Daddy. And I hooked up with the Madisonville team again and played baseball each Sunday. But that was not enough. I had to find something else to do – just as long as it was not the shipyard!

Shortly, I landed a job piloting a paddle-wheel boat in a small amusement park in Covington. It mattered little that I had never piloted a boat but the owner taught me how. Going forward wasn't a problem, but it took me several days to master the art of turning around. For 15 cents a kid could ride the boat down the bayou and back to the landing. I worked from 1:00 - 5:00 PM Tuesday - Friday and all day on Saturday. The owner would meet me each day and give me a money pouch, including some money to make change, and then come at 5:00 PM to collect the daily receipts.

One Friday, after I had been working for a couple of weeks, the owner did not show up at 5:00 PM. I waited until 6:00 PM with everyone else gone from the park. Finally, I took the money pouch and went home, as I had a date to meet some guys at 7:00 PM to go out that night. Shortly after I got home, the boat owner showed up at my house, raving mad because I had "run off with his money". I told him I had waited on him for an hour, had not touched the money and was planning to bring it in the next morning. But that would not satisfy him; so he fired me, leaving me unemployed again. When Daddy came home, I explained to him what had happened. He told me that he didn't feel I had done anything wrong and that I was better off not working for someone like that. That meant a lot to me.

A few days later, I started a new job at Holden's Texaco as a service station attendant. Holden's was a real <u>service</u> station: every customer was guaranteed that he would have his oil checked, his windshield washed, and his tire pressure checked, otherwise the gas was free. Bud Holden, the owner, kept a close eye on the four of us who worked the pumps. The station sat beside the main highway into Covington from the causeway over Lake Pontchatrain and had a steady business. There was often a car at each of the four pumps in front. I worked ten hours a day, six days a week, for 60 cents an hour.

The four guys who worked the "front" were white and young, like me. There were two older black guys who did the oil changes and washed cars. And there was a station manager who worked the cash register and filled in when needed in front. Holden's also had a taxi service -- two cars available for that use. The manager or Bud usually drove the taxis, but as summer went on, I was called on for that duty frequently and got to know the town well in the process. Holden's even had an ambulance service that would respond whenever there was a call from the police. Bud always drove the ambulance, but I got to accompany him on a couple of calls to the site of automobile accidents. Once we had to load a man who was injured into the ambulance and transport him to the hospital, with the siren wailing,

Before I returned to school that fall, Daddy did something unexpected. He told me he was concerned that my old Ford might break down on the road and that he was, therefore, going to give me his car -- a green 1954 Plymouth -- to take with me to Northwestern. He said he was ready to trade for a new car and would use the Ford as a trade-in. I appreciated his generosity and his recognition of my efforts to support myself. With a new set of wheels, I was prepared for the return to school.

Daddy revealed that he was retiring from the ministry and that he and Momma were going to move back to Mississippi. Paul and Henry would provide them with a house on their dairy farm near Union. I was pleased with their decision and knew that they would be well cared for by my brothers and their families.

THE JUNIOR YEAR

Over the summer I had let my hair grow longer and I swept it back in a ducktail, along with a set of sideburns. I think I actually looked like Elvis! I loved his music and would sing his songs when I was by myself, getting in front of the mirror and practicing Elvis' moves.

My Elvis impersonation didn't serve well when I went to the Mississippi High School basketball championship tournament in Jackson that winter. Clyde was the basketball coach at Starkville and his team was in the state finals.I hitchhiked to Jackson to be with Clyde on this special occasion. When Clyde's wife, Vashti, saw me, however, she immediately informed me that I needed to get a haircut! Starkville did not win the championship that year, but it was a thrill for me to be with them and to see the game. And I hoped that my hair was not an embarrassment.

Through Clyde, I had met the head basketball coach at Southwestern Louisiana who was there to scout players. He was driving back to Lafayette after the games on Saturday night and offered to give me a ride as far as Baton Rouge. I figured that I could spend the rest of the night in the Greyhound Bus Station and, then, catch a bus or hitchhike to Natchitoches the next day. But, as we drove over there, another alternative occurred to me. During the previous summer, I had dated a girl named Nelda Mizell, the niece of a lady in Daddy's church. She was a high school senior in Baton Rouge and had spent about two weeks with her aunt. While she was there, we dated several times and had a typical summer romance. We had continued to correspond and I was urging her to enroll in Northwestern the next year. I had her address, which was near downtown Baton Rouge; so I had the coach drop me off there. It was about 2:00 AM when we arrived, but I knocked on her door anyway. Her father came to the door and I explained that I knew his sister, that Nelda and I were good friends, and that I had gotten stranded in Baton Rouge on my way back to Natchitoches. I must have been convincing because he invited me in and showed me to a vacant bedroom. Nelda didn't know I was there until the next morning, but she greeted me happily and her parents had a good laugh about the surprise visit. Her dad even drove me out to the highway toward Natchitoches later that morning and I hitchhiked back to school. Nelda and I continued to write for a while, but she decided not to come to Northwestern; so our paths went in different directions.

THE CURRENT SAUCE

My job on the student newspaper was a very challenging one. Fortunately, Ray Sawyer was still around to help me get started. He introduced me to all the merchants who advertised in the paper and showed me the basics of ad layout. I enjoyed selling the advertising, as well as writing the copy and designing the ads. I also had to oversee the printing of the paper and its distribution on campus to various boxes where students could pick it up. These tasks, as well as the accounting and financial responsibilities, made it almost a full-time job. In fact, when not in class, I was almost always in my office at the newspaper. In the spring, I even took on an additional assignment as a sports writer, writing stories about various athletic events when the sports editor couldn't cover the games. That was not too difficult for me, since I attended virtually all the games anyway.

DORMITORY ASSIGNMENT

For the junior year, Ken Ivy and I lived in West Caspari Hall, a new dorm between the gymnasium and the baseball field. Two of Ken's long-time buddies, Jerry Haynes and Glynn Phillips, lived across the hall from us. I knew Jerry and Glynn well, as they were business students, so the four of us often hung out together. But an event occurred that year that put a little strain on our relationship.

JOINING A FRATERNITY

While Ray Sawyer was showing me the ropes at <u>The Current Sauce</u>, he also talked with me about joining his fraternity. Until that time, I had not thought seriously about being in a fraternity for a couple of reasons. First, before I came to college, I had never talked to anyone who was in a fraternity and didn't know anything about them; it was truly "all Greek" to me. Secondly, whenever I asked anyone in D-Frame or the "jock dorm", they quickly told me that I didn't want to have anything to do with those "Frat Rats". The impression was that they were rich kids who partied all the time.

But Ray Sawyer didn't fit that image at all. A skinny redheaded kid with thick glasses, he made excellent grades and was a very decent fellow. So I agreed to go with him to a rush party of his fraternity, Tau Kappa Epsilon. To my surprise, I found that TKE members included many of the student leaders -- Truman Maynard, the Commander of the ROTC units on campus; Jim Hammons, president of the Junior class; Gerald Paul and Charlie Brown, members of the Student Council; and John Rabb, editor of the campus yearbook. I was intrigued by the "brotherhood" they described and impressed by the Fraternity's principles. When extended a bid to join, I accepted, went through pledgeship, and was initiated into the fraternity at the beginning of the spring semester.

When my friends in the dorm learned that I was thinking about joining a fraternity, they tried to talk me out of it. Then, when I went ahead and did so, they razed me for weeks, calling me a "Frat Rat". There were no fraternity houses at NSC at this time; each of the three chapters on campus instead had a room in the basement of Caldwell Hall that served as a chapter room for meetings. So I continued to live in the dorm with Ken, Jerry, and Glynn and still considered them good friends. Over time, our relationship endured. But a whole new chapter of my life was just beginning.

I will talk more fully about my experience as a Teke in a later chapter. Suffice it to say, that decision to join the fraternity was one of the best choices that I made. I experienced a true brotherhood in TKE, unlike anything I had experienced before, and the membership in the fraternity provided many opportunities for me in later years. I enjoyed being with student leaders like Frank Hudson, Johnny Creech, and Buddy Webb and fraters like Ellis Coutee, a fellow accounting student who also had to work his way through college by being a bookkeeper for a business in Natchitoches throughout his undergraduate years.

TKE introduced me to a more active social life. I had dated several different girls during my sophomore year, usually to go to a ball game or some other campus event. They were cheap dates since students got into all the events free. But now there were fraternity parties to attend. The biggest social event for Tekes each year was the "Barfly" at which TKE would rent a hangar at the Natchitoches Airport, fill it with hay bales to sit on, and decorate it like a Western saloon. We hired a country western band and had a big dance with all of us dressed in jeans, boots, and western apparel.

On the night of the "Barfly" some of the Tekes, knowing that I was an Elvis fan, dared me to sing with the band. I accepted the challenge and cut loose with a rendition of "Lawdy Miss Clawdy". It brought down the house. From that point on, every time we had that band for a party, I would sing with them. "Blue Suede Shoes" was also one of my favorites. Several of the Tekes called the band "Suitcase and the Satchels."

Before the Christmas holidays each year, the Tekes would serenade the girls in the women's dorms. We would gather in the darkness underneath the windows, then light candles and sing Christmas songs. One of the numbers would be a solo of "Blue Christmas" that I would sing while the rest of the group provided harmony. I'll talk more about my interests in music in chapter 16.

THE POLITICAL SCENE

During student elections in the spring, I decided to run again for political office and filed for the position of president of Associated Men Students, representing all the men who lived in the dorms. The person who held this post was also a vice-president of the Student Council. I hoped to eliminate the mistakes I had made in my first run for political office. But no one filed to run against me, so I won the position without opposition. In addition, the Tekes elected me as Secretary for the next year and I was inducted into Blue Key, a leadership honorary and chosen as its vice-president.

With all the student activities in which I would be involved during my senior year, I decided to stay in Natchitoches and go to summer school. That proved to be a good choice, as I reduced my graduation requirements to twelve semester hours, only two courses each semester. And I got a job selling advertising for the Natchitoches Enterprise, to earn some money during the summer.

I decided not to go out for baseball that spring. With the responsibilities I had on The Current Sauce, it would have been very difficult, if not impossible, for me to play, particularly being away on road trips. But Wayne Williamson, a business student who had also played on the Demons freshman team, invited me to play for his hometown team that summer, since I was going to be in Natchitoches. Wayne's hometown was Montgomery, about thirty miles or so south of Natchitoches. The catcher on the team and an excellent player, Wayne assembled a good team for our games each Sunday. When we had a home game, I would often go down to his house and spend Saturday night with him. Wayne became a good friend and went on to a very successful business career in Louisiana after graduation.

FRATERNITY HOUSING

During the summer of 1959, Northwestern decided to convert the "frames" to fraternity housing. There were only three fraternities on campus then, so TKE got A-Frame, Sigma Tau Gamma was assigned B-Frame, and Pi Kappa Phi was located in C-Frame. Poor ole' D-Frame was still stuck out there by itself. The dorms were still college housing, but we were able to install our sign on the outside of the building, use the lounge as our chapter room, and fill the rooms with our members.

Since I planned to live in the house my senior year, I persuaded the Housing Director to let me move into A-Frame as soon as they were finished with the painting and re-furbishing. I did that late in the summer session, selecting a corner room for myself. The director told me I had to move out of the house (I was the only person there) at the end of summer school, as the college would be locking the dorms. That posed a problem for me, as I had another week or so of work with the Natchitoches Enterprise to complete when the college closed. So I unhooked the screen for one of my windows (all the Frames were one story buildings) so I could climb in through the window at night and have a place to sleep while I finished my work.

Then I went home to visit Momma and Daddy, as well as Paul and Henry and their families, in Union before starting my last year at NSC.

THE SENIOR YEAR

There were many times during my senior year when having a reduced course load was a blessing. The first occurred about midway through the fall semester when the sports editor on The Current Sauce resigned. Artie Wimberly, the editor, was in a panic; so I volunteered for the job. I covered the major sports events myself and wrote a weekly column called "Sauce Sports with Suitcase". Then I recruited some other staffers to write some sports stories for me and got the intramural director to turn in information I could use each week.

I enjoyed writing the column, although I got a major scare one day. The Demons had played the McNeese State Cowboys the night before in our gym. It was a particularly rough game, as the Cowboys were trying to provoke the Demons by hard fouls. On one occasion, a McNeese player submarined one of our players, Phillip Haley, as he went in for a lay up. He banged against the floor and had to be helped off the court. McNeese was assessed a technical foul for their flagrant action, as our fans responded angrily. Fortunately, NSC prevailed in the game, 59-57. (The Demons went on to have a 23-5 season, winning the Conference Championship).

The morning after the game McNeese's hometown newspaper had a lead story on the game, headlining the "dirty playing" of NSC. This angered me greatly, so I wrote my column about the game, lambasting the sports writer for his one-sided coverage and the Cowboys for their rough play. Roy Clark, the Director of the News Bureau, served as advisor to The Current Sauce and read the copy before it went to the printer. Mr. Clark came into my office and told me that the President, Dr. John Kyser, wanted to see me.

I had never been in the President's office and had only met Dr. Kyser at various college events. So I went into his office in Caldwell Hall with my knees knocking, thinking that I was in serious trouble. But Dr. Kyser greeted me heartily, telling me that he had read my column, and that I had done a splendid job. He said that I had stood up for the school strongly but in a civil manner. I walked out with my feet hardly touching the floor!

The Current Sauce was well read across campus. I know because I would get calls from angry students when one of our boxes was empty. My sports column was very popular, especially with the guys, judging from the feedback I got each week. People who did not know me personally thought that I was a journalism major, heading for a career as a sportswriter.

The offices for the college yearbook, called The Potpourri, were edited by Frank Hudson, a Teke and were next door to the newspaper. Frank asked me if I would serve as sports editor for the book and I agreed to do so. Since I had all the information and pictures I would need already, I figured that would not be a major challenge.

Working on The Potpourri staff was an attractive young sophomore, Doris Richard from Shreveport. I asked Doris for a date and we began a relationship that spanned most of my senior year. She went with me to most of the Teke parties, including "Barfly" that spring. We enjoyed each other's company and this became my first serious romance.

THE TEKE HOUSE

Living in the fraternity house was a different, but very enjoyable experience for me, being in a residence with guys that I knew well and with whom I shared so much -- the things we did together and the bond we had in the fraternity. I played intramural sports for TKE -- football, basketball, and softball. And I won the intramural tennis tournament. Serving as an officer for the chapter gave me excellent leadership experience. Charlie Brown as president, Gerald Paul as vice-president, me as Secretary, and my good friend and fellow accounting major, Ellis Coutee, as Treasurer comprised the top four officers.

My roommate was Jay Reese, who was also an officer. Jay and I got along well and enjoyed living together. But I found the house pretty noisy; so I did most of my studying in either my office at the newspaper or at the library.

Up until the time that I came to college, I had never smoked or drank. Partly, it was in respect for the beliefs of my parents. But it was also highly influenced by my coaches who had a rule that anyone caught drinking or smoking would be immediately dismissed from the team. So I never took the chance of that happening.

When I got to college, I found that many of the men drank -- or at least said they did. I don't remember the first time that I tasted the beverage of choice, beer, but I definitely did not like it. That posed a problem on occasions when everyone was drinking, particularly at the fraternity parties. But I found that if I took a beer and sipped on it slowly and occasionally talked loud, others would think I was drinking. I finally acquired a taste for beer and could finish a whole bottle or can, but one was almost always my limit. As far as hard liquor goes, I didn't like the taste of it either. I found that, when a mixed drink was expected, I could tolerate bourbon and 7-up and settled on a"7 and 7" as my drink of choice. Later I found that I liked gin and tonic, if there wasn't too much gin in the drink. Fortunately for me, in college and the years thereafter, drinking never became a necessary part of my lifestyle.

THE LAST SEMESTER

I did have some academic work to do my senior year, although by the end of the fall semester I had completed all my required courses. In the spring I could have taken a couple of "crip" courses that would have been easy, but instead I enrolled in an English Literature class. The reading list for the course was formidable -- The Iliad, The Odyssey, and a number of Shakespeare's plays -- and I had a difficult time keeping up. The professor was not a very good teacher, certainly not up to the standards I had experienced in the business courses. So I struggled to make a "C" in the course, one of the few "C's" I received in college. But I was still able to graduate with a GPA of 3.75 and was elected to Phi Kappa Phi, the national scholastic honorary society. The Louisiana Society of CPA's also gave me an award as the top accounting graduate at NSC.

My attention in the senior year began to turn toward what I was going to do after graduation. I had made A's in all of my accounting courses and was being urged by my accounting professors to sit for the CPA exam and to go into that profession. I interviewed with several of the national accounting firms and they were recruiting me aggressively. But another option began to emerge.

Early that spring, I signed up for an interview with Dr. Russell Westmeyer, the Director of Graduate Studies in the Business School at the University of Arkansas, who had come to our campus to recruit graduate students. My advisor, Joe Johnson, had asked me to interview, as they needed additional students to fill Dr. Westmeyer's schedule. Up to that point, I had not seriously thought about graduate school. But I liked what he told me about the University of Arkansas and was enticed by a possibility he described to me. He told me that the federal government had established a National Defense Graduate Fellowship program and that he thought, with my strong academic record and my extensive leadership activities, I would have a good chance of winning a grant to cover tuition and living expenses for three years of graduate work. So I took the NDEA application form, completed it, and mailed it back to him. The Fellowships were designed to increase the production of Ph.D.'s in the sciences and in fields like business to meet a need for college professors. Acceptance of the fellowship involved an obligation to teach for at least two years at the college level after graduate school.

While I was not yet sure that I wanted to be a college professor, I began to realize that the past four years had been, perhaps, the happiest years of my life. I loved learning and the academic environment and all the activities on a campus. So spending another three years in college didn't sound like a bad alternative to me.

Waiting to hear from Arkansas, I got offers of graduate assistantships at both the University of Texas and Mississippi State. I had not interviewed with them; so I figured that they came because Mr. Johnson had recommended me. The offers were for one year to complete an MBA program. I decided, however, that if I went to graduate school, it would be to UA. Finally, a letter from Arkansas arrived announcing that I had been accepted for graduate school and that I had won a NDEA fellowship. I was delighted and looked forward to going to Fayetteville that fall.

GRADUATION AND BEYOND

As I neared graduation, I was selected for the NSC Hall of Fame, one of only four senior men to receive that honor. I had come a long way from the

4

1

7

frightened kid who was afraid to drop the suitcase to become a B.M.O.C. -- A big man on campus -- and it had been an enjoyable journey.

Since I was going to graduate school, the national accounting firms declined interest in hiring me for the summer months. But one of the firms with which I interviewed, Interstate Oil Pipeline Company in Shreveport readily offered me a job in their accounting department, figuring that I might like the work so well that I would change my plans about going to graduate school. On some occasions, I thought that might be an outside possibility. Accepting the job, I agreed to rent a house in Shreveport with two other NSC grads that were going to work with firms there.

But, first, I took a little time to visit with Momma and Daddy in Mississippi. They seemed to be very happy in their house on the farm. I would have liked for them to be at my graduation but realized that it was too far for them to travel. While home, Daddy and I traded the Plymouth I had been driving for two years for a new Chevrolet Corvair. This was the first car I owned in my own name, complete with a bank note and monthly payments to make.

Hopping into my new car with a big smile on my face, I headed to Shreveport. The employment with the pipeline company provided two positive benefits. First, I was able to continue my relationship with Doris, as she was at home in Shreveport for the summer. We dated frequently and I met her folks. Secondly, this enabled me to play another summer of baseball with Wayne Williamson and the team in Montgomery. Each Sunday I would drive to wherever we were playing, with Doris accompanying me on most occasions. We had a great team that summer, including several guys who had played for Northwestern. At the end of the season, we advanced to the finals of the state semi-pro championship before losing. If we had won, we would have gone to the National Semi-Pro Tournament in Wichita, Kansas.

The other aspect of the summer employment was not as positive. Interstate Oil Pipeline was a subsidiary of Standard Oil and, therefore, a big company. I found the accounting jobs that they assigned me boring as hell! Accounting had been an exciting subject for me in the classrooms; I enjoyed the challenge of solving the problems. But posting inventory changes to accounts by hand all day convinced me that going to graduate school presented, by far, the best alternative.

Before I headed for the Ozark Mountains in Arkansas, however, Doris and I came to a major crossroads in our relationship. I felt differently about her than I had about any of the other girls I had dated and seriously contemplated asking her to marry me. But I was looking at another three years of school and Doris had another two years at Northwestern. Furthermore, I knew that her mother wanted her to stay in school and was uneasy about our relationship. So we had a tearful farewell, promising to write to each other and to get together again as soon as possible.

REFLECTIONS

I can't imagine that I could have had a better undergraduate experience than I had at Northwestern. I grew intellectually and socially and had many opportunities to develop my leadership skills. Almost all of the students at NSC were first-generation college students, as I was, and I felt very comfortable there. I had my share of disappointments and experienced the loneliness and anxiety that are common to young people, but these were part of the normal growth process.

NSC was not a prestigious school. Few of the faculty were research scholars. But they were excellent teachers and always available to meet with students individually. I felt that I was well prepared for graduate school. Northwestern as small enough to allow me to participate fully in the extra-curricular activities that were available, which was a distinct asset.

NSC (now Northwestern State University) honored me with an Outstanding Business Graduate award in 1984 and inducted me into The Long Purple Line (the Alumni Hall of Fame) in 1996. I have always been proud to be a Northwestern graduate and appreciate all that the school contributed to my personal development.

In 2006, I had the opportunity to give something back. My classmate, Ellis Coutee, and I headed a campaign to raise monies to endow a professorship in the Business School in honor of Dr. Kenneth Durr, one of our favorite teachers while in school. It was a great thrill to be a part of this effort and to see Karl Moore, Wayne Williamson, and Doyle Williams, other classmates who supported this endeavor. I was particularly touched when Dr. Durr said, upon the presentation of this award, that it was the nicest thing that had ever happened to him.

All of my education to this point had been in segregated schools. I was certainly aware that there were blacks in our communities and that they had their own schools but I was not sensitive to the harm that such a system produced. I just accepted it as the way things were. I had no animosity toward blacks or any other minority, having never heard those attitudes expressed at home and having worked side-by-side with blacks in the cotton fields. But graduate school and the years that followed would bring me into a much more diverse society.

CHAPTER 7:

IN THE LAND OF THE RAZORBACKS

It took nearly all day to drive from Shreveport to Fayetteville, following U.S. Highway 71 up the western side of Arkansas. The last sixty miles wound through the Ozark Mountains over two-lane roads with spectacular scenic views, revealing mountains like I had never seen before. From a distance of ten miles, I could see the twin towers of Old Main, rising above the University of Arkansas campus.

Fayetteville is located in the northwest corner of Arkansas, only a short distance from the borders of Oklahoma and Missouri. Having read all the literature the university had sent me, I was anxious to see the campus and found it to be more beautiful than I had imagined. A centerpiece of the campus is the lawn in front of Old Main that contains sidewalks bearing the names of university graduates and is called "Senior Walk."

Arriving in Fayetteville with all my belongings packed into my new Chevy Corvair, which wasn't much larger than a Volkswagen, I did not have a place to spend the night.I had applied to the university for housing, but received information that dormitories were not provided for graduate students and a list of rooming houses off-campus. So I began driving around, trying to locate some of the places cited.

THE TEKE HOUSE

At the corner of Arkansas Avenue and Maple Street, bordering the campus, I looked up and saw a white three-story frame house with a TKE fraternity sign and three guys sitting on the front porch. I parked my car and then introduced myself as a Teke who was enrolling as a graduate student. They seemed genuinely pleased to meet me and, since it was dinnertime, invited me to stay and join them.

I quickly learned that the group had just been organized the previous spring as a colony. In TKE, a colony must operate for one year and meet certain standards before it is eligible to become a chapter. The group had just rented the house and had worked all summer to prepare it as their place of residence. Because the members of the colony had not yet been initiated, they were excited to meet a "real Teke" and had many questions for me.

When asked where I was living, I replied that I had not yet found a place, whereupon they invited me to spend the night on an empty bunk in one of the rooms. Gladly accepting, I spent the evening meeting and talking with the men in the house, which contained beds for about thirty men, as well as a kitchen and dining room, where meals were already being served. Since the president felt that I could be helpful to him as he prepared the colony for installation as a chapter, I inquired about the costs of room and board and found them to be reasonable. And the location was fantastic. Arkansas Avenue runs right in front of Old Main and it was an easy walk to the business building, the library, and other important places on the campus. Other positive factors were that I would not have to prepare my own meals and would have an immediate set of friends. So I accepted the offer and moved in, launching a tremendous experience for me during my first year at Arkansas.

THE ACADEMIC WORK

The next day I met with Dr. Russell Westmeyer, the graduate advisor in the business school, and learned that I was one of five new National Defense Graduate Fellows who were admitted. We planned my class schedule, enrolling me in fifteen hours of course work for the fall semester. Since I had already taken so many business courses at Northwestern, it was determined that I could complete the requirements for the MBA by passing 30 hours, fifteen in each of the two semesters.

This sounded like a reasonable load, since I had taken 18 hours most of the semesters at NSC. But I soon learned that there was a significant difference between undergraduate and graduate courses. Not only was the material more extensive and more difficult but also each course required a term research paper. I soon developed a routine of going to the library as soon as my classes were over and staying there, except for going back to the Teke House for meals, until 10-12 o'clock at night.

I found the faculty quite demanding but also approachable and helpful. Some of the more effective classroom teachers were Robert Kennedy and

Harold Dulan in finance, Nolan Williams and Doris Cook in accounting, and Robert Hay and Harold Williams in management. Each was an excellent classroom lecturer with very demanding expectations for his students. It was important to come to class well prepared. Dr. Hay later became my principal advisor and, subsequently, the chairman of my doctoral dissertation committee. I experienced tremendous intellectual and professional growth in my courses and in my interaction with faculty.

All the students in my classes were smart and were very competitive. A's did not come easy in that environment, but I applied myself and earned top grades in all my courses. Two of my classmates and ND Fellows, Harvey Lewis and James Hester, went on to significant administrative assignments, Harvey as Executive Vice-President of both Ole Miss and Mississippi State and Jim as the Business School Dean and Dean of the Graduate School at Louisiana Tech.

LIFE WITH THE TEKES

Residing in the fraternity house turned out to be a great benefit. I participated fully in the chapter's activities, going to meetings and parties and even playing on their intramural basketball team. I particularly enjoyed the evening meals in the fraternity house at which our housemother, Mrs. Trilby Dortch, enforced appropriate behavior; she was a fine lady and much loved by the men in the house. After meals, we would sing fraternity songs and I relished in the brotherhood that singing together produced after the grind of graduate work and long hours spent in the library.

Sometimes we would invite members of one of the sororities over for dinner and provide the entertainment, consisting mostly of songs the group would sing. Additionally, I joined with two other guys, Bob Busby and Paul Siepman, to form a trio, called "The Neverly Brothers". We would sing songs recorded by the Everly Brothers, a popular group in the early 60's, usually "Bye, Bye Love."

I roomed with Neil Schmitt, the president of the group during the fall semester, and Bill Cooper, who succeeded him in the spring. Neil and Bill were great guys and I spent many hours talking with them about how the fraternity should be operated. In the spring, I wrote most of the petition for a charter that resulted in the colony being installed as a chapter in mid May, 1961. Neil went on to get a Ph.D. and later became dean of the college of engineering at Arkansas; Bill became an air traffic controller.

WOO, PIG! SOOIE!

Becoming an immediate fan of the Razorbacks, I went to all of Arkansas' home football games -- or at least those that were in Fayetteville. Half of the home games took place in Little Rock, about four hours away. Razorback fans had a lot of spirit and, several times during a game, they would "call the hogs" with a yell of "Woo Pig, Sooie." I, also, attended a few basketball games but football reigned the major sport at UA during this era.

The Razorbacks competed in the Southwest Conference (SWC) whose schools were all located in Texas, except Arkansas. Hence, one of the favorite songs of Razorback fans was "I Don't Give a Damn About the Whole State of Texas." The football coach, Frank Broyles, developed a program that won a national championship in 1964 with sustained success for many years. The biggest rival was the University of Texas.

I also participated in various student activities with members of the fraternity or by myself. Each Friday night before a home football game there was a pep rally in the Chi Omega Greek Theater. All the fraternities and sororities would sit together as groups and try to yell the loudest. The Tekes had a bell that they would ring at the rally. In the spring, the University had a weekend named "GAEBALE" which featured big name entertainment. One year the keynote performer, Ray Charles, had just recorded "What'd I Say", a song that had this line: "Tell your Ma, Tell your Pa, I'm gonna take you back to Arkansas." That brought down the house and the crowd begged him to sing it again and again. In another year, the featured performer was Chuck Berry.

My romance with Doris, my girlfriend at Northwestern, did not make it though the fall semester. At first, we wrote regularly; then the interval between letters grew until, finally, they stopped. I don't remember who wrote the last letter. It wasn't that I had found another girlfriend. Although I had dates, often arranged by other guys in the fraternity, none were memorable. It is just that my life was so full, intellectually and socially, that I didn't have time to look back.

SUMMER, 1961

At the end of the first year at Arkansas, I received the MBA degree and I was ready to start the Ph.D. program. But I was "worn out" academically and wanted to do something different. Four straight years of undergraduate work and then a highly intense year of graduate work without a break had taken its toll. I wanted to get as far away from academics as possible for a while.

I seriously contemplated joining the Marine Corps. Although I had an educational deferment, I had no objections to serving in the military. All my brothers had, except Clyde, and he served for a short time before receiving a medical deferment. The Marines had a program, called the "Platoon Leaders Class", that allowed college graduates to go through a training program and to be commissioned as officers. I talked to the Marine recruiters and they gave me the application forms to complete. Then I talked to Dr. Westmeyer and learned that, if I gave up my National Defense Fellowship, there was no guarantee that I would get it back. I concluded that was too big a risk to take.

The next possibility I explored was to work in a summer camp. Reviewing a directory in the library, I looked up Maine -- about as far from Arkansas as I could get -- and applied to Camp Takajo in Naples, indicating that I could coach baseball or write the camp newsletter. I got a phone call soon afterwards from Monty Goldman, the owner, offering me a job and asking me to do both baseball and the newsletter.

The camp ran for ten weeks and the pay was $300 for the whole session plus free room and board. Fortunately, with the NDEA fellowship, I didn't need to earn money during the summer because the stipend I received was more than adequate to cover my living expenses. In fact, I sent several hundred dollars home to Momma and Daddy each year. Knowing that Daddy's pension from the church was small, I felt they could use the money. Before leaving for Maine, I stopped in Mississippi to visit with them and to get caught up on all the news about the family, none of whom could believe I was going so far north.

At this juncture, the only time I had been outside the Deep South was the trip to St. Louis to see the Cardinals play. So I was looking forward to the venture with great excitement. Driving in my Corvair, I planned a weeklong journey to get to Maine.

My first night I stayed with an old classmate at Northwestern who lived near Atlanta andthe next two nights at a motel in Washington, D.C. I took a tour bus around to see all the sites in the nation's capital and, that night, went to see the Washington Senators play the Detroit Tigers at Griffith Stadium, the first time to see my favorite team, the Tigers, play in person. The next day I got up early and drove to Schenectady, New York to spend the night with Paul Siepman, one of my fraternity brothers at Arkansas. Paul's dad worked for General Electric and they lived in the suburb of Scotia. Then I traveled to South Yarmouth, Massachusetts on Cape Cod to stay with Milton Feltch, another Teke from Arkansas. On the next day, I completed the trip on up to Maine.

The journey up there was an education itself, as I saw many places about which I had only read. The further I traveled north, the harder it was for me to understand what people were saying -- probably because they were laughing so hard after hearing me speak! There truly was a language barrier.

Another cultural difference that I encountered at Takajo was that the campers were all Jewish boys -- about 300 of them -- primarily from New York City and Boston. I should have picked up a clue since the camp owner was named Marty Goldman! In spite of our different backgrounds, however, the campers and I forged a good relationship. They listened to me because they had never heard anyone with such a southern accent.

The counselors came from all over the country, about half Jewish and half Gentile, including at least one other from the Deep South. Jimmy Taylor, from Alabama but currently a student a Mississippi State, was the basketball coach. I was overjoyed seeing him and hearing his voice. We became great pals that summer and are still close; Jimmy went on to become the basketball coach at the University of South Alabama and then a highly successful banker in Alabama.

At the camp, I coached the junior boys in the morning and the senior boys in the afternoon and wrote The Takajo Talk, a mimeographed newsletter that came out each Friday. Two counselors slept in each cabin with ten campers. Our biggest challenge was getting the kids to bed at night at 9:00 P.M. and, then, getting them up at 6:00 a.m. A "Dippy Club", comprised of some counselors and campers would race naked down to the lake, at reveille, to plunge into the icy waters. I was never tempted to join them.

Camp Takajo resided two miles from the scenic village of Naples, thirty miles inland from Portland. Sited on beautiful Long Lake, it was a well-developed camp with a rustic lodge and a dining hall that framed the waterfront with areas for swimming and docks for boats. I found the water too cold and I had never experienced summer weather like this; it was usually mid 70's during the day, but became quite chilly at night. Fortunately, I brought a blanket for my bed, even though I doubted the instructions when told to do so.

The camp staff included about 60 counselors, some veterans who had worked there several summers. We could leave camp after 9:00 p.m., as long as one counselor stayed in each cabin, but the only place to go close was Naples, which consisted of a service station, a Howard Johnson's Restaurant, and a trading post or general store. Many of the guys would hang out at Howard Johnson's, trying to meet female counselors from the girls camp in the area. On the one day a week we got off, I would usually visit some other area in Maine and once traveled to see the Red Sox play in Boston.

Jimmy Taylor and I, however, decided to take a major trip on our next off day. Since neither of us had been to Canada, we elected to go to Quebec. The trip took much longer than we expected. We arrived in early afternoon, spent an hour looking around, and discovered that we couldn't understand anyone because they spoke French; so we headed back. The return trip seemed even longer and we arrived at the border with a major problem -- my Corvair's gas tank was almost empty. We asked the Canadian guard for directions to a gas station, but he did not respond (he may not have been able to understand us!). U.S. Customs, however, said there might be a station in a town called Moose River about five miles below the border, but that there was nothing else for 50-60 miles. Jimmy and I rolled into Moose River around midnight and everything, including the one gas station, was closed up tight. We were sitting in my car, not knowing what to do, when a policeman came up and wanted to know what we were doing. We explained our plight and he advised us that the owner of the service station lived in the house behind it, but he did not hold out much hope for us, as the man had already gone to bed.

Faced with the alternative of sleeping in our car on the town square or risking the wrath of the station owner, we knocked on his door and waited for a long time before a light came on and the owner answered. We told our story of woe, in our southern brogue, including that we had to be back to work by 6:00 A.M. He did not utter a word and closed the door. We stood around there for a while and were preparing to leave when he came outside in a nightshirt and boots, marched over to the gas pump where the car was and filled it with gas. We paid him, thanking him profusely. He marched back to his house, never saying anything. Jimmy and I made it back to Takajo about 3:00 A.M., just in time to catch a nap before reveille.

The summer was truly an enjoyable venture. I didn't read an academic textbook or article the entire time and got to play baseball everyday. Now I was ready to get back to the challenge of doctoral study. On the drive back south, I drove through parts of New York City, going across the George Washington bridge, as I had missed the Big Apple on my way north.

DOCTORAL WORK

Having concentrated in accounting for my BS and in marketing for my MBA, I decided to focus on management and organizational behavior for my Ph.D. work. I chose Dr. Robert D. Hay as my doctoral advisor because I really liked him as a teacher and a mentor. He believed that all organizations, business or non-business, needed effective management to succeed, a principle he called "the universality of management." At this juncture, this was "cutting edge" thinking as most scholars saw the need for management limited to business firms. Dr. Hay helped pioneer the notion that management was just as important for non-profits and organizations of all types.

At the Ph.D. level classes were smaller, but had long required reading lists and term papers. I found that my experience writing for the newspaper in undergraduate school helped me greatly on the term papers. I would do my library research, recording the data on note cards, and then sit down at the typewriter to compose the report. Unfortunately, this was before word-processing technology, so I had to either type a rough draft and then do it over or stop and correct my mistakes as I went.

Some of the courses that I enjoyed the most involved teams of students working with a real project. One semester a team looked at a proposed new business converting chicken manure into garden fertilizer. There were a lot of commercial chicken houses in Northwest Arkansas at this time, creating a ready supply of raw materials. Some of the students had a lot of fun cracking jokes about this study. Another project that I chaired reviewed the operations of largest milk producer in the area.

During my second year, I served as the head resident of Razorback Hall, a large freshman dormitory for men. The job came with a private apartment in the dorm and free board in the dining hall, plus a small salary. My main task was to maintain order in the dorm, with the assistance of three others who were upperclassmen. Although counseling was also offered, few freshmen asked for help, until they are in trouble, and then it's too late. So most of the effort went into keeping the noise down and destruction of property to a minimum. That presented a challenge on weekends when the students would go out and drink too much. But serving in this role also gave me the opportunity to identify several sharp freshmen that I recruited to pledge TKE.

At the end of the first year, I ran for a position as the graduate school representative on the Student Senate and was elected. This role required attending meetings every couple of weeks but got me fully involved in student activities. I also attended sporting events, particular football and got to meet Coach Frank Broyles who would later become a good friend.

INVOLVEMENT WITH TKE

Because I no longer lived in the fraternity house, I was less involved in the day-to day functions of the chapter. I helped form and served on the chapter's Board of Control, an alumni group that oversaw the operations of the Chapter. As the chapter at Arkansas grew, the Board of Control began to look at alternatives for a larger house. We did not have the financial resources to build a new house, but we found an apartment building further down

Arkansas Avenue that was owned and operated by U.S. Senator William Fulbright's company, Fulbright Investment Company. We negotiated a lease with them beginning in Fall, 1962, with the opportunity to renovate the house, installing a kitchen and dining room over the summer, as well as other improvements. With a lot of hard work by chapter members we got moved into the house over the summer. I helped with much of this work while taking one course during the first summer session.

After the first summer session, I went home to Mississippi to visit with my folks for about six weeks, my longest stay in a while. I even hooked up with a baseball team representing Conahatta, a community in Newton County not far from Union. Conahatta is best known as the site of a Choctaw Indian Reservation, but no Native Americans played on our team. Carroll Jones, who subsequently married my niece, Paula, was on the team and recruited me to join them. Our games were played each Sunday.

Upon my return to Fayetteville, I moved into one of two apartments, separate from the main building but on the property we leased for the Tekes. Another graduate student, Mark Mormino, rented the other one. I decided to have my meals in the chapter house and offered to help the chapter in various ways.

SELECTION OF DISSERTATION TOPICS

While I still had several courses to take my third year, a major focus of my attention was upon getting a dissertation topic approved. Dr. Hay agreed to serve as chairman of my dissertation committee, which included two other graduate faculty members as well. I had to submit a proposal, describing the topic on which I wanted to do research and how I proposed to conduct the investigation.

I talked with Dr. Hay about an idea I had that was consistent with his "universality of management" theory. I related my work with the TKE chapter, particularly how I had helped them install good management practices and how the chapter had become more successful. My hypothesis, I proposed, was that better managed chapters would be more successful as a result. Dr. Hay was delighted and reported that he knew of no research that had been done applying management principles to social fraternities. He encouraged me to put this proposal together and bring it to the committee.

As I thought about how I could research this topic, it became clear that I needed access to a number of fraternity chapters and that it would be useful if they were geographically dispersed -- i.e., not at the same university. I wrote to Bruce Melchert, Executive Director of TKE at the national headquarters in Indianapolis, and explained what I wanted to do. Bruce was excited about the idea and offered me a job as a TKE Field Supervisor, beginning in August 1963. He said I could collect the data I needed while performing my responsibilities in that role.

With the arrangements made, I developed a proposal for my committee, outlining the data I would collect to determine how well managed the chapter was and how I planned to measure "success." When I presented the proposal, the committee had a number of questions but, with Dr. Hay's strong support, the committee approved it.

TRIP TO MEXICO

During spring break, 1963, Mark Mormino and I had decided that we would take a trip to Mexico, a place I had never been, and invited three other Tekes to go with us -- Paul Siepman, Milton Feltch and Buddy Spivey. Since Mark was older than me, had graduated from the Missouri Schools of Mines, and was a graduate student in engineering, I figured he would be a very responsible driver and companion -- but that was not always the case. We drove from Fayetteville down through Texas to Monterrey, Mexico in Mark's Chrysler The guys had a big party there that night and were hung over the next morning. But they kept drinking the next day as we drove through Torreon down to Durango, the hometown of Pancho Villa, the famous Mexican bandit.

By the time we reached Durango, I was the only sober person in the car and kept asking Mark to let me drive. But he insisted he was okay. While traveling through town, Mark made a wrong turn and we ended up on a plaza in front of a statue of Poncho Villa. The guys all hopped out of the car and were "toasting" Poncho with their beer cans. I saw a bunch of angry Mexicans starting to gather around the plaza and managed, finally, to get the guys back in the car before that group reached us. Mark drove the car toward what we thought was a street that turned out to be a wide stairway down to a street below. The car bounced down the stairs and, amazingly, was able to run when it reached the bottom. We hurriedly got out of Durango.

If this incident didn't sober up the crowd, the next part of the journey certainly did. Our final destination was Mazatlan on the Pacific Coast. But between Durango and Mazatlan lay the Sierra Madre Mountains. As we traveled over the mountains on winding roads, Mark had to use the brakes for the last 25 miles or so, eventually burning them out. He had to switch to the emergency brake before reaching Mazatlan; by then, everyone was sober and clutching the handles of their seats.

Mazatlan was a beautiful beach town with the mountains in the distance. We stayed at a hotel right on the beach and relaxed for three days while Mark got his car repaired. The return trip was much less eventful as everyone stayed on his best behavior.

RETURN TO TAKAJO

Late that spring, Marty Goldman called me and asked me to come back to Camp Takajo that summer. He needed a baseball coach and a newsletter editor. I wasn't as excited to return as I had been on my initial venture there, but I had nothing scheduled for the summer -- so I agreed.

Prior to departing Fayetteville, I traded my Corvair for a beautiful red 1963 Pontiac LeMans convertible. I had saved enough money from my fellowship to make a nice down payment and felt like I had the hottest car on the road.

On the trip north, I visited with two TKE national officers, Lenwood Cochran in South Carolina and Landis Coffman in Pennsylvania, and with Paul Siepman in New York and Milton Feltch in Massachusetts.

The work at the camp turned out to be pretty much as it was the previous summer. One of my favorite memories is a camping trip that I went on in the White Mountains of New Hampshire. What a beautiful site! One of my least favorite memories is volunteering for the diet table to which were assigned (by their parents) all the overweight kids. They would whine and cry when the other tables got dessert while they got fruit or when others got bagels and cream cheese and they got dry toast. I took on the task because I thought it would help me lose a few pounds, but it was not worth the grief I had to endure from the "fat kids."

With the summer completed, I headed for Indianapolis to begin my new job that would allow me to do the research for my dissertation.

REFLECTIONS

The campus at Arkansas was much more diverse than I had experienced before. Not only had UA been of the first universities in the South to admit blacks, but the campus included many students and faculty from other countries as well. There were also "foreigners" -- like students from New York, New Jersey, Massachusetts and other northern states -- there that were unlike those I had gone to school with before. And the work in Maine, as well as the trips to Canada and Mexico, had broadened my understanding of the world.

My graduate work was unusual in many respects, namely that I got to continue many of my undergraduate activities, particularly my involvement with the fraternity. The demanding courses required me to work hard. But I truly enjoyed my three years in the land of the Razorbacks and felt well prepared for a career in higher education.

In 1994, the University of Arkansas honored me with the Distinguished Alumnus Citation, during my tenure as President of Auburn University. The weekend of the award was a wonderful experience. Friday night included a dinner for the honorees at which I got to speak, thanking Dr. Hay for his tutelage. On Saturday morning we attended a luncheon at which Marlene and I were given "Hog Hats." And on Saturday afternoon I was recognized in a ceremony on the football field at half time in the game between Arkansas and Auburn. I will have to admit some mixed emotions during the game, which Auburn won.

CHAPTER 8:
A TEKE FOR LIFE

Tau Kappa Epsilon fraternity has as its slogan: "A Fraternity for Life." That has truly been the case for me, as from my initiation into the fraternity, I have been continually involved with TKE in some capacity. That is unusual; most men have very little, if any, contact with their college fraternity after graduation.

But my fraternity experience has been a special one and I am indebted to TKE in a number of ways. Specifically:

1. Through my participation in the fraternity at both the undergraduate and graduate levels, I developed leadership and organizational skills that have served me well throughout my career.

2. Through my membership in TKE, I was able to secure employment that permitted me to do the research necessary to complete a doctoral dissertation and earn a Ph.D. degree.

3. Through my employment with TKE, I met Marlene Munden who, subsequently, became my wife and has been my companion for over 40 years.

4. Through my involvement with the international fraternity in a variety of roles over the years, I have had the opportunity to develop close friendships with a wonderful group of men with whom I share a common bond.

Each of these dimensions will be discussed individually.

UNDERGRADUATE AND GRADUATE EXPERIENCE

As described in chapter 6, when I enrolled as a freshman at Northwestern State College in Natchitoches, Louisiana in the fall of 1956, I knew nothing about fraternities and, hence, did not go through rush. It was not until the beginning of my junior year, in the fall of 1958, that I was approached about fraternity membership and attended a TKE rush party. What I learned there was that the group had just been installed as Epsilon Upsilon chapter the previous spring on May 5, 1957. For many years they had been a local fraternity, Lambda Zeta. I had an opportunity to be a member of the first TKE pledge class. What surprised me was the number of Tekes who were in campus leadership positions.And I was particularly impressed by what they said the fraternity stood for -- its Declaration of Principles. At the end of rush, I was extended a bid and accepted.

Contrary to popular opinion and, perhaps, inconsistent with the motivations of many young men, it was not the promise of parties that lured me. I looked forward to the social events, but, most importantly, I wanted to be part of the brotherhood about which they had talked. Because I had grown up with brothers much older than me and had moved a lot, I never had the opportunity to establish close friendships with a group of boys, other than the athletic teams on which I had played. I hoped the fraternity could fill this missing ingredient.

TKE's rush was very successful, as 43 men joined the pledge class. Unfortunately, the pledge program was not nearly as effective. Perhaps as a holdover from the local fraternity, pledgeship consisted mostly of harassment. Each pledge had to make a paddle and secure the signature of each active member after absorbing a whack on the rear end -- and carry out the commands of any active. I had already gone through freshman hazing and didn't relish going through that ordeal again, so I avoided the actives wherever possible. I was not the only pledge who reacted negatively to this treatment. As the time for initiation approached, only nine men remained in the pledge class.

I admit that I thought about dropping out many times myself. I had gone through a tough high school football program and had played college baseball -- and was stubborn to boot -- so I figured I could take anything they dished out. But it was clearly not what I had expected the fraternity to be. The final hurdle was "Hell Night" on the Saturday night prior to our scheduled initiation on Sunday afternoon. The pledges were picked up in cars, blindfolded, and driven around for a long time. When the cars stopped and our blindfolds were removed, we found ourselves in a clearing in the middle of a wooded area around a campfire. For the next several hours, the actives played cruel games with us, individually or as a group. Finally, they blindfolded us again and poured some foul smelling mixture in our hair and, then, left us there.

After the actives had departed, we removed our blindfolds and began to explore the area to find the right way out. We, finally, located a dirt road and followed it until we found a highway that took us back to the campus. Fortunately, we were only a mile or so away, but it was still daybreak when I arrived back at my dorm. I was thankful that my roommate had gone home for the weekend so that he could not see me. I stood in the shower for a long time, shampooing my hair and washing the filth off my body; then I climbed into bed, vowing that I was not going to the ritual initiation ceremony that afternoon.

But, after waking up about noon and having lunch in the cafeteria, my stubbornness won out and I decided to go to the chapter room at the appointed hour. I am forever grateful that I did. The ritual initiation ceremony was beautiful; the officers must have practiced the ceremony many times because they seemed to perform it flawlessly. I was fascinated by the ideals of the fraternity -- Love, Charity, and Esteem -- qualities that seem essential for a true brotherhood to exist. And the statement that "Men should be selected not for their wealth, rank, or honor, but for their personal worth and character," resonated with me. Jim Hammons, the Prytanis of the chapter did a marvelous job and administered the bond to each new member. The setting, the music, the robes and jewels of the officers, and the lighting were all perfect. When I knelt at the altar, assumed the bond, and signed the chapter scroll as member number 48 of Epsilon Upsilon Chapter I felt a warmth that I had never experienced before. Over the years, I have conducted and participated in many ritual initiations, but none have been as powerful as the one I first experienced.

In retrospect, I understood the psychology of having the pledges "go through hell" to get into the fraternity but I did not think that was the best way to build true brotherhood. In fact, I never fully forgave some of the actives who had been especially cruel to me and other pledges. I was selected as the Top Pledge of the class, an award that had to be tempered by the observation that there were only nine of us who survived.

I quickly moved into a leadership role in the chapter, being elected Grammateus in the spring and being appointed rush chairman for the summer to develop a list of prospective pledges for the next fall. I moved into the chapter house for my senior year and fully participated in all activities of the chapter -- the social events, service projects, intramurals, serenades of the sororities, etc. I liked the ritual meetings of the chapter because I felt that they provided a structure and decorum that facilitated conducting business.

I learned important leadership skills within the chapter, such as the need for clear goals and careful planning. I found that organizations and people are not perfect -- some guys were great students and while others struggled to stay in school; some wanted only to party and others concentrated on intramurals. To make a group effective, you have to draw upon each person's talents and make everyone feel included. And I found out that one man can make a difference; I was able to get Hell Night dropped from the pledge program.

When I graduated from Northwestern in spring 1960, and headed to graduate school at the University of Arkansas, I looked back on an enriching experience as a member of TKE. I was selected as the Outstanding Senior and Top Teke of the chapter at the end of my senior year. But I assumed that this phase of my life was over. I, of course, knew that Tau Kappa Epsilon was a national fraternity but the information I had indicated that there was no chapter at Arkansas.

But when I arrived in Fayetteville, as related in chapter 7, I found that the Tekes did have a group there. A colony had been formed the previous spring and was working toward meeting the requirements for installation as a chapter. I ended up moving into the chapter house, working with them to achieve that goal, and participating fully in their programs.

One of the activities that I most remember and enjoyed was the singing that occurred following the evening meal in the chapter house. We would usually sing "The Sweetheart of TKE" and one or two other fraternity songs. And, occasionally, several guys would gather around the piano later and sing more. Singing seemed to elicit a feeling of warmth and togetherness and facilitated the work of the chapter.

As we moved toward the anniversary of the colony's first year and the date where it would be eligible for installation, I helped the chapter write a Petition for Membership that would be sent to all TKE chapters for a vote. Before sending the petition, however, there had to be a secondary inspection by a representative of the International Fraternity to ensure that all standards had been met. The Secondary Inspection Officer was a tall southern gentleman from Greenville, South Carolina, Lenwood Cochran, who was a Grand Officer of the fraternity. Lenwood and I immediately became good friends and have remained so from that day forward. He found that requirements had been met and that the petition was in order; so it was sent to all chapters and received a favorable vote.

In late spring, Theta Xi Chapter was installed and the then Grand Epiprytanis, J. Russell Salsbury, was the Installing Officer. The weekend, complete with the ritual initiation and installation ceremony and a formal banquet, was a great experience for the new chapter and for me. I felt as much a part of the chapter as the members being initiated.

During the three years that I was at the University of Arkansas, I remained active with the chapter, participating in various activities and being available for advice and assistance in numerous ways. Combining my undergraduate and graduate years, I was able to have four full years of fraternity life and to observe those activities that help produce organizational success. I can't think of a better "laboratory" on a college campus in which a young man can learn leadership skills.

DOING THE DISSERTATION

Since my graduate courses concentrated on management and organizational behavior, the work that I was doing with TKE seemed very relevant. My interests had evolved toward the question of "what does it take to make an organization successful?" The textbooks were filled with examples and recommendations for business firms, but very few applications to non-business organizations. But I could easily see that the fraternity had become more successful as it used the basic management practices I taught them. My major professor, Dr. Robert D. Hay, believed that management principles were universal and could be applied in any type of organization. But no one had tested this hypothesis as it applies to social fraternities, so I proposed to Dr. Hay and my committee that I attempt to determine whether "better managed fraternities are more successful."

In designing the research, I had to define the measures of success and, finally, decided upon six criteria: The size of the chapter (# of members and pledges), the rush results (# of men pledged) in the last rush period, the percentage of pledges initiated, the chapter's ranking in scholarship (Group GPA), the success in campus competition (e.g. intramurals), and the public opinion ranking of the chapter. In each case, success was measured via a comparison with other fraternities on that campus. The "public opinion" rankings came from a firm, the College Survey Bureau, run by Wilson B. Heller, that ranked fraternities on each campus. Based on where a chapter ranked in each category, a score was assigned and, therefore, an overall "success score" determined.

To determine how well a chapter was managed, I came up with a list of 33 relevant practices and developed a system for scoring based on whether and how well each practice was used. To collect the necessary data, I needed to study a number of chapters at different campuses. As described earlier, TKE hired me as a Field Supervisor. While I performed in this role, I could also collect the data that my research project required.

During the 1963-64 school year I visited sixty TKE chapters throughout the South and the Midwest. On each visit, I completed my TKE duties and reported back to headquarters on what I found and did. And I did my dissertation research, visiting the Dean's office to get comparative data on the fraternities on campus and interviewing chapter officers about their use of management practices. The normal campus visit was three days and my time was often fully utilized.

My year as a TKE Field Supervisor was very interesting. I was one of eight men serving in that role and we each had an assigned geographical area. The veteran on the staff that year was Charles D. (Chick) Statler from Southeast Missouri State. We began the year with a "Field School" at the International Headquarters where we learned the procedures to follow in conducting a visit and important skills like how to rush or recruit new members. Chick was a very outgoing fellow and helped "rookies" like me get ready to hit the road.

Before heading out, however, all the field staff got to attend the 1963 Conclave in Indianapolis. This three-day affair is held every two years and is attended by representatives of the undergraduate chapters and alumni leaders. They elect the international officers (Grand Officers) of the fraternity and consider legislation concerning the constitution and by-laws of the fraternity.

After this thrilling experience, I began my work at Gamma Chapter at the University of Illinois, a huge campus with over 50 fraternities, arriving just in time for rush week. Talk about jumping into the frying pan! But I made it through my maiden visit and, then, headed south. I spent the entire fall traveling to chapters from Texas to Virginia. I had to call the headquarters once a week to report to Bruce Melchert or Jim Irey, the Assistant Executive Director; otherwise, I followed my itinerary and lived on the road.

First year field supervisors were paid $300 a month, plus expenses, with the expense reports scrutinized carefully by the office. We were supposed to live in the chapter house, if there was one, both to become better acquainted with the men and to save money. Some of the accommodations were fine but others bordered on "hardship duty". In the spring, when I visited chapters in the Midwest, I had my first experience traveling in snow and in seeing how some of my northern fraters lived. On a visit to Ohio State, I learned that all the beds in the house were in a "dormer" (a large open room with rows of double-decked bunks) on the third floor. The OSU fraters slept with the windows open and the bed I was assigned was near one of the windows. Fortunately, the bed had a nice set of blankets on it which helped me endure the snow that had blown in during the night.

When the chapter had no house, fieldmen were authorized to stay in a motel. One of the luxuries at that time was the new Holiday Inns, some costing less than $10 a night. A challenge on the road was taking care of laundry; I either had to find the time to go to a laundromat or drop off my dirty clothes at a laundry as I came into town and pick them up on the way out.

One of the highlights that year was a visit to Findlay College in Ohio. The Prytanis of the chapter, Michael Kazakas, was also the President of the Student Body and had arranged for a popular singing group, The Lettermen, to perform at the college. He had also found out that they were not members of a fraternity and arranged for them to be initiated into TKE after the concert. They came over to the TKE house for the ceremony, which I was able to attend. The Lettermen became very loyal members of the fraternity, recording "The Sweetheart of TKE" and other Teke songs that many of our chapter used for years.

By the end of the school year, I was ready to quit traveling for a while. I had put many miles on my car, had met many outstanding young men and had visited campuses in parts of the country I had not seen before. A benefit of being on these campuses was the opportunity to look for a teaching job, beginning in the fall of 1964. After interviews at several schools, I was offered a job as an Assistant Professor at Georgia Tech in Atlanta and accepted it.

My dissertation research ended up including twelve chapters of other national fraternities, in addition to the 60 Teke chapters. In analyzing the data that I collected, several important findings emerged:

1. There was a significant positive correlation between how well managed a chapter was and how successful it was.

2. Among the success criteria, the most important measure was comparative chapter size.

3. There were about ten managerial practices that were strongly correlated with success, the most important ones being:

    a. The existence of well-known specific short-range goals.

    b. A budget that was in writing, and

    c. The presence of an active, experienced chapter advisor.

It took me two years after the data had been collected to complete the analysis, write up the results, present them to my dissertation committee and defend my conclusions. I received my Ph.D. degree in May, 1966. None of this would have been possible without my membership in and employment by Tau Kappa Epsilon.

Meeting Marlene

Personally, the most important benefit of my association with TKE was the opportunity to meet Marlene Munden, who became my wife. Marlene had grown up in Scottsburg, Indiana, a small town about thirty miles north of Louisville, Kentucky, and had come to Indianapolis to work. When I arrived to attend "Field school," she was serving as secretary to Bruce Melchert, the Executive Director.

Marlene was an extremely attractive young lady who immediately caught my attention. But I didn't have time to talk with her because I was involved in sessions all day and into the night. Also I didn't think it would be a good idea to bother the boss' secretary. Everyone in the office was busy that week, also, preparing for the conclave that weekend. Marlene had a particularly demanding job. Over 300 undergraduates were attending the conclave and there was a big banquet and dance on Saturday night for which the headquarters had offered to arrange dates. Marlene was trying to round up about 300 girls -- calling the sororities at Butler University, the nursing schools in town, anywhere she could find a concentration of young women -- and matching them up with the young men.

As this task was completed, Bruce asked Marlene if she had arranged a date for herself and she replied that she had not but that she would like to ask Bill Muse. Apparently she had noticed me, also. I was delighted to accept, not realizing that I could have a date, thinking that I would be on "duty" for that event. As it turned out, all the staff was working when something needed to be done, but Marlene and I finally got to talk and get acquainted. I liked her immediately, but realized that I was hitting the road the next morning and that there were no immediate plans for me to return to Indianapolis.

Fortunately, at the end of the school year, I received an invitation from Bruce to work in the headquarters over the summer. He wanted me to completely re-write The Teke Guide, a manual for pledge training. That was great with me, as I did not have to be at Georgia Tech for my new job until September. And it would allow me to see Marlene again. Over the summer, our romance blossomed and we were married in late August.

Marlene has been a great asset to me in my life as a Teke. She knows a lot about the fraternity and the people who are a part of it. She has attended many conclaves and other TKE events with me over the years and has enjoyed it almost as much as I have. But our marriage did change one policy in the international headquarters. Field staff could no longer date the secretaries!

INVOLVEMENT IN THE INTERNATIONAL FRATERNITY

My involvement with TKE beyond the chapter level began almost immediately after Theta Xi chapter had been installed at the University of Arkansas, as I became an assistant Province Supervisor for Arkansas and Oklahoma. The USA and Canada were divided into "Provinces" that could include one or more states, or part of a state, depending on the concentration of chapters. The Province Supervisor was an alumnus in the region who agreed to visit the chapters and to conduct a leadership conference each year. My job as assistant was to be responsible for the chapters in Arkansas, which consisted only of the chapter at UA and one at Arkansas State. Since I was already active with Theta Xi chapter, all I had to do was visit the group at ASU -- and I discovered they were a very strong chapter.

In the spring, the Prytanis of the chapter at Arkansas State called me to tell me they had initiated Elvis Presley as a member. I was ecstatic as Elvis was my favorite singer but disappointed that they had not notified me in advance so I could have attended the initiation ceremony. He told me that he knew one of the guys who played in Elvis' band, had attended a party at Graceland, and, while talking with Elvis, had asked him if he would like to join the fraternity. Elvis said yes and agreed to a date to bring the chapter officers and the ritual equipment over to Graceland for the ceremony. On my next trip to Jonesboro I saw pictures taken in the living room at Graceland during the initiation. Elvis was, reportedly, very interested in the symbolism and ideals of the fraternity and talked with the fraters at some length.

The next year I moved up to Province Supervisor for Oklahoma and Arkansas, visiting all the chapters in both states and conducting a leadership conference at Oklahoma State. Later, while teaching at Georgia Tech, I served as a Province Officer in Georgia and when we, subsequently, moved to Ohio University, I was the Province Supervisor for Southern Ohio.

In summer, 1967, I was elected to the Grand Council as the Grand Hegemon, one of the eight Grand Officers who comprise the Grand Council, the supreme governing body of the fraternity. The Grand Council met twice annually, with each Grand Officer participating in numerous fraternity events in between -- speaking at chapter celebrations, leadership conferences, etc. My election occurred at the 1967 Conclave held in the Bahamas. Achieving this goal was a major political task, as the chapter delegates in attendance elect the Grand Officers who make up the Grand Chapter. It was a thrill for me to accomplish this at age 28, with a lot of help from leaders of the fraternity. The research I had done on fraternities gave me a lot of visibility, but it was the support and active campaigning by many friends that assured my election.

Over the next twelve years I served on the Grand Council, moving up the ladder (with two terms as Grand Crysophylos or treasurer), until being elected Grand Prytanis in 1977 at the Conclave in New Orleans. My elation on this occasion was dampened only by the death of Elvis that occurred during that week. In my address after my election I made note of that occurrence and spoke of my admiration for him and my pride in his TKE membership, using the phrase "The King is dead. Long live the King!" And how true that has been; Elvis' music and his image have lingered longer than during his career while he was alive.

During my service on the Grand Council, I tried to help implement the findings that came from my doctoral research. I wrote many articles on chapter management for <u>The Teke</u> and other publications, spoke at many leadership conferences on the subject, and helped start a College of Leadership and Chapter Management, which was held at the biennial Conclave. And, after the results of my dissertation were published, I was invited to speak at the conventions of several other national fraternities and sororities. I think these contributions made a difference in the success of our chapters.

In the summer of 1975, I had a special assignment with the United States Agency for International Development, a federal agency, working with a university in Kabul, Afghanistan. Because of the nature of my responsibilities, I could not return to the states in time to attend the Conclave in August at Lake Geneva, Wisconsin. I wanted to be re-elected to the Grand Council, but felt that would be impossible with my absence from the meeting. But fierce campaigning on my behalf by friends on the council and throughout the fraternity resulted in my election as Grand Epiprytanis; this may be the only time that a Grand Council member was elected in his absence.

One of the initiatives I undertook while Grand Prytanis was to form a Grand Prytanis Advisory Council, comprised of influential Teke alumni. I asked Ronald Reagan, TKE's most famous alumnus, to serve as chairman and he agreed to do so; this was after Reagan had served as Governor of California and before be became President. Reagan chaired a well-attended meeting in Indianapolis that was very successful. And while President, Reagan invited a group of approximately 20 Tekes (including me) to a luncheon at the White House.

At the White House luncheon, I sat at a table with President Reagan and six other Tekes, including an alumnus of Eureka College who was in the TKE chapter with President Reagan. I was amazed at how well President Reagan could remember other men in the chapter and even where they lived in the fraternity house. Throughout his career, even the years as President, Ronald Reagan served as a very active and loyal member of the fraternity.

After completing my service as Grand Prytanis, I have served on two different occasions as a member of the Board of Directors of the TKE Educational Foundation, the fund-raising arm of the fraternity that supports programs to enhance scholarship and leadership development, including a term as chairman of that board. I also served for two terms as a member of the Board of Directors of the National Interfraternity Conference (NIC), the trade association that represents all fraternities, and later as Teke's delegate on the NIC House of Delegates. For my interfraternity service, NIC awarded me its highest honor, the Gold Medal. Additionally, the Fraternity Executives Association presented me with the Order of Fraternity Excellence and Pi Kappa Phi fraternity gave me its Durwood Owen award.

During my years of service to the international fraternity, I have had the good fortune to know most of the men who have been in leadership positions. I did not come along early enough to meet any of the men who founded the fraternity in 1899, but I did meet, L.W. Tuesburg, one of the National Founders who decided to make TKE a national organization. And I met all of the Expansion Leaders -- R.C. Williams, Leland F. Leland, James C. Logan, Frank B. Scott, and Bruce B. Melchert. In the ensuing years I have served with and/or known well, all of the individuals who have served as Grand Prytanis and almost all of the Grand Officers.

The Grand Prytanii under whom I served as a Grand Officer were Don Becker, Lenwood Cochran, Bill Quallich, and Bill Wisdom. The Grand Officers who served on the Grand Council with me who later became Grand Prytanis were Rodney Williams, John Courson, Dwayne Woerpel, and Joel Johnson. The Executive Vice-Presidents and CEO's who provided leadership during my tenure on the Grand Council were Bruce Melchert and T.J. Schmitz.

All of these men added greatly to my life, but there are two that stand out. Lenwood Cochran was the first Grand Officer I met and he served as my mentor through much of my Teke experience. He was a marvelous Grand Prytanis and served for many years as the Chairman of the Nominations Committee at Conclaves. His wife, Jean, has been as devoted to TKE as Lenwood and they both have been the dearest of friends.

Bruce Melchert made it possible for me to work for the fraternity and complete my research. He was, in my opinion, the most effective Executive Director/CEO that the fraternity has had and, subsequently, served as Grand Prytanis. His contributions to the success of TKE are immeasurable. He has been a true friend and frater.

Most men see their fraternity experience relegated to the short time they are in college and, even then, rarely understand the real essence of fraternity -- focusing only on the social life and not what can be learned from the brotherhood that can be developed and the leadership skills that can be acquired. But, for me, my fraternity has been a lifetime experience. I have contributed many hours, my creativity, and my leadership and I received much in return. Tau Kappa Epsilon has honored me with every award available, including the Order of the Golden Eagle, TKE's highest honor. I am grateful for the recognition, but, more importantly, for the friendships I have made and the lasting memories that they have produced.

CHAPTER 9:

MARLENE, MUSSIE, ELBO, AND MISTER V

The family, I believe, is the most important group in our society. It is the source from which most of the values, beliefs, attitudes, and behavior we exhibit emanates and is the most appropriate and effective forum for the raising of children.

I feel fortunate to have had a mother and father who loved me and cared for me and to have had an extended family that has provided support and encouragement throughout my life. It has been my goal to replicate that environment to the degree possible so that my family would benefit from similar conditions.

This, then, is the story of how my family evolved.

MARLENE

The first thing that I noticed about Marlene was her eyes -- big, beautiful, dark brown eyes, accentuated by a pair of black-rimmed glasses. She was slim with dark brown hair, a ready smile, and an infectious laugh. Anna Marlene Munden was born on February 10, 1945 in Scottsburg, Indiana, and lived there until she graduated from Scottsburg High School in 1962.She came to Indianapolis to work and had landed a job at the Teke office. As cited in chapter 8, it was here that we met, with Marlene arranging our first date at the 1963 Conclave.

That date was lovely although we were both "on duty" and had to respond when things needed to be done. But we enjoyed the dinner and the dancing and, mainly, getting to know each other. She even stayed after the event and we talked until after midnight. I learned that she was only eighteen, although she had poise and maturity that made her seem older. Finally, she had to return to her rooming house and I had to get to bed, as I was leaving early the next morning to drive to Champaign, Illinois.

When I got ready to depart the next morning, I felt a sense of loss; I didn't know if I would ever see Marlene but wanted very much to do so. I didn't have her phone number but she had told me where she lived and mentioned that she had to do her laundry on Sunday morning. So I drove over to where she lived, found the nearest laundromat, and hung around there, hoping she would appear. But she didn't show up, so I left on my journey with a heavy heart.

Over the ensuing weeks and months, as I would call into the TKE office, I hoped that Marlene would answer the phone so I could talk with her. We did have opportunities to talk and, when I was in Indiana visiting chapters that winter, I made plans to come to Indianapolis for a date with her at The Embers, a fancy restaurant. We had a great time, which made me want to see her more often. I knew that I would see Marlene at least once more, as I had to come to Indianapolis for a "de-briefing" at the end of the school year.

As noted earlier, I was invited to work in the headquarters over the summer to rewrite the fraternity's pledge manual. This allowed Marlene and me to spend much time together. We went to the Indianapolis 500 together (our first and only time to attend this event); it was five hours of constant noise. I also took Marlene to an Indianapolis Indians baseball game. Chick Statler and I were living at the Teke House at Butler University. He was dating a girl he met in Indianapolis who was studying accounting so Chick called her "the CPA." Marlene and I would get together with them on weekends, once to visit a beautiful lake in northern Indiana.

By mid-summer, my love for Marlene had grown and we began to discuss marriage. She, therefore, invited me to come home with her to Scottsburg to meet her folks. The Mundens lived on Meridian Street, about three blocks from the town square in Scottsburg. Marlene was the oldest of seven children; she had two sisters -- Wynogene and Betty Ruth -- and four brothers -- twins, Ronnie and Donnie, plus David and Ricky. Another brother, Allen, arrived later. Her mother, Virginia, had been born and raised near Gallatin, Tennessee and still had a trace of a Southern accent. Her dad, Preston, was a native of Scottsburg and a salesman for the Jewel Tea Company.

Virginia was a friendly, outgoing woman and I felt that she liked me right away. It was harder to get a reading of how her dad felt. Preston was funny, always joking and telling stories, but I didn't know what he really thought. After the weekend, though, Marlene reported to me that her family was pleased and supportive, so we began to plan for a wedding at the First Baptist Church in Scottsburg on August 22, 1964.

It was a beautiful wedding. My brother, Paul, and his wife, Marie, drove up from Mississippi to represent my family and Paul served as my Best Man. Marlene's sister, Wynogene, was the Maid of Honor. Several staff members at TKE headquarters attended, including Chick Statler who I suspect put Limburger cheese on the engine block of my car.After the wedding on Friday night, we drove to Louisville for the weekend and attended a concert on Saturday night at the Kentucky Fairgrounds that featured Frankie Valli and the Four Seasons.

After the honeymoon, we returned to Indianapolis to work for another week before our move to Atlanta. As I contemplated our life together, I recognized the differences that Marlene and I had: our ages (I was 25 and she was 19), our educational levels (I was nearing a Ph.D. and she had just completed high school), and our geographic origins (I grew up in the South and while her home had been in the North). But I also realized that Marlene was mature beyond her years, that she was more intelligent and more widely-read than most college graduates I had known, and that Northerners were not that different from Southerners (except that people from the North talk too fast and sometimes have a funny accent!).Marlene was beautiful, smart, and could cook! Who could ask for anything more! But, most importantly, we loved each other and I knew we could have a good life together.

Marlene and I have been married for over forty years and she has been a wonderful wife and mother. During the early years of our marriage, she devoted herself to raising our three children, providing the care and direction that helped to produce three outstanding young people. After all the kids were either in high school or junior high, Marlene began to work on a college degree, first at Texas A&M and then at the University of Akron, earning a B.S. degree in education with a specialization in history in 1988.

When I began to assume administrative responsibilities in higher education, Marlene took an active role in the entertaining and other public functions that go along with the job. That was particularly true for the role of the President's wife or First Lady, as that is almost a full-time (uncompensated) job. And she always took an active role in the community where we lived, serving as President of the League of Women Voters in both Omaha and Bryan-College Station, Texas. In Akron, she helped start the Habitat for Humanity Chapter there and served as President of Habitat in Auburn. In addition, she served on the boards of many other community organizations.

I will now discuss each of our three children, in the order of their births. At the outset, let me indicate that I gave each of the children a nickname, a habit that I may have adopted from my brother, Paul. I also had a nickname for Marlene during the early years of our marriage. I called her "Babe", but she complained that I called her that because I could not remember her name! So I dropped it.

AMY MARLENE (MUSSIE)

Amy was born on April 1, 1965 at the Piedmont Hospital in Atlanta, Georgia. She was a healthy, beautiful baby who brought a whole new dimension to our lives. Not having had any younger siblings, I had to learn how to care for a baby, including changing diapers, something I had not experienced before. And those "wake-up calls" at two or three o'clock in the morning took a little getting used to. But holding her in my arms was worth any disruptions that occurred.

When Amy was only five months old, we moved from Atlanta to Athens, Ohio and this is where she spent her pre-school years. In the house we were renting there, Amy's room had hardwood floors and her baby bed was on rollers. At night, she would get on her knees and rock so hard that the bed would roll across the floor, sometimes blocking the door and making it difficult for us to get into the room. This rambunctious behavior earned her the first nickname -- "Amy the Bull." After she began to sleep through the night, I changed it to "Amiable." Over time, I call her "A-mus", then sometimes "Mus", and, finally, "Mussie."

From an early age, Amy demonstrated considerable creativity. She liked to have Marlene and me read to her and to look at her books. As she got older, she developed two imaginary friends, "Koochie" and "Larry Lettuce", with whom she would have animated conversations. After Ellen came along and they were old enough to play together, the girls invented a language called "Ham" in which they communicated and which none of the adults could understand.

We enrolled Amy in the nursery school run by the College of Education at Ohio University when she was three. She was very excited about school from the inception. Amy advanced to the kindergarten program at Appalachian State University when we moved there when she was five, and then began the first grade at Hardin Park Elementary School.

Amy, as well as Ellen and Van, loved to watch "The Brady Bunch" on television each afternoon. When Amy was in elementary and junior high school in Omaha, she wrote plays based on episodes from that program. Then she produced, directed, and starred in the show. She would assign roles to Ellen and Van; they would practice and then perform the play for Marlene and me in our living room. Later, during high school in Bryan, Texas, Amy enrolled in a summer theatre program at Texas A&M University that culminated with a play performed by the students. The production was

"Picnic" and she had the starring role. It was no surprise that, when it came time for Amy to go to college, she wanted to major in theatre.

Amy spent her freshman year at Trinity University in San Antonio, Texas and, then, moved with the family to Akron when I became President of The University of Akron. She enrolled in the theatre arts program, performing in numerous productions and earning a B.A. After graduation, she went to work as an intern at the Playhouse in the Park in Cincinnati, earned her Actors Equity union card and then performed at several professional theatres in both Cincinnati and Dayton.

Wanting to try her hand as an actor on Broadway, Amy moved to New York City and began to audition for roles both on and off Broadway. She supported herself by working as a salesperson at Laura Ashley, a women's clothing store on Madison Avenue. But she was never able to get the big break that she needed in this highly competitive field.

After a year in New York, she moved to Minneapolis, where Ellen was living and working at that time, to act in a summer theatre and, subsequently, to work for the St. Paul Chamber Orchestra in their development department. Marlene and I persuaded Amy to go back to school, so she enrolled at Washington University in St. Louis and earned a Master's degree in English. She, then, came to Auburn University to pursue a Ph.D. in English, teaching as an instructor in the English Department there. Completing a dissertation concerned with women who played the role of Hamlet, Amy earned her doctorate in 1998. One of my thrills as President of Auburn was to present Amy with her degree.

Upon graduation from Auburn, Amy was able to land a job on the English faculty at the University of Minnesota, teaching for three years in a non-tenure track position before moving to the University of St. Thomas in St. Paul as an assistant professor of English. Recently, Marlene and I were visiting Amy and attend her class on English Literature at St. Thomas. We were very impressed with her performance as a teacher, her classroom management skills and her ability to elicit responses from the students. Her training as an actor has, in my opinion, benefited her teaching. In 2007, Amy was granted tenure at St. Thomas and promoted to associate professor.

One of my favorite times with Amy occurred when she and I spent a week together in Greece. Marlene and I were scheduled to host an Auburn Alumni tour of Greece. When conflicts prevented Marlene from going, I invited Amy to accompany me. We had a wonderful time, seeing Athens and the Greek Isles. Amy fell in love with Greece, has learned to speak Greek, and has returned many times to do research and to lead students on study-abroad assignments.

I admire Amy greatly, not only for her intelligence and talent but also for her perseverance and pluck. She has had to deal with disappointments and challenges in her life, but has shown the courage and commitment needed to succeed. Being an actor, with the inevitable unsuccessful auditions, undoubtedly has left a level of resolve that Amy has carried with her to other aspects of her life. She is a warm human being, caring and sensitive to the needs of others.

ELLEN ELIZABETH (ELBO)

Ellen was born on May 31, 1967 in the Sheltering Arms Hospital in Athens, Ohio. Marlene and I seemed to have an easier time with Ellen, perhaps because of the experience we had gained the first time around. Whereas Amy was impulsive as a young child, Ellen was more contemplative; she would observe what was going on until she understood "how things worked" and, then, would jump in and participate.

Amy and Ellen played well together; Amy soon introduced Ellen to her imaginary friends and they would spend hours talking "Ham" to each other. Ellen began school at age three when we enrolled her in the Lucy Brock Nursery School at Appalachian State. She loved learning and soon progressed on to the kindergarten program at ASU. When we moved to Omaha she entered Harrison Elementary, our neighborhood school. Ellen always seemed to be well-organized and very conscientious about studies.

During the 1977-78 school year, the family lived in Alexandria, Virginia while I completed an assignment with the U.S. Department of Education. Ellen was in the fifth grade and had a marvelous educational experience there. She had a teacher, Mrs. Mitchell, who told the class about the research she had done on bees and then asked them to choose an animal and do similar research on it. Ellen chose penguins and conducted a yearlong research project on them. I was very impressed with the work she did and the report she wrote; it was better than that some of my college students had done!

One of the incidents I remember during our years in Omaha was when Ellen was playing softball at the YMCA. Although not naturally athletic, she worked hard at being a good player. In one game, she was asked to be the catcher, a position she did not normally play. I could tell it was not a role she enjoyed, but she hung in here and did a creditable job. This was characteristic of the attitude Ellen brought to anything she attempted; she was determined to succeed, no matter what challenges she faced.

While we were living in Texas, Ellen became a very successful debater at Bryan High School and her debate team won several championships. She also participated in the summer theatre program at Texas A&M, acted in several plays at Bryan High, and was a member of the Shyannes, a dance team that performed at each football game.

My decision to accept the presidency of the University of Akron and move the family to Ohio in the fall of 1984 created a difficult problem for Ellen. She was going into her senior year of high school and wanted to complete it at Bryan. But we did not want to leave her in Texas. Upon investigation, we found that, because she had taken a heavier than normal load each year, she only lacked three courses to complete her diploma. I learned, also, that the University of Akron had an early admissions policy for outstanding high school students and that she could complete her high school courses via correspondence through Texas Tech University. So Ellen applied for early admission to Akron and was accepted because of her almost straight A average and high test scores. She, therefore, moved with us and began her freshman year at UA. With Amy transferring from Trinity to Akron, she and Ellen lived with us in the president's house and enjoyed another year together.

After her freshman year at Akron, Ellen decided to transfer to Indiana University. Her best friend in Texas, Mary Leslie, planned to join her there. Ellen was accepted into the Honors Program and provided a room in the Honors dorm. She majored in theatre and acted in one production during her first year. But, unfortunately, Mary didn't come to IU. In her second year, Ellen lived in a regular dorm and concluded, after the first semester, that IU was just too big for her. She had done very well academically but wanted a more intimate environment.

Ellen moved back to Akron and spent the spring looking at various private liberal arts schools in Ohio, before finally settling on The College of Wooster. For the next two years, she had a great experience, earning a B.A. with majors in both theatre and psychology, graduating as the top student in each field. She was active in theatre and, as a senior project, revised and directed Harold Pinter's play, Betrayal, reversing the gender of the two characters.She also completed her high school credits by correspondence, getting her high school diploma about the same time she got her college degree.

After her graduation from Wooster, Ellen moved to Minneapolis to work in the field of psychology. She landed a job as a counselor in a long-term treatment center for juveniles run by Abbot Northwest Hospital. She also developed an innovative program for girls with eating disorders and was able to put her training in psychology to work in many other ways. Services were provided 24 hours a day and the work was often intense.

After three years in this role, she decided to move back to Ohio and live in Cincinnati with some of her classmates from Wooster. She took a job as a Director of Youth Programs for the Covington Community Center in Covington, Kentucky and entered graduate school at the University of Cincinnati to earn a M.S.W., Master of Social Work, degree. While completing this program, Ellen served as an intern with United Way of Greater Cincinnati, working for Richard Aft, the UW President.

In the M.S.W. program with Ellen was Larry Lindeman. Larry had grown up in Cincinnati and graduated from Xavier University prior to attending UC. Larry and Ellen began dating and married in 1997 following their graduation from UC and have made their home in Cincinnati. They have two children, Henry Muse Lindeman (born in 1999) and Elizabeth Leah (Bess) Lindeman (born in 2001). Ellen advanced to become Director of Development for the Center for Great Neighborhoods (formerly Covington Community Center), while Larry works as a Coordinator of School-based Services for NorthKey Community Care in Covington, Kentucky. In 2008, Ellen assumed a new job as Executive Director of the Kennedy Heights Arts Center in Cincinnati.

One of the joys that Marlene and I have been able to experience in Cincinnati is being with Henry and Bess as they grow up. They are energetic and creative and enjoy being with "Nana" and "Doe-Doe", often staying overnight and going with us to various activities.

Ellen's nickname evolved over time. Two early versions that she did not like were "Ellen the Melon" and "El-Belle." So I shortened them to "El" and then settled on "Elbo." She gave me a nickname also that has survived into the next generation. When she was a baby, Ellen had trouble saying "Da-Da"; it came out "Doe-Doe." So the kids called me "Doe-Doe" as they grew up -- and the grand kids also adopted that name. I also answered to "Pop the Chop" and "Dad the Pad."

Ellen, I believe, has the ability to succeed in the social services field, or any other field she enters. She has strong organizational skills and interacts well with others. She inspires confidence in others and has naturally moved into leadership roles.

WILLIAM VAN, JR. (MISTER V)

After Ellen's arrival, Marlene and I began to talk about the possibility of a third child. I hoped that we could have a son, even kidded that I wanted to name him Tommy Donald -- so that his initials would be T.D. and he would grow up to be a football star. She thought I was serious about the name; so, she adopted a cat and named him T.D. to foreclose that alternative.

William Van, Junior, was born on September 19, 1968 in Sheltering Arms Hospital in Athens. Almost from the inception, Van was a "happy-go-lucky" child, having a good time but finding it difficult to focus on the task at hand -- putting on clothes, eating his food, picking up his toys, or anything else he was asked to do. As he got older, he would make friends easily with whatever group he joined but often found his schoolwork less interesting.

Van followed Ellen through the schools in Boone and in Omaha. I, also, started to get him involved in sports at the YMCA in Omaha, where he played junior basketball and T-ball (baseball). During the year that we spent in Virginia, I signed Van up for youth soccer and agreed to help out with the team. I ended up being asked to serve as one of the coaches, even though I had never seen a soccer match. But I quickly got a book and read up on how the game was played. Van and I had a good time learning about soccer together.

Later, when we were living in Texas, I encouraged Van's interest in baseball. He played a couple of years in Little League and one year in the Babe Ruth league, as a pitcher and first baseman, and developed into a good player. I tried to attend all of his games. One day, while watching one of his Little League games, I noticed that Van was swinging too early. I called him aside and told him to watch the ball carefully and not to begin his swing until the ball was nearing home plate. On that at-bat, he hit a pitch over the fence for a home run. How's that for coaching!

Despite his knack for baseball, Van's primary interest turned out to be tennis. Fortunately, we lived only a couple of blocks from the Country Club in Bryan, so Van and I would go up there to the tennis courts to play. At first, I would concentrate on just hitting the ball back to him to help him develop his strokes. Then we began to play games and keep score. I tried to play at his level, allowing him to win a few points but not the match. Each time we played he got better and I had to step up my game in order to win. I was deliberately pushing Van to get better, using his desire to beat me as motivation. Soon he started to go up to the club to practice and to play other kids and, before long it became harder for me to win. Finally, we reached the point where, even with me playing as hard as I could, Van could beat me. I could sense his satisfaction and was proud of his perseverance to achieve that goal. It was obvious that Van had the same intensity and desire to win, as I did, along with the same frustration and anger at errors and losses. I hoped that he would be able to channel these emotions in a positive way, toward improvement of performance.

Van went on to become an outstanding tennis player. At Stephen F. Austin Junior High in Texas, he played on a doubles team that won the state championship. When we moved to Akron, he went to Firestone High School that had one of the top tennis programs in the state. Van not only made the team but also played number one doubles and won several championships. Later, when he went to the University of Akron, he played on the varsity team for his first two years.

At Firestone High, Van was the editor of the school newspaper and a popular student. But, unlike Amy and Ellen who got A's with an occasional B, Van was satisfied with C's and an occasional B. It wasn't a matter of intellectual ability because Van tested as high as the girls on I.Q.; it was just that academics did not have the same appeal to Van – at least not yet.

When he enrolled at the University of Akron, Van joined the TKE chapter there. One of my proudest moments was Van's initiation into Beta Rho Chapter and my induction as an honorary member in the same ceremony. I agreed to let him live in the fraternity house, which turned out a mistake. He had a great time, but his grades were barely high enough for him to stay in school. We required him to move out of the house to an off-campus apartment and, then, to move back home in order to concentrate on his courses. Marlene even threatened to sign him up for the U.S. Army if he didn't straighten up.

Van's social skills at Firestone High were legendary. Once when Marlene and I went away on a trip, he had a party for many of his high school friends at the president's house. After we found out about this, we strictly forbade any parties in the house while we were away. Some time later, we returned from a trip early to find about 100 kids in our backyard, around the pool. After sending them home, I confronted Van who argued that we said no parties in the house (so he thought outside would be okay!)

After his sophomore year at the University of Akron, Van decided to transfer to Ohio University. We felt that, perhaps, he would do better away from home. When Marlene and I attended his graduation a couple of years later, we were pleased to read in the program that Van was graduating with honors with a B.A. in English. He had finally gotten serious about academics and used the intellectual skills that we knew he had.

One of the most valuable outcomes of Van's years at the University of Akron was meeting Lori McCrobie, an attractive young coed from Boardman, Ohio, near Youngstown. An outstanding accounting student, Lori was active in student activities, including being president of Omicron Delta Kappa. They began to date while in school and continued afterwards. When Lori graduated she accepted a job with Arthur Anderson, a major public accounting firm in Cleveland; Van, after his graduation from OU, moved to Cleveland and worked as a waiter and in a warehouse to be near Lori.

We persuaded Van that he needed to go to graduate school and got him to come to Auburn. He enrolled in the Master's degree program in English with the intent to pursue a Ph.D. Lori then got transferred to the Arthur Anderson office in Birmingham to be near Van. When they got married in 1994, they established their residence in Auburn. Lori got a job with the internal auditing staff at the University, while Van continued his graduate work.

After completing his master's degree, Van decided that life as an English professor did not appeal to him; so he transferred to the doctoral program in educational administration, working for several years in the admission office of the university while completing his degree. While working for the university, Van founded and edited a publication, Horizons, that focused on educational innovations. Lori also went back to school, earning an MBA degree in the College of Business and, then, pursuing a Ph.D. in business with a concentration in management, after teaching a class at a community college and finding that she got a lot of satisfaction from it. All of their work culminated with both Van and Lori earning doctorates from Auburn University.

Following their graduation, they moved to Kalamazoo where Lori began work as an Assistant Professor of Management at Western Michigan University and Van as Director of Marketing at Olivet College. After one semester at Olivet, Van was offered a job as Director of the Center for New Media at Kalamazoo Valley Community College. He subsequently was promoted to Dean of Instruction for KVCC's downtown campus. In 2008, Van and Lori moved to Yorba Linda, California with Van becoming dean of academic affairs at California Design College and Lori assuming a position as associate professor at California State University-Fullerton.

While still at Auburn, Van and Lori had Madelyn Elizabeth in 2000. Marlene and I were very fortunate to be living in Auburn during Madelyn's first 2 ½ years and were able to spend a lot of time with her. In 2006, Sophia Ann arrived. We were able to spend considerable time with her in Kalamazoo during her first two years.

Van's nickname was initially just "V" but as he matured I promoted him to "Mister V". Then, after he got his doctorate, I recognized him as "Dr. V".

Lori has a bright future as a college professor and Van, I believe, has the skills to be an outstanding administrator, even though he disavows any interest in following the direction of his Dad's career. But one never knows what might lie ahead.

OUR FOUR-LEGGED FAMILY

Our family has included a number of four-legged folks at various times. Numerous cats have joined us over the years -- with names like O.C. (Outside Cat), Calico, Catman, Baby Kitty, Vanilla, Catspur, Gracie, and Aubie. But two stood out – for quite different reasons. A gray cat named T.D. came to live with us shortly after Ellen's birth and stayed for about five years. He was good with the kids but had the habit of going out at night, coming back about four o'clock in the morning. He would climb up to our bedroom window and hang on the screen until I got up and let him in. If I had had a gun, I'm sure I would have shot that ornery critter! Finally, as we were moving from Boone, N.C. to Omaha, we were attempting to take T.D. with us, although it was clear that was not his preference. We had him in a cardboard box (with holes for breathing) in the back seat of our car. He cried constantly and kept trying to claw his way out. About an hour into our trip in Elizabethtown, Tennessee, we stopped at a Dairy Queen; as soon as one of the kids opened the back door, T.D. tore out of his box, bounded out of the car, and high-tailed over the next hill -- without even saying goodbye!

The second was Sugar Boy, our last cat, who had beautiful orange and white coloring. He came to live with us as a kitten in Auburn and was very lovable, almost too much so. Sugar Boy could never get enough stroking (Marlene said he must have been taken away from his Momma too soon) and would climb in your lap almost every time you sat down. When we moved from Auburn to Greenville, North Carolina, we took Sugar Boy with us. Unlike T.D., he hardly complained at all and was a model passenger. But when we arrived, a different story emerged. The chancellor's house at East Carolina has an 8-foot high solid wooden fence surrounding the back yard; so we brought Sugar Boy's cage into that area and let him out. He immediately scaled the fence and disappeared down the street. This was about the same time a reporter showed up to do a story on our arrival. So Sugar Boy became a major part of the story and, for a few days, he became the most famous feline in eastern North Carolina. But Sugar Boy found his way back home after about three days and lived with us during our time at ECU. When we moved from there, Sugar Boy went to live with our good friend, Ruth Ann Cook, and still enjoys a pampered life.

The canines that were a part of our household were fewer and less transitory. Our first pup, a beagle named Punch, lived with us in Athens and developed into a good playmate for the kids. Some of Amy's first words when we were away and returning home were "Home, Punch", indicating she wanted to go home and see Punch. When we moved from Athens, we gave Punch to a farmer because he needed room to run around.

While in Boone, we tried to adopt a dog. But that venture lasted only a week or so. One day, we left him in the house while we were out and he tore down all the curtains in the living room. Needless to say, he went back to the puppy farm promptly. For good reasons, I do not even remember his name.

When we moved to Omaha, we purchased the first of three Scottish Terriers who would live with us over the next twenty-five years. They were all identical in appearance and temperament -- black and ornery! The first one, Bonny, loved to play with the kids and chase any cat that came near our property. She also liked to attack the mail; as soon as it fell through the slot each day, Bonny would assault it and scatter it all over the foyer. Bonny moved with us to Texas where she was run over by a car.

The second Scottie, Piper, came from a kennel in Texas. She lived with us there and in Akron before succumbing to liver cancer. Piper loved to take walks with Marlene and would try to attack any dog she encountered, particularly one on a leash, even those considerably larger than she.

The third Scottie, Patrick, came to live with us in Auburn. He loved to attend the cocktail parties in the president's house where he was the center of attention and where people often dropped food on the floor. When we moved from Auburn, Patrick retired to Indiana to live with Marlene's mother, Virginia.

REFLECTIONS

I am very proud of my family. The children are talented and industrious. Each has a good mind and a big heart. They care about others and work well with diverse groups of people. Marlene deserves most of the credit for how well they "turned out", for she devoted a major portion of her life to raising them and teaching them the life skills they needed.

It was important to me to be a good father, so I tried to balance the demands of my profession with the need to be involved with the children's lives. Men (and, increasingly, women) who chose professions that require extensive time commitments often face this difficult challenge. In my case, I became a department head at age 27 and each year that followed brought increasing responsibilities. On top of that, I became a national officer for TKE at age 28 and the nature of my job and my personality led to extensive community involvement wherever we lived. As a result, my days were long and even many weekends were filled with commitments.

While we were living in Athens and the kids were young (4, 2, and 1), Marlene reminded me very adroitly how difficult it was to care for three preschoolers without help. I had been gone for several weekends in a row to attend Teke events when she secured my commitment to be home one weekend, telling me she needed desperately to go to Columbus to do some shopping. On that Saturday, she left with a couple of friends before breakfast and did not return until late that night. So I got to feed the kids all three meals and care for them all day. I don't think there was a single time all day when all three kids were asleep. By bedtime that night, I was worn out and much more appreciative of the task that Marlene had.

From that point on, I limited my time away on weekends and tried to be at home at night, when possible, to help feed them, bathe them, and put them to bed. While in Omaha and all the kids were in elementary school, we had a routine that we followed almost every Saturday. I would take them to the YMCA for swimming, then to a restaurant for lunch, and then to a movie. I think I saw every child's movie made during those years. And I tried to be present for each event (play, ball game, etc.) in which one of the kids was participating, not just out of a sense of obligation but because I was interested in their performances.

As the kids got older, Marlene and I took them many places. In fact, during the year we lived in the Washington, D.C. area, we went to so many sites that the kids begged to say home at least one weekend to watch TV. They were able to go to Afghanistan with us and attended many Teke Conclaves.

When each of the kids reached his or her eighteenth birthday, Marlene and I each wrote them a letter. It was to convey to them our thoughts and feelings about them and to provide advice about their future lives. Each letter was private and personal. I hope it was a meaningful experience for them and that they will do the same for their children.

I don't begrudge the time I spent with the kids. I wish I could have been more available but feel that I did the best job I could of balancing my responsibilities as a father with my obligations to my employer. But only Marlene and the kids can judge whether I achieved that goal.

CHAPTER 10:
UP THE ACADEMIC LADDER

When I assumed my first full-time job in higher education as an assistant professor at Georgia Tech, I was only 25. Over the next six years, I advanced to associate professor and to professor, the highest faculty rank, completing a very rapid rise up the academic ladder. Along the way, I also took on my first major administrative assignment as department head at age 27, followed by an appointment as dean at age 31 and eventually as president at age 45.

Three primary factors influenced my rapid movement up the administrative ladder: (1) the good fortune of having opportunities come my way, (2) my willingness to accept the responsibilities offered to me, and (3) the ability to perform effectively in those roles. The promotion in academic rank came about, I believe, because I was productive in ways the faculty and administration valued, namely the publication of numerous articles in referred journals. Being in a field where the demand for faculty was strong may have also had a positive effect.

In this chapter I will discuss my academic career as a faculty member and as a department head in each of the places where we lived. In doing so, I will deal with dimensions in both my personal and my professional life.

GEORGIA INSTITUTE OF TECHNOLOGY

Personal. When Marlene and I moved to Atlanta, we loaded all that we owned into my Pontiac. With assistance from Georgia Tech, we had located an apartment on the second floor of a beautiful old home at 247 Brighton Road, N.E. in the Buckhead neighborhood not far from the campus. The white Cape Cod styled house had an outside stairway to the second floor in the rear. The unit was nicely furnished and included a bedroom, bathroom, living room, and dining room/kitchen. Our landlord was a very nice widow who lived downstairs.

On one of the first weekends after we had gotten settled, Marlene and I drove over to see my parents. Since their health did not permit them to come to Indiana for the wedding, this was their first opportunity to meet Marlene.I was a little nervous but I should not have been. Momma and Daddy both liked Marlene a lot.

Marlene was learning to cook the things that I liked. That wasn't too difficult since I like most all kinds of food, except liver and fishy fish (like salmon). Before we were married, Marlene prepared me a salad consisting of lettuce, tomatoes, boiled eggs, onions, ham, and cheese. It was what we would now call a chef salad; I had never had one before but loved it. I called it a "Muskatuck salad", after a creek near Scottsburg, and requested it on a regular basis. I also asked her to prepare some rice since that was a staple of my diet in Louisiana. Since she had never cooked rice before, she went to the store and bought some Uncle Ben's Instant Rice. Her first attempt was barely edible but subsequent efforts were steadily better. Marlene turned out to be a great cook, willing to try new dishes, and consistently pleasing my palate.

Two couples that we met at Georgia Tech became our close friends during our time in Atlanta. Bill and Beverly Schaeffer were both economists with Ph.D.'s from Duke. Bill had gone to Tech as an undergraduate and to Duke for his doctorate, then returning to Tech as a member of the faculty. He took me "under his wing" and taught me a lot about Tech and about my role as a faculty member. Beverly taught economics at Olgethorpe College in Atlanta; she and Bill met at Duke while they were in graduate school together. We enjoyed the many times we spent together.

The other couple, Mike and Suzanne Mulligan, had both graduated from Alma College where Mike was a Teke. They had come to Georgia so that Mike could earn his Ph.D. at the University of Georgia. Mike then took a position on the Dean of Men's staff at Tech. Mike and I enjoyed going to baseball games together. Once we went to an exhibition game in Atlanta between the Braves and the Detroit Tigers to visit with Mike's fraternity brother at Alma, Jim Northrup of the Tigers. We lost contact with the Mulligans after leaving Tech but reunited with them many years later after they had settled in Chicago.

After Marlene discovered she was pregnant, we began to prepare for the arrival of the baby. She found an obstetrician named Dr. Robert Gillespie, with whom she was very pleased, who operated out of the Piedmont Hospital, which was just a short distance from where we lived. We bought a baby bed and carriage and kept them ready. Amy was born at 3:52 a.m. on April 1st; I had spent the night in the waiting room and, to stay awake, had prepared lecture notes for my class the next day. After I saw Amy and I was assured that she and Marlene were okay, I went home, took a shower, and went to Tech to teach my classes.

Over the next few weeks and months, Amy commanded our attention. This was a new experience for me, as I had no younger siblings, whereas Marlene had grown up taking care of her younger brothers and sisters. So Marlene taught me a lot about what to do and I tried to be a good student and helper. We took Amy over to Mississippi so Momma and Daddy could see her later that spring. Although they had many grandchildren by this time, the new arrival was well received.

Professional. I had interviewed for the job at Georgia Tech when I visited the TKE chapter there as a Fieldman. Dr. Walter Buckingham was the Director of the School of Industrial Management. I had accepted the offer from Tech, even though I had two or three others at higher starting salaries, because it was a well-known school and would be a good place to start my career.

Being near downtown Atlanta and boxed in by major highways or industrial development on all sides, Tech's campus had a very urban feel. It's outstanding reputation as an engineering school had attracted a student body of which less than 100 were women. In the fall, I had a teaching load of 12 hours (four courses), with three preparations. This means that I had two sections of the same course (that could handled with one preparation) and two other different courses. Since it was my first term of full-time teaching, I had to spend considerable time preparing for each class - studying the textbook and readings, preparing notes for each session, and organizing my presentation.

In the fall, I taught courses in management. But as the spring rolled around, I was asked to teach marketing because of the heavier demand. I did not mind doing so, as marketing was my secondary field. Additionally, my research interests revolved around the questions of how and why people behave as they do, both as members of an organization and as consumers. I was again assigned twelve hours, with three new preparations.

When folks outside of academia hear about a teaching load of twelve hours a week, they think "what an easy job!" But I spent an average of three hours in preparation for each hour of instruction. In addition, there were the many hours preparing and grading exams and other assignments. As I became more experienced and as I taught particular courses multiple times, the time in preparation declined. But by then the expectations for research had begun to escalate.

Furthermore, I knew it was important that I finish my dissertation. The data from my questionnaires had been compiled in the previous summer, but I needed to do some more sophisticated analysis. My objective was to use multiple regression and correlation analysis to determine the relationship between certain variables. The computer center at Tech helped me access the program I needed and, over the course of the year, complete the analysis of my data but I had not had time to begin writing up the results.

With only about 40 faculty, the School of Industrial Management at Tech was too small for individual departments. So my boss was Dr. Buckingham, the director of the school and the person who had hired me. However, about midway through the spring term, Dr. Buckingham died suddenly and Dr. Sherman Dallas, the associate director, was moved up to director. I had had little or no contact with Dr. Dallas. Nevertheless, I was surprised when, toward the end of the spring term, he called me to his office and told me that, while he was pleased with my performance, my raise for the next year would be only $100. My starting salary was $7,500 for nine months. This sounds meager compared to salaries today, but it was much better than the $300 a month I had earned as a Fieldman! I was very disappointed and responded to Dr. Dallas that I had expected a more substantial raise. He replied that $100 was all he could afford and pointed to the fact that I had not finished my dissertation. I wanted to tell him that my teaching responsibilities did not leave sufficient time to make the progress desired but my better judgment prevailed. I did resolve, however, to complete the dissertation as soon as possible.

About the same time, I received a letter from Dean Harry Evarts of the College of Business at Ohio University, informing me that I had been recommended for a faculty position in marketing. I had no idea who the recommender was, but called Dean Evarts and agreed to come up for an interview, driven at least partially by my disappointment over the raise. I liked the campus and the people I met and was particularly impressed with Dean Evarts and his plans for the college. Before I left, he took me to dinner and offered me the job at a starting salary of $8,500. When I returned to Atlanta, Marlene and I talked about the offer and agreed to take it. She was pleased to be getting back closer to home and we both realized that we would likely be more comfortable in a smaller city.

Before leaving Atlanta, however, I had the opportunity to make significant progress on my dissertation. I learned that there were some courses unstaffed for the summer session. As a new faculty member and as someone departing, I was the "low man on the totem pole" for summer teaching assignments. But apparently there was a shortage of faculty desiring to teach that summer. So I was assigned a marketing course that met every day at 7:30 am. I would get to the campus early, teach my class (which, fortunately, was a repeat of a course I had taught in the spring), and then begin writing on my dissertation. I would take a break at noon, play a set of tennis with another faculty member, take a shower, and then come back to the office for a sandwich. I would work until about 4 p.m., then try to beat the rush hour traffic home. By the end of the summer, I had completed a rough draft of the thesis.

Overall, my memories of the year at Tech are mostly positive. In addition to my academic work, I served as faculty advisor to Beta Pi chapter of TKE, an outstanding group. Through this connection, I met Miller Templeton, a Teke alumnus who was a staff member at Tech, and one of the most enthusiastic people I have ever known. The faculty at Tech were not as collegial as I anticipated with most of them coming to the campus, teaching their classes, and then leaving to do research, consulting or other duties. I was thankful for Bill Schaeffer who took the time to mentor me through my first year at a new place.

OHIO UNIVERSITY

Ohio University is located in the town of Athens in the southeastern part of the state. Athens is a small town with the university being, by far, the biggest enterprise there. And the campus sits right in the middle of town, with one being able to walk out the front gate of the campus onto the main street (Court Street).

We arrived after a move that I will never forget. Marlene and I had rented an unfurnished apartment at the Athens Apartments on U.S. 50 just west of the town, intending to purchase the furniture we needed in Atlanta before moving. I saw an ad for a big sale at a furniture warehouse and persuaded Marlene to go there because of the terrific prices. We purchased living room, dining room, and bedroom furniture and scheduled delivery on the day of our move. Meanwhile, being the smart planner that I am, I had rented a U-haul truck and loaded it with all of our personal belongings, leaving ample space for the furniture that was to arrive before noon. When it was not delivered at that time, I began to call every hour always getting the reply that "it was on the way." Finally, about 7 o'clock p.m., with no furniture in sight and having moved everything out of our apartment, we departed with me driving the U-haul and Marlene following behind in the Pontiac. We had left Amy with Marlene's mother in Indiana.

We stopped in North Georgia to spend the night and, then, for the next two days traveled over winding two-lane roads across Tennessee, Kentucky, and West Virginia. Every time I would go around a curve, the contents of the U-haul would slide from one side to the other. By the time we got to Athens, I felt like I had wrestled a bear for two days.

To make matters worse, when I checked the speedometer on the truck with our car, the truck registered nearly 150 miles greater. I explained this to the U-haul dealer when I turned in the truck, but all he wanted was the money, telling me to "take it up with the company." And so I did, and with the FTC, ICC, and various other government agencies. My persistence paid off and I got a refund for the excess mileage. And I got a refund of the deposit we had made on the furniture. But this trip left a bad taste in my mouth – and was the last time I used a U-haul!

Personal. Marlene quickly purchased the furniture we needed and we settled into our apartment. The building housed a mixture of faculty and students, with the students often being loud on the weekends. One faculty member near us was Dean Dudley, a new member of the Finance Department, and his wife, Lenore. They were good friends during our time in Athens.

In that first year, when she was caring for Amy, Marlene spent a lot of time typing my dissertation. Before word processing equipment, typing was a grueling job; one had to stop and correct typing errors or start over. The dissertation was over 300 pages in length and Marlene must have typed the whole thing two or three times before switching to erasable bond paper.

In the spring, after Dr. Hay had read the dissertation and shared copies with the committee, he scheduled my defense. Each doctoral candidate has to defend his research methods and findings before the faculty. The session was scheduled for 10:30 a.m. on a Friday morning; so I flew to Fayetteville on Thursday, departing from Columbus, Ohio, and making several plane changes before arriving that evening. I carried on a briefcase that had the original copy of my dissertation, plus the notes for my presentation, but checked my suitcase with the clothes I would need and my shaving kit. I arrived in Fayetteville but my luggage did not. The airline said they had another flight early the next morning and would deliver the bag to my motel. By 9am the next morning, the bag had not arrived and I was a nervous wreck. I could see myself standing before the committee, unshaven in a rumpled shirt and pants. Finally, the luggage got there about 9:30 a.m., just enough time for me to shave, shower, dress, pack my bags, and catch a taxi to the Business School building.

I was pleased with the job I did in describing the research I had done and the results I found. But then the questioning started. There was one faculty member there who, rumor had it, came to the defenses just to heckle the doctors-to-be. He, obviously, had not read my thesis but that didn't stop him from asking questions. And the committee members had a number of questions, mostly of the "why didn't you do this or that" nature. After this had gone on long enough that I was feeling embattled, Dr. Hay spoke up and said: "I think Mr. Muse has done a fine job on the dissertation and his research will be a significant contribution to the field." Shortly thereafter, there was a motion to approve the dissertation which passed unanimously. Each member of my committee then had to sign the title page of the original copy.

My final task was to take the original signed copy to the Dean of the Graduate School. I arrived about 11:45 a.m., knowing that the office closed for lunch, hoping to get this done before noon so I could get to the airport for my flight back to Ohio early that afternoon. The staff member who accepted the dissertation checked to see if the signatures were in order and then began to feel the paper. She then told me that it was unacceptable because it was typed on erasable bond. I was about as close to the "end of my rope" as I have ever been, but I kept my cool. I got out the regulations the Graduate School had sent me and asked her to show me where it said erasable bond paper was not acceptable. She said, then, that there were some newer regulations. She kept shuffling papers and looking at the clock, obviously wanting to go to lunch. Finally, she relented and accepted the copy. I beat a hasty retreat and headed for the airport.

Another traumatic event occurred that spring when I got a phone call in May telling me that Daddy had died. I drove from Athens to Mississippi, stopping near Memphis the first night and arriving just before the funeral the next day. On the trip down there, I had a lot of time to think about Daddy and what he had meant to me. All the memories described in chapter 2 came flooding back. The funeral was at Rocky Hill, the church where he had the best years of his ministry.

During the summer of 1966, Marlene and I rented our first house on the eastern side of Athens on S. May Avenue. S. May intersects with E. State Street (U.S. 50) and the house was at 10 S. May, just off this main artery. There was a service station on the corner, facing State Street, with our house immediately behind it. The house was a single story, white frame structure with two bedrooms, a living/dining room, kitchen and bath.Our next-door neighbors were Mary and Chuck Culp (who was an administrator at OU) and behind us were Dottie and Lou Spataro (who had just come to OU as head of the Business Communications Department).

In the Spring of 1968, I met a guy who had bought a house just down the street at 39 S. May and was in the ROTC Department at OU. He told me that he had been ordered to Vietnam and had to leave in a few weeks and asked if I wanted to buy his house. He had used a VA loan to purchase the property and he only accumulated $300 equity in the few months he had owned it. He told me that if I would pay him $300, he would assign the mortgage of about $17,000 to me. The house was a white, two-story wood frame structure with a large living/dining room, den, and kitchen downstairs and three bedrooms and bath upstairs. Since Marlene was pregnant with Van at that time, we knew we were going to need a larger place. Marlene and I liked the house and agreed to assume the mortgage, moving in shortly before Van was born.

This proved to be a good neighborhood for us. It was near the campus and several families lived nearby who had children that Amy and, subsequently, Ellen and Van could play with. Martha and Larry Miller, who was on the Business Communications faculty, lived on the next street over. And the lab school that Amy attended when she got to be three was only a few blocks away. I had the house painted yellow with green shutters and was pleased with how it looked.

One of the continuing challenges here was the mystery of the missing "Foe". All the kids used pacifiers, especially to get to sleep. Ellen called the pacifier a "foe", so all the kids adopted that name as well. Invariably, when one of the kids was going to take a nap or going to bed at night, we could not locate his/her "foe". I bought many new pacifiers and put each on a string so the kids could wear them around their necks. But they still lost them. When we moved from Athens, I found "foes" in all sorts of places – e.g. behind couches, under beds, in closets, etc.

Unlike Atlanta, we got to know a lot of people in Athens. We socialized with a number of younger faculty and I joined the Junior Chamber of Commerce (Jaycees) to meet young men both in town and at the university.I played on a city league softball team that included both university and townspeople and also served as an advisor to the TKE chapter at OU.

But, clearly, the most significant events that occurred in Athens were the births of Ellen and Van. Dr. Lester Hamilton, Marlene's obstetrician, delivered both of them. Fortunately, Athens was only 5-6 hours from Scottsburg and we were able to visit Marlene's family several times each year while the kids were young. We bought a Volkswagen station wagon and, subsequently, a Chevrolet station wagon to make our trips as a family more comfortable. The VW had the distinction of having a heater that never put out heat until the trip was finished, making winter travel in Ohio pretty tough. We called the VW "the squareback" because of its shape. The new Chevy wagon was perfect for transporting the kids on trips. There was a large space behind the back seat that the kids called the "back-a-back"; we could put two baby mattresses back there for the girls to lie on and read while on the road so that Van could have the back seat to himself.

Professional. My first year at OU was similar to the year at Tech, at least in terms of workload. I taught twelve hours each semester, with two or three preparations each term, but having a year of experience made it easier to handle this responsibility. In addition to teaching, I attended all the faculty meetings and the various college events. I thought that was what a faculty member was supposed to do.

After I had defended my dissertation and was scheduled to receive my degree, I began to think about getting out of academia and going to work in business, which had been my initial interest. At the end of the spring term, I would have taught for two years and thereby fulfilled my obligation to the National Defense Graduate program. So I began discussions with campus recruiters from Proctor and Gamble and General Foods, both of which had large marketing operations. The recruiters seemed to be surprised that someone with a Ph.D. would be interested in going to work for them, telling me that I would not be happy doing the things they required of new employees. They, instead, thought I should talk to someone in marketing research, an area that would be more suitable for someone of my education.It was the first time I realized that I was overeducated for what I had originally planned to do. But new opportunities were just around the corner!

A few weeks later, Harry Evarts called me down to his office. I began to worry about what I had possibly done wrong to warrant a trip to the dean's office. But, amazingly, he told me instead that my department head, Karl Krauskopf, was stepping down at the end of the spring semester and that he would like for me to be department head. Karl was a very nice guy and had served the department well for a long time. I had no idea that he was planning to retire or that Dean Evarts was thinking of me as his replacement. As the youngest and least experienced member of the marketing faculty, I seemed to be the most unlikely person for this assignment. Dean Evarts told me that he was impressed with what he had seen of me and believed I could provide the kind of leadership that the department needed. Still in a state of shock, I accepted the challenge.

Two individuals had been on the marketing faculty for a number of years, Bob Raymond - a full professor and David Richmond - an associate professor. Either or both of them may have viewed themselves as Karl's successor. Additionally, I am confident they highly resented me being appointed as their boss. So I met with them individually, told them I had not asked for the job but that I would do the best job I could, and asked for their cooperation.I made sure I understood their teaching preferences as to courses and times and tried to give them what they wanted.For example, David lived on an operating farm out in the country and did not like to have early morning classes. Fortunately, Karl agreed to teach for another year before retiring fully and was accessible to me when I had a question. One of our faculty members, John Hewitt, accepted a job at another university and left at the end of the spring term, but I was able to hire Bob Watts, a recent MBA grad, to accept a one-year assignment to replace Hewitt.

The role of department head in the business school consisted primarily of determining the class schedule, making teaching assignments, evaluating faculty performance, making recommendations on compensation and promotion, and recruiting new faculty. The associate dean, Bill Day, handled budgetary matters and the assistant dean, Sherman Hopkins, counseled the students. We had one secretary for the department whom I supervised.

During my first year as the head, I spent considerable time recruiting faculty, as I needed to replace Dr. Krauskopf and John Hewitt. The positions were listed with the American Marketing Association; at the AMA meetings, I interviewed twenty-five candidates and, then, brought five in for campus visits and, eventually, hired Howard Cox and Bob Kegerries, both of whom were completing their Ph.D.'s at Ohio State. From this experience, I learned an important lesson.

Of the two new faculty, I was most excited about Howard Cox who had an undergraduate degree from Brown and an MBA from Harvard; with degrees from such prestigious schools, I was convinced he was bound to be a "winner". Bob, on the other hand, had been the CEO of a chain of variety stores in southeast Ohio, a family business that he had led after graduating from Ohio State and Case Western Reserve. He had gone back to OSU at age 42 to earn his Ph.D. and now wanted to go into teaching. I was fearful that he was looking at higher education as a form of "early retirement' from business, but was still impressed enough with him to extend the offer.

My judgment could not have been more wrong. At the end of their first year at OU, Bob had completed his dissertation, already had a couple of publications, and was a very popular teacher; Howard, meanwhile, was still negotiating about his dissertation topic. In fact, when I left OU in 1970, Howard had still made little progress toward completing his doctorate. In the fall of 1968, Dean Evarts asked me to serve as the director of the Division of Research in the college and I recommended that Bob become department head. He did and, a year and a half later, resigned to become dean of the business school at Wright State. Bob, subsequently, was promoted to vice-president and, then served as president of that institution over a period of ten years.

This experience taught me that one should not judge an individual solely by their age or credentials (e.g. where they went to school) but need to look closely at how well they have performed the jobs they have had and the kind of personal qualities they have.

In the summer of 1967, I was able to get some interesting business experience. Having been selected by an economic education foundation to participate in a program that gave faculty real world business experience, I was sent to work for the Proctor-Silex Company in Philadelphia. I was assigned to the vice-president of advertising and sales, Adam Hepp, and asked to evaluate the company's marketing programs. Given that the length of the experience was two months and that Ellen was just a baby, I went to Philadelphia alone and lived in the TKE house at Drexel University.

Proctor-Silex, a manufacturer of irons, toasters, and coffee percolators, had just introduced a concept of "life-long" appliances. Each product came in modular pieces that snapped together; so if any part of the product failed, the customer only had to unsnap that part and get a new one, rather than a whole new appliance. I interviewed buyers and merchandise managers in department stores throughout eastern Pennsylvania and then presented a report to Mr. Hepp, detailing the problems I'd seen.

Since Marlene and the girls had not been able to accompany me on this adventure, I invited them to come over to Philadelphia as I finished my work. We were able to spend a few enjoyable days on the Jersey shore.

Back at school, even as department head, I still taught nine hours each semester. But, since I was making the schedule, at least I minimized the number of preparations I had. My research and publication output had already started to grow. I published an article from my dissertation in The Academy of Management Journal, the top journal in the management field at that time, and placed several other articles in less prominent journals. As a result, at the end of my second year, OU promoted me to associate professor.

After I was appointed as director of research in Fall, 1968, my productivity increased even more. As director, my responsibilities were to work with the faculty to help stimulate research activity. I disseminated information about funding, assisted in making grant applications, and arranged an annual research seminar where outside scholars were brought in to speak to the faculty. Since I was now teaching only one course per term and had full-time secretarial support, I was able to generate manuscripts for review on a regular basis. Resulting from this was an article in The Journal of Marketing Research and another in The Journal of Marketing that Bob Kegerries and I co-authored. I had two graduate assistants, Michael Hutt and Kenneth Hartung, who did outstanding masters theses, and was able to use the data they had accumulated to co-author articles with them.

When Bob Kegerries left for Wright State in January 1970, I re-assumed the position of Marketing department head as well as director of research. And later that spring I was notified that I was to be promoted to professor with tenure. But another opportunity was already unfolding.

Harvey Durham was an American Council on Education (ACE) Fellow at OU in 1969-70, working out of the provost's office. He was on leave as head of the Mathematics department at Appalachian State University. Harvey attended several of the department heads meetings in the College of Business and we began to talk with each other. He wanted to know how the division of research worked and I, in turn, asked him about Appalachian State. Frankly, I had never heard of the university nor did I know where it was located. Harvey told me that ASU had been a teacher's college but had recently been granted university status and authorized to establish a business school, its first non-teaching degree program. He indicated that they were looking for a Dean and asked me if I would be interested in being considered. Given all the great things Harvey had told me about ASU, I agreed to do so and, upon his recommendation, was invited down for an interview.

ASU is in Boone, North Carolina, a beautiful little town in the Blue Ridge Mountains, just off the Blue Ridge Parkway and near the Eastern Continental Divide. I was astounded by the beauty of the area and impressed by the enthusiasm that officials at Appalachian had for developing the new Business School. And I was flattered that they would consider entrusting such a challenging task to someone as young as me. A few weeks after the visit, I got a letter from ASU offering me the job as Dean with a tenured faculty appointment as Professor of Marketing.

This presented me an interesting dilemma. I could remain at OU as a full Professor with tenure and, perhaps, become one of the leading scholars in the field of marketing. Or I could take a more risky route of trying to develop a new Business School at a less well-known university. I opted for the riskier alternative, as the excitement and challenge of creating a new school appealed to me. How many people get the chance to do that?

My five years at OU had been very productive in terms of both scholarship and administration. I am grateful to Harry Evarts and Bill Day for having faith in me. I also had other wonderful friends and colleagues including Ken Blanchard and Paul Hersey, who wrote a leading textbook in organizational behavior; Dick French, a retired executive who taught in management; Hershall McNabb, an assistant dean; and Richard Vedder, a leading scholar in economics.

OU was an interesting and exciting place in the late 1960's. Vernon Alden who had come to OU from Harvard as President in 1964 was a dynamic leader who brought national recognition to the school. Both the enrollment and the budgetary resources were expanding rapidly, but two forces converged to create major problems at the end of that decade. First, torrential rains caused the Hocking River that ran through the campus to overflow and flood a major segment of the campus. The damage was so severe that the university and the city were able to get federal funding to reroute the river around the campus over the next several years. Second, political, sociological, and cultural forces including student opposition to the Vietnam War created palpable tension between the campus and the community. After months of rallies, protests, sit-ins, and other expressions of disgust and distrust, the campus erupted in the aftermath of the shootings at Kent State, causing the Governor to call in the National Guard and to close the school, terminating the spring semester early in 1970.

It was probably a good time to move.

CHAPTER 11:
BUSINESS SCHOOL DEAN - THREE TIMES OVER

Very few faculty members get to be the dean of their college. Even fewer are able to start a new college. And even fewer still have that opportunity at an early age. When I assumed the position as dean at Appalachian State, I was the youngest business school dean in the country.

In later years, as I reflected on this experience, I often concluded that I would never have taken the job, had I been older, as I would have realized the amount of work and risk involved. But I never considered failure; I had the confidence and the energy necessary to succeed.

I ended up serving as the dean of three different colleges of business, each varying in size, setting, and mission. In this chapter, I will talk about those three jobs from both a personal and professional prospective.

APPALACHIAN STATE UNIVERSITY

<u>Personal.</u> Before leaving Athens, we sold our house, clearing enough to make a down payment on a home in Boone. But since we had not been able to look for housing before I started the job on July 1, ASU offered to lease us a house. The university owned several houses on Faculty Street, across from the campus that were available to incoming faculty on a short-term basis. Although convenient, the house did have one handicap - a coal-fired furnace that I had to be filled and stoked regularly; it would go out in the middle of the night if a stone got stuck in the auger-feeder.

The Mukherjees, Tribid and Debi and their children, Sandip and Misti, lived next door. They had come from India and Tribid was a faculty member in economics. They introduced us to Indian cuisine, which brought tears to our eyes, even though I am sure they had reduced considerably the spices they normally put in their food. Over time, however, we became quite fond of Indian food and the Mukherjees became good friends.

Our closest friends in Boone were the Purringtons, Burt and Sandra and their two girls, Jenny and Laurie. Marlene met Sandy in the League of Women Voters, while I met Burt who was a faculty member in anthropology at the university.Our kids were near the same ages and spent a lot of time playing together. We took vacations to Wrightsville Beach on the Atlantic Ocean with the Purringtons, using a house owned by Julia and Charlie Braswell. While we had some great times together, I got a significant scare one day.

To allow the adults time to read or sleep, we would take turns watching the kids at the beach. I was on "watch" one day while the kids played in the sand. After a while, Ellen, Van and the Purrington girls returned to the beach house, leaving Amy. She was having a good time, playing in the water as the tide rolled in. Because of the warm sun and the cool breeze, I dozed off and when I awoke, Amy had disappeared. I called her and began to run up and down the beach, asking people if they had seen a little girl with blonde hair. I had visions of her being washed out to sea. So I ran as hard as I could to the house where I discovered Amy playing peacefully on the back porch. I was torn between impulses to hug her close or to scold her for leaving the beach without permission. I did neither but it took a while for my pulse to return to normal.

In the spring of our first year in Boone, we bought a house in Blairmont, a subdivision overlooking the golf course. It was a ranch-style house with a full basement and a deck off the second level, four bedrooms, and a study downstairs. The neighborhood ran up a steep hill with each house at a different level. Ours sat parallel to the street with a garage at one end.A steep bank separated our property from the house below us with a wooden fence to keep the kids from falling down the embankment. This created the setting for another scary moment. One day I was working in the yard while the kids played in the driveway. Van, who was about four at the time, had been pretending he was driving our station wagon.The girls had gone back inside the house when suddenly the car began to roll backward out of the garage. Thinking that Van was in it, I ran toward it but saw that it was empty. Arriving at the garage too late, however, I saw the car crash through the fence, plummet down the embankment, and fall into our neighbor's driveway. Fortunately, the car landed parallel to the neighbor's house and did not turn over - and there was no one in our neighbor's driveway.I walked down to the neighbor's house and drove the car back into our garage - making sure that the emergency brake was engaged when I parked it!

Boone lay in a beautiful valley with mountains all around. It hardly ever got hot in the summer; in fact, our house, like most of the others, had no air conditioning at all. In the winter we got plenty of cold weather and snow.Major ski resorts -Beech Mountain, Sugar Mountain, etc. – that were heavily used in the winter surrounded Boone. To insure I could get around in the snow, I bought from my brother, Junior, a 4-wheel drive vehicle, a Jeep Wagoneer, which was particularly helpful in negotiating the steep hill up to our house.

Boone was also a very social place. We knew many faculty and staff at the university, as well as a lot of the townspeople. I joined the Rotary Club and, through this association, got to know two of the town's key leaders: Alfred Adams, president of Northwestern Bank, and Jim Marsh, president of the Watauga Savings and Loan. I also joined the Jaycees and met many of the younger business and professional leaders in the area, including Jim Holshouser, a young attorney who later became Governor of the state.

Additionally, I worked with a local developer, Bob Bingham, to create an event that we called "The Snow Carnival of the South" at Beech Mountain. We brought in professional skiers for an exhibition, as a way to attract more visitors to the region. In the first year, we even had Mickey Mantle as the Grand Marshall of the opening event. I was, also, invited to serve as a member of the Board of Directors of the North Carolina National Bank in Boone.

When I went to Appalachian, the university had no fraternities. So I helped get a TKE chapter organized and installed as the first national fraternity on the campus.

Among our good friends at ASU were the Trussells. I had recruited Larry to be head of the accounting department. He and his wife, Sharon, had two girls, Christy and Micki. The Durhams were also good friends. Harvey and his wife, Susan, had three boys -- Bill, Brian, and David.

The kids loved the schools at ASU. As a former teacher's college, one would expect the programs in education to be excellent. Ellen started at Lucy Brock Nursery School. She would come home everyday, telling us about her activities and her playmates. She particularly liked a boy named "Winters", but his name was not on the class list. Finally, on visitation day, we asked Ellen to introduce us to Winters and discovered his name was Reynolds. (Hey, close enough!) Van also loved Lucy Brock, calling it "Wucy Brock", when he enrolled the next year. Within a week, he knew every kid in the class.

<u>Professional</u>. The chancellor of ASU in fall, 1970 was Herb Wey, a graduate of Appalachian who had worked a number of years at the University of Miami before being chosen as the chancellor at ASU. He was a tall, lanky guy with an outgoing personality who interacted well with external

audiences. He clearly understood how a good business school could enhance ASU's reputation with the business community in the state.

The provost, Paul Sanders, who managed internal operations, was very different from Dr. Wey. He was a quiet mathematician, very detailed in his analysis, and tended to be straightforward in his communications. Even though they were quite different in temperament and approach, I got along well with both Dr. Wey and Dr. Sanders. They were both very supportive of the new business school and gave me the resources I needed to do the job they desired.

In fact, Dr. Wey made it possible for me to have my first employee who was a staff member in the Chancellor's office. Mrs. Ruth Ann Cook became my administrative assistant and was extremely valuable. She knew the internal workings of the university and was able to help me get so much done, following through on tasks and often anticipating what was required.

Another person I added to my staff was Carl Messere who had just resigned as head football coach at ASU, after more than ten years in that post. But, interestingly enough, Carl had a master's degree in business and had been teaching a course in accounting each semester. I asked him to serve as assistant dean in charge of student advising.

The third individual to join my staff just walked into the office one day. His name was John Wilson and he turned out to be one of the most interesting characters I worked with at ASU. John came from a wealthy, old North Carolina family, his father having been a co-founder of Henredon Furniture. John had an undergraduate degree from Princeton, an MBA from Harvard, and a divinity degree as well. He had worked in a variety of jobs, none of significant duration, and gained contacts and experience that would prove very valuable in my future plans. So I hired John to help me develop an internship program for the business students, placing them with companies for a semester as a part of their learning experience.

Since Appalachian was located in the mountains far from the commercial and industrial centers of the state and had historically been a teacher's college, special efforts were needed to give ASU's new business school some visibility and enhance employment opportunities for graduates of the school. A key component of this strategy was the internship program, similar to the cooperative education (co-op) programs that many engineering schools had been using for decades. I figured the best way to let a company know that ASU was producing business graduates was to have students working for them. So John Wilson and I traveled the state, visited CEO's, and persuaded them to employ one or more interns.

John also helped me to establish an Advisory Council of business executives to meet periodically for information on how the business school was developing and to provide advice. We put together a council of about forty executives that was valuable in this role.

A third element in our strategy to make the new school better known was an Executive-in-Residence program. Many business schools brought executives in for a day to speak to students but few, if any, used operating executives as full-time members of the faculty for a term. But I thought such an arrangement would excite the students and raise the school's profile in the business community. I quickly lined up some executives from North Carolina companies; one of the first was David Brunn who had recently retired as CEO of Drexel Furniture. Deciding to "go national" with the idea, I placed a small ad in the Wall Street Journal and was inundated with responses. There were people all over the country interested in taking a quarter off to teach. The salary was meager ($1,200 a month), not much more than I would have paid a graduate assistant, but executives lined up to participate each term.One of the early participants, Jim Hathaway, from Allstate Insurance near Chicago, liked the experience so well that he resigned from Allstate and joined our faculty full time.

At the time I was appointed dean, Appalachian had a business education department for students who wanted to teach in high school. Orus Sutton was the head of that department which consisted of only four faculty members. This unit was absorbed into the business school along with three or four faculty in economics for whom an economics department was created with Barry Elledge as its head. Then I had to develop a Bachelor's of Business Administration (BBA) degree for those intending to work in business. With the assistance of AACSB (American Assembly of Collegiate Schools of Business) guidelines, I formulated the curriculum for this degree and created new departments in accounting and finance and in business administration that included programs in management and marketing.

Larry Trussell was recruited from Eastern Michigan University as head of the accounting and finance department. He had graduated from the University of Arkansas several years after me. To head the business administration department, I hired Shah Mammoud, a graduate of Columbia who had come from Afghanistan. In the second year, finance spun off as a separate department, with Dean Dudley, a colleague I had worked with at Ohio University, being hired as the head.

In the first year, I had to assume primary responsibility for recruiting new faculty, which included transporting them to and from the airport.Most candidates flew into Charlotte or Johnson City, Tennessee, both of which were 1-2 hours away on steep mountain roadsA small airport in Hickory was closer but had very limited flights. In the second year, the department heads assumed the major responsibilities of faculty recruiting.

By the end of the third year at Appalachian State, we had achieved most of the goals I had established for the new school. Enrollment had grown to approximately 1,200 students out of a total of 6,000. Over 40 new faculty had been hired, the curriculum and the academic departments were in place, the internship and executive-in-residence programs were going well, and the business school's visibility had substantially increased. We even had funds appropriated for the construction of a new building to house the school and were on target to achieve AACSB accreditation, which was obtained as soon as ASU was eligible.

The experience of starting a new school and achieving the success that we did was exciting, to say the least. I worked harder in the three years at ASU than at any other time in my career, but the personal satisfaction was tremendous and the learning experience unprecedented. Living in Boone was also enjoyable, as we had many friends not only in the business school but in the university and in the community as well. We loved the setting and all that Boone offered. But a new opportunity soon beckoned.

THE UNIVERSITY OF NEBRASKA AT OMAHA

In the spring of 1973, I was contacted by Dick Ortman, the chairman of the search committee looking for a new business school dean at the University of Nebraska at Omaha. He said I had been nominated for that position and wanted to know if I would consider it. After considerable discussion and exchange of information, I agreed to go out for an interview.

I had never been to Omaha but was impressed with the city. It is the largest city between Chicago and Denver but rarely gets national attention. UNO was one of the three units that comprised the University of Nebraska - the other two being The University of Nebraska at Lincoln (the campus with the Cornhuskers football team) and the University of Nebraska Medical Center (in Omaha). UNO had been a municipal university (The University of Omaha) for many years before becoming part of the UN system in 1968, and had an enrollment of about 15,000 students. The UNO business school was well established with AACSB accreditation.

The job at a salary considerably higher than I was earning at ASU was offered and accepted and we prepared to move to Omaha to start the job on July 1, 1973. The opportunity to lead an established business school in a major metropolitan area was too attractive to turn down.

Personal. Marlene found a great house for us in Omaha in the Happy Hollow area, a residential neighborhood of older homes near the UNO campus. Happy Hollow Boulevard was a beautiful four-lane divided street lined with elm trees, running north and south off of Dodge Street, the main thoroughfare from downtown Omaha going west. Our house was a three-story brick French Tudor style house on Izard Street, just off the boulevard. The first floor had a large living room, dining room, den/TV room, and kitchen. There was a foyer (where Bonnie, our Scottish Terrier, attacked the mail each day) and a wide expansive staircase to the second floor that housed all our bedrooms. The smaller third floor, which had probably served as a maid's quarters at one time, provided a playroom for the kids as well as a storage area. One unusual feature of the house was that its garage, narrow and long, permitted the parking of two cars in tandem. The thick walls and heat by radiators kept it cozy in the winter. We paid $53,500 for the house in 1973; I am sure it would be worth over $500,000 today.

The kids all went to Harrison Elementary School only three or four blocks from our house and were able to walk there except for during bad weather. Amy later went to Lewis and Clark Junior High. On the whole, the kids liked their teachers and Marlene and I felt that Omaha's public schools were excellent.

Our next-door neighbors were the MacNaughtons, Luther and Barb, and their children, Peggy, Jill, Scott and Peter with whom our kids played often. Van, also had a good friend, Jim Kemp, who lived on the street behind our house. Memorial Park where the kids could play and use their snow sleds in the winter was only a short distance away.

Marlene became quite active in the community, serving as president of the League of Women Voters and establishing good friendships with many other women. She also campaigned actively for John Cavanaugh who was elected as our congressman. I joined the downtown Rotary and through it met many of the business leaders in the city. And we joined the First Central Congregational Church in which the whole family participated.

I enjoyed the summers in Omaha, attending a lot of the games of the Omaha Royals, the top farm team of the Kansas City Royals often taking Van with me. I also attended the College World Series each year in Omaha. Winters presented a different challenge, though. The blizzards would come off the Rocky Mountains, hit the plains of Nebraska, and cover Omaha in a blanket of snow very quickly. In our first year there, we had a storm that dumped 24" of snow in 24 hours.

During our years in Omaha, we had two very significant trips. The first took place in the summer of 1975 when we got to spend three months in Afghanistan, working under the auspices of a USAID grant. The University of Nebraska had a Center for Afghanistan Studies, headed by Tom Gouttierre, a creative young man who had worked in that country as a Peace Corp volunteer and as Director of the Fulbright Program. I was able to take the whole family on this exotic adventure. More is written about this in the chapter on international travel.

The second unfolded during a year that we spent in Washington where I participated in the President's Executive Exchange Program and worked in the U.S. Office of Education. This program included a two-week tour of Western Europe on which Marlene and I went. This experience is also covered more fully in a subsequent chapter.

Professional. The chancellor of UNO, Ronald Roskens, had just arrived the year before from a vice-presidency at Kent State.Ron was a tall elegant man who clearly wanted UNO to have a greater presence and stature in the Omaha community. As the first dean he had hired, I thought this was a goal toward the business school could make a significant contribution. But many tasks needed to be undertaken.

The first was to reorganize the college.Stagnant with almost all leadership posts held by senior faculty who had been there a long time, I felt the future of the college lay in the hands of many bright younger faculty who had been very productive. To accomplish the reorganization, I dissolved the departmental structure and formed in its place a number of programmatic areas, each chaired by a faculty member, with faculty being able to participate in more than one program. This enabled me to involve younger faculty like Dick Ortman (accounting), Brad Chapman (management) and Youssef Kouatly (insurance) in leadership roles.

I also enticed Larry Trussell to join me from Appalachian State as associate dean. Since Larry and his wife, Sharon, were both natives of Kansas, I felt they would be receptive to returning to the "Heartland". Larry assumed the responsibility of managing the college's budget and handling much of the internal management.

Consistent with chancellor Roskens' vision for the university, I pursued a goal of making the business school more visible and more important to the Omaha business community.Given that almost all of our students came from the Omaha area and that most of them would want to work in the area after graduation, this was a relevant objective. First, I formed an Advisory Council comprised of local CEO's and met with them individually and collectively to gain their input and confidence.

Other key components of this strategy were:

a.   The formation of a Center for Management Development to offer short-term, non-credit programs for the business community. I was able to attract Harold Gray, a man experienced in developing similar programs, to head the center. Hal was energetic and worked hard to make the center responsive to the needs of the business community.

b. The establishment of a Small Business Development Center, one of the first such centers in the nation. The U.S. Small Business Administration created and funded the program, with UNO being one of the first six programs started. Students under faculty supervision served as consultants to companies, either a new business getting started or one that was experiencing problems. The students would analyze the situation and give the owner recommendations.A terrific learning environment for the students, it usually produced very useful results for the business. David Ambrose directed the SBDC originally, with Bob Bernier succeeding him a few years later.

c. As an alternative to the executive-in-residence program that I started at ASU, we originated a Student-Executive dialogue, bringing executives to the campus to talk with students in classes and in small discussion groups. We offered a full range of evening courses, many taught by local businessmen.

d. To reach many of the up-and-coming executives, we started a Young Executives Organization (YEO) by getting the corporations to designate one or more of their employees to participate. This group would meet monthly for lunch and to hear one of our faculty report on the research they were doing.

e. In cooperation with the business school at UNL, we launched an Executive MBA program in Omaha. We already had a large regular MBA program, offered mostly in the evening but the EMBA was designed for a more exclusive audience of senior-level executives. The idea originated with Ron Smith, the dean at UNL, but he realized that Lincoln was not large enough to support such a program alone so he proposed that we collaborate, attracting students from both markets and splitting the instructional assignments.

I believe that all these programs helped to strengthen the business school's reputation. Our enrollment grew steadily and the university secured funding for the construction of a new state-of-the-art business school building. Additionally, I was able to secure a gift from Northern Natural Gas Company to establish a chair in energy economics.

Not everything was positive about the job. It never is in any major leadership post. One aspect of the dean's job that I liked least involved making tenure decisions. Each year we had to evaluate faculty performance in teaching, research, and service. Research was more clear cut, as performance was based almost totally on publications - whether or not the results of research had been accepted for publication in a refereed journal and how prestigious that journal was. About the only evidence we had about teaching came from the student evaluations which I found useful and informative, but which the faculty often criticized - particularly if they were bad. Service rarely became a major factor in the evaluation unless a faculty member had received some noteworthy recognition.

One of my unpleasant memories of UNO came from a lawsuit over a tenure decision. According to AAUP policies, a tenure decision must be made on a full-time member of the faculty before the end of seven years of employment; to employ an individual beyond that time gives them "de-facto tenure." So decisions are made at the end of the sixth year in order to give the individual one-year's notice before the end of his or her employment. Two faculty in economics - one male and one female - came up for tenure at the same time. Both had very similar records of performance and were recommended by the chair of the program. In my evaluation, the male had a slightly stronger case. But both, I concluded, fell short of the standard we had used for granting tenure in other program areas.So I recommended that neither be approved. The female filed suit against me and the university on the charge of sexual discrimination. I had to testify in state court before the case was finally decided in favor of the university over a period of about three years.

When we went to Washington for my assignment with the U.S. Office of Education in 1977-78, we sold our house on Izard Street and purchased another house in the same neighborhood when we returned. While we were away, Ron Roskens became president of the University of Nebraska System and Del Weber from Arizona State replaced him as chancellor. After our return to UNO, I was approached about the deanship of the business school at Texas A&M. A&M was a much larger university, as was the business school. I felt it was a logical next step in my career and, after visiting and being offered the job, I accepted.

Larry Trussell had served as acting dean during my tours in Afghanistan and in Washington, so it was logical that he be the leading candidate for the job when I left. I was delighted that he was selected as my successor. Larry served in that capacity for a period of nearly twenty years. In addition to the Trussells we had many good friends in Omaha, such as the Kouatlys, the Gouttierres, and the Grays. Of special mention also were the Beers, Ron and

Cara. Ron was vice-chancellor for student affairs at UNO and his family was in our church. We enjoyed our years in Omaha and regarded it as a good place to live and work.

TEXAS A&M UNIVERSITY

Texas A&M is the land-grant university of Texas, so designated by the Morrill Act of 1865 that established an institution in each state to provide instruction in the agricultural and mechanical arts. Originally called The Agricultural and Mechanical College of Texas, it remained an all-male, all military institution for much of its history, not admitting women until 1964. TAMU's campus sits in College Station in Brazos County, about 70 miles northwest of Houston.

By the time we moved to A&M in 1979, it had grown into a large comprehensive university. Although agriculture and engineering were dominant fields, A&M offered academic programs in almost all areas and enrolled over 33,000 students. The business school had been established in 1968 but was already the second largest college on the campus. I was only the second dean in its history.

Personal. We bought a house in Bryan, adjacent to the Briarcrest Country Club. Bryan, the county seat of Brazos County, was originally about five miles from College Station but, over time, the two towns grew together until they operated as one commercial and residential entity. Our white, two-story home had a living room, dining room, kitchen, and master bedroom downstairs and three bedrooms and a game room upstairs.

The move from Omaha to Bryan did not get off to a good start. We traveled in two cars with me leading the way in our Chevy Vega (that I had bought in Omaha) along with Amy and Bonnie as my passengers. Marlene followed in the station wagon with Ellen and Van. We planned to spend the first night with my brother, Paul, and his wife, Marie, at a dude ranch south of Kansas City. I had the only set of directions as to how to get there. Unfortunately, as we were driving through Kansas City, I took the wrong exit off the interstate. Marlene didn't see me do so and kept going. I quickly got back on the interstate but was unable to catch her. Cell phones had not yet been invented; so I had no way to contact her. Amy and I went on to the ranch and spent the night with Paul and Marie. I called friends in Omaha to see whether Marlene had contacted them and checked with the Highway Patrol to make sure she had had no accident. We traveled on toward Texas the next day, spending that night near Denton, and arriving in Bryan the next afternoon. Marlene had stopped along the way for two nights. The family was finally reunited in Bryan, two days after our separation in KC.

We had been moved to Texas only a few weeks when I learned that my mother had died. Momma had lived in a nursing home in Union in the later stages of her life. Marlene and I drove over there for her funeral and burial in the cemetery at Rocky Hill Church of God in a plot that Daddy had saved for her next to his grave, only a few yards from the church where they spent many happy days.

Adjusting to life in Texas also had its challenges. Marlene and the kids liked Omaha and had good friends there. The move was viewed with some anxiety, but they were supportive of my conclusion that this was a good move for me professionally. The schools in Bryan did not seem as good or as challenging as those the kids attended in Omaha and each of them encountered some measure of dissatisfaction. Marlene did not particularly embrace the "cowboy culture" in Texas, but, nevertheless, became very active in the community serving for two years as president of the Bryan-College Station League of Women Voters and running a successful campaign for a friend, Wendy Costa, for a position on the school board in Bryan. The kids, also, coped with their situations, doing well in their school work and becoming involved in other activities: theater for Amy, theater and debate for Ellen, and baseball and tennis for Van.

I joined into the community, serving as vice-president of the Bryan-College Station Chamber of Commerce and chairing the industrial development efforts to attract new companies to the area. I was also elected to the Board of Directors of City National Bank, the largest bank in the city. The Peters family owned it with Bookman Peters serving as chairman and his brother, Mervin, as president. I enjoyed my service on that board and, especially, my friendship with Bookman. City National merged with First City National Bank, a large statewide financial institution, in the early 80's; this turned out to be a bad decision as FCNB went bankrupt in the late 80's.

I was also involved in the Rotary Club in Bryan-College Station and helped to establish a TKE chapter at Texas A&M which, up to that time, had not had a fraternity system. One of the members of the Board of Trustees for the Teke Chapter was Ron Newton, a faculty member at A&M with whom I would later work at East Carolina.

We had a lot of good friends among the business school faculty at A&M - the Mobleys, the Gillespies, and the Roses, to mention just a few. Outside of the business school, the Bryants - Keith and Margaret - became close friends. Keith was dean of the College of Liberal Arts and later joined me in Akron when I became President there. Marlene had a lot of friends through her work in the LWV. A special friend to me was Elizabeth Cowan (now Neeld) who served as executive assistant to president Frank Vandiver at A&M. Elizabeth and I established an immediate kinship when I learned that her father had also been a Church of God minister. I had never met anyone in higher education who came from the same religious background as I had. I enjoyed many hours visiting with her about our common heritage.

<u>Professional</u>. A&M was, by far, the largest university with whom I had been associated with the business school being considerably larger than the units at either ASU or UNO. The enrollment was growing rapidly and we had outgrown the space assigned to us. The immediate challenge was to plan and build a new building for the business school. Fortunately, that process was already underway when I came to A&M and we were able to move into a beautiful new facility toward the end of my second year there.

Clint Phillips, a long-time member of the finance faculty, had served as interim dean prior to my arrival and I had the good judgment to ask him to stay on as associate dean. Clint helped orient me to A&M and assisted with the day-to-day management of the college. To my good fortune, Bettye Kahan, who had been the Dean's secretary for many years, remained in that position. She knew the internal processes of the university well and assisted me in many ways.

The faculty was exceptionally strong, consisting of many well-known scholars in their fields as well as young productive researchers who were establishing names for themselves and the school. My strategy in leading the school was to enhance A&M's relationship with the business community in Texas and to continue to attract talented leaders and scholars to the college.

The University of Texas had been the dominant business school in the state for many years, but we decided that A&M would not take a backseat. I formed an Advisory Council (similar to what I did at both ASU and UNO), comprised of business leaders across the state, and met with them individually and collectively to get their input and sell what A&M had to offer.I spent considerable time in Houston and Dallas, particularly, visiting with banks, accounting firms, and major corporations who hired many A&M graduates. And I gave speeches all over the state about what the school was doing.

Among the talented individuals I helped attract to A&M were:

a. Bill Mobley from the University of Maryland. Bill came in to succeed Don Hellriegel as head of the management department. Don had done a great job of attracting faculty to the department and was moving back to a faculty position. Bill, subsequently, became my associate dean when Clint Phillips moved to the provost's office to become dean of faculties and, then, succeeded me as dean when I became vice-chancellor. To further illustrate Bill's talents, he became vice-chancellor when I went to Akron and later served as president of A&M for several years.

b.   Bob Nelson from the University of Illinois. When Bill Adams retired as director of the Center for Executive Development, I went after Bob who held a similar position at Illinois. I had known Bob for a number of years and was aware of the great job he had done there. He greatly enhanced this center, expanding its programs to serve the business community.

c.   Len Berry from the University of Virginia. Len was one of the leading scholars in marketing and came to A&M to be director of a new Center for Retailing Studies. With Len's help, we attracted major gifts from retailing firms. Sam Gillespie who had done an excellent job as head of the marketing department for many years was promoted to assistant dean and managed the student advising process in the college. Dan Robertson from Georgia State was attracted to replace Sam.

One of my many interesting experiences at A&M came during a visit to the campus by Ross Perot who at that time was CEO of Electronic Data Systems in Dallas. I invited him to come down and see what we were doing in the business school and he did, spending the better part of a day with me and the administrative staff of the college. I had an A&M football jersey with Perot's name on it made up and gave it to him as a memento of his visit.

By the beginning of my fourth year at A&M, we had settled into the new business school building and our enrollment had grown to approximately 6,000 students, making A&M the fifth largest business school in the nation in terms of undergraduate enrollment. We had raised the stature of the school in the state, judging by financial contributions from business firms and the hiring of business graduates. It was at this juncture that another interesting opportunity emerged for me.

Art Hansen, former president of Georgia Tech and Purdue, had been hired as the new chancellor for the A&M System. As a part of his orientation, he asked each college on the A&M campus to prepare a presentation for him. I quickly volunteered because I had made such a speech many times to business audiences, describing the goals of the college and the progress we had made toward them. It was on professionally developed overhead transparencies, the state-of-the-art technology in those days. Dr. Hansen was obviously impressed with the presentation and the discussion that followed. Within a couple of weeks, he had offered me a job as vice-chancellor of academic programs for the A&M System. I moved into that new post in January 1983.

REFLECTIONS ON THE THREE DEANSHIPS

By 1983, I had served as a business school dean for over twelve years and had been quite active in AACSB circles. I even served for a year as president of the Southern Business Administration Association, the Southern business school deans' organization. But I was ready for something different.

The three universities where I had worked were quite different in location, size, and mission. And the business schools differed in age, size, and research orientation, but each had an obligation to be responsive to the needs of the market that it served - the firms that hired its graduates. So I spent considerable time and effort trying to move the colleges in that direction.

My managerial style and philosophy focused on hiring the best people I could find and giving them the freedom to do their jobs. I articulated clear goals that I wanted to achieve and left it to them to decide how best to do that. I usually had good relationships with those who worked for me.

By the time I left the deanship, however, I was concerned about the direction that business education had taken. My feelings were expressed in an article that I authored for the <u>Collegiate News and Views</u>, a magazine that was published by the South-Western Publishing Company and sent to all business school faculties. The article was entitled "If all Business Schools in the Country were eliminated, would anyone notice?" It described the efforts of business school faculty to gain academic legitimacy and acceptability by publishing research in academic journals that were of little interest or relevancy to the business community while at the same time devaluing the efforts of colleagues to work with firms in more highly applied areas. I called for better balance, recognizing the importance of contributions in both arenas. The response was overwhelming. I got over 100 letters or other forms of communication from faculty who had read the article and almost all of them agreed with the conclusions I had reached. By contrast, I had published many articles in prestigious academic journals with rarely any response except for an occasional graduate student citing the article in their research.

TEXAS A&M UNIVERSITY SYSTEM

The move to the A&M System turned out to be a good one for me career wise. First, Art Hansen served as a good mentor and, second, he gave me a significant responsibility to handle. The system at that time consisted of: Texas A&M University; Texas A&M University at Galveston; Prairie View A&M University, a historically black university; and Tarleton State University. Dr. Hansen asked me to serve as the chief academic officer of the system, working with the provosts on each campus to prepare proposals for new academic programs and policies that needed approval of the A&M Board of Regents. I also represented the A&M System to the Coordinating Board for the Texas College and University System, presenting and defending proposals for new degree programs.

Fortunately, I had an excellent administrative assistant, Verna Dewese, who was very knowledgeable about the academic programs and the information required by both the Board of Regents and the Coordinating Board. Presenting proposals to both of these bodies was very valuable experience for me.

During the years that I served as a business dean, I began to think about the possibility of becoming a university president. I had good role models in Herb Wey and Ron Roskens and found that much of the work I did as a business school dean was similar to the work they did, particularly the work with external groups. Art Hansen was a good sounding board, listening to my expressions of interest and encouraging me to pursue opportunities that might materialize.

The first opportunity occurred at Ole Miss. This was a heady experience for me, contemplating the possibility of going back to Mississippi. I ended up being one of eight candidates interviewed by the Higher Education Board. It was initially announced that William Winter, former Governor of the state, was going to be chancellor. But, when he later declined, Gerald Turner was appointed. I was disappointed, yet encouraged that I had gotten this far on my first try.

The second opportunity that later emerged was as president of New Mexico State University. I was one of the three finalists for the post but was informed that the acting president of the University of Arkansas had been selected by a 3-2 vote of the Board of Trustees. In retrospect, NMSU would probably not have been a good location for the family and me.

The third time was the charm. After being nominated for the presidency of the University of Akron and going through the interviewing process, I was selected. I looked forward to the move to the Rubber City and to assuming my first chief executive officer position.

CHAPTER 12:
HELLO, RUBBER CITY!

The anticipation of becoming president of the University of Akron induced considerable excitement. After over 15 years as a part of the administrative team at three universities, my opportunity to be a chief executive officer had arrived. Going back to Ohio also pleased me, as I knew the state reasonably well and had pleasant memories of the five productive years at OU.

The University of Akron had been founded in 1870 as Buchtel College, a private liberal arts college, but changed its name to The University of Akron when the city accepted its assets in 1913. It operated as a municipal university until 1967, when the assets were transferred to the State of Ohio and UA became a part of the state university system.

In 1984, UA enrolled approximately 25,000 traditional and non-traditional students, many of whom worked full time and attended classes in the evening. The campus was conveniently located in the middle of the city, just a short distance from the downtown business district. A nine-member Board of Trustees, each appointed by the Governor governed UA; it had a law school and operated the Northeastern Ohio Universities College of Medicine (NEOUCOM), as a partnership with Kent State and Youngstown State. The university also had a branch campus in the town of Orrville in Wayne County, about thirty miles from Akron.

Akron is located in the heavily industrialized northeast sector of Ohio, close to Cleveland, Youngstown, and Canton. For years it was known as the "Tire Capital of the World", home to Goodyear, Goodrich, Firestone, Mohawk, and General Tire companies who at one time employed over 100,000 people. But after World War II, the tire companies began moving their production facilities to the South and, eventually, to foreign countries in order to avoid high labor costs and to gain proximity to growing markets. By the 1980's, there were virtually no tires manufactured in Akron and the city was looking for a new spark to ignite its economic growth and to boost the city's image.

When I interviewed for the presidency, there were two people who strongly influenced my decision to come to Akron.John Steinhauer, a prominent local attorney, chaired the search committee and had just been named the incoming chairman of the Board of Trustees, replacing Charles Pilliod, who was the CEO of Goodyear Tire and Rubber Company. While I had been impressed with Mr. Pilliod during the interview I knew that I would be working more closely with John and I liked his enthusiasm and approachability. The other person was Mayor Tom Sawyer, a very bright young man who, as I determined from our conversations, wanted to improve relations between the city and the university, which he saw as a catalyst for local and regional development.

I had been close enough to the presidents of the universities where I had worked to understand the nature of the job -- or so I thought. But there is hardly any way a person can be fully prepared for the demands of such a position, particularly in one's first year. Being a university president is different from being the CEO of almost any other organization in that a university (at least a public one) has a large and diverse constituency of faculty, students, parents, staff, administrators, trustees, alumni, elected officials, and business leaders, each of whom feels that they should have access to the president.I also learned that every civic and student organization wanted the new president to come speak to them so that they could to get to know him and possibly influence him about some idea or problem they had. Deans or faculty who have been turned down by the previous president will come calling in hopes the new guy will prove more "understanding". In short, the demands on your time are relentless. And often it is difficult to get good advice from your staff as each person has his own bias about who should be listened to.I, nevertheless, tried to accommodate as many individuals and groups as I could. The Akron Beacon Journal, the daily newspaper, published a copy of one day's schedule -- with appointments from breakfast through an event in the evening -- as an example of how busy I was.

In addition to the requests I received, I asked each college at the university to arrange for a tour of their facilities, a briefing by the dean and department heads, and a meeting with the faculty. A similar schedule was also set up for the non-academic units. These events took a lot to time but they gave me valuable information and an opportunity to meet all university employees.

By the end of this process, I had gained a pretty good understanding of the university's problems, assets, and opportunities. The experience also reinforced the value of listening as a skill. People who came to see me -- or those I went to visit -- were not reluctant to talk and, surprisingly, rarely expected an answer. Usually, all they wanted was to be heard. So that is what I did -- listen and ask questions when I needed more information. Some of the presentations were, of course, self-serving - to gain an advantage or personal benefit. But I found that many people simply wanted to share their insights about the university and suggest future courses of action. From these sessions I began to develop a set of goals and a strategic plan for their achievement.

STRATEGIC GOALS FOR UA

A PARTNERSHIP WITH THE CITY

Because of its history, location, and market, the University of Akron needed to be responsive to the needs of the city and its citizens. Most of our students came from Akron and the surrounding region and a substantial number of alumni lived in the area as well. I wanted the city to see UA as "its university". That was easier said than done; Kent State University was located only fifteen miles away in western Portage County and Ohio State, of course, had a significant statewide presence.

Mayor Sawyer was eager to contemplate various alliances, so we began to discuss how to implement an idea called "Span the Tracks" that had been proposed during the administration of my predecessor, Dom Guzzetta. Between the campus and the downtown business district ran a set of railroad tracks that were recessed into a ravine with a four-lane bridge spanning the gap. The barrier seemed more psychological than physical. We talked about how the university might expand into the downtown area, which, like that of many similar cities, had fallen into decline. Its remaining major downtown department store, Polsky's, had closed and the building sat empty; many other retail businesses had moved to the suburban malls, creating plenty of available space.

I had also concluded that the university campus needed to be enhanced before UA could be perceived as a "major" university rather than a local commuter college. A four lane one-way street ran right through the middle of the campus separating the library and dorms from the major classroom buildings. It was not only noisy but dangerous, as it was difficult to keep students from jaywalking, especially between classes. I wanted a pedestrian campus that looked and felt like a university.

Marlene believed that I could get it done, but hardly anyone at the university (including my own staff) felt that the closure or re-routing of this street (Buchtel Avenue) could be accomplished. The responses were typical -- "we've tried that before. It won't work." And the first reactions of the mayor and his staff reinforced that view. Mayor Sawyer felt that Buchtel Avenue was a major artery into downtown, citizens would protest if it was closed, and downtown would suffer a loss of retail traffic. But I persuaded him to split the cost of a traffic survey conducted by a reputable engineering firm. What they found was that the overwhelming majority of traffic on Buchtel Avenue consisted of students and university employees, rather than people going downtown. The university architect, Roger Ryan, then developed a plan to re-route traffic around the core of the campus to parking areas, permitting the street to be closed through the interior of the campus.

But there was still much work to be done before this goal could be reached. To entice the city to agree to the plan to close Buchtel Avenue, I agreed that the university would move major operations into the downtown area, including the vacant Polsky's building, if it could be acquired at a reasonable price. In the middle of these negotiations, Tom Sawyer decided to run for U.S. Congress and was successful. Fortunately, his successor was Don Plusquellic who had been the president of the City Council. Don was a strong advocate for the partnership with the university and we developed an excellent working relationship. In fact, my key staff (particularly those in charge of physical facilities) and I met with the mayor and his staff on a monthly basis to discuss the projects on which we were working. With the support of the mayor, the City Council approved the closure of Buchtel Avenue and construction to make this an attractive pedestrian mall began.

Consistent with my promise, I flew with the mayor and the economic director, Jim Phelps, to St. Louis to visit with executives of the May Company, the department store chain that owned the Polsky property. The property included not only the building but a large parking deck. We found that the May Company was anxious to dispose of the property - so much so that they agreed to "sell" it to the university for $1. Now UA owned a major piece of real estate right on Main Street. But I needed to raise the money to refurbish the building, including the removal of asbestos. It took a lot of effort to persuade the Ohio Board of Regents to approve the project and to convince the Ohio legislature to fund it but, eventually, approximately $34 million was appropriated. When the project was finished, we moved the university's community and technical college, a two-year program offering associate degrees in a number of technical fields and serving a working clientele into the building. Additionally, a number of administrative units re-located their operations there. The parking deck responded to the growing demand for spaces for students and staff.

In another move, UA purchased a vacant building that had housed a Greyhound bus station and constructed a new College of Business Administration on the site. Additionally, law offices next door were purchased to house the university's personnel offices. All of these facilities were in the downtown area but adjacent to the bridge over the tracks.

I also worked with the city to help attract the National Inventors Hall of Fame to Akron and to select a site for their attractive new museum, across the street from the UA Business School and at the entrance into the campus. The university also supported an effort to build a new convention center just a couple of blocks from the entrance to the campus. The partnership between UA and the city became substantial, thanks to the excellent leadership of Mayor Don Plusquellic. Downtown Akron today is a more vibrant place because of the work that we did in the 1980s.

As a part of the effort to make the university an integral part of the city, I accepted several major leadership roles outside the university. I served on the Executive Committee and for two years as chairman of the Akron Regional Development Board (ARDB), a three-county economic development agency that also served as Akron's Chamber of Commerce. On behalf of ARDB, I traveled to Japan to help lure Japanese companies to Akron. I also served as president of the Akron Roundtable, a major public forum that brought in speakers of national stature monthly. Two major companies - National City Bank of Akron and A. Schulman, Inc. - asked me to serve on their Boards of Directors. And I also served on the boards of six different civic organizations in the community.

While I was on the board of the Akron Roundtable, I initiated an effort that received a lot of local attention. Since Akron was undergoing a renewal of sorts, transitioning from a "Rubber City" to a "Polymer Capital", I proposed that we invite the mayors from cities that had seen the greatest turnaround in their economic conditions over the past ten years to come and describe the strategies they had used to achieve that growth. I got the Center for Urban Studies at UA to research this matter and come up with a list of cities; then I began to contact them to schedule them for their participation in this series. The Roundtable, then, had a year- long "Turnaround Cities" program that was well received, boosting the spirits of Akron's civic leaders and inspiring them to believe that they could achieve similar results.

DEVELOPING ACADEMIC PROGRAMS OF NATIONAL STATURE

In order to be seen as a university of national prominence, an institution has to have some academic programs that rank among the very best in the nation.

Even among the most prestigious universities, many of their programs are average at best. But, when we look at the institution from a distance, we only see those programs that stand out (what I call their "peaks of excellence") and assume all other programs there must be of similar quality.

Therefore, in order to raise UA's prominence, we needed to identify a few programs that could attain national stature. In my review of the institution, I found two programs that seemed capable of attaining that goal. One was industrial psychology, already among the best in the nation with a strong Ph.D. program and housing the Archives of the History of Psychology. The second was the field of polymer science, particularly important as the "rubber city" now was trying to find uses for polymers other than producing tires.

UA had a department of Polymer Science in the College of Arts and Sciences and a department of Polymer Engineering in the College of Engineering. The university had been involved in polymer research since World War II when the War Production Board had established a laboratory to develop synthetic rubber, using tire company and university scientists. Dr. Frank Kelley headed the department of Polymer Science and seemed to be the ideal person to lead an increased emphasis in this area. During my years at Akron, we accomplished the following things:

a. The separate departments of polymer science and polymer engineering were combined into a new college with Frank Kelley as the dean.

b. Funding was obtained from the Ohio legislature for a new state-of-the-art research and classroom building located in the pathway of the closed Buchtel Avenue, near the entrance to the campus from downtown. Designed by architect Richard Fleishman, the modernistic steel and glass structure rises 18 stories into the air and can be seen from miles away, showcasing the importance of this discipline to the university and the city. The building won recognition from Northern Ohio Live Magazine in 1991 with its Award of Achievement in Architecture.

c. The State of Ohio designated polymer science as one of its Centers of Excellence through the Thomas Alva Edison Partnership Program. An organization called the Edison Polymer Innovation Corporation (EPIC) was formed to bring together researchers from the University of Akron, Case Western Reserve University in Cleveland, and industries in northeast Ohio to develop new products and enhance technological development.

All of these efforts not only helped the University of Akron solidify its position as one of the top three polymer programs in the nation but also spurred the development of new products and companies in the region. Akron even began to call itself the "Polymer Capital" of the country.

Polymer Science was not the only academic discipline to receive support, as over $7 million was obtained through the Ohio Board of Regents Fund for Selective Excellence for various other academic programs. And twelve new endowed chairs and professorships were established to attract and retain outstanding faculty, more than doubling the previous number.

In an effort to showcase UA's academic excellence throughout northeast Ohio, we began a TV advertising campaign. Research showed that the reputation of UA was enhanced by this effort. And I believe it helped attract good students to the university as well.

MAKING THE CAMPUS MORE DIVERSE

One of the things that most surprised me when I came to Akron was that the black enrollment at UA was only 6% in a city where the black population was nearly 25%. I began to listen to the black students and to seek the counsel of the black leaders in the community, particularly Vernon Odom, president of the Urban League. I concluded that black students did not feel welcome at UA for a variety of reasons, including the low number of black faculty and administrative staff.

To counteract this attitude, I began to speak to black organizations in the city and to black churches on Sunday morning. But most importantly I created a position of assistant to the president for minority affairs and hired an outgoing and articulate lady from Mississippi to handle that responsibility. Dr. Sebetha Jenkins had been in a similar position at Mississippi State. Over the next several years we worked to further diversify the campus and improve relationships with the community. Black enrollment increased by 44% (from 1,710 to 2,465 students) and the number of full-time black faculty rose from 8 to 28. Furthermore, the black administrative staff expanded from 11 to 47, including four deans, one of which was Isaac Hunt who headed the law school and, later, became a commissioner of the Securities and Exchange Commission (SEC).

But these changes did not occur easily. I took a fair amount of grief both from those who felt the changes were too slow or inadequate and from those who resented the opportunities that were given to minorities. Dr. Jenkins and I had a marvelous working relationship and I admired her poise and courage.

Eventually, she went on to become president of Jarvis Christian College in Texas.

UPGRADING THE ATHLETIC PROGRAM

Clearly the most controversial component of my strategic plan was upgrading the athletic program.Athletics generates an emotional response and a creative tension always exists between academics and athletics on a campus. Many faculty resent the attention that athletics gets and/or feel the money should be used for more important things, like increasing their salaries.

But the fact is that the visibility and stature of a university are highly influenced by the level at which it competes in athletics and by the success it achieves.Many universities are regarded as "outstanding academic institutions" primarily because they are successful at the highest levels of athletic competition. Those making those assumptions (parents, prospective students, the general public, and even many faculty members) often know very little about the quality of the academic programs at those institutions.

This situation exists because approximately 75% of the media coverage of the average university goes to its athletic programs, according to knowledgeable sources. Almost everyone has heard of Notre Dame, for example, because of its athletic prowess and may conclude, naturally, that it is a great university. Therefore, a way to raise UA's visibility would be to compete, athletically, at a higher level.

When I went to Akron, the Zips were members of the Ohio Valley Conference and were competing at the Division I-AA level in football. Other sports played at Division I, except women's softball, which operated in NCAA Division II. Akron and Youngstown State were the northernmost members of a conference that was concentrated in Kentucky and Tennessee. When Gordon Larsen, the long-time athletic director retired, David Adams from California was hired to succeed him in my first year at Akron.

As Dave Adams and I discussed how we might move the Zips up a notch, we concluded that the primary change had to occur in football. Schools that played at the I-AA level got very little national coverage and were often, perhaps unfairly, regarded as "lower level" universities. So a move up to I-A seemed to be the logical step. The trouble was that, at this juncture, no university had ever moved from I-AA to I-A. We studied the I-A requirements from the NCAA: a stadium with at least 25,000 seats (we had that in the Rubber Bowl with a capacity of 30,000); average attendance of at least 17,000 over five years (we did not meet this requirement but felt that we could); and a schedule that included at least six I-A opponents each year (that would require some major changes). Another alternative was to join an

I-A conference; there were schools that did not meet the I-A criteria (such as average attendance) but were regarded as I-A schools because they belonged to a I-A conference. The logical move would have been into the Mid-America Conference (MAC), as it included schools in Ohio, Indiana, and Michigan against whom the Zips often successfully competed. But movement into the MAC was considered to be another one of those "can't be done" deals.

In the meantime, we looked at all our other sports. We had an excellent Division I men's soccer program. We often made it into the NCAA playoffs and one year got all the way to the championship game, playing Duke in the Tacoma Dome in Washington. The Zips lost the match, 2-1, in a heart breaker. Women's softball was very strong in Division II, also playing for a national championship in 1985. But that achievement gained moderate local coverage and almost none outside the area. The program that had the best opportunity to raise Akron's profile nationally was men's basketball. A new on-campus arena had just been built and a new coach, Bob Huggins, had just been hired. We felt that Huggins would develop a winning program and he did, capturing the OVC title in his second year. Akron went on to the NCAA tournament, playing the University of Michigan in the first round. The Zips lost by four points after a tremendous battle before 25,000 fans in the Metrodome in Minneapolis. Over the next three years, Akron won at least 19 games each year and went to the NIT twice. After five years, Huggins moved to the University of Cincinnati where he had an outstanding record. Coleman Crawford, who had served as an assistant on Huggins' staff, succeeded him as head coach and led the Zips to winning records in the Mid-Continent Conference. Crawford was the first black head coach in Akron's history.

But, in 1985, movement into the MAC seemed to be a very attractive alternative that would benefit all sports, particularly football. I had a number of discussions with the MAC Commissioner who reviewed this matter with the presidents of the institutions in the conference. Things looked very good for a while but when the proposal came up for a vote, at least one school opposed Akron's admission. Since only one negative vote could defeat such a motion, we were left out in the cold. The only alternative left to us, if we wanted to move to I-A, was to meet the requirements playing as an independent. We would have to withdraw from the OVC in order to get a schedule with six I-A opponents.

In order to make this significant change, Dave Adams and I felt that we needed a football coach who had the contacts to recruit players with the ability to compete at the I-A level and bring national visibility to Akron. Gerry Faust had just resigned as the head coach at Notre Dame after five years with a winning record (but not good enough for ND). He was from Ohio and had been one of the top high school coaches in the nation at Moeller High School in Cincinnati. Adams and I held several discussions with Faust to determine whether he might be interested in coming to Akron. When it appeared that could happen, I talked to Jim Dennison, the current coach, and asked him to move into a position as associate athletic director, clearing the way for us to hire Faust. I had no animosity toward Dennison and felt he had done a good job at the I-AA level. But we did not believe that he was the coach we needed to take Akron to the next level. Dennison later moved up to athletic director after Adams resigned a couple of years later.

The day we announced Gerry Faust's appointment as head football coach at Akron the media coverage was, without a doubt, the greatest that had ever occurred in the University of Akron's history. Almost all of the national coverage was positive, but there was a strong negative reaction from the sports department at <u>The Akron Beacon Journal</u>. I believe this was a result of their being caught completely off-guard and because of the personal relationship that the primary sportswriter had with Jim Dennison, whom he felt had been "wronged".

For the first season under Faust, the Zips had to compete at the I-AA level in the OVC, before embarking on an independent schedule, achieving a 7-4 record. But the next five years were tougher, as they had to play I-A powerhouses like Tennessee, Florida, Auburn, and Virginia Tech in order to meet the scheduling requirements. Moreover, all those games took place on the road. The best the Zips could do as an independent was 4-7 and many sportswriters and fans put the blame on Faust. But he had almost an impossible task. I admired Gerry for how hard he worked to build a competitive program and garner support in the community.

For my part, I was criticized by the faculty for spending the additional money to compete at a higher level. But the funds came primarily from increasing the fees that students pay to attend all athletic events. My reasoning was that UA students would be the primary beneficiaries of the higher profile the university attained - i.e. the better known the university was, the more valuable would be their diploma and the more job opportunities they would likely have.

At the end of the five years as an independent, Akron had met all the I-A requirements and was, at that point, invited to join the Mid-American Conference. The goal we had sought had been achieved, albeit by a more difficult route than we anticipated. Although I absorbed a lot of criticism for the decision, I believe this move was in Akron's best interests over the long term.

ENHANCING THE CAMPUS ENVIRONMENT

In order for Akron U (as it was often called locally) to be perceived as a major university, the campus environment needed to be improved. But that was difficult to do because the campus was "hemmed in" on all sides: by the downtown to the west, by a major highway to the east, and by commercial and residential areas to the north and south. We spent a fair amount of time investigating real estate that came available near the campus - either for parking or to house some university operation.

Under the direction of Roger Ryan, the university architect, a master plan for campus development was formulated and presented to the board. Over the years I was at UA, a total of over $75 million was invested in facility and campus improvements, including the projects that emerged from our partnership with the city -- the closure of Buchtel Avenue, the new business school facility, and the renovation of the Polsky's building. The new polymer science building was clearly the most significant new structure. The pathway of Buchtel Avenue was made into a brick pedestrian mall with significant landscaping and a major fountain. A statue of John R. Buchtel, the founder of the university, was installed in front of Buchtel Hall, the main administration building. There was much more that needed to be done, but the changes that were effected made a major difference.

We were able to house only about 2,400 students in campus dorms, so a majority of the residential students lived in off-campus apartments many of which were converted residences. The biggest off-campus housing area was south of Exchange Street and consisted mostly of old houses, many of which I feared were unsafe. But the university had no authority to tell the students where they could not live nor to require the landlords to improve their property. Finally, what I feared happened. A house caught on fire and a student was fatally trapped in a third story loft without a fire escape. We used this death to pressure the city to enforce housing codes in the area. As it turned out, one of the biggest landlords was a major drug dealer currently serving time in prison. I received a letter from him, threatening to sue me for the problems I was causing him. It did not happen; I guess he had bigger problems to deal with.

GETTING THE FACULTY ONBOARD

Having trained to be a member of the faculty and having entered the profession in that role, I felt that I understood and valued the importance of the faculty in a university. The strength and stature of any academic program depends on faculty accomplishments. As a dean, I interacted with the faculty in my college regularly and attempted to attract, support, and retain the best.

As a president, however, I quickly learned that the faculty was only one of several important constituencies that included the students and staff on campus and the alumni, parents, community leaders and taxpayers beyond. Providing access while balancing the influence of each group was always a challenge. But maintaining a good relationship with faculty should always be high on a president's agenda. During the 1980's, an oft-repeated mantra was "shared governance", implying that faculty ought to have a special role in running the institution. As a practical matter, that was a very difficult concept to implement for a couple of reasons.

First, faculty committees or councils do not make decisions easily or quickly. That is due, I believe, to the way faculty are trained and evaluated. To complete a doctoral program, one must find a unique niche in which to do research for a dissertation and then, to gain tenure and promotion, must spend the rest of his career attempting to differentiate himself from others by the unique contributions he makes to the discipline thru research, writing, and teaching. It should not be surprising, then, that faculty tend to have sharply defined and strongly held opinions. For example, a faculty member trained in the liberal arts is apt to see the world—and almost any issue—differently than one trained in the sciences. I often joked that I could meet with any ten faculty and get at least eleven different opinions!

Secondly, the responsibility for most decisions ultimately rests with an appropriate administrator accountable for that area of the university's operations. For example, search committees are appointed for almost every employment opening and are charged with evaluating applicants for the position, interviewing finalists, and recommending the best-qualified candidates for consideration. It was sometimes difficult to convince a committee that they were not making the actual hiring decision rather than the administrator to whom the employee would be reporting. But, of course, if the new employee did not perform well, it was clearly the administrator who had to deal with the situation.

Nevertheless, I believed that faculty should have input into any decision that affected them, whether the appointment of a new administrator or the adoption of a new policy. Process is extremely important to the faculty, whether it be following the prescribed procedures or the agreed-upon plan. I think most understood that their input represented an opinion or recommendation—not the final decision—but felt it was critical their voice be heard.

So I listened to input both individually and collectively. A Faculty Senate consisting of members from each college, in proportion to its size, as well as others who served by virtue of their positions represented faculty leadership at the institution. This body met monthly during the academic year and I made it a practice to attend each session in order to address current issues and answer questions. I remember one senator, Don Gerlach, a professor of history, who relished the opportunity to ask the president a vexing query at every meeting. These sessions, while not always pleasurable, were, I believe, an important opportunity to neutralize the faculty's inherent inclination to distrust the university administration. This distrust, I believe, arises out of the realization that their voice is not the only one to which the administration has to listen and the fear that it might not be perceived as the most important one. Additionally, faculty are trained to be critical; so their first reaction is almost always skeptical. But because they are at the heart of any university, it was essential that faculty input be carefully considered.

I made good progress in bringing the faculty and administration closer together, but never felt that I closed the gap entirely. Some objected to the decisions to elevate the level at which athletics competed. Others resented the special emphasis that some academic programs received. Still others worried about all the changes designed to move Akron from a municipal university to one that served a broader audience and had some national visibility. Some faculty even tried to form a union but could not get the votes needed to call an election. This was, I felt, something of a victory since the faculties at both Kent State and Youngstown State were already unionized. While tensions always existed, I enjoyed the opportunity to work with many outstanding leaders on the UA faculty.

EXPANSION OF PRIVATE SUPPORT

In order to accomplish many of the university's goals, I believed that greater private support was needed. UA had had only one fund raising campaign in its history that raised approximately $10 million. After conducting a feasibility study, we announced a campaign to raise $50 million. The individuals who led that campaign were Paul Martin, an alumnus and very successful automobile dealer, the chairman, and John Shorrock, the university's director of development.

Mr. Martin was very generous with his own gifts and helped direct us to other good prospects. John Shorrock and I called on virtually everyone who was considered a major prospect. At the end of the campaign we had raised $52 million and, in the process, increased the university endowment from $10 million to $50 million. These gifts helped to fund endowed chairs and professorships, scholarships, and campus improvements.For example, some of Paul Martin's gifts funded the fountain on Buchtel Mall, a new campus gateway, and major improvements to the University Club, a dining and meeting facility, which was later named the Martin Center.

LEADERSHIP SUPPORT

The achievements described above that occurred during the years of 1984-92 would not have been possible without an excellent leadership team and a supportive Board of Trustees. Each of those bodies will be discussed.

THE LEADERSHIP TEAM

I was fortunate to attract an outstanding group of individuals to work with me in the pursuit of the goals we set and enjoyed my relationship with them both individually and collectively.

Several have already been discussed: Sebetha Jenkins, who led the effort to achieve greater diversity on campus; Roger Ryan, the university architect and vice-president for administrative services, who led the initiative to beautify the campus; and John Shorrock who directed the capital campaign. Many others also played key roles.

Charlene Reed, a bright young woman who had been editor of The Buchtelite, the student newspaper, and now working for the university's Office of Communications, interviewed me for an article in the faculty and staff newsletter on one of my first days on the job. I was impressed with her work and asked her to become an assistant to the president to write speeches for all the engagements that were accumulating. When the volume of speeches dropped to a more normal level, Charlene assumed other tasks. And when George Ball, a long-time university employee who was secretary to the board, retired, I moved Charlene into that position. For the remainder of my time at Akron, she handled communications with the trustees, prepared the agenda for the meetings, and distributed the minutes, along with many other duties.

Kathy Stafford joined the team when Richard Wright retired as the university's chief lobbyist and director of government relations. Dick was well known in the legislature and I needed someone who had equal skill and knowledge. Dr. Stafford was then serving as the executive director of the Inter-University Council (IUC) in Columbus, a lobbying group representing all the 4-year institutions of higher education and I asked her to come to work for me to be in charge of government relations. She did well and was eventually promoted to vice president of institutional advancement, with responsibilities for government relations, alumni relations, development and communications.

After I had been at Akron a couple of years, I decided that I had to have a more effective secretary to the president and recruited Dottie Schmith, secretary to the dean of education. It was one of the best decisions I made. Dottie did a superior job of handling my schedule and the volume of communications and visitors to my office. She had excellent knowledge of the university's functions and exercised good judgment in the performance of her duties.

Don Bowles, a long-term university employee, was very knowledgeable about the administrative side of the campus, particularly physical facilities. He served as vice-president for administrative services for several years before becoming executive assistant to the president. Don often accompanied me on trips to Columbus and we became close personal friends. Dr. H. Kenneth Barker had a long and distinguished tenure as dean of the College of Education at UA. After he retired from that position, he became my executive assistant to assist me in local community relations. Ken seemed to know everyone of importance and enjoyed setting up lunches and other meetings.

Dr. Faith Helmick was the person on campus to whom we turned whenever we had a problem or need in information systems. I eventually moved her into a position of vice president of human resources and information services and she provided important leadership in this role. Karla Muglar became director of special events, making arrangements for the many public events and social affairs that we hosted. She handled this taxing responsibility with great poise and competence. A bright young lady, she earned her doctorate and, later, advanced through the administration to associate provost and dean of University College.

When I arrived, the position of provost and vice-president of academic affairs was vacant. I appointed Dr. Jack Watt, a veteran education professor to serve in that role on an interim basis. Following a national search, Frank Marini was selected for that post. A bright individual, Frank had been dean of Arts and Sciences at San Diego State and had a good understanding of academic programs and processes. He and I had a good working relationship but his standing with deans and with key faculty leaders deteriorated over time. When Dr. Marini moved to a faculty position, Dr. Mark Auburn was selected to succeed him. Mark, the son of a former Akron president, had a distinguished academic record and had been provost at one of the campuses of Indiana University. He served as provost during the remainder of my term at UA and we worked well together.

The important roles of vice-president for business and finance and vice president of student affairs were held by veteran administrators Wayne Duff and Richard Hansford, respectively, for a long time. When they retired, their big shoes were filled by Darryl Bierly, chief financial officer, and Bob Dubick, as chief student affairs official. Ted Mallo, as general counsel, headed a three person legal staff. The last executive assistant that I had was Dr. Marion Ruebel who had served as dean of the University College for many years. Rube was appointed as interim president after I left Akron. He had been at UA a long time and was well qualified to continue the work.

BOARD OF TRUSTEES

UA's Board of Trustees very effectively operated as a governing board, concentrating on oversight and policy formation and eschewing involvement in day-to-day operations of the university. In addition to John Steinhauer, I was blessed with excellent chairs of the Board -- Ben Ammons, Gene Graham, Janet Purnell, and David Headley. Charlene Reed and I would meet with the chair prior to each board meeting to discuss all items on the agenda and we updated the board regularly about issues within the university.

Each year the board would elect a chair for a one-year term, but both John Steinhauer and Ben Ammons served two terms each. They provided excellent leadership for the board and wise guidance to me. I enjoyed working with them and consider each to be a good friend.

The nine trustees each served a nine-year term, with one term expiring each year, so the board was constantly changing. When I arrived at UA, Republican James Rhodes had just finished two 4-year terms as Governor and the board was made up of eight Republicans and one Democrat. For the eight years I was there, a Democrat, Richard Celeste, was Governor and the board switched gradually to eight Democrats and one Republican. But the attitude and operations of the board did not change materially, as the board members did not see their role as a partisan one. And even though almost all the board members lived in the Akron area and read the local newspaper containing frequent stories about controversies on the campus, they did not try to interfere or intervene -- with one exception.

The university had established a Ray Bliss Institute of Applied Politics to do research on political issues. Ray Bliss was a former chairman of the UA Board of Trustees who had also served as chairman of the Republican National Committee. I indicated that I planned to appoint Vern Cook, a strong Democratic leader in the Ohio House and a member of UA's Political Science faculty, as director of the institute. George Wilson, a member of the Board of Trustees who had worked in the Rhodes Administration, told me that a Republican should serve in that role. I told him that the director had to be non-partisan and that the best way to acknowledge that was to appoint a Democrat and, furthermore, Vern Cook was well qualified and already a member of our faculty. Mr. Wilson went to the newspaper, telling them how much he disapproved of my decision and that I "needed to be fired." The chairman of the board responded that the appointment of the director was the president's decision. And he met privately with Mr. Wilson and told him that such behavior was inappropriate for a board member.

Board members came to the meetings well-prepared and engaged in lively discussions. Although they frequently challenged me to justify proposals and explain the university's results in particular areas, they always applauded my leadership and that made the job satisfying. Among the board members that I remember most fondly were: Chuck Taylor, an executive with British Petroleum in Cleveland; Kathryn Hunter, a local savings and loan owner; Jane Quine, a former county Democratic chairman; Joe Kanfer, the CEO of a large manufacturing firm based in Akron; and Dr. Melvin Farris, a distinguished local physician.

PLEASANT MEMORIES

I have many pleasant memories of our years in Akron, a good place to work and to live both for the whole family and me. Some of the things that come to mind are:

MY INAUGURATION

My inauguration as president of the university was held in UA's beautiful performing arts hall, E.J. Thomas Hall, which sits right at the entrance to the campus from downtown. The ceremony included all the normal "pomp and circumstance" -- an academic procession, welcoming speeches by all sorts of dignitaries, beautiful music, and my presentation of future plans for the university

But the incident that I remember most was an exchange between my brother, Clyde, who spoke on behalf of my family, and Dr. Gabe Campbell, the pastor of the First Congregational Church, who gave the benediction. In his remarks, Clyde had described how Daddy wanted both of us to go into the ministry and how he had justified his choice of education as a career by telling Daddy that there wasn't much difference between "preaching and teaching". Dr. Campbell, before he delivered the benediction, said he wanted to point out to Clyde that there <u>was</u> a significant difference between preaching and teaching and it was <u>tenure</u>. Needless to say, that brought down the house!

FIRST CONGREGATIONAL CHURCH

Marlene and I became active members of the First Congregational Church, serving on boards and attending services on a regular basis. The church is in a beautiful old stone building located right on the edge of the University of Akron campus. We enjoyed our relationship with many members of the Church and, especially, with Gabe Campbell and his wife, Sandra. Gabe was an excellent preacher and we looked forward to his sermons each Sunday. Gabe and Sandy became, and still remain, among our closest friends.

INVOLVEMENT IN THE LIFE OF THE UNIVERSITY AND THE CITY

The whole family was involved with UA, as both Marlene and Amy earned bachelor's degrees there while Ellen and Van both attended Akron for a brief time. Marlene and I entertained community leaders and university officials on a regular basis and attended a university or community event almost every evening. We particularly enjoyed artistic performances and athletic events. The president, of course, was expected to take an interest in all aspects of the university.

One of our benefits was being able to see Amy and Ellen perform in the university theater. As a theater major, Amy was always in a play or rehearsing for one. When Ellen was at The College of Wooster, we got to see her perform there too. And even Van got into the theater venue, acting in a play at a Catholic girls' school that had to import male actors from Firestone High.

When we were leaving Texas to move to Ohio, we were frequently asked "Why are you moving to Ohio?" as Texans couldn't believe anyone would willingly leave their state to go anywhere else. Surprisingly, when we got to Akron, we were often asked the same question, implying that they also wondered why anyone would move from Texas to Ohio. Many folks in Akron, perhaps because of the economic decline in the area, had negative impressions of their hometown. But Marlene and I found that the area had many great assets -- one of the best park systems that we had encountered, an excellent art museum and symphony orchestra, and a tremendous ballet company that was housed at UA. E.J. Thomas Hall brought a rich array of cultural entertainment to Akron on a regular basis. I enjoyed the beautiful golf courses in the area and was a member of The Portage Country Club.

In addition to the volunteer boards (United Way, Salvation Army, etc.) on which I served, Marlene served on several boards including Summit County Family Service, Blick Mental Health Clinic, and Arlington Ministries. And she helped organize a Habitat for Humanity chapter there. In short, we were actively involved in the community.

RELATIONSHIP WITH THE BUSINESS COMMUNITY

In addition to the two corporate boards on which I served and my role as Chairman of ARDB, I enjoyed my relationship with many of the top business executives in the city. They included the CEO's of the three rubber companies in town: Bob Mercer at Goodyear, John Ong at Goodrich, and John Nevin at Firestone. All three companies provided major support for UA's polymer programs. One of the achievements was a $3 million gift from Firestone to establish the Strive Toward Excellence Program (STEP) to bring youngsters from low-income families to the university in the summer for three years, beginning in the sixth grade. Those completing the program received scholarships to attend the university. John Nevin had been impressed with our efforts to diversify the university and wanted to support that initiative. Ben Ammons, UA Trustee and executive vice president of Firestone, was also influential in securing this gift.

I also had a good relationship with David Brennan, a senior partner in one of Akron's largest law firms and a major entrepreneur as well. Dave owned a number of companies that he had purchased, including one, Romeo Rim in Romeo, Michigan, on whose board I served. He had also bought a huge steel mill in Gadsden, Alabama. In one of the interesting trips we took, Dave chartered a plane and took about 25 friends to visit the mill and, then, on to Auburn to see the Akron-Auburn football game. Marlene and I sat in the Auburn president's box for the game; ironically, a few years later, I was serving as president of Auburn. Dave had big ideas and strong opinions; I always enjoyed interacting with him.

SIGNIFICANT CHALLENGES

NEGATIVE REACTION TO CHANGE

After a few years at Akron, I concluded that: "Things are the way they are, no matter how bad they may appear, because someone wants them that way and is benefiting from that arrangement." Usually the beneficiaries are individuals who have been in power for some time and, therefore, react negatively to changes that would disrupt that relationship. I guess I knew that even before the Akron experience, as I had been an activist leader from a very early age. But I had never dealt with stakes that were so high and so public. In a university, almost every major decision is pushed to the top "where the buck stops." Even when that decision is supported or recommended by others, it is the president who takes the blame when problems occur. Faculty members, particularly those who are tenured, have no reservations about publicly criticizing the president. It is simply an occupational hazard.

Therefore, when I began to make changes at Akron -- personnel changes, modifications to the campus, changed emphasis on certain programs both academic and athletic -- there were negative reactions. The press frequently covered such protests, encouraging the disgruntled even more. The most highly visible and emotional reactions were to the changes in athletics.

Through this whole experience my resolve as a leader was seriously tested. But I did not deviate from the goals that had been set. I took the role of leader/president seriously and believed that, if an organization was going to improve, the support for change had to come from the top - and the criticism that resulted had to be absorbed there. So I stuck to the plans we had laid out. And I believe that the University of Akron was a much better university when I left.Not only that, but I also had a much tougher hide.

RELATIONSHIP WITH THE PRESS

Another challenge that I had to deal with was reading in the paper each morning what I had done or said and what people were saying about me. I, of course, had received press coverage before in other positions but it was normally just the printing of a news release that had been written by the university. But being the president of a major public university is a totally different situation.

As a result, the changes being made at UA and the reactions to those changes received extensive media coverage. Among the newspapers, <u>The</u>

<u>Akron Beacon Journal</u> provided the most ink with <u>The Cleveland Plain Dealer</u> weighing in heavily on the changes in athletics (covering the controversy, mostly, it seemed). The coverage by <u>The Beacon Journal</u> was understandable, given that the paper's editorial offices were only a block off campus and very accessible to anyone who had a gripe. Moreover, the changes at the university frequently constituted the "biggest story in town."

In all fairness, I must point out that I had a good relationship with the management of <u>The Beacon Journal</u>. I had great respect for Paul Poorman, the editor, and David Cooper, the associate editor. David and I worked together on the Akron Roundtable and other civic projects. Additionally, Diane Evans, a senior reporter who came to Texas before the move and wrote a story for the Sunday magazine and who covered UA for the first couple of years, always wrote a comprehensive and fair story..

The difficulties arose during my third year at Akron when a young reporter, Patrick Cole, was assigned to the UA beat. Admittedly, it was at this juncture that all constituents of the university had realized that I was not going to be a president who just sat in his office and "presided" but planned to make some real changes. But it seemed to me that the emphasis in the coverage was tilted toward the criticism of the changes rather than the long term benefits to the university. The story that I considered most unfair concerned repairs to the president's house and the "expenditures" that had been incurred. I considered it unfair because of its placement (top of page one on Sunday) and the implication that the changes were for personal rather than institutional benefit and that university funds had been inappropriately used. The facts were that the house was university property; the modifications were to allow larger gatherings, a major step in gaining community support and raising money; and most of the "expenditures" were a charge-off of the time of university employees who worked on the project (and would have been employed otherwise working on some other university building). But Cole got his byline on many major stories during this time, then moved on to a larger newspaper elsewhere.

THE PRESIDENT'S HOUSE

The president's house was a beautiful stone and wood structure located about four miles from the campus in a neighborhood between Merriman Road and Portage Path. It was situated on about ten acres of land along Eaton Avenue. Russell DeYoung, a former CEO of Goodyear Tire, had given the property to the university. He was also a UA alumnus and a former chairman of the trustees. The second floor had four bedrooms and a study, while the first floor was almost all "public space" -- a kitchen, formal dining room, small

TV room, living room, and a large room that we modified to accommodate about 60 people for seated dinners and 150 or so for receptions. The lower level or basement had a informal parlor and an indoor swimming pool. The property also included an outdoor patio and pool.

The outdoor pool was not very practical as there were only a few months of the year when its use was comfortable. But I used the indoor pool almost everyday. There was an elevator from the second floor to the pool; so I would go down each morning and swim for a half hour or more as a part of my exercise routine.

The modifications that were made to the house were on the first floor to make the hosting of larger groups possible. The house was regularly used for community events and to entertain groups of faculty and community leaders. The house also needed a number of repairs in order to maintain its value and to deal with damage from a leaky roof.

Partly because of the criticism and as a way to lower costs, I persuaded the Board of Trustees to sell the house and property and to give me a housing allowance instead. The house fetched a market price, while much of the surrounding acreage was sold for a housing development. Marlene and I bought a smaller house a few blocks away and lived there for about a year before the move to Auburn.

TO GO OR TO STAY

The average length of the tenure for a major university president is about five years. That is understandable, given the nature of the job. The saying among many presidents is: "If you haven't accomplished your goals in the first five years, the chances of doing so after that are pretty slim." The 24/7 aspects of the job can also lead to "burn out."

In my case, I was not unhappy at Akron and, in many respects had gotten through the roughest period. But after seven years, I began to think seriously about moving on to another challenge. I had often thought about the desirability of being the president of one of the universities in the Southeastern Conference (SEC), since this was the area of the country where I had grown up. I got my chance when, after a series of interviews, I was offered the job at Auburn University. I looked forward to this new chapter in my life and was grateful for the opportunity I had had to lead the University of Akron. Marlene and I made, and still have, many friends there.

In 2008, the University of Akron dedicated a clock and a garden on campus in my honor. This form of recognition for my service to the institution was deeply appreciated. Particular thanks goes to my good friend, Paul Martin, whose gift financed this investment.

Henry (in Navy), 1941

Billy at Goodwill
Church, 1942

Muse Family, 1941Clyde, Paul,
Mary Elizibeth, Mose Lee, Floyd,
Junior nd Bill (in front)

Brother and Sister Muse

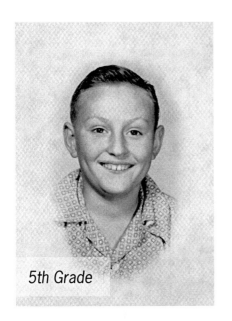

5th Grade

7th Grade

High School Senior

James Ray Jones & Billy (age 14)

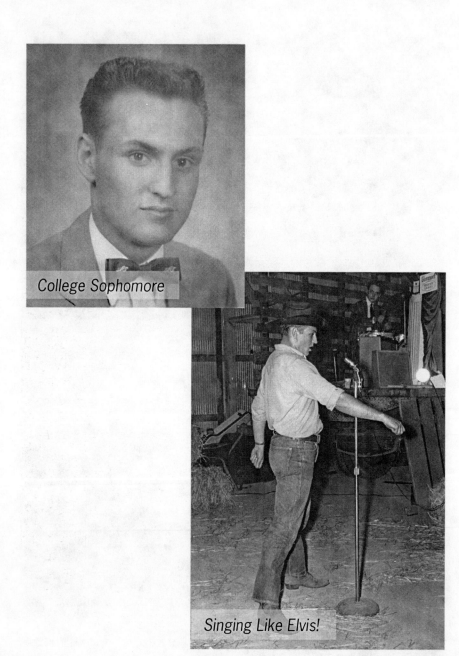

College Sophomore

Singing Like Elvis!

Wedding in Scottsburg, 1964
L-R, Preston and Virginia Munden, Marlene and Bill, Marie and Paul Muse

TKE Grand Council, 1977Seated (L-R), Rodney Williams, Bill Muse (Grand Prytanis), John Lourson Standind (L-R), Dwayne Worrel, Joel Johnson, Bruce MeLehert, Dan Laird, Jim Kane

Meeting with Fraternity Brother, Ronald Reagen, 1978

Family Photo in Texas, 1984

In President's Office at Auburn, 1998

With AD Mike Lude at Auburn, 1992

Clyde and Bill, 1998

Marlene and Bill with Gabe Campbell in Akron, 1985

The William V. Muse Family at Christmas, 2006

Sophia Ann, Born 2007

CHAPTER 13:
FIRE ON THE PLAINS

On the afternoon of May 2, 1994, I sat in my office in Samford Hall on the Auburn University campus interviewing a candidate for the deanship of the School of Pharmacy. My secretary interrupted me to tell me that the president's house was on fire! Knowing that Marlene was at home, I bolted from the office, jumped in my car, and dashed the two blocks to the house. Arriving, I found smoke streaming out of the attic windows but, fortunately, Marlene had been safely evacuated.

The Auburn fire department was already on the scene, pouring water into the attic, having been alerted by a passing motorist even before Marlene had smelled smoke. We were not able to remove our personal belongings, but, thanks to the quick response from the firemen, we lost only those items we had stored in the attic, although there was extensive smoke and water damage to the wall coverings, rugs and furnishings. And we had to subject all of our clothing to a deep steam cleaning,

For the next six months, Marlene and I lived in a small apartment about a block away while renovations took place. Eventually, the mansion was restored to an even better condition with new floor and wall coverings, new paint, and many new furnishings before we moved back in.

The fire had begun while university workers were using blowtorches to remove paint from the large two-story wooden columns that supported the front portico of the house. Apparently, the inside of one of the columns had ignited, sending a spark into the attic and starting the blaze.

This blaze was one of many "fires" I had to deal with during my years as president of Auburn. The heat that I was to experience was revealed even during the search process.

THE SEARCH AND HIRING PROCESS

The chairman of the search committee notified me in the summer of 1991 of my nomination for the Auburn presidency. I did not and still do not know who placed my name in nomination, but indicated that I would be interested in being considered and forwarded a copy of my resume, assured that the names of the candidates would not be made public.

Being a candidate for another job while one is president of a university is a risky proposition. Although corporate executives seem to change jobs with little, if any, furor, a university president is identified inextricability with his employer and is expected to be its strongest fan and advocate. To go to another university seems to many alumni, students and other supporters as a form of disloyalty. Therefore, universities often use executive search firms or other means to keep the identity of candidates secret.

I had experienced this phenomenon in 1990 when I had been a candidate for the position of chancellor of Louisiana State University. The names were kept private until five finalists were chosen and invited to the campus for interviews. I agreed to go forward with the public interviews because I felt I was better qualified than the other finalists and believed that my experience living and going to school in Louisiana would give me an edge. But when this news reached Akron, it caused quite a bit of consternation on the campus and in the community. As it turned out, I did not get the LSU job; I later learned that the individual selected had been consulting with the Governor for several months before the search and that the die had probably already been cast. So I had to deal not only with my disappointment and embarrassment but also with the "ruffled feathers" back in Akron. I didn't want to go through a similar experience with the Auburn search.

Having grown up in the Deep South and being a sports fan, I was well aware of Auburn. But, interestingly enough, I knew very little about the university and its current condition. And I did not know anyone on the campus who might have been able to share information with me. The first time I had visited the Auburn campus was in 1963 while I was working for the national office of TKE. And I had gone to the 1964 Orange Bowl to see Auburn play Nebraska with an Auburn alumnus and former Teke fieldman, Bruce Ivey. The only other time I had been on campus was when I came with the Akron football team in 1986. The Internet did not have the volume of information in 1991 that it has today; even if it had, I still would have been uninformed since I was "technologically-challenged" and did not use this modern marvel. So my knowledge of the situation at Auburn was very limited.

In late October, 1991, I was invited to interview with the search committee on a Sunday early in November at a hotel in Atlanta. By holding the meetings in Georgia, Auburn could avoid Alabama's open meetings law and keep the candidates' names private. The day of the meeting followed the University of Akron's football game with Army at West Point. I had agreed to go to the game and to join the Superintendent of the Academy in reviewing the troops before the game; so I did not want to miss this event. I arranged to travel to New York City after the game with an athletic staff member, spend the night there, and fly to Atlanta the next morning for the interview, and then fly back to Akron Sunday evening.

The search committee consisted of about twenty faculty, staff, and students and one trustee, Mike McCartney, who was president pro tempore of the board. He chaired the meeting but did not participate in the questioning. After nearly eight years as a university president, I was able to answer confidently all the questions that were posed and felt that the interview went well. Toward the end, I was asked about my personal interests and began to discuss my love for baseball, describing the Detroit Tigers' Fantasy Camp that I had attended a year or so earlier. Everyone seemed to get a big kick out of that. Dr. Jerry Brown, head of the journalism department at Auburn and a member of the search committee, told me a few years later that the conversation about baseball "humanized" me and was a significant factor in the interview.

A couple of weeks later, I heard from Dr. Gerald Leischuck, chairman of the search committee, that I had been selected as a finalist; the board had scheduled another round of interviews in Atlanta and Marlene was invited to accompany me. We flew to Atlanta on a Saturday morning, got a room at the hotel where we would be meeting, and prepared for the interviews later that day.

I was interviewed in three small groups of three or four trustees each, while Marlene met with the trustees' wives. I had not met any of the board before, (except Mr. McCartney) and didn't know anything about them except their names and occupations. But that did not worry me, as I had worked with a very diverse board at Akron and felt that I could work with almost anyone. Although I got little feedback from the board members, I thought that the sessions went very well.

I met Marlene back at our room and just as we prepared to head for the airport, Mike McCartney appeared and told me that I was the choice for the job. He offered me a salary that was slightly lower than what I was making at Akron; so I negotiated for a higher figure to which he agreed. He, then, told me that I would have to come to Auburn for a public interview and the appointment by the board in an open session. I knew that the appointment would become official on that day, but as far as I was concerned, it was a "done deal". So Marlene and I traveled back to Akron, not telling anyone about our decision. I was excited about the new challenge, moving back to the south as president of one of the universities in the SEC.

The date for the interview and appointment was set for December 17, 1991. The news of this event broke the night before and, on the morning of our departure, the <u>Akron Beacon-Journal</u> carried the news in a front-page story. We flew to Atlanta where we were met by Emily Leischuck, an assistant to the president, and continued to Auburn in a university plane.

The meeting took place in a large conference room in the James E. Foy Student Center on the Auburn campus. When we arrived, we found the room packed with people. In addition to the trustees seated around a large rectangular table, spectators filled every seat, and the press was in ample supply, including at least three TV cameras. There was even a reporter from Akron who had flown down to cover the event.

I grabbed a seat at the table with the trustees and the interview began. The questions were all on material we had covered previously, including potentially sensitive topics like racial diversity and academic freedom, and I felt that the discussion went smoothly.

Finally, after about an hour, Mr. McCartney asked Gerald Leischuck to escort me and Marlene to a room down the hall while the board continued the meeting. I assumed that we would be there only a few minutes while the board voted, and then would return to the meeting for the formal announcement. As it turned out, the wait took much longer. Dr. Leischuck kept going back and forth between the meeting and our room, looking worried but only reporting that the board was "discussing some matters."

After a span of fifteen or twenty minutes, we were brought back in to the meeting and I was introduced as the 15th President of Auburn University to much applause. Then followed many handshakes and numerous press interviews before we got on the plane for our flight back to Akron.

It was not until many months later, after I was on the job at Auburn, that I fully understood what happened after my interview. One of the trustees moved that I be appointed as president and the motion was seconded. But then, Bobby Lowder, another trustee, moved that the motion be tabled and it was seconded. Reportedly, Mr. Lowder had supported one of the other finalists and had not given up that he might still get him appointed, arguing that the board needed to consider other candidates. Some people speculated that Lowder had thought that any delay would be embarrassing enough to get me withdraw, leaving the opportunity to get his candidate elected. But, after much discussion, the trustees who supported me prevailed, defeating the motion to table by a 5-4 vote. After that, the motion to appoint me as president was unanimously approved. The motion to table, I was told later, failed because one trustee, Jim Tatum, who was expected to vote with Lowder, changed his mind.

Marlene told me later that she did not feel good during the wait and thought to herself that we ought to "get out of there." But having faced many controversies during my years at Akron, I felt that I could handle anything that arose and was excited about the challenge. The vote of the board, however, was an indication of the significance of the struggle that awaited me.

PREPARING FOR THE MOVE

While I was elated about the new job, the return back to Akron confronted Marlene and me with the pain associated with leaving. We had made many good friends in Akron, both at the university and in the community. They wished us well and understood the move in terms of career advancement, but parting was still difficult. I had invested tremendous energy into making UA better and identified strongly with the progress that had been made during our time there. The Akron trustees wanted me to finish the academic year (until June, 1992), as it would permit them to conduct a search to find my replacement. However, I felt that an earlier move to Auburn would be best for me.

Dr. James E. Martin, an Auburn graduate and former president of the University of Arkansas, had served as president for Auburn for about eight years. He had announced his plans for retirement and was flexible as to the date he would depart. I took a couple of trips to the campus to visit the staff and assess the situation. And I found all sorts of problems that called for immediate action. There was significant racial turmoil on campus. A controversy had arisen over the chartering of a gay-lesbian student group. The faculty had passed a "vote of no confidence" on the president. AU was under investigation by the NCAA for rule violations in football. There were major financial problems because the Governor had declared proration (a reduction in the state appropriation by a set percentage). And Auburn was the defendant in a higher education desegregation lawsuit. Otherwise, things appeared to be in great shape!

Rather than change my mind, though, I decided to go ahead and jump into the fray as soon as possible. So I negotiated an early departure from Akron and agreed to start at Auburn on March 1, 1992. We had placed our house in Akron on the market and it sold in March, allowing us to move our household goods to Auburn by the end of that month and for Marlene to join me at that time.

THE FIRST
ONE HUNDRED DAYS

It is said that a chief executive faces his most difficult challenges and has his greatest opportunities to effect change during his first one hundred days in office. My first one hundred days at Auburn provided me with such an opportunity to demonstrate how I would deal with many perplexing problems. The issues were all "on my plate" at the same time, but a brief discussion as to how each was handled might be instructive.

RACIAL UNREST AND THE OLD SOUTH PARADE

One of my first meetings at Auburn was a workshop on racial diversity.Not only was the percentage of black students on campus low, they also perceived the environment on campus as hostile. I immediately began to envision what could be done, since I had faced very similar problems at Akron.

The most powerful symbol of racial discord was the annual "Old South Parade" conducted by Kappa Alpha fraternity. The KA house sat at one end of South College Street, a wide avenue that marked the eastern boundary of the campus. Each spring for as far back as anyone could remember, the fraternity (who claimed as one of its national founders, General Robert E. Lee) had donned confederate uniforms and ridden horses up the street, waving their rebel flags, while accompanied by a float carrying their girlfriends clad in antebellum dresses. They traveled down College Street to Toomer's Corner (the main intersection between the campus and the town), turned around, and came back to their house. The parade, according to reports I received, drew tremendous crowds each year. There were black students who wanted me to stop this event but I declined to intervene because Kappa Alpha was a private organization and, having never witnessed the parade, I had no way to judge whether the stories I had been told were accurate or exaggerated.

As the day of the parade, a beautiful Friday afternoon in April, arrived, around 10,000 people lined both sides of College Street with the press, including a number of TV trucks, in ample supply. About one block from the KA house stood a crowd of black students, including some from Tuskegee University, a historically black university only about 20 miles away.

As the KA parade passed this location, there was significant booing from the black students and cheering from the white students on the other side of the street. After the parade passed, black students moved into the street and sat down to block the parade's return route. And a huge black man snatched a confederate flag from an on-looker and set it afire. The black students cheered and the makings of a major confrontation began to unfold.

Fortunately, the university and city police were alert to the dangers emerging and managed to redirect the parade back down a side street, thereby avoiding conflict. By the time the parade viewers became aware of what had happened, the KA's were back at their house and the event was over. But the press recognized this as great "theatre" and the parade was carried as front-page news in every major newspaper and TV station in the state, as well as by many outside.

I had seen enough. Herb White, the university's savvy director of public relations made up a huge board displaying all the press clippings and I asked the officers of the KA chapter to meet with me the next week. Standing before the board of press clippings in the president's conference room, I told them, first, that I was a fraternity man, not just a member, but a former national president and, therefore, I understood the value of fraternities and respected their desire to have certain traditions. But I also challenged them to rise above their status as fraternity men and recognize their obligations to their university as Auburn Men. They could readily see from the press coverage the damage they were wreaking on Auburn's academic reputation. Next, I asked them to contemplate what would have happened had the police not been alert enough to divert them on their return route; a riot would likely have occurred with significant injuries both to themselves and to others.

At the conclusion of the meeting, I asked the officers to consider what we had discussed and to come back to me within a week with their recommended solutions. A few days later the officers held a chapter meeting that ran late into the night and finally voted to discontinue the Old South Parade. The parade in 1992 was the last one held. I greatly respected the men of KA for the decision they made, reportedly in the face of considerable pressure from their alumni to continue the event.

Stopping the Old South Parade did not solve Auburn's racial problems, by a long shot, but it certainly was a move in the right direction and created expectations that things would improve. And they did. I created a position of assistant to the president for minority advancement, a first for AU, and hired Dr. James Brown from Mississippi State to fill that role. Efforts were made over the next several years to increase minority recruiting, bring black alumni to the campus, and pay more attention to black student activities. An advisor for international students, Nejla Orgen, assumed responsibilities for working with black student organizations and became very effective in that role. As a result of all these efforts, black student enrollment increased significantly, a black man was elected Student Government Association (SGA) president and a black woman was elected as Miss Auburn, the highest honor for a female student. And the Auburn Alumni Association formed a Black Alumni Association. Changing an institution's racial climate requires sustained efforts over a long period of time. Stopping the Old South Parade allowed that process to begin.

AUBURN GAY AND LESBIAN ALLIANCE

Prior to my arrival, a gay and lesbian student organization (AGLA) had formed and had petitioned the Student Government Association for a charter so that they could use university facilities for meetings. The SGA had denied the request and the group had appealed to President Martin for reconsideration, but he approved the granting of the charter. The SGA was still not happy, alumni were angry, and some members of the state legislature were threatening to pass a bill that would deny the group access to public facilities.

Shortly after my arrival, all of these groups converged on me, demanding that I reverse President Martin's action. I listened to their pleas, but I knew that Dr. Martin's decision had been correct. Similar cases had arisen at other universities, including some that had gone to court, who had consistently ruled that universities could not deny students their freedom of association – as long as the groups met all established requirements – nor could they deny students the use of facilities provided for all students. So I refused to overturn the decision made.

But I went beyond just letting the action stand. I wrote an article that called for tolerance for diversity and respect for the rights of those who are different. I discussed the needs for our students to learn how to live and function effectively in a diverse culture and contended that it was inconsistent to demand freedom for themselves while denying it to others. The article ran as an op-ed piece in all major newspapers in Alabama. My ideas were hardly new nor revolutionary, but having the president of Auburn – or any public official in Alabama – say them publicly apparently was! This stance settled the AGLA issue and, I believe, helped contribute to a more tolerant attitude on campus.

FACULTY UNREST

There was considerable animosity among the faculty toward the administration and the board of trustees when I arrived. The vote of no confidence in Dr. Martin had stemmed from his decision to deny tenure to a distinguished but controversial professor of religion who, reportedly, had been hired with the promise of tenure after his first year. The faculty felt that President Martin had succumbed to pressure from some trustees in taking this action. They were also upset by the fact that the university was on the censure list of the American Association of University Professors (AAUP) for an earlier case involving a faculty member who had been denied tenure after being employed beyond the probationary period and by their perception that the administration was doing nothing to remove this status.

I agreed to meet with the General Faculty on one of my trips to campus and walked into a large auditorium that was packed to capacity. After a few opening remarks, I threw the floor open and fielded questions for over an hour. I was not intimidated because I had been through this experience many times with the faculty at Akron. I answered their questions with examples of what I had done at Akron and by promises to review issues about which I was not yet fully informed. By the end of the session I believed that we had reached a modest level of mutual respect.

Fortunately for me, the incoming chair of the Faculty Senate was Dr. Barry Burkhart, a professor of psychology and a well-respected member of the faculty. Like most of his colleagues, he was skeptical about the prospects for improvement. But we forged an excellent working relationship during my critical first year and this set a precedent for the senate chairs that followed him. I made the chair of the Faculty Senate a member of the President's Cabinet, attended most of the senate meetings to brief the members and answer questions, and met with the officers on a regular basis. Over time, my relationship with the faculty leadership became one of the strengths of my administration.

NCAA INVESTIGATION

Prior to my arrival, I had learned about the possibility of NCAA football rule violations in a rather dramatic fashion, a feature story on the national television program, "60 minutes." It described one of the former players, Eric Ramsey, who claimed that he had received cash and other illegal benefits. The NCAA initiated an investigation and Auburn hired one of the largest law firms in the state, Balch and Bingham of Birmingham, to assist in its defense. John Scott, the lead lawyer, was very helpful and forthright in his review of the matter.

I realized early on that Auburn was highly vulnerable because the head football coach was also the athletic director; that is, the person who was supposed to be overseeing the operation was also running it. Pat Dye had been a highly successful coach during his years at Auburn, winning SEC championships and beating Alabama but he had paid little attention to the administrative aspects of the dual role. The combined coach/AD job was an imitation of the Paul "Bear" Bryant era at Alabama when the football coach controlled everything; few major schools employed that arrangement anymore.

In addition, I felt that an athletic department as large and as complex as Auburn's needed to have full time administrative leadership. So I met with Coach Dye, explained the conclusions I had reached, and asked him to relinquish his title as athletic director. He was cooperative and readily agreed to do so. My next step was to hire a new athletic director. We needed someone who was experienced in managing a "big time" athletic program, but I recognized that it would be difficult to attract such a person given the situation we had.

I called Frank Broyles, the long time athletic director at Arkansas, and asked him for his advice. I had met Frank during my student days while he was the football coach and had used him as a consultant at Akron when we moved the Zips from I-AA to I-A. He told me that he knew "the man that I needed"; his name was Mike Lude and he had been the highly successful athletic director at the University of Washington for sixteen years. Mike had retired and was now the Executive Director of the Blockbuster Bowl in Fort Lauderdale, Florida. I called Mike and invited him to meet in Atlanta; after two hours of intense conversation, I was convinced that he was the man that we needed. Although he was nearly 70 at the time, Mike was very alert and energetic and had the experience and skills that would allow us to tackle the challenges ahead. I offered Mike the job, asking him to give me two years to get the house in order at Auburn.

This was just the beginning of an intense dimension of my job at Auburn. I had to give extensive time to athletics, not only because of the unique situation at Auburn and but also because athletics was the most visible (and, to many people, the most important) part of the university's operation.

FINANCIAL CRISES

I had to learn quickly how higher education in Alabama was funded (or, more accurately, under-funded). The legislature would often approve a state budget that had unrealistic revenue estimates, but which allowed them to look good by awarding increased appropriations. The Governor had the authority to declare "proration" and, thereby, to reduce appropriations by the percentage needed to balance the budget. But, since proration likely occurred midway through the fiscal year, adjustments in spending patterns became difficult.

This is what had happened in 1991-92 when Governor Guy Hunt had declared proration and the state appropriation had been cut, shortly before I arrived. Since the university had used much of its increase to improve salaries for faculty and staff at the beginning of the year, we were currently operating at an $8 million deficit. At this juncture, little could be done other than tap into financial reserves to cover the shortfall. But I knew that was not a viable long term solution.

Our dilemma was further exacerbated by the way capital improvements had to be financed. The state would not appropriate funds for new buildings; instead, universities had to issue bonds and pledge tuition revenues for their repayment. A number of new buildings had been constructed during the Martin administration and I found that Auburn was currently paying out 16% of its tuition revenue for debt service. This further restricted and complicated financial decision making.

It was obvious that Auburn's financial problems would not to be solved overnight. But the most important step I took in that direction was to appoint Donald L. Large as vice president of business and finance. A longtime VP and chief financial officer had retired and Don, who had been his assistant, was the acting vice president when I arrived. Don was an impressive young man who had graduated from Auburn and worked in public accounting before returning to the university. Although a number of people urged me to conduct a search to fill the position, I liked Don's knowledge and willingness to consider alternative solutions and, therefore, appointed him to the post. This was one of the best decisions I made. Don became the best chief financial officer I ever worked with in higher education and, together, we were able to confront the financial challenges the university faced.

DESEGREGATION LAW SUIT

The federal government had sued the State of Alabama to force desegregation of its institutions of higher education. Judge Harold Murphy, U.S. District Judge in Georgia, had jurisdiction of the case and Auburn had to file regular reports on its progress in recruiting minority students and faculty as well as in other areas.

The lawsuit would require attention over several years. Judge Murphy had appointed a court monitor, Carlos Gonzales, and had impaneled a group of four former university presidents (from Michigan, Ohio State, Penn State, and Prairie View A&M) as consultants. So I met with Judge Murphy, Mr. Gonzales, and the consultants on several occasions. Fortunately, the aggressive plan that I put together to recruit minority (almost exclusively black) students and faculty and the impressive progress made quickly dismissed this as an issue.

The focus then, of the lawsuit turned to the merger of the cooperative extension systems at Auburn and Alabama A&M University. Auburn had been established as a land grant institution under the provisions of the Morrill Act of 1862, while A&M had received similar designation in 1890. This came about because of segregation in the southern states, which resulted in two cooperative extension systems, one for white farmers and one for black farmers. The court had mandated that these two systems merge in Alabama.

Auburn had extension offices in every county while A&M maintained offices in about fifteen counties; therefore, there were duplicate offices in these locations. I initiated meetings with the interim president of Alabama A&M, Dr. Virginia Caples, to begin discussion about how this could be done. Our staffs met on several occasions for many hours with little progress being made. It was apparent to me that A&M distrusted Auburn and that integration of the two extension systems was not their preferred solution. But, after nearly a year of discussion, Dr. Caples and her staff had arrived at a level of trust that enabled us to lay the framework for the merger to evolve.

The court had approved the hiring of a person to head the Alabama Cooperative Extension System and to oversee both the Auburn and A&M operations. Dr. Steve Jones was recruited to fill that post and worked hard over the next several years to make the new system function, appointing a number of A&M staff to system leadership positions and trying to get all staff working together. Dr. Jones later went to North Carolina State as a vice-chancellor and, subsequently, to the University of Alaska as chancellor. He is due considerable credit for progress that was made in Alabama.

The president who followed Dr. Caples, Dr. John Gibson, worked with the system we had put in place but, in my judgment, was not very enthusiastic about the concept of merged operations where Auburn was clearly in charge. But we met the mandate of the court and did our best to serve all citizens of the state in need of extension services.

The problems confronted during the first one hundred days required attention throughout my tenure. But, by the time my official inauguration occurred on May 29th, it felt like I had been already been at Auburn for a lifetime. The "baptism by fire", however, was just a preview of the fireworks that were to occur throughout my years at Auburn.

PUTTING AU ON
THE RIGHT TRACK

It should be noted that Auburn – both the university and the city – is a special kind of place. The university was founded in 1856 as East Alabama Male College, a school affiliated with the Methodist Church. It struggled during its early years, even closing during the Civil War when the students all left to join the confederate forces. In 1872, the state of Alabama agreed to establish a land grant institution in response to the Morrill Act of 1862 and selected Auburn and the EAMC campus for its site. The school's name initially was Alabama Agricultural and Mechanical College but was changed to Alabama Polytechnic Institute in 1899 to reflect a more technical approach. It was not until 1960 that the name was changed to Auburn University, adopting the name of the town where the school is located.

A defining characteristic of the university is the "Auburn Spirit", a feeling of loyalty and identification that alumni who attended Auburn possess and that new students quickly acquire. It is most visibly exemplified through their support for Auburn's athletic teams, particularly football, but goes much deeper than that. To many individuals it is a love for Auburn, the place and their memories of it.

I regarded this as a great asset of the university and looked for ways to more firmly inculcate it. While at Texas A&M, I had been fascinated by a program called "Fish Camp" that all incoming freshmen had to attend during the summer before their first semester. Fish Camp taught them about the history and traditions of the school and what it meant to be an "Aggie"; it seemed to help produce tremendous spirit in the students. I suggested that we implement something similar at Auburn and what finally emerged was "Camp War Eagle", a summer program for incoming freshmen with objectives parallel to those at A&M. Deborah Shaw, a staff member in student affairs, was largely responsible for establishing and managing this program during its early years. It is still a very important part of new student orientation at Auburn.

I enjoyed my interaction with the students at various gatherings and many unplanned encounters around the campus. I made the president of the SGA a member of the president's cabinet and met with student leaders several times a year. I was always impressed with the individuals that the students elected.

Interactions with alumni were also an integral part of my job. This included meeting with individuals in many different settings as well as speaking at alumni gatherings. The Auburn Alumni Association had many active clubs and I spoke to nearly all of them, some every year, during my years there. Betty DeMent was director of alumni affairs and, subsequently, vice president of alumni and development, and we would often travel together to these functions. The program would normally include a presentation by one of the coaches--the head coach in football at the larger clubs--followed by my remarks. While recognizing that the primary and, likely, most exciting connection that the attendees had was with athletics, I would tell them about the important things that were happening in academics in which they could also take pride.

I attended all the alumni board meetings as an ex-offico member and pushed the association to inaugurate a slick alumni magazine to replace the current tabloid newspaper. Under the editorship of Mike Jerrigan, the <u>Auburn Magazine</u> won numerous awards for its design and content. I got to know many alumni personally, attended all sorts of events – golf outings, tailgates, pep rallies, etc. – and was always buoyed by the enthusiasm and support of the Auburn faithful.

But students and alumni were not the only members of the Auburn "family". The faculty and staff, many of whom were not Auburn graduates, got into the spirit, and even many town folks who had not attended Auburn adopted the school as well. After my first year, a group of faculty, staff, alumni, students and townspeople "inducted" me into the Auburn Family at an "Appreciation Day" in my honor. While the AU family – as all families – sometimes had its quarrels, I was always proud to call myself a member. On the occasion of my first anniversary I was quoted as saying "Auburn is a special kind of place…an institution worth working for, an institution worth fighting for."

And there was certainly much to work for and fight for in the years ahead.

DEALING WITH THE FUNDING PROBLEM

It did not take me long to understand the funding problems at Auburn, but a solution proved much more elusive. As with most public universities, operating funds came from two main sources: state appropriations and student tuition.

State funding was inadequate, inequitable, and inconsistent. The inadequacy was illustrated by a formula for funding higher education that had been developed by the Alabama Council on Higher Education (ACHE), a coordinating agency. It was similar to those in other states, including Ohio. But, whereas Ohio had fully funded the formula each year, except one, while

I was at Akron, Alabama regularly funded the formula at only about the 75% level.

The funding was inequitable because it did not reflect changes in an institution's enrollment or programs offered; instead each school would get the same percentage increase, whenever an increase was provided. As a result, Auburn's appropriation was normally about 65% of what the formula indicated it should receive, while a few of the schools were being funded near to or above the 100% level.

Inconsistency was reflected in the fact that the original state appropriation might be prorated or cut back; moreover, there were years when the appropriations were not increased and once when they were even reduced. This made any kind of long range planning difficult.

Both higher education and K-12 education were funded out of the Alabama Special Education Trust Fund (ASETF) from state sales and income tax receipts. But the federal courts had ordered the state to provide better funding for its public schools and, as a result, higher education's share of appropriations from the fund (which were traditionally about 33%) dipped to 27% during the 1990's. In addition, Alabama's ad valorem (property) taxes, the primary source for funding public schools in most states, were the lowest among the 50 states, placing even more pressure on the ASETF. And, to complicate the situation ever further, Alabama had expanded its system of four-year and two-year institutions beyond what the state's population could justify.

To illustrate the results of this arrangement, in 1995-96 Auburn received approximately $4,900 per student from the state while the University of Georgia and Georgia Tech were each appropriated $7,800 per student. Such disparities made it difficult for us to compete with comparable universities in the region.

When I arrived in 1992, there was an effort underway to achieve "tax reform". This, as I learned, was not the first time such reform had been attempted, but there was some optimism that the present effort might succeed. Alabama's corporate leaders despite ample opposition from farm and timber groups were supporting it. To achieve reforms of the types proposed, amendments to the Alabama Constitution were required. Therefore, along with other university presidents, faculty and business leaders, I went around the state promoting the changes. But, in the end, no action was taken by the Alabama legislature.

Our only recourse was to lobby the legislature each year to get Auburn's share of the pie and/or to protect its interests.

In 1992, Auburn had a full-time director of government relations, Hamilton Wilson, a former head of the Alabama Cattlemen's Association, who was based in Montgomery, the state capitol. When Ham retired about a year later, I appointed Buddy Mitchell to handle this important function. With Buddy's help, I met with the Governor and legislative leaders each year to present our case; I also spent a lot of time with individual members of the legislature. We established offices near the capitol and next door to the University of Alabama System with whom we often cooperated in lobbying for support. The chancellors of the University of Alabama during my years at Auburn (Phil Austin and Tom Meredith) were good friends and responsible partners in this process. We, also, teamed up with all other four-year institutions to form the Higher Education Partnership to lobby for all schools.

But, in the final analysis, about all we were able to do was to "protect our turf" and occasionally make modest gains. There was even a period during the mid-90's, under the Fob James administration, when higher education had to endure a cut of 7.5% in its base budget in one year, followed by two years of no increase in appropriations.

With respect to our other source of revenue -- tuition -- we were able to make significant gains. Dan Large, the VP for business and finance deserves a lot of credit for the changes that we were able to make, particularly in out-of-state tuition. When I came to Auburn, students from out-of-state were able to gain resident status after one year by doing some rather simple things, like getting a local driver's license. Most did, meaning that the university collected out-of-state tuition (which was three times the in-state rate) for only one year. Don and I prepared a proposal to tighten residency requirements and the board approved it.

Some felt that this would result in a significant drop in out-of-state enrollment. But, to the contrary, tuition revenue from non-resident students expanded tremendously. This allowed us to cut the debt service, as a percentage of tuition revenue in half (to 8%) over the next several years, even while issuing additional bonds for new capital construction.

The financial challenges never seemed to end at Auburn, but they became particularly acute during Governor James' administration. As indicated earlier, he cut the universities' budget by 7.5% in his first year and then provided no increased funding for the next two years. To cope with the cut, we offered an Early Retirement Incentive Program (ERIP) to our employees and did not fill the positions vacated unless absolutely necessary. We contracted out student heath services to a private physicians group, thereby saving the cost of operating and staffing a clinic. Under this new arrangement, students either used their parent's insurance policy or subscribed to one that was made available to them. Dr. Bettye Burkhalter, a new vice president for student affairs that I appointed, designed this program and worked hard to put it in place.

HEALING THE FACULTY RELATIONSHIP

It was clear from the beginning that faculty leaders distrusted the administration. So I worked consistently and patiently over the first several years to repair that relationship, attending senate meetings, including faculty leaders in planning sessions, and holding open and frank discussions with the faculty about the problems facing the university.

All of these things, I believe, helped to heal the relationship. But two accomplishments stood out and were highly applauded by the faculty. The first was the removal of Auburn from the AAUP censure list, a distinction that had embarrassed the faculty for many years. I was surprised that many trustees showed little or no concern about this status. Nevertheless, I initiated discussions with the national office of AAUP about how the removal could be effected. Many of the actions I had taken during the first 100 days as well as the increased confidence of the faculty in the leadership I was providing contributed to a more favorable environment.

A highly publicized incident involving tenure also contributed to the favorable response of AAUP. A distinguished professor of history, Wayne Flynt, spoke about the efforts of the Alabama Farmers Federation, perhaps the state's most powerful lobbying group, to hold down property taxes, leading to very poorly funded public schools. The head of AFF called for Dr. Flynt to be fired. I respectfully declined to do so.

The second achievement was the establishment of a Phi Beta Kappa chapter at Auburn. Membership in Phi Beta Kappa is considered the premier recognition for a student's academic achievements. A group of faculty had tried unsuccessfully in the past to get the national office of the society to grant a chapter to Auburn. The major criteria involved the university's academic reputation – e.g. its research, library holdings, quality of entering students, etc. Being on the AAUP censure list, I believe, was also a black mark. I encouraged another application and wrote a strong letter of support. Eventually a Phi Beta Kappa chapter was established and I was rewarded with membership in this prestigious organization.

The thing that I most wanted to do, however, was bring the faculty salaries at Auburn up to the average for major public universities in the South. We did make some progress but the inadequacy and inconsistency of state funding made achieving that goal problematic. I was gratified with the number of distinguished faculty at Auburn who remained at the university in spite of non-competitive salaries. I believe that the environment that I helped to create at Auburn in which faculty were valued and their views considered contributed to that result.

BUILDING THE UNIVERSITY'S REPUTATION

Like many major public universities, particularly in the South, Auburn had considerable national visibility because of its athletic program, primarily in football. But its academic reputation outside the region was not nearly as well known. And even at home there were often negative issues that were prominent.

When I arrived, Auburn seemed to be attracting a lot of bad press. But, it was also providing a lot of material for such stories. With the assistance of Herb White, the director of public relations, I decided to meet the problem head-on and try to turn the perception of Auburn around. I went to every major newspaper in the state, met with its editorial board, and made myself available to its reporters. I emphasized my plans for the future and touted our outstanding academic programs. Over time the press coverage became more positive. A year or so after my arrival, The Birmingham News, the state's largest newspaper, even published an editorial, entitled "Mighty Muse", citing the progressive changes that had been made.

On a national scale, I felt that Auburn was a much better university than its reputation might suggest. It had been named by Money magazine as one of the "Best Values" in higher education, offering an excellent education at a reasonable cost, but was ranked by U.S. News and World Report among the second tier of public universities in terms of its academic standing or reputation.

We began to look at the factors that went into the USNWR rankings and to work toward improving Auburn's performance in those areas. By the end of my second year, the university had been moved up to the "Top Fifty" public universities, USNWR's top tier. Auburn continued to be ranked in that category throughout my presidency, rising as high as 38th on the list. Additionally, AU began to appear in other national rankings as well: as one of the "Most Wired" campuses by Yahoo Internet Life, as one of the top ten "Most Efficient" national universities (USNWR), and as a Top Public University by Kiplinger's Personal Finance Magazine. The publication, The Guide to 101 of the Best Values in America's Colleges and Universities designated Auburn as one of its 34 "National Flagship Universities."

What pleased me most was that individual academic programs had also begun to attract attention on the national stage. Perhaps the best example was the Rural Studio in the School of Architecture. Under the leadership of D.K. Ruth and Samuel "Sambo" Mockbee, the faculty took senior students in architecture to the poorest county in Alabama and gave them the task of designing homes for its poorest citizens, using whatever materials were available. Some beautiful structures were designed and built and the project received numerous national awards. Over the years, the Rural Studio has gotten significant coverage in <u>The New York Times</u> and many other news outlets; it is still operating and bringing positive recognition to the university.

During the mid-90's, with the assistance of Pete Pepinsky, Herb White's successor, Auburn launched an advertising campaign on the major television stations in the state. The ads featured the university's research that helped the state attack its major economic and social problems. It was designed to strengthen Auburn's reputation with the legislature, as well as raise its visibility among potential students. Our research indicated that it did both.

I saw my role as president to be an advocate for and a promoter of the university and its various components. Therefore, in my speeches around the state and across the nation, I cited Auburn's achievements and its future plans consistently. I believe that the university's reputation grew, both with state and national audiences, because of all the promotional efforts undertaken and the positive changes put in place.

DEVELOPING A STRATEGIC PLAN

I believed that one of my most important roles as president was to articulate a vision for the university and develop a strategic plan to guide our efforts. I laid out an initial framework in my inaugural address, calling for Auburn to be true to its land-grant mission but not limited by it; to value diversity; to become increasingly significant internationally; to be more aggressive in seeking private support; and to continue to operate a very strong athletic program but within the context of a top-notch academic institution.

To convert this framework into a plan of action, in July 1992, I appointed a Twenty First Century Commission composed of trustees, administrators, faculty, students and alumni. I chaired the commission and participated in numerous discussions during which all constituencies had ample opportunity to contribute their views; reports were heard from all vice-presidents, deans, and heads of other administrative units.

In March 1997, the Commission presented its recommendations to the Board of Trustees, including a new vision statement, mission statement, and institutional goals in instruction, research, outreach, student enrollment and fiscal support. There were also recommendations for each major segment of the university, including AUM, Auburn's campus in Montgomery. The Commission had met on 17 occasions for nearly 50 hours of formal deliberation.

I was quite pleased with this planning effort, which provided a comprehensive "road map" for the years ahead. Auburn would maintain undergraduate programs of high quality as its primary focus and concentrate its graduate programs and research efforts around centers or peaks of excellence consistent with its existing strengths, the needs of the state, and opportunities for external support.

When I presented the commission's recommendations to the trustees, they were accepted but not without some opposition. It was obvious that some trustees wanted to focus on other issues. Mr. Lowder, who had been off the board for about 18 months wanted to know how we were going to cope with the limited funding. Actually, vice president Large, provost Paul Parks and I had done a lot of work on that issue, following on the heels of the cuts in the state appropriations under Governor James; so we promised to bring such a plan to the next board meeting.

Our funding proposal addressed the goals recommended by the 21st Century Commission with a major focus on bringing faculty salaries up to the Southern Regional Education Board average and increasing spending on deferred maintenance (improvement of facilities) each year. To do so, we laid out a five-year financial plan that called for the elimination of academic programs that did not meet viability standards of the Alabama Commission on Higher Education (ACHE) and for 2% of the budget to be reallocated each year toward the priorities established. We also assumed that state appropriations would be increased by an average of 3% per year and that tuition would be brought up to the average for SREB institutions.

Judging by their reaction, I concluded that the trustees were stunned by the depth and specificity of our planning. Mr. Lowder seemed to be particularly vexed, asserting that he did not feel that this plan went "far enough" and that major cuts in academic programs were needed. Some other trustees felt that the plan to raise tuition to the regional average was unwise. As a result, no action was taken on the proposed plan.

What occurred next represented what I considered to be a major threat to the academic programs of the institution and one that required skill in handing. Mr. Lowder asked me to come to see him the next week, a meeting at which he reasserted that he did not think the Twenty-first Century Commission "had gone far enough". More specifically, he claimed that Auburn had too many academic programs and academic departments and that the relationship between AU and AUM, the campus in Montgomery, needed to be studied. Furthermore, he suggested that I "step aside" and let the trustees handle this reorganization.

I indicated to Mr. Lowder that, while I did not object to these issues being studied, I felt there should be representation from the campus, particularly the faculty, in any discussions. I knew any consideration for dismantling programs or departments would be sensitive matters and should, therefore, be dealt with objectively and openly. The compromise that we reached was a new commission, called the Commission on the Role of the University in the 21st Century (thereafter to be called the "Role Commission"). It would consist of five trustees and five individuals I would appoint from the campus.

At the first meeting of the commission, an effort was made by the trustees to make the sessions private. Major objections by the faculty on the commission to this proposal kept the meetings open.

To respond to the requests of the commission, I formed a group to study all degree programs using objective criteria such as the costs of the program, number of graduates per year, etc., and to recommend which programs should be eliminated or phased out. Another group reviewed proposals for reorganization, such as combining departments or eliminating units. Still another group looked at how the relationship between AU and AUM could be improved.

The recommendations to the Commission were extensive:

(1) Approximately 100 academic programs were recommended for elimination, the bulk of which were majors with very few students where the faculty involved could be used in other areas.

(2) A number of academic departments were combined with a savings of administrative costs. Perhaps the most controversial was the merger of journalism and communications, viewed by many as a slap at journalism because the student newspaper had been very critical of the trustees. However, I felt that such a merger could be done without injuring a strong journalism program.

(3) The nursing programs on the two campuses were combined into one College of Nursing under the dean based at AUM, thereby taking advantage of the greater demand for nurses and the increased opportunities for internships in the Montgomery metropolitan area.

My goal was to comply with the mandate of the trustees, but at the same time, to protect the integrity and viability of the institution. I knew that, if I "stepped aside" and let the trustees do what Mr. Lowder wanted to do that a major fight between the trustees and the faculty would erupt that would have been very destructive to the institution. So, at some cost to myself, I worked hard to achieve a delicate balance in which all the actions taken, except one, met with my approval and major damage to Auburn was avoided. I knew that Auburn was already one of the most efficient major universities in the nation in terms of costs per student. While some of these changes reduced costs, the viable academic programs remained largely intact.

The one action that I disapproved of was the elimination of the Ph.D. program in economics. The program met all criteria for viability and had an excellent reputation. The Program Review Committee recommended that it be retained, the provost did also, and I supported their proposal. But the trustees voted to drop the program. There may have been other reasons for this action but a principal one, I believe, was an effort by Mr. Lowder to retaliate against John Denson, another trustee who had strongly supported the program and who often opposed Lowder.

Over the next three years we tried to implement various components of the strategic plan, including the Peaks of Excellence program. Several programs were selected for emphasis through a vigorous process and were allocated additional funds. But there was never enough funding to fully support the concept. Efforts to raise tuition to the regional average met opposition from the board, limiting the revenue that could be generated from that source.

DEALING WITH ATHLETICS

Athletics, particularly football, generated more fire – both positive and negative – than any other area of Auburn's operations.Anyone not raised in the Deep South might find it difficult to fully understand the importance that people attach to college football. It is discussed year round and produces very intense feelings. One's personal identity is largely formed by where he went to school and/or which team he supports.

I have heard various explanations for the origins of these intense feelings. Some say it is because Alabama has no NFL, NBA, or MLB teams and, therefore, all the sports loyalty is focused on the college teams. Others say that it comes from a feeling in much of the South that they are "looked down upon" by other regions and the realization that the primary means to gain national standing and recognition comes from the success of their football teams. The example most often cited is the national championships in football won by the University of Alabama under Coach Paul "Bear" Bryant during a time when the state was receiving a lot of bad publicity because of racial strife.

For whatever the reasons, a very high percentage of the population is interested and involved in college football. A lot of that interest in Alabama is sparked by the rivalry between Auburn and the University of Alabama. The winner of that big game has "bragging rights" for the next 364 days and the feelings between the fans of the two schools often approach hatred. One legend has it that young boys (and, perhaps, girls too) had to decide who they were going to root for by the fourth grade; therefore, the rivalry was not limited to the alumni of the two schools. Both Auburn and Alabama draw over 85,000 fans for their home games (often on the same day) in a state with a population of only 4 million people.

It was into this environment that I came. As an avid sports fan, I was not unaware of the Auburn-Alabama rivalry and had experienced something similar at Texas A&M. But the atmosphere in Alabama was more intense than anything I had encountered before. I loved the enthusiasm and loyalty of the Auburn fans but also recognized that virtually any conversation about athletics would produce a tidal wave of opinions.

On the day that I was hired, the Auburn Board of Trustees adopted a resolution declaring that the president had full authority and responsibility for athletics, including hiring the athletic director and the head coaches for both football and men's basketball (previously, they had been hired by the board). I welcomed that "clarification", as the NCAA and the Knight Commission were strongly advocating that presidents should have the same authority over athletics that they have over academics. As I was later to learn, however, things don't always function as they are described on paper. But I began to operate on the authority that had been declared. First, I moved quickly to remove Pat Dye as athletic director and brought in Mike Lude to handle that responsibility. Mike performed just as I hoped he would, establishing a clear organizational structure and putting in place the procedures and systems that were vitally needed. He made a number of important personnel decisions, including the hiring of Barbara Camp as associate athletics director and senior women's administrator. Mike and I developed an excellent working relationship, and I believe he performed a very valuable service to Auburn in his two years in this post.

Overall, I enjoyed the "athletic part" of my responsibility, partially because I am a sports fan but mainly because of the Auburn people – the outstanding student-athletes, the excellent coaches, and the enthusiastic and supportive alumni. I tried to let the athletic director run the program just as I let academic administrators manage their areas. This was very difficult in athletics because of the desire of some trustees to be intimately involved in the decision-making.

Marlene and I hosted about 75 people in the president's box at each home football game, a seat that was highly prized. We also attended each home basketball game – men's and women's. I also tried to go to as many baseball games as I could and to attend at least one contest of each sport during the year –both to see what was happening and to let the coaches and athletes know that the administration was interested in them.

I have many great memories of Auburn athletics: the 11-0 football season in 1994, the football bowl games, winning the NCAA national championship in men's swimming twice, the SEC tournaments and the NCAA playoffs in basketball, going to the College World Series twice with the baseball team and being with the wonderful Auburn fans in both victory and defeat. The faculty at Auburn were amazingly supportive of athletes, particularly under the able leadership of Jane Moore and Dennis Wilson as chairs of the Faculty Committee on Athletics.

I also enjoyed my work with the other presidents in the Southeastern Conference and with our commissioner, Roy Kramer. My work included a term as president of the SEC. Under Kramer's leadership, the SEC emerged as one of the premier athletic conferences in the country.

Over the course of my years at Auburn, there were several key decisions, in addition to those earlier described, that required considerable time. They were:

(1)   The Resignation of Coach Dye as Football Coach

As the 1992 football season played out, it was clear that Pat Dye was going to have another "unsuccessful" year, by the standards expected at Auburn. After wining four consecutive SEC championships in the 1980's, Auburn had gone 5-6 in 1991 and was headed to an eventual 5-5-1 record in 1992. In addition, I became increasingly concerned about what was being revealed by the NCAA investigation. Clearly, Auburn was guilty of NCAA violations; and, although there was limited evidence that Dye was personally involved in the transgressions, it would have been hard for him, as both coach and AD, not know what was going on. So Mike Lude and I became convinced that action – removing Dye as coach – needed to be undertaken at the end of the season.

While we were waiting for the season to end, some members of the Board of Trustees acted unilaterally. On Monday of the week preceding the season-ending game with Alabama on Thanksgiving Day – the Iron Bowl in

Birmingham – I was attending a meeting in Birmingham when I got a call from Dr. Gerald Leischuck, who was secretary to the Board of Trustees. He informed me that Mike McCartney, the president pro temp of the board, and Bobby Lowder, the chairman of the board's athletic committee had met with Coach Dye and had asked him to resign. They wanted to know if I was in agreement; I indicated that I was.

While I was relieved that the trustees had taken the preemptive action – in that I had anticipated that Dye might be difficult to deal with – I was also conscious that this had taken place without my involvement or even consultation and that the policy adopted by the board was of little value. I contacted Mike Lude to let him know the news. Then negotiations were begun with Dye's attorney, Sam Franklin, about the terms of the resignation. Dye was to announce to the team his intentions right before the game on Thursday, hoping to motivate the team, and then to make a public statement following the game. However, by the time we met with Coach Dye to finalize the agreement on Wednesday night at the Sheraton Hotel in Birmingham, the news had leaked (Dye had told his assistant coaches) and the press was converging on the hotel.

Auburn called a press conference for ten o'clock that evening at the hotel and, when I arrived, the room and hallway were packed with reporters – every major newspaper in the state and all the television stations. The press conference was carried live by each of the network TV stations on their ten o'clock news. After making a statement confirming the rumors of Dye's resignation, I answered numerous questions about the search for a new coach.

Following the game, which Auburn lost, Marlene and I took off for the beach, trying to capture a few days of peace and quiet over the Thanksgiving holidays. I asked Mike Lude to begin to compile a list of possible candidates for coach that we could review on Monday. But I got a call from Dr. Leischuck on the day after Thanksgiving, informing me that McCartney and Lowder were very upset about the names of possible coaches that were surfacing and that I was not do to anything until I conferred with them. According to Mr. McCartney, "hiring the right football coach at Auburn was not a matter of life and death; it was more important than that!"

(2) The Hiring of Terry Bowden

When I arrived back on campus, I was summoned to a meeting with Mr. McCartney at his business in Gadsden. I proceeded to tell him what I planned to do – form a search committee with myself as chairman and including three trustees (McCartney, Lowder, and Charles Glover), the athletic director, the student government president, the chair of the Faculty Committee on Athletics, a representative of the Alumni Association, and a former student athlete. Then I was going to have the athletic director present candidates for our review.

Mike Lude did a great job of contacting people around the country and came up with an impressive list of possible candidates, including many head coaches of major schools. I asked him to add Terry Bowden to the list. Terry had been an assistant coach to Gerry Faust at Akron while I was there before he went to Samford, a I-AA school in Birmingham, and compiled an excellent record. I didn't know if Terry was ready to move to "the big time" but I felt he was going to be a great head coach and wanted to give him consideration.

When the search committee met, Mike presented a list of about twenty candidates. We eventually selected six head coaches for interviews, including (to my surprise) Terry Bowden. Mike contacted the candidates and we proceeded to interview them individually over a two-day period at a hotel near the airport in Atlanta. The location was kept private in order to protect the identity of the candidates.

While we were in Atlanta, Mr. McCartney approached me about adding Wayne Hall, an assistant coach and defensive coordinator under Pat Dye at Auburn, to the interview list. He argued that he and Mr. Lowder felt we ought to have at least one inside candidate. I talked to Mike Lude about this and we were both uneasy. Although Hall was an excellent coach, there were too many implications in the NCAA investigation that was underway that Wayne might be involved in the violations. But I reluctantly agreed, figuring that we had several candidates who would overshadow Hall.

As it turned out, Bowden was the candidate that stood out above all the rest. He was enthusiastic, articulate, and well prepared, with excellent answers to all the questions. Following the interviews, we took a break for lunch and then reconvened to see if we could reach a conclusion. During the break, Lude and I conferred. We both felt that Bowden was the best choice but we were convinced that McCartney and Lowder would push for Wayne Hall.

Before I reopened the meeting, McCartney whispered to me that he "was impressed with Bowden and thought he would be a good choice." I was not sure what had precipitated this conclusion, but I was delighted to hear it. I indicated that I would give each committee member the opportunity to express his/her opinion and, then, we would vote and started with McCartney. To my surprise, every member of the committee, including Lowder, said that Bowden was his or her choice. So the vote was unanimous. I, then, asked Mike Lude to contact Terry and, assuming he accepted the offer, to arrange for a press conference in Auburn the next morning at 11:00 a.m.

As I was preparing to leave Atlanta, McCartney informed me that it would be necessary to "clear this appointment" with the athletic committee of the board. I expressed concern about the logistics of doing that within the short time span we had, but he told me not to worry about that – that Lowder, as chairman of the committee, would have everyone at a conference room at AUM at 9:00 a.m. the next morning. I needed to make sure Terry was present and that this could be done before the press conference.

I showed up there the next morning to find Terry and the committee already there. The meeting went very smoothly, with the committee seemingly very enthusiastic about Terry. Terry and I, then, arranged to meet Mike Lude in Auburn for the press conference.

The reaction of the press and of the Auburn fans was one of surprise and, to an overwhelming degree, negative. I received over 400 letters and emails (I quit counting at that point!) about the appointment and at least 75% of them were negative. Fans thought Auburn should have hired a "big-name" coach from a major school and I was the person to blame for this mistake. But I was still convinced that we made the right decision.

What I was to learn over the next few days, however, about Lowder's involvement did trouble me. It was reported to me that Lowder had met Bowden through his daughter who worked for Terry at Samford, that he contacted Terry while we were in Atlanta and told him what questions to be prepared for during the interview, and that he called Terry before Mike Lude could contact him to tell him he had the job. Furthermore, he invited Terry and his wife to spend the night with him and his wife in Montgomery before the press conference. All of this served to convince Terry that he got the job because of Lowder. I was never able to disabuse Terry of this notion. In spite of my assertations that he had unanimous support of the committee and had won the job on his own merits, he always believed that he owed this job to Lowder. And that perception affected his actions throughout his tenure as coach.

Another interesting aspect of the appointment of Bowden is that I continued to receive a lot of criticism for the decision – that is until Bowden went 11-0 in his first season. But it was at this juncture that Lowder, through an interview with a sports columnist, let it be known that it was really he who had attracted Bowden to Auburn.

(3) NCAA Probation

While these changes were occurring, the NCAA investigation was being completed. There was clear evidence that Eric Ramsey had received cash and other illegal benefits. It was hard to believe that Ramsey was an isolated case, but none of the other athletes interviewed would admit receiving payments. We knew, however, that the NCAA needed only one transgression to find Auburn guilty. I was just hopeful that the changes we had made in the leadership positions of athletic director and head coach would persuade the association to be more lenient.

Our hearing before the NCAA Infractions Committee was scheduled for late spring, 1993 in Kansas City. I asked Terry Bowden to attend, even though he was not involved, because I wanted him to see what happened when NCAA rules were broken. Mike Lude and I represented Auburn along with John Scott, our attorney. The hearing went two full days. There was little doubt as to the verdict; the only question was the nature of the penalty. That decision was not forthcoming until late in the summer.

When notice from the NCAA arrived, we learned that the major penalties were a two-year ban on post-season competition and a one-year ban on television coverage for the football team. The television ban required some quick changes as Auburn had several games already booked for TV coverage. Because we anticipated a rebuilding year under a new coach, the TV ban did not appear to be that hurtful, but the ineligibility to participate in the distribution of conference revenue from TV and post-season bowls would be difficult to handle and would injure the whole program.

To everyone's surprise, the Tigers under Terry went undefeated in 1993 and became the team everyone wanted to see but couldn't because of the TV ban. Auburn's opponents were also hurt by this ban. In the final game against Alabama in Auburn, the campus police told me there were at least 25,000 fans there who could not get a ticket but just wanted to be near the action. This is the last case where the NCAA has used a TV ban as a part of the penalty for rule violations.

With a new athletic director, a new coach, and the uncertainty of the NCAA investigation behind us, I thought that Auburn was ready for a fresh start and a brighter future. But I also knew that any additional violations in the football program would subject Auburn to the "Death Penalty" by the NCAA – the cancellation of the program for a period of time, such as what occurred at SMU. I was determined not to let that catastrophe happen at Auburn.

(4) Trustees Involvement in Athletics

Before my first year at Auburn was completed, I was convinced that the trustee's resolution on the day I was hired was meaningless. A subgroup of the board – specifically, the athletics committee – had firm control of athletics and did not plan to relinquish it.

The athletics committee was an official committee of the board but it never "officially" met – that is, its meetings were not announced or open to others and no minutes were kept. But it met on a regular basis, usually every couple of months or more frequently if needed. The chairman of the committee was always Bobby Lowder with the other four members being those who were close to him and most interested in sports. The meetings were held off campus, often in a conference room at AUM near the chancellor's office.

At first, I thought these meetings were intended to keep the trustees informed about athletics but quickly learned that the committee expected all major decisions to be brought to them for approval. Each meeting consisted of a detailed review of operations and specific conclusions as to the actions to be taken. Arrangements for the meetings were made between Mr. Lowder and Gerald Leischuck, the secretary to the board and my executive assistant, with the athletic director and I being requested to attend. Most of the conversation was between the trustees and the athletic director; my input, it seemed, was tolerated but not essential. I decided to go along with this arrangement because I was convinced that the committee would meet without me if I objected. I thought that it was important to "stay on top of" what was happening in athletics to prevent the reoccurrence of NCAA violations.

I surmised that Lowder had probably been the "unofficial" athletic director during the time Pat Dye held that post, since Pat seemed to have little interest in the administrative aspects of the job. Initially, I found this hard to believe. Lowder was the CEO of the Colonial Bank, a multi-bank holding company with many other enterprises, and would not have seemed to have the time to devote to this task. But he had few other outside interests and was not involved in civic leadership in Montgomery where the bank was headquartered. He had every intention of keeping a firm grasp on this activity, because football was one of the most important activities in the state.

Mike Lude was equally appalled by the role that the athletic committee and Lowder played but we resolved to work through it as best we could. Lowder approached Mike after Mike had been on the job for a while and invited him to counsel directly with him. Mike informed Lowder that he reported to the president and that he did not think that would be a good idea. This led to subsequent efforts to undermine Mike and to put pressure on me to "get rid of him." But I had made a commitment to Mike for two years and felt that his leadership of the department during this critical time was essential.

(5) Hiring of David Housel as Athletic Director

As Mike neared the end of this two year term, I began to think about the search for a replacement. Given the situation at Auburn, I was uncomfortable about bringing someone in from the outside and concluded that David Housel, the longtime sports information director at Auburn, was the best man for the job. SID's don't normally become AD's, but David was a special case. He was probably the best known individual in Auburn athletics, was adept at handling public relations, and was much-loved by the Auburn people. More importantly to me, I believed he was a man of integrity who would not agree to anything that might damage the institution. Furthermore, Terry Windle, a CPA and excellent financial manager, had been appointed associate athletic director and could handle that area which was not David's strength.

Given the "way of doing things" at Auburn, I knew that I had to discuss this appointment with Lowder, which I did. He was in agreement, which pleased me. But I also realized that he would likely contact David to inform him that he was his choice to serve as A.D. in order to establish a dependency or obligatory relationship that he seemed to desire. I, then, met with a search committee I had appointed and got their concurrence on David's appointment, which was well-received by the Auburn family and around the state.

David and I developed an excellent working relationship. I had a lot of respect for him and trusted him to do the right thing. Knowing that some trustees, particularly Lowder, would approach him directly, I told David to listen to them, to find out what they wanted him to do, but not to take any action until he consulted with me. To my knowledge, he always did so. And the athletic department, under David's leadership, had some of its most successful years in terms of athletic victories, facilities improvements and financial stability.

(6) <u>Changing of Basketball Coaches</u>

Basketball clearly played "second fiddle" to football at Auburn. Interestingly, the women's program, under Coach Joe Ciampi, had been consistently good, winning SEC championships and playing for the national championship on two occasions. By contrast, the men's program had a brief period of success under Coach Sonny Smith but had experienced few other winning seasons.

The men's basketball coach at the time I arrived was Tommy Joe Eagles. He seemed to be popular with the fans – the few that there were – was a good recruiter, and seemed to be developing a stronger program. In my third year at Auburn, Eagles was in the last year of a four year contract. In that year, he had an excellent record – by Auburn standards – finishing with a 15-12 record and playing in the post-season NIT. He also had most of his starters returning for the next season.

As the season was ending, I was summoned to a meeting of the athletic committee where they "decided" not to review Eagles' contract. I don't remember being asked for input on the issue. So I met with Eagles on two occasions. He pleaded with me to give him another chance, particularly with the players he had coming back. The more we talked the more I became convinced that that was the right thing to do. So I negotiated a two-year extension with him. Then I informed Jimmy Samford, who was president pro temp of the board at that time and a member of the athletic committee, what I was going to do. Lowder called me and told me that was not how "we did things" at Auburn and that I would regret that decision. But I went ahead with the appointment.

This story did not have a happy ending. The next season turned out not to be the success that Tommy Joe and I predicted. In spite of a lot of talent, including one player (Wesley Person) who played a number of years in the NBA, the Tigers had a losing season. Eagles was appropriately apologetic and accepting when I dismissed him at the end of the season. But I thought enough of him as a man and as a coach to help him land the head-coaching job at The University of New Orleans. Unfortunately, Tommy Joe suffered a heart attack and died in his first month on the job. Although retaining Eagles created discomfort with Lowder and the athletic committee, I never regretted the decision to give Tommy Joe the extension. I still feel it was the right thing to do.

The search for a new basketball coach involved an interesting turn of events. In contrast with the search for the football coach, I took a less active role. David Housel, the athletic director, began the process of identifying candidates and I appointed a search committee, headed by trustee Jimmy Samford, to recommend an appointee. The committee subsequently recommended Mike Brey, who was at that time an assistant coach at Duke. We brought Brey and his wife to Auburn for a private visit that included a small dinner party at the president's house. I made sure that among the guests were Bobby Lowder and his wife, figuring that Lowder's interaction with the candidate would be a critical step in the process.

Brey indicated that he was interested in the job but wanted to wait until after the Final Four weekend to announce his decision. The next week I was at North Carolina State as a member of a Peer-Review Term of the Southern Association of Colleges and Schools (SACS) and invited Brey to meet with me at the hotel where I was staying. I took a draft copy of a contract we had prepared and discussed the terms with him. He was in total agreement and very enthusiastic about coming to Auburn. We concurred that he would fly to Auburn the day after the national championship game for a press conference announcing his appointment.

By the time I had arrived back in Auburn a couple of days later, however, Brey had left a message with Housel's office that he was withdrawing. Efforts to reach Brey were unsuccessful and a brief telephone conversation with his wife revealed that she was upset and uninformed about the decision. What happened is a mystery to me. Some felt that

Lowder got someone to call Brey, letting him know that he was not wanted and could not be successful at Auburn.

Whatever the reasons for Brey's withdrawal, we were suddenly back in the market for a coach. Lowder came forward quickly to suggest that Cliff Ellis, who was the head coach at Clemson, would be an excellent choice. Ellis had a winning record at Clemson, although there were rumors of a possible NCAA investigation because of rule violations. Nevertheless, I agreed to an interview with Ellis and instructed Housel to find out what he could about the situation at Clemson. He reported that, while there might be violations at Clemson, there was no evidence that Ellis was directly involved. So a deal was quickly cut with Ellis and the new basketball coach announced.

I learned later that Lowder had known Ellis when Cliff was coach at the University of South Alabama and, in fact, Ellis had served as a director of Lowder's bank there, so their relationship went back quite some time. And, from the beginning, Ellis behaved as though Lowden was his benefactor. However, I must admit that Ellis was an excellent coach. Auburn won the SEC championship during his tenure and went to the Sweet Sixteen in the NCAA playoffs twice. But, after my departure from Auburn, Ellis eventually fell into disfavor with Lowder and was dismissed.

Brey, in the meantime, took the head coaching job at the University of Delaware, building a strong winning program there. He subsequently moved on to Notre Dame where he has had a consistently winning record.

(7) The Departure of Bowden

The event at Auburn during my tenure that created the greatest attention and turmoil was the abrupt departure of Terry Bowden. After winning twenty straight games in his first two seasons (but not able to go to a bowl game because of the NCAA probation), Terry's Tigers had three winning seasons, including a bowl game after each – the Outback Bowl against Penn State in 1995, the Independence Bowl against Army in 1996, and the Peach Bowl against Clemson in 1997.

During these years, Bowden had maintained a close relationship with Lowder. Lowder's daughter continued to work for Terry on a personal basis and Lowder's bank provided the financing for a house that was bought for Bowden in Auburn by the Alumni Association. But a crack in that relationship seemed to develop when Terry fired Wayne Hall, the defensive coordinator and long-time Lowder associate. He brought in Bill Oliver, a former defensive coordinator at Alabama, to replace him.

The 1998 season did not get off to a good start. Many reasons were suggested – a new inexperienced quarterback, some key injuries, the failure of some athletes to meet academic requirements, etc. For whatever the reasons, the Tigers had an uncustomary 1-5 record going into the Homecoming game with Louisiana Tech. But, while all Auburn fans were disappointed in the record, I had encountered no one who was calling for Bowden's ouster. In fact, because of Terry's past record and enthusiastic personality, he was still quite popular with the Auburn alums I met.

On Monday of the week before the Homecoming game, however, a columnist in a Huntsville paper reported that an "unnamed source" at Auburn said that Bowden would be fired at the end of the season. I did not see that story but Terry did. He came to David Housel on Tuesday, wanting to know who the source was. Housel, either in that conversation or a subsequent one, informed Terry that the source was Lowder. On Wednesday, Bowden came to Housel and told him that he wanted to resign immediately and that his attorney would be in touch with David to negotiate the termination of the contract. David immediately contacted me to tell me what happened. I was en route from Birmingham to Auburn after a luncheon speaking engagement.

When I got back to Auburn, I began trying to reach Terry. He had gone to practice with the team and then disappeared. I left messages for him at home and his office that I wanted to talk to him. Finally, about ten o'clock that night, Terry called me at home. He described what he had found out, concluding that "Lowder had hired him and he could fire him" and, therefore, he should leave. I tried to persuade him that, while the current season was a disappointment to me and to everyone else, I thought he still had a chance to salvage a winning season and that, furthermore, I thought he had the ability to win consistently at Auburn. Furthermore, I emphasized that no individual trustee, including Lowder, had the authority to fire him; admittedly, the trustees as a whole, in a public meeting, could do so, but I didn't think that would occur.

On Thursday, Terry came in to Housel and told him he was staying. Bowden ran the team practice that afternoon and appeared on his weekly radio show that evening, sounding very upbeat and enthusiastic about the upcoming game. But something happened between then and Friday morning. I believe that Terry had further conversations with Lowder or with someone representing Lowder. In any case, by Friday morning Bowden reported to Housel that he was "outta here" and David spent a good part of that day negotiating with Terry's attorney, and deciding who was going to coach the team the next day.

On Saturday morning, we held a press conference at the stadium to announce Terry's departure and Bill Oliver's appointment as head coach on an interim basis. The Auburn community and the sports world generally were shocked by the news they received, as one might expect, in extensive coverage. One of the topics that provoked much comment, both immediately and in the weeks that followed, was Lowder's involvement in this matter. This was unusual as Lowder normally worked "behind the scenes" and was rarely identified as the individual who "pulled the trigger" or was involved in a major way. The reaction of most people was negative toward one individual exercising that much power. This included much of the press, particularly the student newspaper.

In spite of all the turmoil, the Auburn Tigers won the Homecoming game and went on to win one more game under coach Oliver to finish with a 3-8 record. Toward the end of the season, I asked David Housel to begin the search for a newhead coach.

(8) <u>The Hiring of Tuberville</u>

In the early days of the search conducted by Housel, he expressed to me a preference that Oliver be named the coach. But, then, he uncovered damaging personal information about Oliver that led him to change his opinion. We talked about Tommy Tuberville, admiring the job he had done at Ole Miss and agreed to contact him as soon as the season was over. The day after Ole Miss' last game, Tommy flew to Auburn for an interview and was offered the job.

I do not know if there were any discussions with Tuberville involving Lowder or any other trustee prior to the campus visit. I only know that Tommy acted in the beginning as though he was "his own man" and continued to exhibit that attitude as long as I was there. He developed a program at Auburn that is consistently competitive and is often ranked in the top ten.

CONCLUSIONS

Although the work with football and basketball dominated my time and the press coverage, I admired greatly the work of some of the coaches in other sports, namely: David Marsh, perhaps the best swimming coach in the nation, who won two national championships while I was there and who won many others after I departed; Hal Baird, the baseball coach, who had consistently strong teams, including two trips to the College World Series; and Joe Ciampi, the women's basketball coach, who was one of the best in the nation, consistently making the NCAA tournament and once making it to the Elite Eight during my tenure.

Most of all I will remember the Auburn fans for their undying loyalty and love for the university and its teams and the outstanding young men and women who represented Auburn in athletics.

While there was always a lot of competitive "fire" and fiery disagreements involving athletics, there was one actual fire that should be mentioned because it was covered live on national television. It happened on a lovely Saturday night, September 21, 1996, when Auburn played LSU in Jordan Hare Stadium.

It is hard for one who has never attended an Auburn football game to fully comprehend the scene. The stadium sits in the middle of the campus with totally inadequate parking for the 85,000 or so fans who attend. So the fans park anywhere and everywhere they can, arriving early to get a prime spot, and having full-scale tailgates while they wait for the game. On the night in question, the campus was totally covered with tailgaters, including several around the old gym near the south end zone of the stadium. This building which once housed the arena for the basketball teams was now used for faculty offices, storage and various other purposes.

There was a rain shower about an hour before game time, forcing the tailgaters to find cover. Some near the old gym apparently moved their grills under an overhang at one end and left them there when they set off for the stadium, with at least one of the grills not completely extinguished. From this source a fire started and, midway through the second quarter of the game, flames could be seen rising above the stadium and, on television, appeared to be lapping at its side. Fortunately, the wind was blowing away from the stadium; so there was little threat that the fire would spread that far.

Jim Ferguson, my vice president who had responsibilities for the campus police and facilities, reported to me immediately and gave me his assessment of the situation. I came out of the president's box to see first hand what was happening. Our greatest fear was that panic would erupt in the stadium with an attempted evacuation. With the campus locked in with cars and people like it was, that would have been a disaster. But, fortunately, the fans were much more interested in the battle on the field than the fire outside. To my knowledge, no one left the stadium! And, with Ferguson's coordination, we were able to control the fire and prevent major disruptions.

THE ROLE AND FUNCTIONING OF THE BOARD OF TRUSTEES

There was no group at Auburn that produced as much heartburn for me nor as much fodder for controversy as the Board of Trustees. Primarily a few individuals created these conditions but their influence was sufficient to create major distractions that eventually led to my departure.

At the time I came to Auburn, the Board of Trustees was comprised of ten individuals appointed by the Governor with confirmation by the Senate, one from each congressional district plus an additional appointee from the district in which Auburn is located; the Governor who was chairman of the board; The State Superintendent of Education; and the Auburn Student Government Association President as an ex-offico, non-voting member. The ten appointed members served for twelve-year terms with no limit on the number of terms they could serve. The Governor rarely attended meetings, therefore, the board elected a president pro tempore who presided at the meetings.

I did not know much about the board when I took the job, yet despite some nervous moments about the process for my appointment, I felt I could work effectively with them. This attitude stemmed not only from a confidence in my own ability but also from my experience at Akron, where I had worked with a board that went from almost totally Republican to totally Democratic during my tenure and was, moreover, very diverse in terms of gender and race.

But I failed to grasp two important differences: (a) the importance of athletics at Auburn to many of the trustees and their desire to control its operations and (b) the willingness on the part of the individual trustees to exercise their perceived authority. The structure and authority of the Auburn board is spelled out in the constitution of the State of Alabama. The powers given to the board are enormous; the board can make practically any decision concerning the university that it desires. But a key factor is that the board can only make decisions when it is represented by a quorum and is meeting in a public session. An individual trustee has no authority.

This was not an issue at Akron. The trustees left the day-to-day operations up to the president, requiring regular reports on operations and progress toward goals. Any effort on the part of an individual trustee to move from oversight to involvement in operational decisions was quickly dealt with by the chairman. But, as I was to learn, at Auburn it was a totally different ballgame.

A lot of the issues involving the trustees at Auburn concerned athletics. The board met five to six times a year, with one of the meetings being at the Montgomery campus. Each meeting required a lot of preparation. Dr. Gerald Leischuck, who served as secretary to the board and as executive assistant to the president, was very helpful to me during my early years at Auburn as he knew the board members well and was skillful at putting together the agenda materials.

I had very few problems in working with the board as a whole. Every proposal that I brought forward was eventually approved, although some items such as a tuition increase might require two or more meetings to produce agreement and sometimes issues were tabled and then brought back with revised provisions. I can recall only one matter that was approved by the board over my objection and that was the discontinuance of the Ph.D. program in economics.

Additionally, I had good relationships with many individual trustees for whom I had a great deal of admiration, including: Emory Cunningham, a former CEO of Southern Progress Corporation; John Denson, an attorney from Opelika who later became a District Judge; Jim Tatum, an attorney from Huntsville; Jack Venable, a newspaper publisher from Tallassee and a member of the state legislature; Charlie Glover, a businessman from Cullman; Besse Mae Hollaway, a retired school administrator from Mobile; and Wayne Teague, a State Superintendent of Education. The two trustees with whom I had the most difficult working relationship were Bobby Lowder, the banker from Montgomery, and Lowell Barron, the president pro tempore of the Alabama Senate. In most states, a member of the state legislature is not permitted to serve on a public university board, this being considered a conflict of interest since the legislature makes decisions about funding for the university. But that was not regarded as a conflict of interest in Alabama.

As I had done in Akron, I tried to keep the board well informed about operations of the university. About every two weeks I would send board members a report called "Memo to the Board" that described things that had occurred as well as matters that were being discussed. I used this venue to provide background information on proposals that would be coming to the board for approval and to let them know about the activities in which I was involved. Furthermore, I took every opportunity to visit with board members one-on-one in order to get to know them better.

It did not take me long to realize that Lowder was the key player on the board. One would not have readily observed that by attending board meetings; Lowder rarely made a motion or spoke more than anyone else at these public sessions. His influence was wielded outside board meetings in two ways: a) first, by talking with other board members with whom he had influence and having them present and/or support the measures he wanted to see pass or held up and b) secondly, by insuring that the president pro-tem was a person who would carry out his requests.

When I went to Auburn, Mike McCartney, who owned a company engaged in highway construction in Gadsden, was the president pro-temp. Interestingly enough, Mike came to me during my first few weeks on the job to tell me that he was "independent" – i.e. not under the influence of Lowder. But my observations and experiences over the next several months did not confirm that assertion. In later years, Jimmy Samford served as president pro-tem. Jimmy was a very likable individual who was a descendent of a family that had long been associated with Auburn; he was a lawyer/lobbyist in Montgomery who had Colonial Bank as one of his clients and whose office was in the Colonial Bank building. While easy to deal with, Jimmy, in my opinion, made very few decisions without consulting with Lowder. There was a brief period when Emory Cunningham served as president pro-tem, but that was a very unusual situation.

During my initial years at Auburn, I worked hard to cultivate a good relationship with the board in order to get the approvals that were needed. I even traveled to Montgomery on several occasions to meet with Lowder privately. Unlike other board members, Lowder never came to see me. And, in most cases, he only spoke with me at his request. For example, he would call Gerald Leischuck in my office and have him tell me to call him. This, perhaps, gave Lowder a psychological advantage as I was always "coming to him" and he was in control of the conversation, but I just accepted that as a condition of doing business with him. He always, it seemed, wanted to be in control. In spite of this, I did not dislike Lowder. I tried to find out what he wanted and tried to recognize those wishes in any proposals or plans that were being developed. But he never seemed to be open with me; rather the attitude that I detected seemed to emerge from his feelings that I was not his choice as president and that he would work with me only to the extent it was necessary to get what he wanted.

During the first couple of years when I was dealing with many significant challenges and resolving them effectively, I received almost no feedback from the board as a whole, either publicly or privately, although individual board members, like Cunningham and Denson, gave me compliments and encouragement. During my second year, I had a private session with the board at which I provided detailed information as to the progress I felt had been made in five areas: improved relationships with the faculty, enhanced diversity of enrollment and employment, strengthened finances, greater private support, and resolving major issues with athletics. Then, I expressed my concern about the lack of feedback from the board and called for their cooperation in establishing a set of goals we could all work toward. I also described my concern about the level of involvement by some board members in managerial decisions.

Although I was very straightforward in laying out my thoughts and concerns, the conversation was mostly one-way. I got very little reaction from the board. So I did what I concluded was the only thing I could do: I continued to manage the operations of the university as I felt a CEO should, bringing matters to the board that required their approval, and working through the situations – mainly in athletics – where board members were involved to ensure that the best interests of the university were achieved.

The big change in board relations occurred in 1995, triggered by the expiration of Lowder's term on the board in January. This was preceded by a gubernatorial election in the fall, 1994. The candidate who was elected, Fob James, was an Auburn graduate and a former football star for the Tigers. He had served a previous term as Governor as a Democrat, but ran this time as a

Republican. James allegedly told several Auburn alums that he did not plan to reappoint Lowder to the board.

The provisions in the state constitution provided that an Auburn Trustee would continue to hold his appointment until the Governor had named his successor and until that person had been confirmed by the State Senate. So Lowder, pending action by the Governor, continued to serve beyond the expiration of his term. Finally, in September, 1995, the Governor appointed Phil Richardson, a businessman in Montgomery, to fill Lowder's seat. By that time, however, an effort to forestall confirmation by the Senate had been effected, reportedly aided by political contributions and assistance from Senator Barron, who had replaced Mike McCartney on the board. The plan was for the Governor's appointments not to be acted upon by the Senate Confirmations Committee, comprised of five senators. Several months passed with Lowder continuing to serve on the board, along with Jim Tatum whose term had also expired.

Finally, the Governor's patience ran thin. He called a special Board of Trustees meeting in Auburn and what was to follow was "grand theatre" at its best. Arriving at the meeting with two State Troopers in tow, the Governor assumed the chairmanship of the meeting and indicated he was removing Lowder and Tatum from the board under a legal opinion he had obtained that an appointee could not occupy a position beyond a "reasonable time" after the expiration of his term. He, then, installed his appointees on the board. Lowder and Tatum left the meeting with Lowder being obviously agitated by the Governor's actions.

The Governor's appointees began to serve, even though the Senate had not and never did confirm their appointments. Emory Cunningham was elected president pro tem and provided a totally different style of leadership. He was very open about issues coming before the board, wanting to know what was in the best interests of the university. He also challenged me to look at how Auburn could best impact the state economically and culturally. I met with him prior to each board meeting to review the agenda and was always encouraged by his insightful questions and supportive comments. It was interesting also that, with Lowder off the board, the tenor of board meetings and the work of the body was entirely different – much less divisive. It was, without a doubt, the most satisfying period for me at Auburn in terms of board relations.

It was during this juncture, also, that Gerald Leischuck retired as secretary to the board. I nominated Lynne Hammond, a member of my staff, to assume those responsibilities and the board approved her. From my past experience, I had learned that the position of secretary to the board can be problematic, unless that individual reports to the president and performs his/her duties –

preparing the agenda, taking and publishing minutes, communicating with the board, etc. – under the president's supervision. In most universities, the board secretary has other responsibilities as well. If the individual reports to the board, he/she is likely to feel, inevitably, that they are "above" the President; if he/she reports to both, there will be many awkward moments when the secretary is "caught in between" the president and the board. Ms. Hammond performed these duties in an exemplary fashion, as a member of my staff, over the next several years.

But Lowder did not take his removal from the board "lying down". Instead, he began to work to overturn the Governor's action. He filed suit in state court, claiming the Governor had overstepped his authority. And, he became a strong supporter of Don Siegelman who had emerged as the Democratic candidate to oppose James in the 1998 election. In fact, according to published reports, Lowder was the largest individual contributor to Siegelman's campaign.

As it turned out, Siegelman won the election and Lowder won his law suit. After losing in the district courts, Lowder appealed the case to the State Supreme Court and won a decision by a 5-4 margin and was reinstated to the board. And, when Siegelman was installed as Governor, he appointed Lowder to another full twelve-year term as trustee. Furthermore, it appeared as though the Governor gave Lowder considerable influence in filling the vacancies that occurred on the board. The terms of three trustees not aligned with Lowder (Cunningham, Denson, and Hollaway) expired and were replaced by individuals who had a business and/or personal relationship with Lowder. This gave him effective control of the board.

Lowell Barron came on the board in 1994 to replace Mike McCartney. A non-practicing pharmacist from the Sand Mountain area of Alabama, Barron had found his niche in the State Senate, rising to the role of president pro tem. As with most politicians, Lowell was very outgoing and easy to get along with as long as his interests were being addressed. My primary concerns with Barron were the many real or potential conflicts of interest in which he was involved. He was appointed by the board as chair of the property and facilities committee that oversaw the awarding of contracts for architects and for capital construction on the campus. Selection of architects was very competitive with the firms often lobbying heavily for their appointment. Additionally, a firm headed by Barron's son got contracts for supplying the windows for all the dorms in a complex that was being remodeled. The contracts were competitively bid and Barron's firm had the low bid, but the situation still left me uneasy.

But my relationship with Barron deteriorated primarily over two personnel matters. The first involved the appointment of a new vice president for outreach to administer Auburn's many off-campus projects. The leading candidate from the search was David Wilson, an African-American who had grown up in Alabama, graduated from Tuskegee, received a doctorate from Harvard, and was currently at Rutgers. Lowell lobbied hard with me against hiring Wilson, but both the search committee and I were impressed with him and felt he was the best man for the job; so I made the appointment, as the president had the authority to fill all positions without board approval, except for the chancellor at AUM and the provost at the Auburn campus. Wilson did a great job for Auburn, developing programs that gained national attention, particularly those that were directed toward the Black Belt, the state's most poverty-stricken area. He later went on to serve as chancellor of the state universities within the University of Wisconsin system.

The second case involved the chancellor of the Auburn University-Montgomery campus. AUM's role in the university was to serve the needs of students in the Montgomery area. Most students commuted to the campus, although there was one dormitory on campus and some apartments available nearby. The campus had been built northeast of Montgomery, just off I-85 toward Auburn. AUM was separately accredited by the Southern Association and by disciplinary groups, offering both bachelors and masters degrees as well as cooperating with the Auburn campus on some doctoral programs. The chancellor served as CEO of the campus and reported to me.

I believed that AUM was an important part of Auburn and visited the campus often to attend events and to talk with the leadership. Jim Williams, a long-time university employee, was chancellor when I arrived and managed the affairs of the campus efficiently. The Board to Trustees paid limited attention to AUM and there were few agenda items from the campus that came up for approval.

When chancellor Williams retired in 1994, a search was conducted to find his replacement. I appointed Bobby Lowder as the trustee from Montgomery, to serve on the committee, wanting to insure that the person in this position met his approval.Roy Saigo, a Japanese-American serving as provost at Southeastern Louisiana University, emerged as the leading candidate. He impressed the committee in the interviews and generated considerable enthusiasm. With the committee's recommendation and the approval of the bond, Saigo was hired.

Roy was very personable and gained significant support in the community, a dimension of his job that I felt was important. I suggested to Lowder that he appoint Roy as a director of his bank in Montgomery to expand his involvement in the local business community and he agreed to do so. Roy's support on the campus was mixed, but considerably influenced by our budgetary woes. During his first year, the Governor declared proration, necessitating a 7.5% cut; this was followed by two years of no increases. So Roy had very few resources to address faculty desires for salary increases or department's requests for funds for other purposes. But the problems with Saigo stemmed from two incidents, one involving Lowder and one with Barron.

During the time when Lowder was off the board and the Governor was trying to get his appointments to the board confirmed, the trustees had a meeting on the AUM campus. After the meeting, Saigo was interviewed about some item affecting AUM by a reporter from a Montgomery TV station. The reporter also asked Roy to comment about the dispute about board appointments and, apparently, said something to the effect that the Governor ought to be able to get his appointments confirmed. This interview appeared on the evening news. Afterwards, Lowder allegedly called Roy and told him he did not appreciate his comments. The next morning, a representative of Colonial Bank visited Saigo and told him that he had been removed from the bank's board.

The incident with Barron involved an MBA student at AUM from his district who complained to him about a grade she had received. She had enrolled in a course during the time she was moving from Montgomery to North Alabama and persuaded the professor to let her complete the assignments through independent study. He agreed and spelled out all the things she would need to do; when she completed none of the assignments, the professor first gave her an "incomplete" which became an "F", according to university rules, when no work was done during the next quarter. She requested that the grade of "F" be removed. When Roy got the request, it was forwarded to the academic vice chancellor, then to the dean, then to the department head, and finally to the professor who had taught the course. Changing a grade at a university is a very sensitive issue and the authority to do so lies with the professor who gave the grade. In this case, the professor reported that he had been very clear with the student about what had to be done and that he had given her every opportunity to comply with those requirements; hence, he refused to change the grade. When Barron learned of this, he was angry, claiming that this was something Roy should have "taken care of".

When Lowder came back on the board, he and Barron began to lobby me and other board members to "get rid of Saigo", claiming that he was not doing a good job. I agreed to investigate the matter fully and did, spending about two full days on campus, having private meetings with administrators and faculty leaders and meeting with a community advisory group. The external sources were very supportive but the internal assessments were clearly mixed, something that was not unexpected given an environment where the

CEO has to make difficult decisions and has very few resources with which to reward others.

I reported to the board that I did not feel there were sufficient grounds for dismissing Saigo but I would work with him to improve the situation. What I told Roy was that he needed to find another job, given the individuals opposed to him. Over the course of my career in higher education, I had to fire a number of people but I never enjoyed doing so, whether the person was a secretary or a vice-president. Unless there was clear malfeasance or a disruptive situation, I tried to give the individual an opportunity to move to another job. Over the next year, Roy was a candidate for the CEO position at two or three other schools, but, unfortunately, was not offered a job.

In the meantime, pressure from Lowder and Barron for me to fire Saigo was unrelenting. The executive sessions prior to each board meeting became a venue for cross-examining me about what I had done. The crowning blow occurred in the president's box during a football game. Auburn was losing to Alabama for the first time in Jordan Hare Stadium and feelings were low. Barron decided to take all his frustrations out on me, telling me that if I did not fire Saigo soon, he would make sure that I got fired.

Concluding that I had given Roy ample time to find another job, I told him that I was going to replace him as chancellor and on an interim basis, installed Guin Nance, a former vice chancellor for academic affairs and an interim chancellor before Roy arrived. He had a tenured position as a Professor of Biology to which he could move, but he requested a leave of absence to care for his mother who was near death in San Francisco and, upon his return, resigned. Fortunately, during that time frame, Roy was offered the job as chancellor of St. Cloud State University in Minnesota, a post that he held very capably over the next seven years before retiring.

My efforts to protect Roy so that he could leave with grace and continue his career elsewhere cost me dearly with Lowder, Barron, and other trustees they influenced. But I felt that Roy was a decent man who had done a decent job; while a change in leadership may have been desirable and, perhaps, even necessary, he did not deserve to be humiliated. And the campus was not harmed by the delay in the transition of leadership. Dr. Nance was appointed chancellor and served very capably in that role for my remaining years at Auburn.

LOOKING FOR THE EXIT

In most respects, Auburn was everything I had always wanted in a university – bright students, dedicated faculty, loyal alumni, and a beautiful campus in a supportive community – but the tension with the board of trustees had a deleterious effect over time. And it did not take me long to realize "what I had gotten myself into" and to question whether I had made the right decision in coming to Auburn.

In fact, by the end of my first year, after confronting and resolving so many problems with no plaudits from the leadership of the board, I had begun to seriously consider leaving. Appalachian State was looking for a new chancellor and I had received a letter from the search committee. Even though this would have been a "step down" in terms of the stature of the schools involved, I recalled very fondly my earlier experiences at ASU. But, while I was thinking it over, Barry Burkhart, chair of the Faculty Senate, orchestrated a "celebration" at the Auburn Alumni Center to recognize my first anniversary on March 1, 1993. This warmth and support from the campus leadership buoyed my spirits and prompted me to not respond to the ASU opportunity.

Over the next three years, I plowed all my energies and attention into improving Auburn in every aspect, dealing with whatever challenges surfaced. Then in 1996, an executive search firm contacted me about the presidency of the University of Minnesota. I was unaware that that job (or any other job, for that matter) was open, as I was fully focused on the tasks at Auburn.

I gave this opportunity a second glance, however, for several reasons: first, Marlene and I had visited Minneapolis-St. Paul on several occasions when both Amy and Ellen worked there and were favorably impressed by the culture and ambiance of the city; second, Minnesota was one of the top ten universities in the country in research and several other dimensions; and third, the environment at Auburn was unsettled with Lowder's board seat still under dispute. So I agreed to consider this option, with assurances that my candidacy would be kept confidential.

After several weeks, the search committee invited me to Minneapolis for an interview. It was my understanding that 8-10 candidates were interviewed with three to be selected for further consideration. Although I felt my interview went well, I was not optimistic about my chances because of the competition. To my surprise, however, I was one of three finalists recommended to the UM Board of Regents. All three finalists were to be interviewed on the same day with the board making its decision immediately afterwards. Unfortunately, someone in the press got access to the names of the finalists, resulting in a major story in Minnesota and quickly became"front page news" in Alabama. Reporters from Minnesota came down to do feature stories on me and there seemed to be daily stories or editorials in Alabama newspapers speculating whether I might leave and what that might mean for Auburn.

Marlene and I had arranged to fly to Minneapolis for the interview, but two efforts were underway in Alabama that would make that trip unnecessary. The first was the work of Emory Cunningham, then President Pro Tem of the Auburn Board of Trustees, to persuade me to stay at AU. I had tremendous respect and admiration for Emory and our working relationship was outstanding. He focused on what it would take to get me to remain at Auburn; I told him it was not money but rather the lack of a long-term contract that troubled me. The State of Alabama required ten years of service to vest in its retirement system; I wanted assurance that I could achieve that goal, if I stayed. So Emory, working with a law firm, developed a five year contract that would take me to the 10-year vesting period, as well as providing some salary improvement.

Meanwhile, a local committee arranged a major "appreciation" reception for Marlene and me to thank us for the leadership we had provided to the university and the community. There was a large turnout, overflowing the ballroom at the AU Hotel and Conference Center. This was a very emotional experience for both of us, seeing all the people we had worked with on campus and in the community and feeling their outpouring of love and respect. We were being urged to stay, although many felt we were already "gone" (after all, who would turn down such a great opportunity?). When I tried to speak to the crowd, I was overcome with emotion and realized what a special place Auburn occupied in my heart.

This event, Emory's offer of a contract, and my assumptions about future board composition (at that time, Lowder's law suit against the Governor had not been successful in the lower courts and it seemed unlikely he would come back on the board) led me to tell Emory that I would stay at Auburn if the contract was approved. He, then, got Governor James to call a special meeting of the board, with the Governor flying back from a hunting trip in Canada to chair the session. The contract was approved unanimously with all board members attending except Barron, who was quoted as saying he did not approve because he thought I was too liberal for Auburn.

I notified Minnesota that I was withdrawing as a candidate and, therefore, not coming for the interview. Another candidate, the president of Portland State University, subsequently withdrew to accept the presidency of the University of Vermont, leaving only one candidate, the provost at the University of Texas, who was appointed to the post. Although I do not know for certain that I would have been selected, all indications both public and private were that I was the leading candidate for the job.

After that emotional episode, I dug back in on all the fronts that required attention. But my assumptions about the board composition turned out to be false. When Lowder came back on the board, the tenor changed dramatically toward an even more contentious atmosphere than before. Jimmy Samford was elected to replace Emory as President Pro Tem.

The request by Lowder to establish the Role Commission after his return was intended, I believed, to narrow the scope of the university and to "get at" certain academic areas. Lowder and some other board members expressed a disdain for the faculty, particularly in liberal arts, that troubled me. For example, some felt that the journalism faculty had influenced the student newspaper to write negative stories about Lowder and the board. Improving the university's efficiency was not the primary focus as Auburn had already been identified as one of the most efficient institutions among major universities and our expenditures per student were considerably below those of our peer group. So I worked hard to carry out the mandate of the commission while trying to prevent major changes that would be harmful to the institution. And, to a considerable degree, I think that was done.Lowder may have felt I was "stirring up the troops" but what he did not understand was that the groups whose programs were threatened would have been much more vocal had I not insisted on an open process.

After my highly public consideration of the Minnesota job, I was contacted a number of times by executive search firms. Most of their openings were not of interest to me, but I did have preliminary discussions with a few schools where my potential candidacy could be kept confidential. One particularly attractive opportunity to me was the presidency of the Ohio State University, as it would have taken us back to Ohio. I pursued that option to the point of becoming one of five finalists. I was not selected, but fortunately the process was kept entirely confidential.

By 1999, after the terms of three trustees who were not a part of the "Lowder coalition" had expired and their posts filled by Lowder loyalists, the atmosphere on the board became even more contentious. It finally reached a point where I requested a meeting with Samford and Lowder to express my concerns about trustees going directly to university employees – vice-presidents, coaches, deans or directors – rather than bringing their concerns to me. I asked them to realize what an awkward situation this created for the employees who would feel they could now "report to" the board rather than their immediate supervisor. This made my job and that of other administrators much more difficult. I assured them that I was concerned not just for myself but also for the entire organizational structure of the university.

At the beginning of the discussion, I had told Samford and Lowder that I did not intend to stay in the job beyond the length of my current contract; I would either take another job or move into my tenured faculty position at Auburn. I thought this assurance might help them look more objectively at the long-term consequences of their actions. I had written out my comments, citing specific examples of my complaints, and requested an opportunity to discuss them with the full board at the executive session prior to the next trustees meeting. As I recall, I got almost no feedback from either Samford or Lowder at this meeting but they agreed to discuss this matter at the board meeting.

When the board meeting came, however, I was requested not to distribute my comments and to leave the executive session while my meeting with Samford and Lowder was discussed. I never learned what the nature of that discussion was, but the behavior of board members interfering directly in university operations seemed to intensify, not lessen. In Lowder's case, it seemed to me that, now that he knew these interventions irritated me, he pushed even harder in that direction.

Within this environment, then, I began to mull over whether I could "stick it out" to meet the ten-year vesting requirement. Qualifying for this pension would represent a significant degree of financial security. Then an opportunity emerged in mid-2000 that I felt I should explore, even though the process would be entirely open. The University of Florida was looking for a president, and I was contacted about being a candidate. Recognizing UF as an excellent university, I decided to pursue it and ended up as one of the finalists. After spending two days on campus for interviews, however, I realized that I did not feel a "connection" to the university. Furthermore, all indications were that the Florida Board of Regents, to which the president reported, was going to be eliminated by the legislature and new campus-based boards were to be appointed by the Governor. It was important to me to know to whom I would report. In addition, I had thought there was a chance I could purchase the additional time I needed to qualify for the Alabama retirement system but, upon full investigation, learned that could not be done. So I withdrew as a candidate and Florida continued with its interim president.

Unlike the Minnesota search, there were no efforts by the board to persuade me to stay. And among the faculty, staff, and alumni that I knew, there were few who blamed me for considering other jobs. I stayed focused on the tasks at hand, as I feel I always had during my time at Auburn with the objective of serving out the remaining year or so on my contract.

In late January 2001, however, Samford and Jack Miller from the trustees came to my office. Miller was a new board member and an attorney whose firm represented the Colonial Bank. Samford informed me that the board had learned that I had been looking at other jobs and that they wanted me to resign. I reminded Samford that I had told him and Lowder that I did not intend to stay as president beyond the contract term and that I would likely move to another job; so my exploration of other opportunities should hardly be a surprise. I also reminded him of the contract the board had approved and he assured me that, if I resigned, all the benefits under the contract would still be paid to me.

I asked when they wanted this to take place. Samford indicated that he wanted me to announce my decision at the upcoming board meeting in February with the change to be effective June 30th. I pointed out that we planned to announce a donation of $25 million to Auburn for the College of Engineering and that Sam Ginn, the benefactor, was to be present at the February meeting. Knowing the press in Alabama, I argued that, if I resigned at that meeting, all the headlines the next day would be about the resignation with Ginn's gift, the largest in the history of the university, relegated to a footnote. The provost, Bill Walker, a former dean of engineering, and I had flown to San Francisco to work out the details of the gift and planned to propose that the engineering school be named for Ginn. So we wanted the spotlight to be on him.

It was agreed, then, that I would make an announcement by March 1st and that Jack Miller would draft an agreement for my review. By this time, I had concluded that the situation at Auburn was not going to get any better and that extracting myself from this leadership role was probably the best thing to do. Interestingly enough, the only other job I was considering at that time was a small liberal arts college in Michigan, Alma College. Mike Mulligan, a good friend and fraternity brother (and Alma alumnus) had urged me to look at it and I had talked with a search consultant who was working with Alma's board. Although this would have been a drastic change, I had often felt that the presidency of a small liberal arts institution might be a nice way to end my career.

Interestingly enough, on the same day that I met with Samford and Miller, I received a call from an executive search firm, asking if I would be interested in either of three presidencies they were seeking to fill. Two of the schools were of no interest to me, but the third, East Carolina University, had some appeal. I recalled the earlier experience I had in North Carolina at Appalachian State and remembered the state as a progressive one. The consultant told me that she thought I was exactly what the ECU board was looking for and that they would want to move quickly.

Within two weeks of that phone call, I had flown to Raleigh to interview with the search committee. ECU had sent a plane to Auburn to take Marlene and me to Greenville to visit the campus and town. I had been offered the job and gone to Chapel Hill to meet with the UNC Board of Governors to accept the appointment. In the meantime, I had worked with the Alabama retirement system and found that, by using my accumulated sick leave and unused annual leave, I could qualify for the pension by August 1, 2001. Therefore, I accepted the ECU job to start on that date. I had also flown earlier to Michigan to interview with Alma but felt that the ECU job was a better fit.

While I had also considered the option of staying at Auburn and moving to a tenured faculty position, it seemed that leaving the institution was the best alternative. I felt that I could be very helpful to ECU during the remaining years I wanted to work and that I needed to get away from the conflict with the AU board that was wearing on both my mental and physical health. And I figured that the leadership of the Auburn trustees would be delighted with this solution to their "problem" – i.e. I would be leaving and they wouldn't even have to buy out my contract. But their reaction was unexpected and unfortunate.

THE SEPARATION AND THE AFTERMATH

I arrived back from accepting the ECU job late on a Friday afternoon only to discover that a special meeting of the Board of Trustees had been set for Monday morning. Before my trip to North Carolina, I had sent a memo to the board informing them that I would be meeting with the UNC Board of Governors and that I would likely be accepting the job. I indicated that I would be staying at Auburn through July and that I would be happy to assist with the search for the new president. No one from the board spoke to me prior to the meeting on Monday, although the secretary to the board, Grant Davis, met with me briefly on Monday morning to tell me the trustees planned to remove me as president immediately.

When I arrived at the meeting room in the Foy Student Center, I found that it was packed with faculty, students, and staff from the campus. The board moved quickly to pass resolutions removing me as president and installing provost Walker as interim president. They also passed a resolution allowing Marlene and me to continue to live in the president's house, use automobiles provided to us, and receive other benefits described in the contract. I was not offered an opportunity to speak but Lindsey Boney, the Student Government Association President, rose to the floor, extolling the leadership that I had provided and condemning the actions by the board. His speech was met with a standing ovation from the crowd assembled. At first stunned by the reaction, the trustees then rose to join the applause; that is, all except one – Lowder – who remained seated. At least he was consistent.

Of course, these actions by the board were totally unnecessary. Outgoing presidents frequently continue to serve until their successor arrives or until they have to depart. I served as president of the University of Akron for nearly three months after I had accepted the Auburn job. This action, in my opinion, was intended to be one final slap to embarrass me. But it had the opposite effect.

The press coverage the next day was negative toward the actions by the board as was the editorial opinion and many feature articles to follow, including a story in <u>The Chronicle of Higher Education,</u> the most highly-read newspaper in university circles. Groups representing every constituency at Auburn – students, faculty, staff, and alumni – passed resolutions condemning the actions by the trustees, with many calling for the resignations of the board. There was a huge student protest rally in front of Samford Hall, the administration building.

I moved out of the president's office and into a small office down the hall where a wonderful lady and friend, Lois Graves, served as my secretary for the remaining months at Auburn. It took me nearly two months just to answer all the correspondence I had received from Auburn people, thanking me for the leadership I had provided and apologizing for the way the trustees had treated me. I had many wonderful meetings with individuals and groups on campus and around the state during this time.

The fallout from this action over the next few years was significant, particularly in the higher education community. Earlier, a group of concerned Auburn alumni had formed a political action committee and led an effort to amend the state constitution, changing the terms of office and the process by which Auburn trustees were appointed. This was a Herculean endeavor as it required getting approval of the legislature, putting the amendments on a state-wide ballot, and winning the support of the electorate. But they were successful in reducing the terms from twelve to seven years, limiting an appointee to two terms, and forming a committee to nominate appointees to the Governor. This committee was comprised of two representatives from the Auburn Alumni Association, two representatives of the Board of Trustees, and a representative of the Governor, with the committee's work being a public process. The events that seemed to trigger and sustain the alumni campaign were Lowder's involvement in the "firing" of Coach Bowden, his attempt to take control of the alumni association through a slate that he promoted, and his success in stacking the Board of Trustees with individuals with whom he had a significant relationship.

The fallout from my removal, however, went well beyond the campus and state, leading to an investigation by the Southern Association of Colleges and Schools (SACS), the accrediting agency for Auburn's academic programs. The investigation, including sending a team from the higher education community to Auburn, was influenced by the number of complaints received from Auburn faculty and alumni and resulted in Auburn's accreditation being threatened.

While the complaints about these events were undoubtedly influential, SACS already had a "thick file" of complaints about the behavior of the AU Board of Trustees, according to a conversation I had with a member of a peer-review team that had visited AUM in 1998. AUM was up for re-accreditation and was experiencing difficulties because of the review team's conclusion that Auburn's board violated the SACS principle that trustees ought to "set policy and not be involved in the administration" of the university. I reported that no violations of that principle had occurred at AUM and, since AUM was accredited separately from the Auburn campus, this should not be an issue. This is when the "thick file" was mentioned. But it took a special appearance by me, chancellor Roy Saigo, and Ed Richardson, representing the Board of Trustees, before a SACS panel at its annual meeting in Atlanta to get the matter dismissed.

There may have been trustees who felt that I prompted the SACS review in 2002 and beyond. That was not the case. Although I had been active in serving on SACS peer-review teams to other universities, I made no complaint to SACS nor was I involved in the investigation in any way. SACS had plenty of material without my input. It is my understanding that the matter was resolved though the active involvement of Governor Bob Riley and with the eventual appointment of new trustees who had a higher degree of independence.

There were other repercussions, also, of a more personal nature. Within weeks after the board's action to remove me as president, I suffered some difficulties with my heart. While working out on the treadmill early one morning, a practice that I followed almost every day, I began to experience chest pain. I discontinued the exercise. The same thing happened the next morning and the next. I was slow to respond because, up until this moment, I had encountered no heart problems – e.g. low cholesterol, normal blood pressure, no pain. But, after the third episode, I called my personal physician and great friend, Dr. David Hagan.

Dr. Hagan examined me and, then, sent me to a cardiologist, Dr. Michael Williams, right away. The tests revealed a significant blockage of one of the arteries to my heart. Dr. Williams performed a catherization and, using the angioplasty process, removed the plaque, and placed a stent in the artery.

While this operation was successful, it began a process over the next two years that would include several catherizations and, eventually, a by-pass operation. I can't help but believe that the stress of dealing with the AU Board of Trustees contributed to the health problems that I encountered.

AUBURN, SWEET AUBURN

As I reflect on my nearly ten years at Auburn, I am flooded with pleasant memories of the wonderful people with whom I worked and the special place that Auburn is. I can truly say that I loved Auburn from the first day I came there and will always love her. The hurtful experiences with some of the trustees will never be forgotten but they fade in their importance over time, overcome by pride in what was accomplished during those years and the positive relationships with people that developed and still endure.

Any recitation of great memories from Auburn will be incomplete as each day brought with it many pleasant experiences, but there are several dimensions of that relationship that must be described.

MY AUBURN FAMILY

Almost any discussion of Auburn will lead to a reference to the "Auburn Family" -- all those who are affiliated with and care about the institution. I was certainly a part of the Auburn Family as the president of the university, but Auburn became a real family as eight members of my family or Marlene's family earned degrees from Auburn while we were there. They were:

(1) Our daughter, Amy, who earned a Ph.D. in English and taught for several years as an instructor in the English Department while finishing her degree. Her major professor, Dr. Paula Bachscheider, was very helpful in guiding Amy through the process and instilling in her the skills that were needed for academic success.

(2) Our son, Van, who earned a Master's degree in English and, then, an Ed.D. in higher education leadership. Van worked in the admissions office as well as other posts in student affairs while completing his degrees. He also edited a publication, The Auburn Horizon, and was a frequent commentator

on a sports talk program on the campus radio station. Van enjoyed, as well as profited by, his time at Auburn.

(3) Our daughter-in-law, Lori, came to Auburn to work as an internal auditor after employment with Arthur Anderson, the public accounting firm. She completed her MBA degree and, then, her Ph.D. in management through the College of Business Administration.

(4) My grand niece, Jennifer Cole, completed a bachelor's degree in economics and international studies before going to New York to work for <u>Time</u> and <u>Travel and Leisure</u> magazines before coming to Birmingham as a travel editor for <u>Southern Living.</u>

(5) Another grandniece, Glenda Jones, of Birmingham earned a bachelor's degree in marketing.

(6) A grand nephew, Seth Muse, completed a bachelor's degree in aerospace engineering.

(7) Marlene's nephew, Richard Munden, got a bachelor's degree in electrical engineering. Rick played in the Auburn Knights, the university's dance band and was its manager one year.

(8) Marlene's niece, Diane Munden, came to Auburn after graduating from Purdue and earned both a master's and doctoral degree in pharmacy.

We enjoyed having our children as well as other relatives attend Auburn and share the Auburn spirit with us.

MY SUPPORTIVE STAFF

No CEO can be successful without a talented team of leaders to carry out the plans that are developed. I was fortunate to have the opportunity to fill all the vice-president's posts, as well as nearly all the dean's positions, while at Auburn and benefited from the expertise that these individuals brought to their respective tasks. Several of the VP's and directors have already been mentioned – athletic directors Mike Lude and David Housel, vice presidents Don Large, Betty DeMent, Bettye Burkhalter, David Wilson and Extension Director Steve Jones – but there are many others who deserve to be cited. I will mention just three:

(1) Paul Parks had served the university for several years as graduate dean and vice president for research. He became the university's first provost and served very capably in that role. His quiet demeanor and reliability helped to resolve many internal issues.

(2) Jim Ferguson, a Texas A&M graduate, came to Auburn as vice president for administrative services and had responsibilities for police, parking, facilities, and a variety of other functions. Through his leadership, the Tiger Transit, a campus bus system, was developed as a partial resolution to an onerous parking problem.

(3) Thomas Samford, the university's chief legal counsel, was a descendant of the Samford family that included a former Governor and many others involved in the university. His wise counsel and impeccable integrity was always an asset. Thomas retired during my last year and died shortly thereafter. His successor, Lee Armstrong, has followed in his footsteps.

But the individuals who are most memorable are those with whom I interacted daily and on whom I depended for so much support. Gerald and Emily Leischuck were very helpful during my first few years as members of the president's staff because they were so knowledgeable about the university and the Board of Trustees. Lynne Hammond did a marvelous job as secretary to the board and as my executive assistant for several years before becoming director of human resources. Pat Wingfield managed the president's box for football games and assisted Marlene with all the entertaining that we did. And Joan Astin, who was my secretary, performed all the tasks required with an amazingly positive attitude.

AU's Strong Faculty

The strength of any university resides in its faculty. The faculty not only structures the academic programs and helps students gain the knowledge and skill they need to be successful but they build the institution's academic reputation through their research and scholarly work. Auburn was fortunate to have a distinguished faculty, many of whom had spent much of their academic careers there and who were very dedicated to the institution.

As has been reported earlier, when I came to Auburn there was a hostile relationship between the faculty and the administration. I worked hard to overcome that and, with the help of Dr. Barry Burkhart, was able to make great progress in that direction. Barry had just been elected chair of the Faculty Senate when I arrived. He was not an easy person to convince, but through the many challenges I encountered the first year and my efforts to include the faculty leadership in important discussions, the ground work was laid for an unusual relationship, particularly for Auburn.

Over the years at Auburn, I was blessed to work with an outstanding group of faculty leaders. The chair elected each year was different in many respects but each was effective in presenting the faculty's view and in working with me and others to find the best solution to the problems we confronted.

As an indication of the mutual respect that we shared, when I was inaugurated as chancellor of East Carolina, nearly every Faculty Senate chair with whom I worked at Auburn was there for help celebrate the occasion.

THE LOCAL COMMUNITY

The university is located in the town of Auburn, but the local community also encompasses the town of Opelika, the seat of Lee County. Marlene and I had many friends in both towns. While my responsibilities took me all over the state, Marlene was very involved in local civic endeavors. She served on the boards of the Boys and Girls Club, the Lee County Youth Development Center, and the local Habitat for Humanity affiliate.

We were both active members of the Auburn United Methodist Church and we were great friends with the pastor, George Mathison. Dr. Mathison asked me to give the Sunday message on several occasions and, while I found that to be an intimidating task, I was pleased to do so. George, along with Bob Baggott, the pastor of a local Baptist Church, served as chaplains for the football team when Terry Bowden was the coach. I always enjoyed being with George and Bob during the away games when we traveled with the team.

An important member of the local community was a former Auburn President, Harry Philpot. Having read Auburn's history, I greatly admired the leadership that Dr. Philpot had provided during Auburn's transition to a major university. Harry became a valued friend and confidant and I always enjoyed and appreciated the opportunities to talk with him.

Auburn was blessed in that there was no town-gown conflict with the local community. There were certainly issues to deal with because the university was such a major part of the economy. But local leaders were very proud of the university and supportive of its programs.

INVOLVEMENT IN THE STATE

I got to travel to every corner of Alabama and to meet people from local farmers to titans of industry. I spoke to Auburn clubs throughout the state, visited county extension offices, and toured experiment stations (farms for agricultural research).

During my second year at Auburn I was selected as a participant in the Leadership Alabama class. This was a yearlong program designated to educate us about the state as well as develop and nurture future leadership. I met many wonderful folks in this program and was pleased to be selected a few years later as "Alumnus of the Year".

One of the benefits of being president of Auburn was being asked to serve on corporate boards. I served on four and each was as special experience. Alabama Power Company, the state's primary public utility, had a very distinguished board. The CEO was Elmer Harris, an Auburn graduate, and one of the state's most progressive leaders. I was also asked to join the board of the American Cast Iron Pipe Company (ACIPCO) in Birmingham, a very unusual company. ACIPCO was employee-owned and governed by a board comprised of four representatives of management, four representatives elected by the employees, and four outside directors. This was a very well run, profitable enterprise that clearly demonstrated some of the advantages of employee ownership.

I was also a member – at different times – of two bank boards. When I moved to Alabama, I got reacquainted with my old friend, Jimmy Taylor, with whom I had worked at Camp Takajo. Jimmy had bought several banks and was combining them into a holding company called Alabama National Bank. He asked me to become a director and serve with a wonderful group of guys that Jimmy had assembled. Alabama National became so successful that it merged with another bank in Birmingham. With the merger, Jimmy Taylor gave up his chairmanship and I, eventually, went off this board. Then I was invited to become a director of South Trust Bank, one of the largest banks in the Southeast. Led by a very colorful and effective chairman, Wallace Malone, SouthTrust was an impressive organization. I continued to serve on this board after I moved to North Carolina and until I retired. SouthTrust later merged with Wachovia to become one of the largest banks in the country.

The most prestigious recognition I got in the state, however, was being elected to the Alabama Academy of Honor, whose membership is limited to 100 living Alabamians plus all the living past Governors of the state. It is designed to recognize individuals for their lifetime achievements. On the year that I was selected, there were four inductees, one of whom was Rosa Parks. As one might expect, the membership of the Academy for many years had been all male and all white. But those barriers as many others in Alabama were being broken and recognition was finally being extended to a person long associated with the civil rights movement who, through a single act of defiance, had changed the course of history.

Mrs. Parks, who was in poor health and nearing age 90, was not able to attend the ceremonies that are, ironically, held in the old House Chambers of the State Capitol in Montgomery where the resolution for Alabama to secede from the Union was passed. I was asked to speak on behalf of the new class of inductees. While a great honor, it was also a daunting assignment.

WAR EAGLE ALUMS

Alumni of Auburn are among the most loyal and supportive in the nation, both in terms of contributing to the university and participating in events. Marlene and I got to know alumni whenever we traveled and were always impressed with their genuine enthusiasm and love for Auburn. I could not begin to name all the wonderful alums that we met and who became very special friends. But I do want to cite one couple because of the magnificent thing that they did.

Albert and Jule Smith lived in Houston, Texas. Albert had graduated from Auburn in engineering and founded a company that he later sold to Westinghouse. Jule had attended AU but left without a degree after marrying Albert. Marlene and I first became acquainted with Albert and Jule on an Auburn Alumni trip to the Yorkshire area of England. We found them to be a delightful couple.

Albert had already given $1 million to endow a chair in engineering and was identified as a major prospect in our capital campaign in the mid 90's. The Smiths hosted a campaign event at their home in Houston for alums in that area and, while there, I noticed the fine art collection throughout the house. When I commented on it, Albert told me that was one of Jule's interests. I filed that away in my memory because we were trying to raise money for an art museum as a part of the campaign.

There were a number of individuals at Auburn, led by Taylor Littleton and Gordon Bond, who had campaigned for many years to establish an art museum. The university had a significant art collection but nowhere to display it. They also argued, and I agreed, that a university of the size and stature of Auburn should have such an asset. The museum was included in our campaign projects, but it was apparent to me that there was very little enthusiasm among trustees for this idea. In fact, I had three alternative sites for the museum turned down by the board.

But a phone call to me from Albert Smith was the catalyst that made the art museum a reality. Knowing of our interest in the museum, Albert called me to say that he would be willing to give $3 million, if the museum could be named for Jule. Albert and Jule were going to celebrate their 50th wedding anniversary and he wanted this to be his gift to her. I told Albert that he was setting a very high standard for other husbands who were approaching their Golden Anniversary, but I thought the naming could be accomplished. And it was. The gift motivated the board to name the museum and to agree to the site we had first recommended.

The Smiths later gave another large gift for the museum and, with additional contributions from Susan Phillips and other alums the art museum was built and furnished. Today it is a beautiful building on an attractive site and is a treasure for the university and the community.

AFTER THOUGHTS

In the years since leaving Auburn, I have sometimes wondered what I could have done – and would have been willing to do – to achieve a different, perhaps more satisfying outcome. But I'm never sure there is an answer to that question.

Part of my difficult relationship with Lowder stemmed, I believe, from the fact I was not his choice to be president. That is something that I, obviously, could not change nor, it seemed, overcome. I could have let Lowder "run" the university, including athletics or any other area that interested him, by simply doing what he wanted done. But I would not do that for several reasons.

First, I understood that Lowder (or any other individual trustee) had no legal authority. If I let an individual trustee do something that was illegal or improper or did it at his request, I would be the one held accountable. If, for example, further NCAA violations occurred in the football program sufficient to warrant the "death penalty", I would have been blamed for a "lack of institutional control". I was determined not to let that happen, if I could prevent it.

Secondly, my management style was always to hire the best people available and let them do their jobs. I believed in being clear about my expectations and goals, then leaving it up to the manager to find the best way to meet them. Naturally—and perhaps naively--, I expected to be treated the same way. I could not have been a "figurehead" and retained any self-respect.

Thirdly, it was my observation that doing whatever Lowder wanted was not a guarantee of continual support. In several cases individuals who felt obligated to Lowder and did what he asked were eventually fired or shunted aside anyway. It seemed that, if Lowder "owned" you, he would eventually have to "sell" you, if for no other reason than just to demonstrate that he was in charge. I did not want to place myself in that position.

So the fact that I survived as long and made as much progress as I did, especially with the turmoil that occurred, is certainly something to celebrate.

My goal when coming to Auburn was to finish my career there, as a member of the faculty after my term as president was completed. That was still an option, although the circumstances at the time were not how I would have preferred them to be. But one factor did weigh heavily in my consideration. While I was being recruited to come to ECU, I was also negotiating with Samford and Miller about the terms of my "resignation" as president. In the first draft of an agreement sent to me by Jack Miller was a "gag order" – i.e. a clause that prohibited me from speaking or writing anything critical about the Board of Trustees. While I had no plans to complain publicly about the board, this provision turned me off completely. The agreement did little other than ensure that I would receive the benefits entitled to me by my contract and my tenured faculty position. I marked out the "gag order" provision and returned the agreement, but there was no further discussion about it prior to my acceptance of the offer from East Carolina.

So, in retrospect, I am pleased with what I was able to accomplish at Auburn and will always be thankful for the wonderful experiences I had there.

CHAPTER 14:
ECU AND RETIREMENT, TOO

The State of North Carolina consists of three major geographic regions that differ greatly in terrain, culture, and commerce. The western region, often called simply "the mountains", encompasses the Blue Ridge and many remote areas and beautiful sites. We lived there when I was the business school dean at Appalachian State in the early 70's. The middle region, called the Piedmont, comprises rolling plains ranging from Charlotte to Raleigh. It is the economic engine of the state, home to the largest percentage of the population, and contains both rich farmland and centers of high technology such as Research Triangle Park.

The eastern region or Coastal Plain extends from Raleigh all the way to the Atlantic Ocean. Some consider Interstate 95, which cuts a diagonal line from Virginia to South Carolina, east of Raleigh, as the western border of "Eastern North Carolina". The east was the first area of the state developed and contained the capitol of colonial North Carolina. With shipping ports on the Atlantic, huge tobacco and cotton plantations inland, and a society that grew from the wealth accumulated, the east was clearly the cultural, economic, and political center of the state for the first couple of centuries. By the end of the twentieth century, though, economic and population growth had moved westward and with it, political power. Eastern North Carolina was left with some of the most poverty-stricken counties in the state.

East Carolina University is located in Greenville near the center of the eastern region. Originally founded in 1907 as East Carolina Teachers' Training School, it functioned for many years as East Carolina Teachers College (ECTC). But under the aggressive leadership of President Leo Jenkins in the 1960's and 70's, the institution began to grow and broaden its mission, becoming first East Carolina College and, then, East Carolina University.

Jenkins skillfully marshaled political support and gained state funds for expansion of facilities and programs at the university. His biggest coup occurred in the mid 70's when he persuaded the legislature to establish a medical school at ECU over loud objections of the University of North Carolina. It was this achievement, many believe, that prompted the University of North Carolina to expand its system to include ECU and to bring Jenkins under the "control" of Bill Friday, the president of UNC and a legendary leader in higher education.

By the time I arrived in 2001, ECU was one of sixteen "constituent campuses" of the University of North Carolina with an enrollment of nearly 20,000 students. This placed it third in the state behind only UNC – Chapel Hill and North Carolina State in Raleigh. The medical school was celebrating its twenty-fifth anniversary, and the university supported a broad range of programs including many at the masters and doctoral levels.

THE SEARCH

As reported earlier, I received a phone call from an executive search firm about the ECU job on the afternoon following my meeting with the two Auburn trustees who were seeking my early retirement. While I had the option of moving to a faculty position at Auburn, I was heartsick over the way I had been treated by the leadership of the board and felt at that point that leaving the university would, perhaps, be the best alternative. Had the phone call come a day earlier, I likely would not have been receptive to the ECU opportunity.

But, in addition to the timing, several other factors led me to entertain the idea of moving to ECU. First was a very positive experience Marlene and I had had in Boone and at Appalachian State. I had become well acquainted with North Carolina while promoting the new business school at ASU, and I thought that the state had progressive leadership. Secondly, I reasoned that, with my experience as a president, I could make a difference in the last 3-5 years I hoped to serve as a university CEO.

The third factor was the aggressive manner in which I was recruited for the job. In all the other searches, I had been one of several candidates and had to sell myself during the interview process. But now, it appeared as though the search committee had already decided that I was their man and went after me "fast and furious". In fact, within days of my first phone conversation with the consultant, a meeting with the ECU search committee had been arranged.

I flew to Raleigh on a Sunday and was met by Phil Dixon, the chairman of the ECU Board of Trustees and chair of the search committee. A local attorney, Dixon drove me to Greenville for a tour of the campus and of the city. Throughout this time, he aggressively sold the university and the opportunity it represented. Although I appreciated his enthusiasm, by the time we got back to Raleigh that evening, I was exhausted.

During the night, I had "second thoughts" and met with the search consultant early the next morning to tell her I wanted to withdraw as a candidate. She was shocked and a look of sheer panic crossed her face. She pleaded with me to just go through with the interview process with the committee before making a final decision. I finally agreed. The search committee turned out to be an interesting and hospitable group, and the issues they described sounded very familiar. By the end of this process, I was more receptive, feeling that ECU might be a place where my leadership skills could be productive and appreciated.

At the end of that week, Phil Dixon had arranged for a private plane to fly Marlene and me to Greenville to close the deal. He had set up a tour of the medical school with a presentation on their research and arranged for a reception with community leaders. He had also asked Dr. Robert Morrison, the chair of the Faculty Senate, to accompany him on the flight so that we would have a chance to visit. All of this convinced me to accept the job.

On the following Wednesday I flew back to Raleigh to meet with president Molly Broad who presented the offer. She was the head of the UNC system to whom the chancellors of the campuses reported. On Thursday, I met with the UNC Board of Governors for confirmation of my appointment and, then, traveled to Greenville to spend that night. On Friday, I addressed a convocation at Wright Auditorium, held a press conference, and met with a variety of groups from both the campus and the community. By the time I flew back to Auburn Friday afternoon, I was all excited about the new challenges.

But there were still several months before I formally began the new job. During that time at Auburn, I made several trips to Greenville and received extensive information about ECU through mail, e-mail, and telephone. By the time the move took place, I felt I was "up to speed" on a lot of issues and ready to "hit the ground running".

HITTING THE GROUND RUNNING

The chancellor's residence at ECU is located on 5th Street, a tree-lined avenue that marks the northern boundary of the "old" campus. The traditional campus was located between 5th and 10th Streets, but had expanded over the years to accommodate a growing enrollment. The residence was an attractive house originally built as a private home and was part of an established residential neighborhood.

When our moving van arrived on August 1, the press was there to cover the event but "Sugarboy", our orange-colored cat, stole the limelight. He had caused us no difficulties on the journey; but, when we deposited him in a back yard with a high wall around it, Sugarboy scaled the fence and "high-tailed" it down the street, not to return until three days later. Sugarboy's escape was the lead in the stories about our arrival and the focus of many questions I got in the days that followed.

As I had done at Akron and Auburn, I set to work getting to know the campus, the community, and the region. I met with each of the colleges and schools, as well as with all other major units, and filled my schedule with speaking engagements to various groups both on campus and throughout eastern North Carolina. If the mission of the university was to serve this region, I reasoned that I needed to get to know it.

With the help of Austin Bunch, my executive assistant and later chief of staff, we put together a series of "Hometown Tours" to every population center in the region, always taking with us an ECU student from that town. Our schedule typically included an interview with the editor of the local newspaper, a meeting with the mayor, a visit to the high school from which our student had graduated, a speech to a local civic club at lunch, and a reception hosted by ECU alums. We traveled in a van decorated with ECU signs and flags so everyone would know we were in town. The trips were fun; they allowed me to meet leaders around the region, and almost always resulted in a major story in the local paper.

During my time at ECU, I worked to help people see us as "The University of Eastern North Carolina", the institution that was not only graduating individuals with the knowledge and skills to meet employment needs but also helping communities solve their problems. We emphasized the outreach mission, particularly as it pertained to economic development.

But in the midst of all these efforts, a major event occurred that shocked not only ECU but the world as well.

9-11-01

In the second month on the job, my staff had planned a trip to Washington, DC so that I could meet and get acquainted with members of the North Carolina congressional delegation. With Tom Feldbush, the vice chancellor for graduate studies and research, and Al Delia, our federal liaison person, I flew out of the Raleigh-Durham airport around 8:30 am, planning to arrive in the DC area around 11:00 am. Austin Bunch had driven ahead to DC and was going to meet us there.

As our flight was proceeding toward DC, the pilot announced that a plane had crashed into the World Trade Center in New York. Someone commented, "some guy really got off his flight pattern"; we all assumed it was an accident. But, then, later the pilot reported that another plane had hit the World Trade Center and that all planes were ordered to get out of the sky. As our flight headed back to RDU, all passengers seemed to be deep in thought, figuring that something serious was happening. By the time we got back to the terminal, we found it packed with other returning passengers, all crowded around the TV's in the waiting areas. We learned that another plane had flown into the Pentagon about the time our plane would have arrived in the DC area.

When we got back to the campus, I began to meet with various university officers and groups as we discussed what actions we should take. A candlelight vigil was organized for that evening and counseling staff began to meet with students who were affected by the tragedy. Classes the next day were cancelled and a university-wide convocation was set for noon. For this event, Wright Auditorium was packed. The university choir sang some patriotic songs, a minister prayed, followed by speeches from the Faculty Senate chairman, the Student Government Association president, and myself. I asked the students to be calm, to call their parents, to talk with their friends, and to reflect on the fragility of life. But, I was most impressed with Sadie Cox, the SGA president, as she delivered a very mature and personal message to her fellow students.

After the convocation, we arranged opportunities for students to meet in small groups to talk out their feelings. Most students seemed "shell-shocked" by the events, unable to fully grasp what was happening to their world. We tried to ease back into our regular schedule the next day, giving students something else to occupy their minds while being flexible on attendance requirements, particularly for those students who were impacted in some way. But I'm not sure our campus or the world ever returned to normal.

THE STRATEGIC PLAN

By the time of my official installation as chancellor on March 8, 2002 (the date the institution annually celebrated its founding), I had formulated a strategic plan for the university that was described in my inaugural address. I didn't form a large committee as I had at Auburn, but instead listened carefully to all the groups with whom I met and attempted to be responsive (within the limits of our resources) to the needs and desires they expressed.

I called for the university's academic mission to be built around four areas of emphasis: teacher education, human health, fine and performing arts, and economic development. I felt such a thrust would be consistent with both the institution's strengths and the region's needs. I, also, described ten conditions or goals toward which I wanted ECU to aspire. Finally, in closing, I coined a phrase that became a part of our marketing theme in the months that followed. I said that "East is the direction one has to face to see the rising sun – to see tomorrow" and that East Carolina needed to help others see and achieve a better tomorrow.

Austin Bunch chaired the installation committee and arranged an excellent inaugural ceremony. I was pleased that my brother, Clyde, and my pastor in Akron, Gabe Campbell, were present and participated in the program, as they had done at my inaugurations in both Akron and Auburn. Marlene and I had many friends and family who attended. Our grandson, Henry, was quite enamored with the ROTC Color Guard. In a very nice touch, a delegation from Auburn flew to Greenville in the university plane to attend the ceremonies, including my good friends, Don Large and David Housel, as well as most of the chairs of the AU Faculty Senate with whom I had worked.

At this juncture, I was feeling good about the move to ECU and excited about the opportunities that lay ahead. But with those opportunities came many challenges, as I was soon to learn.

THE ORGANIZATIONAL STRUCTURE

One of the first things I encountered in North Carolina was a university system somewhat different from any I had worked in previously. I had been in "systems" before, even served as vice-chancellor for academic programs for the Texas A&M system when it consisted of four universities and several state agencies. But the UNC "system" was considerably more complex and diverse. It consisted of one of the top universities in the nation, the UNC campus in Chapel Hill, that most people in the nation and the state regarded as "The University of North Carolina" and one of the premier land grant institutions, North Carolina State University. In addition, it had three campuses that served major geographic areas (ECU, Western Carolina, and Appalachian State); four campuses serving metropolitan areas, (UNC–Asheville, UNC–Charlotte, UNC– Greensboro, and UNC–Wilmington); five historically black universities; one campus historically focused on serving the Lumbee Indians; and the NC School of the Arts.

In spite of these differences in size, mission, and region served, the president of the "system", Molly Broad, insisted that UNC was <u>not</u> a "system" but instead "one university with sixteen campuses". The difference was much more than a variation in phrasing. To operate as one university required a large central staff and President Broad had reporting to her a group of vice-presidents with responsibilities that paralleled those of vice-chancellors on the campuses – e.g. academic affairs, finance, research, information systems, legal affairs, etc. These vice presidents were talented individuals who tended to cultivate relationships with their campus counterparts, creating an inevitable informal reporting system. Likewise, all lobbying of the state legislature was to be done by a UNC vice-president for legislative affairs.

The UNC governing board, the Board of Governors, consisted of thirty-two individuals who were appointed by the Governor and who had to approve virtually very personnel decision and programmatic change. The Board of Governors met every month over two days in the UNC offices located near the UNC–Chapel Hill campus. President Broad met with the campus chancellors and her vice-presidents at the beginning of the two-day period with the session typically dominated by issues presented by the various vice-presidents. Then the Board of Governors committees would meet in the afternoon, followed by the full board meeting the next day. At the Governor's meeting, all the chancellors were seated at chairs near the back of the room and had no role in the meeting except to be introduced by President Broad at the beginning. The board, comprised mostly of UNC–Chapel Hill and NC State graduates, rarely dealt with issues that were unique to the other campuses. In my two years attending these sessions, not once was I asked to address the board or respond to an issue under consideration.

In addition to the Board of Governors and the president's staff, the organizational structure included a Board of Trustees for each campus. This board consisted of twelve individuals appointed by the Board of Governors for six-year terms. The Trustees elected their own chair. By the time I arrived, the chair that had recruited me, Phil Dixon, had completed his term and was off the board. Charlie Franklin, the head of a regional mental health agency, was now the chair of the trustees.

The powers delegated to the trustees by the Board of Governors fell into two primary areas: athletics and the campus physical facilities, including the approval of architects and the awarding of contracts for campus construction. The board was meeting each month over a two-day period and padding the agenda to include reports concerning many areas of the university over which they had no official jurisdiction. I finally persuaded them to streamline their meetings into one day and not to meet every month. But, in the areas where the trustees had jurisdiction, they were heavily involved, both through their committees and as a full board.

The board committee for campus facilities spent considerable time inspecting architectural proposals, often insisting on changes that would lengthen the process and result in increased costs not only from the changes but also from the inflated bids from contractors because of the delay. This was in spite of a talented and experienced staff at ECU responsible for this area. Likewise, in athletics I would have the athletic director come to board meetings to provide a report that always resulted in detailed questions about many issues. And there was tension between the AD and some members of the board, largely because of bad feelings between the AD and the head football coach. So the board took a lot of my time and energy in both preparing for the meetings and refereeing the various disputes that arose.

In addition, the chair of the trustees, Charlie Franklin, was very active, visiting the campus often and frequently talking with staff members whom he had known for a number of years. This often resulted in rumors Charlie picked up on the campus concerning internal matters about which he would want to talk. My staff and I sometimes joked that it would be nice if Charlie had a "real job" so he did not have time to come to campus so often. While Franklin was a likeable guy, all of these issues required considerable time for research and response and his behavior encouraged individuals on the campus to go to the trustees to get their problems solved.

In retrospect, the organizational structure did not mesh with my managerial style and this would ultimately contribute to several mistakes I made. The first was that, because of their proximity and intense interest in ECU, I gave a disproportionate amount of my time and energy in responding to the demands of the Board of Trustees. But, when I needed support, the board did not reciprocate.

The second was an assumption that President Broad, with sixteen chancellors and about as many vice-presidents and central office staff reporting to her, would welcome someone who could function without much guidance. I met with President Broad during my first month on the job for what seemed like a perfunctory session and, thereafter, did not meet with her individually. She did not request that I, or the other chancellors, to my knowledge, meet with her one-on-one, apparently preferring to interact with us as a group. I took this as an indication that she wanted us to "take the ball and run with it" – i.e. chart a course for our institutions and pursue it. So that is what I did. That didn't turn out to be the best strategy.

The organizational structure and culture seemed, also, to minimize the role of the chancellors, although that may not have been intentional The vice-presidents in the central office often communicated and dealt directly with the vice-chancellors on the campuses so that decisions were sometimes made without consultation with the chancellors. This seemed to be particularly true in the financial area. While the decisions weren't necessarily ones with which I would have disagreed, the flow of work and the resulting relationships created the impression that vice-chancellors reported to their respective vice-president.

ALL PIRATES ON DECK

Much of East Carolina's support throughout the region and most of its visibility nationally came from its athletic program. The Pirates excelled consistently in baseball but it was football that generated the most attention.

East Carolina had been a football power in the "small college" division of NCAA in the 60's and 70's. Interestingly, one of the coaches who built up its strong program was Pat Dye who was at Auburn when I arrived. When ECU moved up to Division I-A competition, however, there was no conference with which to affiliate; so the Pirates played for over 20 years as an independent, occasionally beating powerhouses like Miami (Fla.) and other major schools. By the time I arrived, ECU was a member of Conference USA for all sports.

In fall, 2001, ECU was ranked in the Top 25 in the pre-season football polls and the fans were expecting a great season. The Pirates had gone 8-4 the year before, including a bowl game. The head coach, Steve Logan, was innovative, particularly on offense, and had achieved considerable success over the past ten years. As the season unfolded, however, it became clear that we could score but had a hard time keeping the opponent from scoring as well. This problem was best exemplified in the GMAC bowl game against Marshall at the end of the season. The Pirates led by over 30 points at halftime, but ended up losing the game, 64-61, in the highest scoring bowl game in history and finished with a 6-6 record.

The next season was even worse as the Pirates finished 4-8. It seemed that they lacked the talent to compete and/or the coaching to utilize the talents they had. In any case, the athletic director, Mike Hamrick, believed that a new coach was needed and I gave him permission to hire one, after the Pirates' last game of the 2002 season. It appeared to me that ECU was not recruiting the caliber of players needed to compete at the C-USA level.

A search committee interviewed several candidates for head coach and recommended the hiring of John Thompson, then the defensive coordinator at the University of Florida. Thompson, who was the choice of AD Hamrick and associate AD Nick Floyd, had an impressive record as a defensive coordinator at several schools and came well prepared for his interview. After the hiring decision was made, however, Hamrick came under some criticism for firing Steve Logan.

I felt that Hamrick had done a good job as athletic director. He had operated the department in the black, no easy task since ECU derived very little income from the conference. He had helped to develop excellent facilities – a beautiful strength and conditioning center at the football stadium; a new baseball stadium, one of the finest on a college campus; and many other facilities that compared favorably with those at larger and more prestigious universities. And he had maintained good relationships with all the coaches, except Logan. But Hamrick eventually decided that a move to another school might be the best decision for him and I assisted him in securing the AD's job at the University of Nevada–Las Vegas. Nick Floyd was then appointed as the interim athletic director and served in this capacity for the remainder of my time at ECU.

A major issue concerning football that emerged during 2003 was the realignment that was occurring in conference membership. Two schools – Miami (Fla.) and Virginia Tech – had left the Big East Conference to join the Atlantic Coast Conference (ACC), and a third – Boston College –was considering a similar move. This left the Big East with the need to add schools, in order to have eight schools with football programs. There were a number of ECU supporters who wanted to push for membership in the ACC. I knew that was highly unlikely but, nevertheless, arranged a meeting with John Swofford, the ACC commissioner that included one of the ECU trustees, Steve Showfety. The meeting was very cordial and helped convince the Pirate faithful that we had, at least, tried that option.

Membership in the Big East was, I believed, a distinct possibility. All indications were that fellow C-USA members Louisville and Cincinnati were going to be invited to join and that the Big East would need another football-playing school as well. The most frequently mentioned alternatives were ECU, Memphis and South Florida. I felt that ECU was the best choice, given our geographic fit and the traditional strength of our football program. So we prepared an attractive proposal that was sent to all Big East schools. I also hired Roy Kramer, former commissioner of the Southeastern Conference (SEC) to lobby for us, particularly with the Big East commissioner, Mike Transgeese. But, after I had left ECU, the Big East selected South Florida on the strength and size of their media market. It was hard for eastern North Carolina to compete with Tampa in that regard.

Marlene and I both enjoyed basketball at ECU. The coach of the men's team, Bill Herrion, a native of Massachusetts, was hard working and innovative. I felt that he got the most out of the talent he had, but the dominance of the ACC in basketball in North Carolina made it difficult to attract good players to ECU. The Pirates did not have a winning season during my time there, but they won some big games and the admiration of fans with their scrappy play.

Baseball was my love and I saw an excellent exhibition of it at ECU. In the season prior to our arrival, the Pirates had gone to the NCAA playoffs and fell one win short of going to the College World Series. The coach was an outstanding young man named Keith LeClair about whom an unforgettable saga would unfold. Toward the end of the 2002 season LeClair began to show signs of ALS, the so-called "Lou Gehrig's disease". He went through numerous tests and treatments, but the paralysis continued to worsen. Finally, he had to move to a wheelchair and then to a bed. Mike Hamrick and I arranged to continue Keith as an advisor to the baseball program so that he could be on the payroll and, more importantly, continue to have medical insurance. A new coach was hired but, during the 2003 season, Keith often came to the games in a specially equipped van that he parked near the bullpen, allowing him to view the play on the field.

That year, the Pirates won the C-USA tournament that they hosted at the minor league stadium in Kinston, about thirty miles from the campus. ECU's new baseball stadium had not yet been built. In the final game on a beautiful Sunday afternoon, the Pirates were locked in a tight battle with Houston. The van containing Coach LeClair was parked down the right field line. When ECU prevailed, the team had its mandatory celebration around home plate and, then, ran down and surrounded LeClair's van and gave him a resounding cheer. It was an emotional moment for everyone connected with ECU.

I visited with Keith as his health continued to deteriorate, finally to a point where he could only communicate with a specially designed computer that followed the movement of his eyes. I was always impressed with his courage and his positive attitude. Keith passed away after I left ECU, but I will always remember the example he set.

Beyond the athletes, coaches, and fans, there were two people who made a significant difference in Pirate athletics. The first was Dennis Young, the executive director of the Pirate Club, the booster organization for ECU athletics. Dennis was a very personable and energetic individual who had built a network vital to the university both in terms of money raised and the tickets sold for the various athletic events. Dennis and I traveled to many Pirate Club functions together and I always enjoyed his company.

The second was Walter Williams, perhaps the number one Pirate supporter. A native of the area and a graduate of ECU, he owned an oil company that operated a chain of service stations throughout eastern North Carolina. The basketball arena carried his name and his financial support was pivotal in the building of a new baseball stadium. But, most of all, Walter was a very decent man who attended almost every game. I enjoyed his friendship and valued his support.

SCHOOL OF MEDICINE

One of the unusual features of ECU was the medical school, established through the exceptional efforts and political skills of Leo Jenkins in the mid-70's. The school focused primarily on family medicine. producing general practitioners to serve the small towns and rural areas of eastern North Carolina. Of course, not all students chose that path. But a large percentage did, with ECU ranking fifth in "rural medicine" and 20th in primary care among medical schools nationally.

The medical school had joined forces with the Pitt County Memorial Hospital (PCMH) to create a major medical facility about two miles west of the main ECU campus. The medical school was part of the health sciences division that also included the School of Nursing, the School of Allied Health Sciences, and the medical library. Nursing and Allied Health were currently located on the main campus, but plans were well underway to construct facilities for these programs on the health sciences campus.

The vice-chancellor for health sciences had resigned right before I arrived and Phyllis Horns, the dean of nursing, was serving in this role on an interim basis. An exceptionally talented and personable administrator, Dr. Horns performed this function remarkably well but did not wish to be a candidate for the job on a permanent basis. Therefore, a search was conducted and Dr. Michael Lewis, the vice-chancellor for health sciences at West Virginia, was hired to fill this position. Dr. Lewis had extensive experience overseeing programs similar to those at ECU and appeared to be the right person to lead this area. When he arrived in the spring of 2002, one of his first jobs was to fill the position of dean of the medical school. Serving as acting dean was Peter Kragel, the former head of the department of pathology who performed this role in 2001-2002. I gave Dr. Lewis three options to consider: a) appoint himself dean and vice-chancellor (as the previous vice-chancellor had done), b) continue with Dr. Kragel as dean (as we agreed he had done an acceptable job), or c) hire a new dean from outside. He elected the third option, bringing in a distinguished physician in family medicine from the University of Iowa in the summer of 2003.

I recognized the importance of the health sciences division both to ECU and to the eastern region that, according to numerous statistics, was unhealthy and significantly underserved. I pushed for new schools of pharmacy and dentistry but these efforts met with little success. However, the most energy was put into securing approval and funding for a "Heart Institute" at ECU and PCMH. Eastern North Carolina ranked as one of the worse areas of the nation in cardiovascular disease and this institute would address the need both for medical facilities and services as well as training of physicians.

Pitt County Memorial Hospital (PCMH), led by its highly effective CEO, David McRae, was very supportive and ECU's excellent team of heart surgeons and cardiologists were excited about the idea as well. Foremost in that group was Dr. Randolph Chitwood, the head of the ECU department of surgery and chief of surgery at PCMH. Dr. Chitwood had developed an international reputation in heart surgery through the use of his daVinci robot to perform a number of surgical functions. He saw the heart institute as something that would not only enhance ECU's reputation but address an important need in the region as well.

To make the case for the heart institute, I had to violate the UNC policy about lobbying the legislature, but I felt this was necessary to get the issue considered. With the help of several legislators, we were able to get bills introduced in both the NC Senate and the House to provide $60M for this project. We also teamed with UNC–Chapel Hill to support their efforts to get $150M for an expansion of their cancer center, partly to defuse their possible opposition to the heart institute. We even put together a plan to fund both the heart and cancer centers by a tax increase of 2¢ per pack on cigarettes; given that North Carolina's tax on cigarettes at that time was one of the lowest in the country, I thought it had a chance to succeed and lobbied for it with both the Speaker of the House and the President of the Senate. In the end, the bill did not make it through the legislature, but these efforts laid the groundwork for the subsequent funding of a Heart Center at ECU after I had departed.

MAJOR PROBLEMS TO BE SOLVED

In addition to the task of developing a strategic vision and plan for ECU and raising its visibility in the state and region, there were several areas that represented significant challenges and, in some cases, major problems. Although they were all interrelated, I will discuss them separately.

a. <u>Filling leadership positions</u>. There were several major leadership positions that needed to be filled during my tenure at ECU. I have already mentioned the vice-chancellor for health affairs, a position to which Mike Lewis was recruited. Another opening that occurred in my second year was the vice-chancellor for institutional advancement with responsibilities for alumni affairs, development, and publications. This was a critical position in that we were ready to launch a major capital campaign. For this post, I was able to attract Bill Shelton who had served for ten years as president of Eastern Michigan University and, prior to that, had been vice president for institutional advancement at Kent State. I had known Bill when he was at Kent and persuaded him to leave a faculty position at EMU to join us in summer, 2003.

The most significant role to fill, however, was that of provost or chief academic officer of the institution. I had created the position in response to faculty requests that the vice-chancellor for academic affairs take a more active and aggressive role in shaping the academic mission. So I moved the graduate school and the division of student affairs under the provost, giving that individual responsibility for all academic programs and for student life, both academic and non-academic.

The other major unit affected by these changes was the division of research, economic development, and community engagement. Tom Feldbush led this division which became the university's major "outreach" arm working with communities and organizations to make ECU a major player in the economic revitalization of the region. A longtime university employee, Richard Brown, headed the division of business and finance.

Unlike the two vice-chancellorships – health sciences and institutional advancement – mentioned earlier, I did not take a personal role in recruiting for or filling the position of provost because of a strong desire on the part of faculty leaders to be involved. I appointed a search committee that advertised the opening, reviewed candidates, selected and interviewed finalists, and made a recommendation to me. One of the finalists was Bob Thompson who had served as acting vice-chancellor for the past year. I felt Bob had done a good job and would have been pleased to have him continue in that role but he had aroused significant faculty opposition. Another finalist was an individual that I had worked with previously and would have favored but she also had faculty opposition.

The candidate who was the unanimous choice of the search committee and who had the greatest faculty support was Dr. William Swart, the dean of engineering at Old Dominion University in Virginia. During his interview, I was impressed with how well organized he was and concluded that he might be the sort of "take charge" person that the faculty leadership had said they wanted. And take charge he did! Joining ECU at the beginning of the 2002-2003 academic year, Swart made a number of significant changes over the next twelve months – e.g. a major reorganization of the academic colleges, developing programs to permit motivated students to complete their degree programs earlier, and formulating plans for a bachelor's degree in engineering. Swart had conducted a number of open meetings for the faculty to give input on the proposals he developed and, impressively, the Faculty Senate approved the academic reorganization he proposed within only a few months. But there was opposition developing to his aggressive managerial style that I did not fully recognize until later.

b.   <u>Heart Work</u>. Following the heart catheterization operation in Auburn in the spring, 2001, I had worked hard at maintaining my health, exercising each day and trying to eat properly. And once I arrived at ECU, the pace of work was always brisk. I had been lined up with a fine cardiologist, Dr. Joseph Babb, and a general physician, Dr. Jack Rose, both on the ECU medical faculty. I had a great deal of confidence in both men, but, to my surprise and consternation, I began to experience chest pain again near the end of 2001.

Dr. Babb decided to do a catheterization in late January 2002, and found that scar tissue had grown inside the stent in my artery, a condition known as "re-stenosis", almost blocking the flow of blood. To remove the scar tissue a new form of radiation was required that the PCMH was not licensed to perform. So I had to be transported to Bowman Gray Hospital in Winston-Salem where a physician from the Wake Forest School of Medicine did the procedure.

Throughout 2002, I experienced episodes of chest pain, resulting in two additional catheterizations, one to clean out the artery and one to place an additional stent in that vessel. But the most intense pain occurred in late December while Marlene and I were celebrating Christmas holidays with our daughter, Ellen, and her family in Cincinnati. As soon as we returned to Greenville, I went to my doctor and was placed in the hospital that day. It was determined that I needed to have an operation to bypass the artery that continued to clog. Fortunately for me, at this point, I had suffered no damage to my heart, but unless this problem was solved, such damage could occur.

Dr. Ranny Chitwood, the renowned heart surgeon, was chosen to do the operation. Because the clogged artery was located behind my heart, my chest had to be opened and my heart lifted out to gain access. The procedure took about ten hours and, when I awoke, I found tubes coming out of my chest to drain off the fluids. I remained in the hospital for about three days after the surgery and reports to me were that the operation had been very successful.

When I got back home, I went to bed and slept for an extended period. Then I discovered just how weak I had become; since I could not use the muscles in my chest, I needed help just to sit up and, certainly, to get out of bed. Visions of returning to the office in a few days were quickly discarded. After about two weeks, I began to meet with staff members at the chancellor's residence, as I felt strong enough to work for a few hours each day. After about a month, I was able to return to the office for a few hours each morning and a few hours in the afternoon with lunch and a nap in between. Though I pushed myself to get back to full speed (there were so many things that needed to be done!), it was mid year before I felt fully recovered.

c.   Internal Auditing. As CEO of the organization, I got copies of all internal audit reports and had to respond as to whether the findings and recommendations were accepted. At both Akron and Auburn, the internal audit staffs were excellent and I rarely had any questions about the reports. At ECU, however, this emerged as a problem. At first, I had reservations about the quality of the reports I saw. There were also some complaints about favoritism as to who got audited and how they were treated. I finally decided to investigate, interviewing each member of the auditing staff, and concluded there were grounds for the dismissal of the head of that department. The result was a negotiated resignation on the last day prior to the beginning of the

Christmas vacation period, 2002. I appointed one of the audit staff members as the acting director. This decision began a chain of events over the next several months that brought me considerable unease and some embarrassment.

The first event occurred on the first day the university was in session after the Christmas and New Year's break. I was in the hospital getting ready for the bypass operation that was to happen the next day. Richard Brown, the chief financial officer who carried the title of executive vice-chancellor and was in charge during my absence from campus, called me to report that an employee in the housing division had provided him with evidence that Emanuel (Manny) Amaro, the director of housing, had been embezzling university funds. He felt that Amaro should be dismissed as soon as he returned to the campus. I asked Brown if he had sufficient evidence to support the charges and he assured me that he had. I, therefore, authorized him to proceed with the dismissal.

Manny Amaro was an individual with whom I was quite familiar, as he had been the subject of several conversations during my time at ECU. Manny was a young man, probably in his late 30's, who had an infectious laugh and a bubbly personality. He lived on campus in an apartment in one of the dorms and always seemed to be available to assist with whatever was happening. For example, whenever there was a reception at the chancellor's house, Manny was there to greet guests, hang up coats, and introduce people around. He would even stay to help clean up. He was an asset in these settings and I thought he was a part of K. Woolard's "hospitality staff" who made all the arrangements for social events.

A few months after I arrived at ECU, Dr. Garrie Moore, the vice-chancellor for student affairs, visited me. He reported to me that a "lot of people" were upset that Manny Amaro was attending events at the chancellor's house. I asked why and he said that Manny bragged about this to others on his staff. I replied that, as far as I knew, Manny was working there but that if he did not think this was appropriate, he could tell Manny not to do so since Manny reported to him. I later checked with Austin Bunch and learned that Manny had volunteered to assist at these events, that this had been going on for several years, and that the staff thought his help was valuable. So I did nothing about the arrangement, actually being somewhat amused that some people would resent others who got to work at these events for no compensation.

Several months later, Dr. Moore came to see me to report that he believed that Amaro was a homosexual and felt we needed to remove him from his position. I admitted that I would not be surprised if Manny were gay, as he was unmarried and had some mannerisms that might lead one to that conclusion; however, I pointed out that university policy prohibited discrimination on the basis of sexual orientation. On the other hand, if there was evidence that Manny had taken advantage of a student or someone who reported to him that could be grounds for dismissal. A week or so later, Moore reported that a male student had admitted to one of his counselors that he had had an affair with Amaro. Recognizing that these were serious charges that could result in litigation, should Amaro be dismissed, I ask Garrie to get some documentation – perhaps a signed statement from the student. We could keep the student's identity confidential, but such evidence could be important should it become a legal matter.

A few days later, a student came to my office and asked to see me. When I agreed to meet with him, he told me that he was aware that Dr. Moore had come to me about Manny Amaro and that he wanted me to know that his comments to the counselor had been misinterpreted. He said that he was an officer in the Student Government Association and that Manny was the advisor to SGA, hence he knew him well -- but that they had not had a sexual relationship. To my surprise, he even gave me a letter, affirming what he had told me in writing. I subsequently reported this to Dr. Moore who seemed to be unhappy with this news. I told him that he could remove Manny as SGA advisor and put someone else in that role, if he wanted to, but the matter certainly did not warrant dismissal.

Reflecting on the events concerning Amaro, I realized that Dr. Moore – and perhaps others at the university – wanted to get rid of Manny. Being somewhat perplexed, I looked at his performance as housing director and it appeared to be excellent – e.g. student satisfaction surveys revealed that they were very pleased with on-campus housing and there was much greater demand for dormitory space than we could accommodate; in fact, we had a planning process well underway that would substantially increase on-campus housing. Surely his work at the social events couldn't produce that much resentment. Or could it? I observed Manny at these functions and everyone seemed to know him and enjoy his company, including trustees and other university officials who were often in attendance. So I did nothing about the issue.

When contacted by Richard Brown the day before my heart bypass surgery about the charges of embezzlement against Amaro, I was stunned. But I trusted Brown's judgment as to the strength of the evidence, and therefore, did not hesitate to authorize Manny's dismissal. After I was home from the hospital, I learned that Amaro had been fired and the evidence turned over to the state for possible criminal prosecution. Over a period of about eight years, Manny had followed a process of having work done by the university (e.g. printing, etc.) for a national housing association of which he was an officer and then having the reimbursement check from the association made out to him. The amount each year was not huge but totaled in excess of $100,000 over the time period. Amaro, subsequently, negotiated a settlement with the state, repaying all the monies by cashing in his retirement benefits. To my knowledge, he never came back to the campus and I never saw him again.

I asked that a complete investigation take place to determine how this embezzlement could occur over such an extended period of time. It was also intriguing to me to learn that the housing division had been audited four years earlier by internal auditing who had not detected this misuse of funds. It also seemed to me that the resignation of the director of internal auditing and the reporting of the embezzlement, occurring on consecutive business days at the university, might not have been coincidental.

Indeed, the internal audit report, when I finally received it, produced significant disappointment. It did not address why the embezzlement had gone on for nine years without detection nor why an internal audit of the division had not discovered it. Instead, it placed "blame" on Amaro's relationship with the chancellor – i.e. that he was "protected" in the eyes of those who might have been able to reveal the transgressions. I found that conclusion unwarranted and did not accept the report. While I had been at ECU only a little over a year at that point and could not speak for the previous chancellor, I just could not see how that finding could be justified. But the audience with whom I was dealing – the internal auditing staff, the chief financial officer, the university's attorney, and the vice-chancellor for student affairs – all had some culpability in the matter and were anxious to see the blame placed elsewhere.

Also during 2003, another internal audit was conducted of the Telemedicine Center in the Medical School. This center was directed by Dr. David Balch, a nationally-known faculty member who had pioneered in the development of networks that could transmit patient information such as x-rays by a closed circuit from remote locations, thereby permitting doctors in small towns to consult with experts at a medical center. Dr. Balch had received a major grant from the National Library of Medicine. His work was impressive and he was gaining considerable national recognition.

The audit was precipitated when three female assistants in the center complained about mismanagement and the mistreatment of staff. All indications were that Dr. Balch was not a good manager; he was often gone from the campus, and was verbally abusive of the staff when he was there. The audit report recommended a number of managerial improvements but also called for Dr. Balch to be dismissed. In my reply, I indicated that changes in the managerial procedures were needed but that personnel changes were not within the scope of the audit team authority. I asked Tom Feldbush, the vice-chancellor for research, to consult with the manager of the federal grant at NLM to determine if any of the audit findings were of concern. The NLM manager indicated that he was very pleased with the work Dr. Balch was doing and that the grant funds had been used appropriately. Nevertheless, Balch resigned from the university.

I felt that both audits had been poorly conducted and that new leadership for that unit was needed. But I also felt vulnerable because of the Amaro case, as any action by me would be seen as retaliation. So I did nothing, hoping the issue would go away. But, of course, it didn't. Someone told Charlie Franklin, the chairman of the trustees about the Amaro audit and he demanded a copy of the internal audit report. I refused to provide it because it was an incomplete report and a confidential document. But, then, someone mailed a copy of the report to President Broad. We talked at length about the case on the phone and I thought she was comfortable with the actions I had taken.

d) <u>Relationship with President Broad</u>. Overreaching all of the problems with which I was dealing was a relationship with President Broad that never felt completely satisfactory to me. A partial contribution may have been the way I was appointed – e.g. emerging as a candidate at the last minute and being the only candidate recommended by the committee. President Broad may have felt she had no other choice. Another factor was the organizational structure with so many people, including sixteen chancellors, reporting to her. I felt that my best strategy was not to "bother" her with issues I felt capable of handling, so there was little cultivation of the sort that would normally occur.

The relationship was exacerbated about a year after going to ECU by my willingness to consider the presidency of Mississippi State University. My good friend, Jimmy Taylor, a banker who was a MSU grad, persuaded me to meet with a group of business leaders in Mississippi at his place in Birmingham. Mississippi State was looking for a new president and this group felt I would be the ideal candidate, given my roots in the state and my experience as a university president. I had some trepidation about leaving ECU after only one year but felt this might be a "chance of a lifetime" to go back home. Within a few days, a plane picked me up in North Carolina and transported me to Jackson to interview with the Board of Trustees for Institutions of Higher Learning, the governing board for all public universities in Mississippi. The interview seemed to go well except for a couple of trustees, who had heard that I had met with the business leaders and were very upset that this group was trying to interfere in the selection process.

After being flown back to North Carolina, I called the search firm involved and found that the board had not been able to make a decision. I therefore, decided to withdraw. In spite of the supposed confidentiality of the process, a story appeared in a Mississippi newspaper that I had been interviewed for the job. President Broad was very upset that I had done this and let me know in no uncertain terms.

There were other incidents that did not improve the relationship, coming primarily from my efforts to promote ECU. I realized later that my actions were likely under greater scrutiny because of ECU's historical role as a "maverick" that didn't want to stay in "its place". One episode that I recall evolved around my visit with the ACC commissioner about ECU's possible membership in the conference. I set up the meeting just to appease ECU fans but, unfortunately, in an interview I had referenced efforts by the Governor of Virginia to get Virginia Tech admitted to the conference and indicated it would be nice to see the Governor of North Carolina make similar efforts on ECU's behalf. Governor Easley did not like that at all, fearing that ECU fans would lobby him to do so. He called President Broad to express his concerns and she voiced her displeasure with my actions.

The issue that caught me most by surprise, however, was her objection to a car I had purchased. When I came to ECU, I was assigned an automobile that was being leased by the ECU Foundation. A Lincoln Continental, it was the car that had been used by the outgoing chancellor. When the lease was expiring in mid-2003, the head of the foundation asked me if I would prefer a car allowance. I indicated I would as I could have a car to take with me when I retired. While looking for a new car, I happened to be with Don Parrott, the mayor of Greenville, and liked the car he was driving. It was a Lexus and he reported that he bought it second-hand through the local Toyota dealer. I met with the dealer and he said he could find me a similar "pre-owned" auto at a substantial discount off the new car price. We made a deal and I was very pleased with my purchase. And it did not cost the university or foundation any more that if I was driving a Volkswagen. But president Broad saw if differently, letting me know that a Lexus was not an appropriate automobile for a university chancellor to be driving. At this point, I was convinced I could do nothing right!

A PREMATURE EXIT

As the fall semester, 2003, was getting underway, I took a trip to Washington to visit with some members of North Carolina's congressional delegation, along with several other community leaders from Greenville. I had ridden up there with Austin Bunch. About the time we were getting settled into our hotel rooms late Monday afternoon, I received a call from President Broad demanding that I be in her office at 8:00 am the next morning. I explained that I was in Washington and that I would need to go back home to Greenville before driving to Chapel Hill. She was not very sympathetic to my logistical problems but agreed to postpone the session until 10:00 am and asked me to meet her at the president's house.

Austin and I had dinner and then drove back to Greenville, arriving late Monday night. Then I got up early the next morning for the two-hour drive to Chapel Hill. Marlene accompanied me to provide support, which I welcomed, although she was not invited to attend the meetings that followed. In our meeting, President Broad complained about the Amaro audit, which was about to be covered by the News and Observer. I agreed that any negative publicity could be embarrassing, but maintained that I had done nothing inappropriate. She also talked about complaints she had heard about provost Swart's managerial style. I admitted that he was, perhaps, attempting to make changes too rapidly for the culture at ECU but that I thought most of the things he proposed were needed.

Then she asked me to follow her down to her office where Jim Talton, now chairman of the ECU Board of Trustees, and the chair of the UNC Board of Governors joined us. President Broad went over much of the same material and I responded much as I had earlier. After this session, I met briefly with Jim Talton and asked him what was going on. He said that he did not know. So Marlene and I drove back to Greenville.

By the next morning, I received notice that president Broad had called an emergency meeting of the ECU trustees for Wednesday evening at a Raleigh hotel and that I was expected to be there. Marlene and I drove to the hotel, planning to join the group for a dinner that began the meeting. But we were informed that we were not invited to the dinner and that I would be called whenever the group wanted to meet with me. So Marlene and I checked into the hotel and had dinner in our room.

Finally, about 10 pm, we were called down to the conference room where the meeting was held. Marlene was asked if she wanted to say anything. She made several positive statements about our time at ECU and then proceeded to give her perspective on the Amaro case, since she knew Manny well from his work at the house. When she finished, she was asked to leave and I was given a chance to speak. I indicated that I found the whole process confusing and somewhat unorthodox, since I did not know what they had been discussing nor what "charges" may have been levied against me. I asked what questions they had and received a query about the Amaro audit. I replied in some depth, emphasizing that the event that triggered the exposure of Manny's embezzlement was the removal of the head of internal auditing and that the conclusion that Amaro was "protected" by his relationship to the chancellor was illogical. I got another question about the Balch audit, wanting to know if this endangered our federal funding in medicine. I described our consultation with the NLM Manager of the grant and expressed my judgment that no such danger existed. I was then excused. I later learned that the board had reviewed an extensive set of documents supplied by the president's office (that I never saw) at the beginning of the meeting.

At 6:00 am the next morning, I got a call from Jim Talton informing me that President Broad wanted me to resign. I asked him if the Board of Trustees agreed with that decision. He acknowledged that there were several who objected but that the majority felt that "if that was what President Broad wanted, then that is what I should do". I thanked Jim and immediately called President Broad, telling her that if she wanted me to resign I would do so. I expressed a desire, however, to continue as chancellor until the end of the year, allowing a smooth transition. She indicated ECU would pay me at my current salary for the remainder of 2003 but she wanted my resignation as chancellor to be effective immediately. Furthermore, she wanted me to vacate the chancellor's house by September 30th. I pointed out that this would be an extreme hardship, as Marlene and I had no other place to move and we would have to make all these arrangements within about two weeks. She evidenced no willingness to negotiate; so the statement "To hell with it" would best describe my attitude at this point. She faxed a resignation letter to me; I signed it, and faxed it back to her.

After we drove back to Greenville, I went to my office, collected all my personal belongings, and said goodbye to the staff. Over the next two weeks, Marlene and I packed our stuff and arranged for it to be stored in Greenville. Then we hit the road toward retirement.

The newspaper article that President Broad feared did appear in the News and Observer about two days after my resignation. It had no input from me and was embarrassing. I was told that a secretary on warning status because of poor performance had released the Amaro audit report to the press, thereby becoming a "whistleblower" which protected her from being fired. Whether that was true or not, I do not know; but, if so, it seemed clear to me that she had some assistance from one or more people inside the university in order to do this.

I was pleased that Greenville's newspaper that usually covered ECU extensively, The Daily Reflector, did not repeat the story, nor comment on it. Before we left Greenville, I called the associate editor in charge of the editorial page and offered to meet with the editorial board on the condition that the entire interview would be printed. I felt that the entire story needed to be heard to clarify any misconceptions that people might have. The interview was conducted and printed in the next Sunday edition.

As far as I know, nothing further developed on the Amaro case and, I suspect it was forgotten fairly quickly; likewise with the telemedicine audit. Bill Shelton was named the interim chancellor, a wise choice given his previous experience as a CEO. But he was not ultimately selected to be the chancellor on a continuing basis. Bill Swart was removed as provost; his managerial style and the pace of change he was pushing did not mesh with the culture of ECU. He was likely hurt also because I had recommended a significant raise for him; this created resentment from others in the administration. Even Tom Feldbush, the vice-chancellor of research was moved back to the faculty after I departed. Tom, whom I felt was doing an excellent job, apparently clashed with the UNC vice-president for research over some of ECU's initiatives. Slowly the leadership team that I assembled was dismantled.

Did I make a mistake in going to ECU? There have been many occasions when I felt that I did. I certainly made mistakes that contributed to my downfall. But I did not fit very comfortably into the system and my desire to make a difference was not always consistent with what others wanted. Perhaps if I had adopted a "go with the flow" attitude, I would have lasted longer. But that was not and had never been my style.

But it is important to look on the positive side of this experience.

A WALK ON THE POSITIVE SIDE

While my tenure at ECU did not end in a way that I hoped or envisioned, I will still treasure many positive dimensions to the experience.

First, I worked with many wonderful people, several of whom represented a "reunion" of sorts. Ruth Ann Cook, who had been my assistant at Appalachian State and who had moved on to several administrative posts at UNC–Greensboro, was persuaded to join me at ECU as an assistant to the chancellor. Ron and Mary Newton, whom we had known at Texas A&M, had moved to ECU where Ron headed the department of biology. Jim Bearden, who had been the business school dean at ECU when I started the business school at ASU and had been very helpful to me, was now a distinguished professor at ECU. We had many good times getting reacquainted with these wonderful friends.

We also made many new friends both at ECU and in Greenville. A brief sampling would include Mike and Susan Dorsey who lived down the street from us. Mike is an accomplished artist and was dean of the school of art; Marilyn Sheerer, dean of education and one of the most skilled administrators with whom I worked; Cindy Kittrel, one of the most enthusiastic development officers that I know; Austin and Wanda Bunch – Austin was my effective chief of staff and a trusted friend; Walter and Marie Williams, great sports fans and dear friends; and Gene and Sylvia McCreary, close friends in the community.

Overall, I had a good working relationship with the ECU Board of Trustees and with the two chairmen under whom I worked, Charlie Franklin and Jim Talton. I particularly appreciated the friendship and support of trustees Mike Kelly, Betty Spier, Tom Bayliss, and Margaret Ward. My only regret was the failure of the board as a group to stand up for me when I needed it.

Although my time at ECU was only a little over two years, I was pleased with what was accomplished. Virtually all of the university's numbers were positive: increasing enrollments each year, rising SAT scores for entering freshman, record donations to the ECU Foundation. I successfully led the university through both reaccreditation by SACS and recertification by NCAA. ECU made major progress in developing courses and degree programs to be offered via distance education technology (e.g. teaching via the internet), becoming the leading UNC institution in that category. Significant advances were made in planning efforts with the city of Greenville and mayor Don Parrott, including plans for a "10th Street Connector", a boulevard that would connect the health sciences campus and the main campus and provide more direct access to ECU from the west. Relationships were established with leaders throughout eastern North Carolina to position ECU to be a player in the economic revitalization of the area.

RETIREMENT

When retirement arrived, we were not ready for it – at least not physically. Over the years, I had envisioned that after my service as a university president was completed, I would move to the faculty and teach for a number of years. I had the opportunity to do that at Auburn and at ECU but elected not to do so. I was weary from all the battles that had to be fought and ready to move on. Since we had lived in university-furnished housing for the previous twenty years, Marlene and I had no place of our own to move back to. We had looked at properties in the mountains near Boone and along the Atlantic coast in North Carolina, as either a vacation retreat and/or eventually as a retirement site, but had never found anything we liked. When we were in Auburn, we had occasionally looked for a place there, but again, never bought anything. So as we approached retirement, we had to count ourselves among the homeless.

Interestingly enough, only about three weeks prior to the meetings with President Broad at UNC, I had thought – perhaps for the first time – seriously about retirement. Marlene and I were spending a week with our dear friends, Gabe and Sandy Campbell, at their place on Crystal Lake near Frankfort, Michigan. The setting was so peaceful and the weather gorgeous. As I sat gazing out at the clear blue water, being massaged by a gentle breeze, I thought how nice it would be to have the time and freedom to relax and really enjoy life. The past two years of dealing with health problems and the increasing stress of university administration was beginning to weigh on me. My next birthday, I reasoned, would be my 65th year and I needed to "hang it up". But, then, my rational side stood up and reminded me that I needed to stay at ECU at least five years to complete the work I had started.

As Marlene and I discussed where we might live, family emerged as the most important factor. We wanted to spend time with our children and grandchildren, so that pointed us toward the Midwest since all the kids lived in Michigan, Minnesota, or Ohio. We had lived longer in Ohio than in any other state, Ellen and Van had been born there, all three kids had gone to college in the Buckeye State, and Ellen and Van had married spouses from Ohio. Furthermore, Marlene had grown up in southern Indiana and many of her relatives, including her mother, still lived there.

So we headed to Cincinnati to visit with Ellen and Larry and to consider buying a home. Larry's parents, Don and Rose Lindeman, had a very nice apartment in their lovely home that they offered to let us use while we inspected the real estate in the area. Fortunately, we found a nice home in Montgomery, a northern suburb of Cincinnati, and were able to move in before the end of December. The house has a contemporary design with lots of windows overlooking a tree-shaded lot, a large living room with fireplace, and a large finished basement that I have been able to use as an office and TV room. The basement provides ample space for me to display the mementos I've collected over my career and, more importantly, provides a great out-of-the-way place for the grandchildren to play.

After our first winter in Cincinnati, we decided to go to Florida for the month of March. I wanted to attend spring training to get my baseball blood flowing and Marlene wanted to visit with several of our friends who were now living in the Sunshine State. One of our stops was in Vero Beach to spend a few days with Gabe and Sandy Campbell. They lived in a retirement community called Vista Royale that consisted of a number of two-story buildings, each containing fourteen condos, spread around an 18-hole golf course. We liked the place and decided to purchase a unit that had just come on the market. It was a fully furnished, two-bedroom unit, overlooking the twelfth green. I think Marlene and I were both surprised that we acted so quickly. It had taken us two months to find a house in Cincinnati.

By the time we returned to Vero Beach in November 2004, two major hurricanes had hit the area causing extensive damage in that section of the Atlantic coast, including Vista Royale. Fortunately, our condo suffered only some broken windows and soaked carpet in an enclosed back porch area. We returned to Cincinnati for Christmas, going back to Vero for January to April. There was plenty of time to enjoy the sun, read and go to movies and museums, and I was able to play golf and tennis on a regular basis. But, by the end of March, Marlene had decided she did not want to be away from the grandkids for such an extended period. So we put the condo on the market and sold it quickly for about a 40% profit. We were into and out of the vacation real estate market quickly!

In addition to deciding where to live, retirement also confronts one with the decision of what do to. I believe men have the most difficulty because their identities are so tied to the job they have held or the profession they have practiced. In my case, there was the added challenge of moving from a community where I was well known to one where no one knew me. I had spent most of my career as a "public person". As a college president in a college town, you can hardly go anyplace without being recognized, a situation that is both comforting and confining.

One of the things I did not miss from presidential years was the seemingly endless string of receptions and cocktail parties. I'm sure that aspect of the job may appear glamorous to some, but believe me, it is hard work. At these obligatory functions, Marlene and I would stand near the door to greet guests as they arrived and to say goodbye as they departed. In between, I would make it a point to try to visit briefly with each guest or, more likely, listen to what they had to say. Rarely did we get a chance to sit down or eat until the guests had left. It should not be surprising that I have a bad set of feet and, in retirement, avoid cocktail parties whenever possible.

My transition to retirement was also made easier by a diverse set of interests. I was actually looking forward to having time for reading and reflection and to a slower, less stressful pace, particularly because of the difficulties with my heart. I had always liked to read, but rarely had the time to do so – for pleasure, that is. Now in retirement, I have averaged reading 100 books a year across a wide variety of topics. And, as a sports fan, I have finally had the chance to watch my favorite teams on television or travel to see a major league baseball game in Cincinnati, Cleveland, Detroit, or Chicago.

But my leisure did not last long, as friends came seeking my involvement in a variety of ventures. In Cincinnati, I was asked to serve on the Board of Directors of the United Way Foundation of Greater Cincinnati. Dick Aft, a former United Way CEO whom I had met when Ellen worked for him while completing her master's degree in social work at the University of Cincinnati, persuaded me to take on this assignment. I became vice-chairman of the board and have helped to affect a partnership with the Greater Cincinnati Foundation to create an endowment for human services to supplement the annual fund drives.

My friends from Tau Kappa Epsilon came quickly to ask me to serve on the board of the TKE Educational Foundation. In that role, I have chaired a search committee to hire a new CEO for the foundation and helped to launch a major capital campaign. TKE also asked me to serve as the fraternity's representative on the House of Delegates of the North-American Interfraternity Council.

Perhaps my most significant involvement has been with the Kettering Foundation, headquartered in Dayton, Ohio. I have served on the Board of Directors of the National Issues Forum Institute, a part of the Kettering operation. NIFI produces discussion guides on topics of national importance and promotes citizen forums around the nation. Additionally, I have served as the Richard D Lombard Fellow at the foundation, allowing me to participate in their many programs studying democracy and how it can be made more effective.

I have also helped a good friend in Akron, Diane Evans, launch a new enterprise, SunLit Communications, to promote the reading and sale of books. In between, there have been several consulting assignments. And who knows what other new and interesting opportunities wait around the corner?

But, clearly, the most important benefit of retirement has been the freedom to spend time with family and friends. As our kids were growing up, much of my time was consumed by the kinds of jobs and outside leadership roles that I accepted. Nevertheless, I tried to be a good father and to spend as much time with the kids as possible. I loved them and I think they knew that. I am pleased with the relationship I now have with each of our three children and enjoy the time I am able to spend with them as adults, much like the time that I wish I had had with my own father. And, perhaps, the greatest role in life is that of grandparents, being available to observe the marvelous process of the growth and development of the human beings who are a part of your legacy – watching the emergence of their personalities and their efforts to learn what they need to know in order to survive and succeed. Lastly, retirement has provided time to visit with old friends. Marlene and I are fortunate to have many wonderful friends scattered all across the nation with whom we can communicate and visit.

CHAPTER 15:
BASEBALL: MY LIFELONG PASSION

Most men (and, perhaps, women as well) engage in some activity - separate from their jobs - that brings them considerable pleasure. For many men that activity is hunting or fishing or playing golf. For others, it is a spectator sport where they follow their favorite team or a hobby that occupies their time and attention.

For me that activity has been baseball, both as a player and as a fan. I have watched thousands of games in person or on TV and read hundreds of books and articles about the sport - and I never tire of doing so. I read a newspaper everyday and, during baseball season, will pour over the box scores of my favorite teams to see how each player performed. During all the years I played the sport, it brought out a passion in me unlike any I had encountered before.

I first "discovered" baseball in the summer of 1950 when I was eleven years old, living in the Rocky Hill community in rural Neshoba County, Mississippi. I had played some version of baseball at the rural schools I attended -- usually a game called "workup", consisting of two or three batters and everyone else in the field. When the batter made an out, he went to right field and tried to work his way up to batter. On a few occasions, we chose up sides, but there were often too few players and too little time to play more than a few innings.

It never occurred to me as a kid that baseball was a game that was played by grownups - -for a living! This may seem strange but I had lived all my life up to then in rural Mississippi far from any city. We did not receive a newspaper nor any magazines and no one I knew had a television set. But at school I came across an issue of _Life_ magazine, a popular publication in those days that had lots of pictures and minimal text. That issue included a story about a battle between the New York Yankees and the Detroit Tigers for first place in the American League with lots of pictures about a series in Detroit that the Tigers had won. The story also featured George Kell, one of the stars of the Tigers, who hailed from Swifton, Arkansas. This added a personal dimension for me, as Swifton was not far from where I had lived in the Mississippi Delta. It was exciting to learn that baseball was a game played by grownups in front of large crowds and even involved people who grew up in the rural South, just like me.

I also discovered that baseball games were broadcast on the radio; the Mutual Broadcasting Company often had a "Mutual Game of the Day". I tuned in when I could, always hoping that the Detroit Tigers would be on. Baseball on the radio opened up a whole new world for me. Listening to the broadcasters describe the stadiums as "green cathedrals", I pictured them in my mind and heard the roar of the crowds. Radio, perhaps, has the ability to inspire imagination as no other medium can.

Throughout the summer of 1950, the Tigers and Yankees fought for first place and went into the last weekend of the season tied. It was not until Monday, however, when I went with Daddy to a store and saw a newspaper that I discovered the Yankees had won.Heartbroken, I resolved, from that day forward, to root for the Tigers and hate the Yankees! And I knew that I had found my calling in life and that was to be a major league ballplayer.

MY CAREER AS A PLAYER

With my new career objective in mind, I got Daddy to order me a baseball glove from Sears Roebuck and started the process of developing the skills that I needed. I read every book or article I could find about baseball and spent hours throwing a ball against a brick wall and fielding grounders. We had moved to Meridian in the fall of 1950 and, since I had no one to play with, I invented all kinds of ways to play by myself. Learning to hit by oneself is very difficult; I would put the ball in a sock and hang it down from the clothesline on a piece of twine. But that was a poor substitute for swinging at a thrown ball.

My first participation in baseball in an organized fashion took place in the summer of 1951 when I tried out for a youth league in Meridian. To my surprise, I was far ahead of many of the kids when it came to catching a ground ball, because of all the hours of practice.Hitting the ball was a bit more challenging, but I began to advance in that skill as well. As a result, I became a member of the Meridian Stars, a team sponsored by the daily newspaper, and was selected as the team's captain. All the hard work had paid off!

That summer the Stars won almost all of our games and the championship of our league. In addition to playing infield, I pitched on several occasions and showed up for every practice and game. Life could not have been better!

From that point on, I played baseball every summer. And I never tired of playing, always striving to get better. I had an intensity about baseball that far exceeded any other dimension in my life. There was always so much room for improvement; even the very best hitters only get a hit about one third of the time and no one catches every ball hit to them. But I kept pushing myself toward perfection. I would invent games, playing alone, in which I would set a goal of catching 50 grounders bouncing off the wall without an error and, if I missed one, would start over and continue until I reached that goal.

Dealing with such intensity continued throughout my playing career. When I made an error or struck out, I would be so angry with myself that I would often throw my glove or bat. Once when I was in high school, I struck out with the tying run on third base and we lost the ball game. As I drove home in my uniform, I was boiling inside. After parking the car, I got a bat out of the garage, went to a big tree in the backyard, and began to hit it as hard as I could. In a few minutes, I was wet with sweat and totally exhausted, finally collapsing and lying on the ground under the shade of the tree. Momma, who had been listening to this racket, emerged from the house, looked at me lying on the ground, and asked a simple question: "If it makes you so mad, why do you do it?" Then she turned and went back into the house.

Momma's question was a fair one. But the possibility of not playing baseball had never occurred to me. Instead, the solution was, obviously, that I needed to get better so I would not incur such disappointment again. I had an intense competitive drive to excel -- for my team to win and for my performance to meet high standards. I was not a "good loser"; any defeat or poor performance on my part hurt and it took me a while to get over it. My anger was always internalized - i.e. directed at myself rather than my opponent. At the same time, I was a "good winner", never too demonstrative or "rubbing it in" to the loser.

The competitiveness that emerged while playing baseball was also demonstrated in the classroom. I always wanted to be the best student and frequently was. And I suspect this drive to excel was a significant factor in the advancements in my profession. Throughout my playing career I had to work at controlling my anger and became better at it, although it would still "boil-over" on some occasions.

As I have described earlier (Chapters 4, 5, and 6), playing baseball was an important part of my experience growing up. Advanced in school for my age, I usually had to compete with older and bigger boys for a position on the team and against older players on the opposing teams. But I made the varsity as a freshman in high school and was a valuable component of the team for all four years.

Rarely the "star" of the team, I was primarily known a sure-handed infielder, able to catch virtually any ball I could reach. Second base was my natural and preferred position, but the coaches would often ask me to play either third base or shortstop. I really did not have the quickness or range needed to cover the shortstop's territory, but often the coach was willing to give up range for skill at fielding.

As a batter, I never hit a home run in a game. People often called me a "contact" hitter in that I would get my bat on the ball and rarely struck out. I hit near .300 at every level I played with most of my hits being singles or an occasional double. I was an ideal number two batter, the place I normally filled in the batting order. I frequently got walks, could bunt, and hit to the opposite field. Naturally a right-handed batter, I began to switch-hit in high school because of something that happened in the field.

During my senior year, I was preparing to play shortstop in an early season game. In pre-game infield practice, I moved to my right to field a ball in the hole. But just before the ball got to me, it took a bad hop and caught me in the left eye. The eye swelled shut as I sat on the bench with an ice pack on it and I had a classic black eye for several days. As it turned out, I had some permanent damage to the left eye and had to begin wearing glasses when I got to college. At this juncture, however, the noticeable difference became the difficulty "picking up the ball" batting right-handed, since the injured eye was my "front eye", closest to the pitcher. So I started to bat left-handed; I had always taken a few swings left-handed in batting practice, but had not hit this way in a game. I found I could see the ball better and batted left-handed against right-handed pitchers. Against left-handed pitchers, I would go back to batting right-handed but think I was a better hitter left-handed overall.

I have so many great memories from playing baseball but there is one that sticks out because it involves redemption, an opportunity that baseball often provides. Delhi was playing Rayville, our arch rival, in a key district game my senior year. We were playing at home before a big crowd and were leading by one run in the top of the ninth. Rayville had the bases loaded with one out when the batter hit a ground ball to shortstop, giving us the opportunity to make a double play and end the game. I was playing second base and took the shortstop's throw to get the force out at second. But as I pivoted to throw to first, the base runner slammed into me and my throw went over the first baseman's head, enabling two runners to score. I was crestfallen, as I had worked on that pivot endlessly and was usually able to avoid the runner coming into the base. I blamed myself for this error and putting Delhi in a position to lose the game.

In the bottom of the ninth, however, I got my chance at redemption, coming up to bat with two out and two runners on base. Batting left-handed, I hit a fastball on the "fat of the bat" and sent a line drive over the right fielder's head and off the right field wall. Both runners scored and we won the game! Even today, approximately fifty years later, I can still feel how it felt to hit that ball and remember the sound that it made.

Another incident that I remember well involved the only time Daddy saw me play. As described in an earlier chapter, my parents did not come to see me participate in sports because the church did not sanction such activities. One day while playing for the American Legion team in Delhi, I was called on to be the starting pitcher since the scheduled starter had not arrived. I sometimes served as a relief pitcher but rarely started. After warming up down the right field line, I was ready to go. Before I went to the mound, however, one of my teammates told me that my Daddy was in the stands. I looked and, sure enough, there he was. This totally floored me, as it had never happened before. Going on to the field, my heart raced; I wanted to do well, to show him what a good player I was. But, nervous and unsettled, I walked the first two batters, gave up a hit, and, then, an error allowed two runs to score. I finally got the side out but, on the way to the dugout, I glanced into the stands only to find that Daddy had departed.

By the second inning the intended starter had arrived and took over the pitching, while I went to my normal position at second base. I don't know why Daddy showed up that day and I never talked to him about it, too embarrassed by my performance to bring it up. I suspect he was in town on another mission and just dropped by for a minute. When he saw how unnerved I was, he probably felt it was best to leave.

Another memory that is still with me occurred even earlier -- I was only fourteen and playing in a summer league for Locke Station, a rural community near Marks, Mississippi. I was the youngest member of the team; there were one or two older high school boys, but most of the team were "grownups" in their twenties and thirties who were farmers or factory workers. Herman Flemmons, who owned the general store in Locke Station, was the manager and sponsor (he supplied the balls and bats) of the team. For those of us who did not have transportation, we showed up at the store and rode to the game in Herman's pickup truck. Herman was a big fat guy in his thirties who never played in the field but would sometimes pinch-hit.

On this particular Sunday, we played another community about ten miles away. I walked to the store and then rode in the open bed of the pickup to the game, as there were several players there for a ride. We had no uniforms. We just wore whatever clothes we had to play in. At the game, I was inserted in the lineup at shortstop because Herman had seen that I was a good fielder but he put me near the bottom in the batting order. But in my first at-bat, the opposing pitcher threw me a fastball about knee high and I hit a line drive into centerfield for a hit. In each subsequent trip to the plate, the pitcher threw me the same pitch and each time I hit safely. In the game, I was 5 for 5, the first and only time I ever got five hits. I just wish I could have had that pitcher for every game!

After my first year at Northwestern State where I was the starting second baseman on the freshman team, I worked the night shift at the shipyard in Madisonville, Louisiana, playing for the Madisonville baseball team on Sundays. The league in which I competed included a lot of college players as well as several who had played some in the minor leagues. It was a tough league but I held my own. Then a big break came.

Buddy Lewis, a scout for the St. Louis Cardinals, saw me play and invited me and a left-handed pitcher on our team to come to a tryout camp in Ponchatoula. The camp ran for two days, Monday and Tuesday. This worked well for me, as I could go to the camp all day Monday, work my job Monday night, and come back on Tuesday, if invited. From the beginning, I had dreamed of being a professional baseball player and, now, I was getting my "shot".

When we reported for camp, we signed in and got a number pinned to the back of our uniform shirt. Buddy Lewis described the schedule and said he would be posting a list at the end of the day of the numbers of the players he wanted to come back on Tuesday. There were about 50 guys at the camp, including 10-12 black players. This was 1957 and I had never played against a black player or even seen one perform in person.

It did not take me long to realize how fast and how strong many of the black players were. In fact, almost everyone at the camp was very skilled. After we had all warmed up our arms, Lewis divided the players into three groups: he took the pitchers and catchers to the bullpen area, one assistant took the outfielders to hit them fly balls, and another guy took the infielders. The two assistants were, I suspect, high school coaches in the area.

I, of course, joined the infielders for an hour or so of infield practice. There were two other second basemen there, so we alternated playing that position. I did well in this drill as I expected to do. Then we spent the rest of the morning in batting practice with each player getting twelve swings in the batter's cage. I hit several line drives but they were nothing compared to how some of the kids were banging the ball over and off the fences.

After a break for a sack lunch and a rest period, the afternoon session began with each player being timed in a run from home plate to first base. Lewis had a stop watch and wrote down each player's time. I knew that I was slow and, compared to the guys there, felt even slower. But I ran as hard as I could.

We were then divided into two teams and played a game with each player getting a chance to perform. I played four innings at second base, handling all the chances I got, and batted twice. On my first trip to the plate, I hit the ball solidly but right to the center fielder. On my second at bat, I faced a tall black boy who threw the ball harder than I had seen before. All I got was one foul ball before striking out. Lewis sat up in the stands, watching the game and recording notes in his book.

By the end of the day, I suspected that my number would not be posted on the list. I was simply not as good as most of the players at the camp. As feared, the list did not include my number or that of the southpaw from my team. So I drove to my job at the shipyard, working that night in a daze. When I got home early Tuesday morning, I was totally exhausted and slept most of that day.

How does one deal with a dream that has burst? My hopes may have been unrealistic but they were, nevertheless, real. I hurt and couldn't talk about the experience for quite some time. Daddy and Momma both asked me how the camp went and I simply said "okay" and nothing else. The pitcher on my team who also attended the tryout camp never talked about the experience and, if anyone else on the team knew we had gone, they never asked about it. So I just kept on playing because I loved the sport but with some level of diminished intensity.

Fortunately for me, my dreams were not totally one-dimensional. I often told myself that I needed to plan for a career, albeit one that I could "fall back on" when my playing career ended. So my performance in the classroom was excellent. I returned to college in the fall with a renewed commitment to my academic goals. My love for baseball was still very strong but somewhat more realistic. After playing my sophomore year at NSU as a reserve infielder, I decided to give it up because of all the other leadership activities in which I was engaged on the campus. But I played each summer in a semi-pro league and loved each minute of it. Even thru my years in graduate school, I played baseball in some form each summer.

As I reflected on my playing career years later, I realized that my dream of being a major league player had been unrealistic. I had neither the speed nor strength to compete at that level. My skills were self-taught, the result of hours and hours of practice. I never had any instruction. My coaches just observed the players and put the best ones in the lineup. Even at the high school level, the baseball coach was often an assistant football or basketball coach who knew little about baseball. I did have an excellent baseball coach in college, Alvin "Cracker" Brown, but at that level you were expected to already know how to play. The area where this lack of instruction hurt the most was in hitting. I could teach myself to be a good fielder playing alone, but learning to hit a ball correctly requires a much different kind of practice. But, through hard work and determination, I maximized the skills that I had.

The final year of my "playing career" came in 1989. I had read about several of the major league "fantasy camps" where individuals could play baseball for their favorite team. As a present for my 50th birthday that year, Marlene purchased a trip to the Detroit Tiger camp for me, something I probably would not have done without her initiative.

The camp took place during the first week of February at the Tigers' spring training facilities in Lakeland, Florida. President of the University of Akron at the time, I began to work out in the gym to get in shape for this experience. In addition to running, I found someone to throw with and even got the baseball coach to let me hit some in a batting cage that was set up in one section of the gym for the baseball team that was practicing for their upcoming season. Since I had not played baseball in over 25 years, I wanted to prevent embarrassment when I finally got on the field in Florida.

We were to arrive in Lakeland on Sunday with the camp concluding the next Saturday night. About 80-90 "campers" each paid $2,500 to attend and about 20 former Tigers served as coaches. On the first night, the former Tigers were introduced at a reception. In our room at the hotel, each of the campers found a Tigers uniform with his name on the jersey.

The first day at camp consisted of tryouts with each of us working out at the positions we designated as well as taking batting practice. Everyone who had pitched or wanted to be a pitcher was urged to go to the pitching area, also, as each pitcher would be limited to two innings a day in order to minimize injuries; therefore, each team would need several pitchers. Two former Tiger greats, Frank Lary and Virgil Trucks, served as the pitching coaches. So after working out in the infield (at 2B, 3B and SS), I went down to the bullpen to pitch.

During batting practice, each of the pitchers got a chance to perform, while one of the coaches timed the deliveries with a speed gun. When I approached the mound, Mickey Lolich (a great Tiger pitcher in the 60's) was manning the speed gun and calling out the speed after each pitch. My competitive spirit surfaced, so I began to throw much harder than I should have. Near the end of my session, I felt something pull in my right shoulder and experienced pain in my arm. In addition, throughout the day, I kept feeling pain in my toes. Since I had thrown away my old baseball shoes, I bought a new pair for the camp. But they were a little too big which caused my big toes to collide against the front of the shoes as I ran.

After batting practice, I went to the trainer's office and discovered that my big toes were bloody from all the banging and that both big toenails were almost off. The trainer wrapped the toes to help save the nails and gave me a bag of ice for my shoulder. That evening the coaches held a draft and selected players for each team.Six teams were staffed with players and two former Tigers as the coaches, my team being led Mickey Lolich and Joe Ginsberg (a catcher in the 50's).

Using the multiple fields in the training complex, each team played two games each day (one in the morning and one in the afternoon) over the next four days. With my toes in their delicate condition, I had a difficult time running. And with the pain in my shoulder (which was later found to be a torn rotator cuff), I had to throw mostly sidearm. But I played every day and even pitched on one occasion. The injuries weren't over, however. During one of the games, while running to first base, I pulled a groin muscle. Again, the trainer gave me a bag of ice.

Finally, in our last game against a team with which we were tied for second place in the standings, I came up to bat in the last inning in a tie game with the winning run on third base and two outs. I hit a ground ball between first and second base that I thought was going through for a hit, but the first baseman went in the hole, drove for the ball and knocked it down. Then it was a race to the bag between him and me. In spite of my banged-up toes and pulled groin, I ran as fast as I could. We arrived at the base at the same time and collided, with the ball being jarred loose in the collision. I reached the bag safely, winning the game. But I jammed the little finger on my left hand which swelled, necessitating another bag of ice.

On Saturday, the final day of camp, each of the teams got to play the former Tigers with the games being held in Joker Marchant Stadium, the place where the Tigers' spring training games are played. Each team played three innings or until each player had batted. When I got a chance to bat, Frank Lary was pitching for the Tigers. In spite of his age, (I think he was near 60 then), he could still throw the ball hard. But, luckily, I hit a ground ball back through the middle for a base hit.

I counted the whole camp as a great thrill. In spite of bloody toes, a torn rotator cuff, a pulled groin, and a jammed finger, I can truly say I had a great time! In addition to the players I have already mentioned, I enjoyed meeting and being around former Tigers like Jim Northrop, Willie Horton, Gates

Brown, and Steve Kemp. And I met Ernie Harwell, the Tigers' announcer. I just wished that George Kell had been there.

Most of the campers were younger than me - in their thirties and forties. But I held my own, even in my wounded condition, hitting .375 for the camp. But, most of all, I had memories I would treasure for years to come.

After returning to Akron, I went to an orthopedic surgeon and learned that I had torn a rotator cuff in my right shoulder. He said that, if I made my living playing baseball, he would recommend surgery. Instead, he recommended a program of rehabilitation that I undertook with the guidance of the athletic trainer at the university. The nails on my big toes were saved and my groin healed. But I still have a crooked little finger and my right shoulder never returned to normal.

But, since I had undergone spring training, I decided to play baseball that summer in an over 40 league in Akron's summer recreational program. Because of my right shoulder, I played first base to limit the throws I would have to make. But, near the end of the season, I finally ended my career after pulling a hamstring, trying to stretch a single into a double. I think my body was telling me "enough is enough". But that still didn't keep me from playing slow-pitch softball whenever I had the chance.

I played baseball with a passion, complete with all the cheers and the tears it produced. I never realized my dream to play professionally and make it to the major leagues, but I loved every minute of the journey. Nothing matched the satisfaction of hitting the horsehide on the nose and watching it soar into open spaces or to fielding a grounder deep in the hole and making a perfect throw to first base. Those memories are always with me.

In 2006, I traveled to Louisiana for the 50th reunion of my high school graduating class at Delhi. The event was held in Monroe, the nearest big town, but I drove thru Delhi on the way there and stopped by the baseball field where I had spent so many hours. The park looked about the same although the covered bleachers behind home plate and down the foul lines had rusted and the green wooden fence around the outfield had been replaced with a chain-link one. No one was there, so I walked all around the field as memories of the past flooded my mind. As I stood at home plate, I could hear the familiar sound of wood on horsehide and feel the tingle in my hands as the ball soared into the outfield. And walking around the infield, I felt again the sting of the ball as it smacked into the pocket of my glove. I was thankful no one was there to see the moisture in my eyes.

My Career as a Fan

From the summer of 1950, I have been an avid Detroit Tiger fan. Everyday during the season, when I see the baseball scores, I feel a surge of joy if the Tigers have won or a pulse of pain if they have lost. I have supported them through "thick and thin", with more years being thin than I would have preferred.

I have always followed another team as well, the team nearest to where I lived. Growing up in Mississippi and Louisiana, the closest major league team was the St. Louis Cardinals. And they were the only team I could get on the radio consistently. So I listened to and rooted for the Redbirds. Later I rooted for the Kansas City Royals when we lived in Omaha, the Houston Astros when we were in Texas, the Cleveland Indians while living in Akron, the Atlanta Braves when in Auburn, and now the Cincinnati Reds while living in Cincinnati. But the Tigers have always been first in my heart.

The first baseball game I ever witnessed (other than the ones I had played in) came in 1951 when the coach took our Meridian Stars team to see the Meridian team play in the Class C Cotton States League. I was fascinated by how beautiful the field looked and by the stands where the people sat. Later while we lived in the Mississippi Delta, I went to Memphis on several occasions to see the Memphis Chicks, a team in the Class AA Southern Association.It was a tremendous thrill to go to a game on Sunday afternoon when the stands were packed. I became such a fan that I listened to almost all of the Chicks' games on the radio.

The first major league games I saw were in 1956 following my senior year in high school. I played for an American Legion team in Delhi that won the regional championship. As a reward, the American Legion took the team to St. Louis for a four game series between the Cardinals and the Dodgers. I was starry-eyed to see the Cardinal players in person that I had listened to so many times on the radio. In one of the games, Sandy Koufax pitched for the Dodgers. I think this was his rookie season. We also went to Stan Musial's restaurant for a meal and met "Stan the Man" and got an autographed picture of him.

The first time I saw the Tigers play in person was in 1961 after my first year in graduate school and while I was driving to Maine to work at Camp Takajo. In Washington, I saw the Tigers play the Senators in Griffith Stadium. The Tigers won on a key hit by Dick MacAlliffe.

Over the years I have attended major league games in most of the cities in the east, south, and midwest, including: Boston (Fenway Park), New York (both Yankee and Shea Stadiums), Philadelphia (Old Connie Mack Stadium),

Pittsburgh (Three Rivers Stadium), Baltimore (Old Municipal Stadium), Washington (Griffith Stadium and RFK Stadium), Atlanta (Fulton County Stadium and Turner Field), Houston (Astrodome), Dallas (Old Rangers Stadium), St. Louis (Sportsman Park and Busch Stadium), Kansas City (Royals Stadium), Minneapolis (The Metrodome), Chicago (Wrigley Field and Cellular Field), Detroit (Tiger Stadium and Comerica Park), Cleveland (Cleveland Stadium and Jacobs Field), and Cincinnati (Riverfront Stadium and Great American Ball Park). Unfortunately, my travels to the west have not been during the baseball season, so there are many parks in that region at which I have not attended a game.

Some of the memorable games that I have seen are:

1. <u>My first game in Tiger Stadium</u>. This was in 1978. We were moving back to Omaha from Washington, D.C. after spending a year there. Marlene and the kids drove back through Indiana to visit with her folks, while I stayed to get the moving van loaded and, then, drove back to Nebraska. On the way back, I stopped in Detroit to see the Tigers play. It was a tremendous thrill for me just to be in this storied old ballpark that I read so much about. I don't remember who the Tigers played or who won the game. Just being there was enough.

2. <u>Tigers win American League Championship in 1984</u>. The Tigers got off to a great start in 1984 and led all the way to win the division. They faced the Kansas City Royals for the league championship and won the first two games (in a best 3 of 5 series) in KC. The third game was in Detroit. We had just moved to Akron a few months before and a great friend, John Courson, who had served on the TKE Grand Council with me, invited me and Van up to go to the game with him. His son, Christopher, was about the same age as Van. John, a mortgage banker, had just gotten a new Buick that he drove to the game. All the way there, John kept telling me about this great parking place he had found. It was across the expressway from Tiger Stadium in a neighborhood where we did not have to pay and could walk across the bridge to the stadium.

The game was a thriller, a one-run game (2-1, I think) that the Tigers won. After the game, the Tiger fans celebrated; this was the Tigers' first pennant since 1968. But, then, the celebrations got out of hand; cars were overturned, fires set, and other damage done. The streets were filled with people and police were patrolling on horseback.

When we finally got back to the area where we had parked, we found that John's car had been stolen. The police found it a couple of days later, completely stripped. In all the confusion and turmoil, we found a cab to take us to Bloomfield Hills where John lived.

3. Meeting Sparky. Following that game in 1984, I have traveled to Michigan every summer to see the Tigers play. After we hired Gerry Faust as the football coach at Akron, he told me that he knew Sparky Anderson, the manager of the Tigers, very well from the days when Gerry was a high school coach in Cincinnati and Sparky was manager of the Reds. He offered to set up a meeting with Sparky for me. Gerry told me to go to the players' gate, give the guard my name, and someone would take me to Sparky. Marlene and I arrived an hour or so before game time and, while she went on up to our seats, I went to see Sparky.

I went into the Tigers clubhouse underneath the stands to Sparky's office. He was extremely friendly and talkative, inviting me to join him in the Tigers dugout to watch pre-game batting and infield practice. I got to see all the Tigers players up close and even got to meet Tony LaRussa, the opposing manager of the Oakland A's, who came over to talk to Sparky.

I still remember something that Sparky told me on that occasion. He said that the very best major league teams rarely win more than two-thirds of their games in a season and that the worst teams rarely lose more than two-thirds. The work of the manager, then, is to win as many games of the third in the middle as possible.

On another occasion, Gerry arranged for Marlene and me to sit in the owner's box at Tiger Stadium. He knew Tom Monahan from his work with Catholic charities and his years at Notre Dame. The box sat right behind home plate (and seemingly, almost on top of it). What a place to watch the game. Mr. Monahan was not there, so I did not have the opportunity to meet him.

4. Seeing Tim Hudson pitch in Tiger Stadium. Tim Hudson was an outstanding player, both as a pitcher and an outfielder, for the Auburn Tigers during our years there, taking AU to the College World Series in 1997. I met Tim on a few occasions and Amy had been his English teacher. In 1998 Marlene and I had planned our annual trip to Detroit. Our good friends, Gabe and Sandy Campbell from Akron, have a summer home on Crystal Lake (just south of Traverse City, Michigan). They invited us each summer to come for a visit; so we would fly to Detroit for a game and, then, fly on up to Traverse City. This year the game was against the Oakland A's, but, at the time we scheduled the trip, Tim was still in the minor leagues. As fate would have it, however, by the time we got to Detroit, Tim had just been called up

and was the starting pitcher for the A's in the game. And, furthermore, Amy (who was teaching in Minnesota) joined us in Detroit for the game.

Tim pitched a marvelous game that night, being the winning pitcher. After the game, we all went down to the Oakland dressing room and I sent a business card into Tim, telling him we wanted to see him. Shortly, Tim emerged and immediately spotted Amy, his former teacher, speaking to her before anyone else. We had a nice visit with Tim and have followed his professional career with interest.

5. Two World Series games. My first time to see a World Series game in person came in 1992 when the Atlanta Braves lost to the Toronto Blue Jays in the sixth and final game. Van and I attended that game in Atlanta. The second time was when the Braves met the New York Yankees in the third game in 1995 in Atlanta. My good friend, David Housel, at Auburn was able to get us tickets. The Braves had won the first two games in New York and came back to Atlanta with the chance to win the series there. In this game, the Braves had a good lead and the crowd was festive. Then, Mark Wohlers, a hard throwing reliever, was brought in to protect the lead, only to give up a three-run homer. The Yankees went on to win the game as well as the next three to win the series.

In addition to the games in the major league parks, I have traveled to Florida in March many times to watch spring training, always including a visit to Lakeland to see the Tigers. Once, when we were in Akron, Van and I used our spring break to see the Akron Zips open their season in Florida and to attend games at several of the spring training sites. When Marlene and I were living in Vero Beach in 2005, we were there the entire month of March and I attended a game almost every day.During other years, we have gone down for a week or two. Over the years, I have been to almost all of the spring training parks in Florida.

On another occasion, Van and I were in Los Angeles to see the Akron Zips softball team compete in a big tournament and, while there, drove over to Palm Springs to see the Angels and Brewers in a spring training game. I have always loved the laid-back feature of spring training, plus the beautiful weather.

During my years as a teacher and administrator, I followed the university's baseball team, often sneaking out of the office to watch an afternoon game. While at Ohio University, I saw a young Mike Schmidt (now a Hall-of-Famer after a great career as a third baseman for the Philadelphia Phillies) play shortstop. And, while at Auburn, I went with the team twice to the

College World Series and saw Tim Hudson, Mark Bellhorn, and Gabe Gross (among those who made it to the major leagues) play.

I realize that many people find baseball boring. The games are often slow-paced and not filled with tension, as is often the case with football and basketball. Baseball does have its tension-filled moments but a lot of time it appears nothing is happening. I love the pace of the game -- it is both relaxing and intellectually stimulating. Each pitch is a battle between the pitcher and the batter and each batted ball a contest between the fielders and the batter. And, as the game unfolds, the strategy employed by each manager is interesting. And there are regular breaks between innings to go to the bathroom or get refreshments. Who could ask for anything more than that!

Baseball is perhaps the only team sport that requires and measures both teamwork and individual performance in such exacting ways. Each player gets his time at bat and his performance is recorded in great detail (e.g. batting average, slugging percentage, on-base percentage, etc.) and, likewise, has a specific area of the field to cover with accompanying measures (fielding percentage). But it takes teamwork to win games. A great batter needs runners on base to get RBI's (runs batted in) and great hitters need pitchers who can get the opposing batters out.

I believe that the athletic skill to hit a baseball moving at 90 mph from a distance of approximately 60 feet is one of the most exacting in sports. And when the pitcher is able to make the ball break sharply in various directions and at different speeds, even greater hand-and-eye coordination is required. I have great respect for those players who can play the game well and deal with the many times they fall short of perfection.

But my greatest thrill in baseball came not from watching a game but from meeting a hero. Remember George Kell? He was the player back in 1950 who helped pique my interest in baseball. George had a very distinguished career as a player, resulting in his election to the Baseball Hall of Fame. Then he spent 38 years as a broadcaster for the Tigers, teaming with another Hall-of-Famer, Al Kaline, to do the Tiger games on television.

In the summer of 1998, Marlene and I made our annual trip to Detroit to see a Tigers game and were waiting in the airport for a flight to Traverse City to visit with the Campbells. I walked into a bookstore there and happened to see a book entitled, Hello Everybody, I'm George Kell, George Kell's autobiography. I purchased it immediately and, over the next two days, I read it completely.

I knew, of course, about George's playing career and, generally, about his work as a broadcaster. But I didn't know about his life growing up nor about his life after baseball. I was so impressed to learn that he had never left

Swifton and that he had done so much to improve the community there. After we got back to Auburn, I wrote him a letter. I just addressed it to "George Kell, Swifton, Arkansas", figuring that everyone there knew him. To my surprise, I got a lengthy reply from George including an autographed copy of the book.

This was the beginning of a continuing correspondence with George. When Auburn played Arkansas in football at Fayetteville in 1999, I invited George and his wife, Carolyn, to meet Marlene and me in Little Rock for dinner on Friday night before the game. It was a great experience for me. George was 77 by then and his knees limited his mobility but his memories about baseball were as clear as ever. I think we could have talked all night. One of my prized photos is of George and me together that evening.

In addition to our correspondence, I went to visit George in Swifton in May, 2005, after a speaking engagement I had at the University of Arkansas in Fayetteville. I had learned that George had a severe automobile accident earlier that year and was pretty badly injured. Given that he was in his early 80's now, I wanted to make sure he was okay. We had a good visit and I found that, while the injuries had been painful, his spirits were high.

It is quite a joyous experience to meet your boyhood hero and to find out that he is just the kind of person you hoped he would be. George is very "down-to-earth" and humble about his accomplishments, truly a good man.

OTHER SPORTS I'VE PLAYED AND/OR WATCHED

I think it is fair to say that I have always been an avid sports fan. Although baseball is my passion, there are a number of other sports that I have played and/or enjoy watching. Here is a brief discussion of each of them, pretty much in the order of their interest to me:

(A) Basketball. Basketball is the first sport I played, shooting at the goal Clyde nailed to a tree at Rocky Hill and playing on the dirt courts at Dixie School. In spite of being short and slow, I played three years of high school basketball. I was rarely a starter, but got to play when the game was already decided. My highest scoring game netted six points. But I loved to play the game and was on intramural teams in college and in pickup games when someone needed a player.

As a fan, I have loved college basketball, rooting for the team where we were. Having grown up in Indiana, Marlene is also an ardent basketball fan. Starting when we were at Texas A&M, we attended college games on a regular basis. Two of our greatest thrills were (1) when the Akron Zips met Michigan in the opening round of the NCAA tournament and (2) when the Auburn Tigers made it all the way to the Sweet Sixteen before losing to Ohio State.

I have never been much of an NBA fan and have seen only a few games in person— in Los Angeles, Omaha, Houston, Atlanta, and Cleveland. I usually watch some games on TV after the playoffs start but have no particular team that I root for.

(B) <u>Football</u>. I played two years of high school football, making myself into a fairly decent player by hard work. I can't say that I enjoyed football; it was more a "rite of passage" into manhood than an activity from which I derived pleasure. Being a part of a championship team, however, made the sweat and pain tolerable. But I have enjoyed watching football, particularly the college variety.

I went to the games while I was in college, both at NSU and at Arkansas, and attended most of the home games at the universities where I have worked. As a university president, the home football games were a venue for entertaining guests and cultivating donors so the events involved both work and pleasure. While at Auburn, I went with the team to several bowl games - the Citrus, the Outback, the Peach, and the Independence bowls. But my favorite bowl is the Sugar Bowl. When Auburn was not in a bowl, I would go to the Sugar Bowl as part of the SEC party since the SEC champion played there. It was my good fortune to know Jerry Romig and his son, Mark, both of whom served as Presidents of the Sugar Bowl.

I follow the NFL but don't have a favorite team like the Tigers in baseball. I rooted for the Houston Oilers when they were a part of the AFL because two of my classmates from Northwestern State (Charlie Tolar and Charlie Hennigan) were stars on the team, as well as followed the Oilers when we lived in Texas. When we were in Akron, I rooted for the Cleveland Browns. I have attended NFL games in Houston, Dallas, Cleveland, and Atlanta. I enjoy watching the games on TV, particularly the playoffs, and am now a Cincinnati Bengals fan.

Sports like football and basketball (as well as hockey and soccer in other countries around the world) seem to bring out behavior in adults that would be considered juvenile in almost any other setting. They scream, pump their fists in the air, and dance, as well as sometimes wear outlandish costumes or paint their bodies. I have concluded that one of the appeals of such sports is that they allow an adult (as well as younger folks) to behave in this fashion and still be considered "normal" or acceptable. There are few other venues in an adult's public life where this is possible.

(C) <u>Tennis</u>. I started playing tennis in undergraduate school and have always enjoyed the game. Because of the hand-and-eye coordination I developed in baseball, I became a fairly competitive player, although the game frustrated me when I did not do well. I played tennis on a fairly regular basis up until I tore the rotator cuff in my right shoulder in 1989. After that injury, it was more difficult for me to serve effectively. So I haven't played much tennis since. I don't regularly watch tennis, except for some major tournaments, like Wimbledon, on TV.

(D) <u>Golf</u>. Golf is, unquestionably, the most frustrating sport I have attempted to play. In spite of good hand-and-eye coordination, I have never been able to master the technique of "swinging down to make the ball go up" and "swinging easy to make the ball go far". Even when I hit the ball well, it too often landed in the wrong place. The aspect of golf that I have found enjoyable is being outside in beautiful weather among beautifully landscaped greenery with good friends. Now if I could only play a little better! Maybe break a hundred more often.

I played my first golf when I was in graduate school and have never played the sport on any kind of consistent basis. Perhaps that is one explanation for my lack of proficiency. I probably played golf most often when we were in Akron, as there were frequent outings involving politicians and alumni in which I was invited to participate. As a result, I played almost all of the beautiful courses in that area, including the world famous Firestone Country Club. Once I got a chance to play with Greg Norman in a Pro-Am at Firestone.

Greg Norman in the late 1980's was among the very best golfers in the world. He was in Akron to compete in the NEC World Series of Golf at Firestone. I was in a foursome in the Pro-Am the day before the tournament began. Through a lottery, my foursome got first choice as to the pro to play with and we selected Norman. What I didn't realize was that we would get to tee off first and that there would be a big crowd there to witness the event – and that there would be an announcer who would introduce each player as he approached the tee. When my turn in the tee box came, my knees were knocking. I feared that I would miss the ball entirely! But, somehow, I got off a respectable drive that landed in the fairway. As it turned out, Norman was "laid-back" and a lot of fun to play with, joking with us as we played the course.

(E) <u>Swimming</u>. I have never been a good swimmer and, certainly, have never competed in that sport. But, while at Auburn, I enjoyed watching the swimming meets because the Tigers had such outstanding teams. The men's team won the NCAA National Championship in both 1997 and 1999. I traveled with the team to Minneapolis (1997) and Indianapolis (1999) to see the championships. The coach at AU, David Marsh, was superb and subsequently won additional national championships in both men's and women's competition.

(F) Women's Softball. I loved to watch the women's team at Akron compete, as they had an outstanding team. And I watched some games at both Auburn and ECU. I marveled at the athletic ability exhibited by the outstanding women players.

(G) Track and Field. I went to several track meets while an undergraduate as I had to cover the events as sports editor for the paper. While events like the 100-yard dash and the 440 (or 400 meters) run were exciting, there was a lot of waiting between events. When the Olympics were in Atlanta in 1996, we went to a track event there - as well as competition in basketball, swimming and tennis.

(H) Soccer. Although I did not play soccer as a kid, I ended up coaching a team that Van played on when he was in elementary school. While at the University of Akron, I went to several matches as the Zips had an excellent team. One year they played for the NCAA Championship against Duke and I traveled to Tacoma, Washington for that game. But overall, I have never understood soccer well enough to enjoy the game.

(I) Horse Racing. I have been to a couple of race tracks - Scarborough Downs in New Hampshire and AK-SAR-BEN in Omaha - but have never found the sport fascinating. Perhaps if I had attended the Kentucky Derby at least once I would feel differently.

(J) Auto Racing. Although we lived in North Carolina on two different occasions, I have never been to a NASCAR race and have absolutely no interest in the sport. Marlene and I did go to the Indianapolis 500 one year and I found it boring and loud.

(K) Hockey. Perhaps because I grew up in the South and never tried to skate on ice, I have no interest in hockey. I did take Van to a hockey game once in Omaha (The Omaha Knights were a minor league team there) but it just seemed like a skating party interrupted by occasional fights.

(L) Hunting and Fishing. Sports that are the lifeblood of lots of men have never held any appeal to me, especially hunting -- mainly because I do not like guns and don't think I would enjoy killing animals. On the other hand, I have sometimes enjoyed fishing as a peaceful activity, if it is in a lovely setting.

(M) <u>Boxing</u>. While I was in high school, I used to watch professional boxing on Friday nights on TV, sponsored by Gillette. And the big heavyweight championships, especially when Muhammad Ali was champ, were always a big event to anticipate and to see, if you could. But I never had any interest in boxing as a participant.

There are other sports – skiing (both water and snow), lacrosse, wrestling, gymnastics, and polo - that do not even register on my interest scale. But I have had plenty of sports to keep me involved as a fan. I recognize also that the interests and passions of others may differ from mine. What is important is the enjoyment that following a sport and a team provides.

CHAPTER 16:
MUSIC AND OTHER INTERESTS

I am not a musician. Have never played an instrument, except the "air guitar." The one opportunity I had to take piano lessons, I found playing ball more interesting. In my mid-thirties, I wanted to learn to play the guitar but, after several lessons, found it more difficult than it looked and the practice time more demanding than I could spare. But music has always been an important part of my life.

Music is the purest form of communication. It can elicit feelings of joy or sadness, of great energy or quiet peacefulness, perhaps more completely than any other sounds. It is hard to think of love and romance without some musical accompaniment. And music can produce feelings of identity, togetherness, and patriotism; there is little wonder why countries, nationalities, universities, fraternities, and other organizations use music and songs to build allegiance and solidarity.

I believe that each of us identifies with and resonates to the music we grew up with, particularly the music that we heard when we were teenagers and young adults. That is the time when music was central to our daily lives and the feelings we were encountering. Therefore, each generation has its "own" music and often has difficulty understanding why the next generation can like or even stand the sounds they find most appealing.

My musical heritage emanates from three major sources: the church, the rural South, and the Mississippi Delta. Each shaped my musical tastes as they evolved over the years.

THE CHURCH

The first music that I remember came from the church, a central part of life during my pre-school and elementary years. I attended church services three times a week, with singing being a significant component of each session. Accompanied by piano, the congregation began with several hymns. No formal choir performed; instead the whole congregation joined in, led by the minister or a song leader.

It seems like the congregation sang the same 5-10 hymns each meeting. Among those that I remember are: "Amazing Grace", "The Old Rugged Cross", "Give Me That Old Time Religion", "Love Lifted Me", "In The Sweet By and By", "When We All Get to Heaven", and "This World is Not My Home." People would sing to the top of their voices, often not needing a hymnal, as they knew the words by heart. The hymn that would best unleash the congregation was "I'll Fly Away," as it frequently led to dancing and speaking in tongues. By the time the singing ceased, the congregation was all warmed up for the preaching.

As I grew up, I joined in the singing, hearing and feeling the "joyful noises" reverberate throughout the church. Even today, when I hear one of the old time hymns, my soul is touched in a very special way. The modern day hymns sung in churches today do not reach me in a similar fashion.

The church revivals, held once or twice a year, involved lots of singing and each service concluded with an altar call that invited people to come to the altar and be saved. The song that most often persuaded the sinners to come forward was "Softly and Tenderly".

A special event at churches in rural Mississippi during my youth was "All Day Singing and Dinner on the Ground." It encompassed a Sunday in which the morning service would include congregational singing and a short sermon, followed by everyone partaking of food laid out on tables under trees in the church yard. After "dinner", everyone would go back to the church to listen to soloists, duets, trios, and quartets perform. Groups would come from other churches to participate in this program. Momma and Daddy would often sing a duet and my brother, Clyde, would sometimes sing with them or with another group.

Another venue in which singing played a big part was the annual "camp meeting." This was a statewide event held in a large auditorium or under a large tent at the state fairgrounds. There would be services day and night for about three days that would involve singing groups from all over the state. There would also frequently be well-known quartets, like the Blackwood Brothers, who would perform at the camp meetings.

THE RURAL SOUTH

Since I grew up in rural Mississippi, it should not be surprising that the next kind of music I encountered was country or better known in those days as "hillbilly." Most of the songs told stories about poor people struggling to survive, women who had done their man wrong, and both men and women searching for love. The Grand Ole Opry, on the radio each Saturday night live from Nashville, became the citadel of country music with featured performers like Roy Acuff, Hank Snow, Little Jimmy Dickens, and Eddy Arnold.

Hillbilly or country music involved singing with acoustical guitars, a bass, and fiddles. Sometimes groups would employ a steel guitar. Another form of country music that I heard often was "Blue Grass" that would also feature banjos and mandolins with performers like Bill Monroe and Lester Flatt and Earl Scruggs.

The country singer that I most enjoyed was Hank Williams. He was a poor kid from South Alabama who wrote and sang songs that spoke directly to the heart: "Lovesick Blues", "Take These Chains From My Heart (And Set Me Free)", and "I Can't Help It (If I'm Still in Love with You")．My favorite Hank Williams song was "I'm So Lonesome I Could Cry" which had lyrics like these:

> "Hear that lonesome whippoorwill,
> He sounds too blue to fly;
> That midnight train is whining low,
> I'm so lonesome I could cry."

Perhaps the lyrics and the sound reminded others and me in the rural South of our isolation. And I think it touched a part of me that felt alone as I grew up without siblings near my age and with few close friends as we moved numerous times. When I listen to the song, even today, I want to cry.

Over the years, I have had a number of favorite country artists. They and my favorites among their songs are:

a. Johnny Cash - "Ring of Fire", "Understand Your Man", "I Walk the Line", "Suppertime", "Folsom Prison Blues", and "I Still Miss Someone".

b. Merle Haggard - "Mama Tried", "Okie From Muskogee", "I Take a Lot of Pride in What I Am", and "Sing Me Back Home."

c. Patsy Cline - "I Fall to Pieces", "Crazy", and "Sweet Dreams."

    d.   Dolly Parton - "Coat of Many Colors", and "I Will Always Love You."

    e.   George Jones - "He Stopped Loving Her Today", "Green Grass of Home."

    f.   Lefty Frizzell - "The Long Black Veil."

    g.   Freddy Fender – "Until the Next Teardrop Falls" and "Wasted Days and Wasted Nights"

My preferences as to country music are with the "old-time" sound. Although there have been many recent and current artists - and individual songs -- that I have liked, the modern sound just does not have as much appeal to me. Some of the artists who have the old-time sound, but who are more recent include Willie Nelson, Waylon Jennings, Tammy Wynette, and Loretta Lynn.

THE MISSISSIPPI DELTA

In the early 1950's, I became aware of another musical genre that was not easy to access. It was often called the "Delta Blues" because most of the artists had grown up in the Mississippi Delta before migrating to Chicago. Also called "Rhythm and Blues", the music had performers with colorful names like Muddy Waters, Howlin' Wolf, Lonesome Sundown, Big Joe Turner, Ivory Joe Hunter, and Bo Diddly.

    None of the mainline (white-owned) radio stations in the South would play recordings of these black artists. Finally, some stations began to play their records late at night. The two that I remember were WLAC in Nashville that had a show after 10 p.m., sponsored by Randy's Record Shop in Gallatin, and WDIA in Memphis with a program after 10 p.m. called "Red, Hot, and Blue" run by a disc jockey named Dewey Phillips.

    When we were living in the Mississippi Delta, I would often spend the night with James Ray Jones, my best friend. James had a battery-operated radio that we would put under the covers at night (so his mother wouldn't hear) and listen to WDIA until we fell asleep. My favorite performers were Jimmy Reed and B.B. King. Jivin' Jimmy had an unusual sound with a driving bass guitar and a harmonica with songs like "Take Out Some Insurance on Me, Baby", "Caress Me, Baby", and "Going to New York." His biggest hit was a number "Big Boss Man" that was copied by several other performers. B.B. King had a mournful sound with his electric guitar, piano, bass, drums and saxophone and had many big hits in later years, like "The Thrill is Gone", and "If You Love Me."

    White performers copied many of the songs of the black artists. For example, Bill Haley and the Comets made Big Joe Turner's "Shake, Rattle, &

Roll" into a big hit. And, of course, Big Mama Thornton's version of "Hound Dog" became a blockbuster hit when recorded by Elvis Presley.

The only source that I had for hearing country music or Delta blues was the radio, as I owned neither a record player nor records, and could not see the performers in person. When we were living in the Delta, I remember seeing old beat-up shacks where the blacks would gather on Saturday night to play music, dance, and drink bootleg whiskey. The white folks called them "juke joints."

THE EMERGENCE OF ROCK 'N ROLL

In the early 50's there began to emerge a musical sound that seemed to borrow from and build upon the traditions of gospel, country and the blues. It used guitars, drums, piano, and other instruments to create a faster beat that appealed to young people and began to unleash the fantastic black talent that had been largely obscured. The artist that is given the most credit for bringing about this marriage and transformation of these diverse sounds is Elvis Presley.

Elvis was born in Tupelo, Mississippi and grew up in a fundamentalist church hearing the same gospel music I experienced while also being exposed to the country or hillbilly sounds of that day. And he surely encountered the Delta blues as well. He created a sound that captured the fancy of young people, including me.

The first time I heard Elvis sing was in the early summer of 1954. We were living in the Mississippi Delta and I was returning to Marks from a visit to Sardis Dam, a popular recreational site. I stopped at a café in Batesville for lunch and heard this song, "That's All Right, Mama", on the jukebox. Some guy had played the record several times. I went over and asked him who the singer was and he replied "some ole boy from up around Tupelo named Elvis."

From this introduction I became an enduring fan, listening to his records and following his career with interest, even going to almost all his movies, inane as some of them were. Elvis' music "spoke to me." It had rhythm, energy, and soul. I used to sing his songs when I was alone and, even on a few cases, with a band. I even tried to look like him for a time, wearing side burns and ducktails.

I can't think of a single Elvis recording that I did not like, but the ones I liked best were "Return to Sender", "Heartbreak Hotel", "I Just Can't Help Believing", "Trying to Get to You", "Blue Christmas", and "I Can't Help Falling in Love With You." His recordings of gospel songs and Christmas songs were truly outstanding.

I regret that I never had the opportunity to meet Elvis personally, although I did see him perform in person. Marlene and I flew to Las Vegas in 1972 to see his show at the Las Vegas Hilton. It was outstanding! After Elvis' death, I visited Graceland and his gravesite there. As described in an earlier chapter, the best opportunity to meet Elvis personally would have been when he was initiated into TKE fraternity in the living room at Graceland in 1962. Had the chapter notified me, as they should have, I would have been there. They needed the approval of the national office to initiate Elvis that, as a Province Officer, I would have given them. But they were afraid that they might be turned down, so they went ahead and did it without asking. Little did they know! I would have been a strong supporter.

Elvis' arrival on the scene was met with considerable resistance in some segments of society who deplored this new "boogie-woogie" or "rock 'n roll" music. But it seemed to unleash a style of music and distinctive sound that came from all directions and would not be deterred. The period from the mid-50's to the mid-60's was the "golden era" of rock 'n roll, in my opinion. This coincided with the years that I was in high school and college, so this is the music that I remember best.

Another of the pioneers of rock n' roll that I almost got to meet was Jerry Lee Lewis. In the mid-50's when I was in high school in Louisiana, I became friends with the son of the Church of God minister in Ferriday, only 30 miles or so from Delhi. He kept telling me about his friend, Jerry Lee, who went to the Assembly of God Church and could really play the piano. He told me that if I would come down to see him, we would hang out with Jerry Lee. But I never did.

Many years later in 1982 when we were living in Texas, I heard that Jerry Lee was going to perform at the Starlight Ballroom in Snook. Snook was a small town of a few hundred people located about ten miles from College Station where Texas A & M is located and where I was working at the time. The "Ballroom" consisted of a band shell and a concrete pad located in a cow pasture. Amazingly, they were able to book top talent and would often draw thousands of students from A&M. Marlene and I talked about going to the concert, but did not, concluding that Jerry Lee would not likely show up since he had just been released from a hospital. Our daughter, Amy, who was a senior in high school, did go, however. She not only got to see Jerry Lee perform, but also got to shake his hand and got a kiss on the cheek! I did get to see and hear Jerry Lee perform a few years later when he played a club in Akron. Even as an elder citizen then, he could still pound the piano and sing. But I didn't get to shake his hand nor get a kiss on the cheek!

By the time I had gotten to my last two years of high school -- and on into college -- I had learned how to dance and could even muster up the courage to ask girls to dance with me. Among the "slow songs" that I liked to dance to were: "Earth Angel" (Penguins), "The Great Pretender" (Platters), "In the Still of the Night" (Five Satins), "Sincerely" (Moonglows), "You Send Me" (Sam Cooke), "Stand By Me" (Ben E. King), "When A Man Loves A Woman" (Percy Sledge), "Hey Jude" and "Yesterday" (The Beatles), "Please, Please, Please" (James Brown), and "Nights in White Satin" (Moody Blues).

Among the "fast" songs that I loved to "jitterbug" to were: "Long, Tall Sally" (Little Richard), "Short Fat Fannie" and "Bonie Maronie" (Larry Williams), "Whole Lotta Shaking Going On" (Jerry Lee Lewis), "Shake, Rattle, and Roll" (Big Joe Turner), "Blue Suede Shoes" (Carl Perkins), "Suzy-Q" (Dale Hawkins), "Kansas City" (Wilbert Hawkins), "Jim Dandy" (LaVern Baker), "Johnny B. Good" (Chuck Berry), "The Twist" (Chubby Checker), "Satisfaction" (Rolling Stones), and "Devil With the Blue Dress On" (Mitch Ryder and the Detroit Wheels).

There were many other performers and songs that I liked from this era, including Roy Orbison ("Candy Man", "Pretty Woman", "Only The Lonely", "Crying"), Fats Domino ("Blueberry Hill", "Ain't That A Shame"), The Everly Brothers ("Dream"), Ray Charles ("I Got A Woman", "Georgia"), Otis Redding ("Sitting On The Dock Of the Bay"), Wilson Pickett ("Mustang Sally", "In the Midnight Hour"), and Aretha Franklin ("Chain of Fools", "Respect"). "The Duke of Earl" by Gene Chandler (which may have been his only hit) was also a favorite. And how could I forget "Seventh Son" by Johnny Rivers.

Preceding and continuing along side the rock 'n roll era was a sound called "popular" music (as though all other types of music were unpopular?). It included many black artists that were acceptable to mainline listeners: Nat King Cole ("Mona Lisa"), Johnny Mathis ("Chances Are"), Brooke Benton ("The Same One", "It's Just a Matter of Time"), Roy Hamilton ("Unchained Melody", "You'll Never Walk Alone"), and Dinah Washington ("What a Difference a Day Makes", "I Remember You"). White artists such as Frank Sinatra, Dean Martin, Perry Como, Tony Bennett, Andy Williams, Patti Page, and Peggy Lee joined these singers.

After I was married, had a family, and became immersed in my career, I was not into the music scene as much as before. And there were musical styles emerging -- heavy metal, psychedelic, punk rock, rap, hip-hop -- that I did not find appealing. But I had to always remember that there were others for whom the sounds and the lyrics were very meaningful.

There were, however, some branches of rock music that I did enjoy, such as folk (Peter, Paul, and Mary, Bob Dylan) and mo-town (The Supremes, The

Temptations, The Four Tops). And I liked Cajun music, now called zydeco, with the strong influence of the accordion.

During the 1970's, there were several groups that I liked, particularly Credence Clearwater Revival ("Have You Ever Seen the Rain", "Proud Mary"), The Eagles ("Hotel California", "Take It Easy"), The Bee Gees ("Staying Alive"), The Allman Brothers ("Rambling Man"), and Simon and Garfunkel ("Bridge Over Troubled Waters", "Sounds of Silence"). The song, "Imagine", by John Lennon is a classic, along with "Maggie May" by Rod Stewart.

In every decade, there have been certain songs and singers that I have enjoyed, but none of the sounds resonate with me like those I heard growing up. In addition to Elvis and Jerry Lee, there were several performers that I got to see live: Chuck Berry, Ray Charles, Willie Nelson, Merle Haggard, James Brown, and EmmyLou Harris. I even got to go backstage and meet Emma Lou and get an autographed picture. But a performance that I would long remember was by a group called KISS.

This occurred in the mid-70's when we were living in Omaha. Amy and Ellen were big fans of KISS; so, after hearing that the group was going to be in Omaha for a performance a couple of days after Christmas, I decided to surprise them by buying them tickets for the event. But, since they were too young to go by themselves, I purchased a ticket for myself, also. I didn't know anything about the group, but I suspected they would be loud; therefore, I selected tickets in the upper deck (in the Omaha Municipal Auditorium that also served as a basketball arena) and beside the stage -- assuming that the sound would be thrust forward. To my surprise, when we arrived, I found huge amplifiers (the largest amps I have ever seen!) stacked beside the stage and only a few yards from our seats. When the band blasted out, I could feel my bones rattle! I wished I had brought earplugs. But, as one might suspect, the girls loved it! And that mattered most.

A singer that I met but did not see perform was Hank Williams, Jr. He was in Montgomery, Alabama for an event honoring his father. The Alabama legislature designated a portion of Interstate-65 near where Hank grew up as the "Lonesome Highway" after one of Hank's songs. I liked many of Hank, Jr.'s records (particularly "A Country Boy Can Survive") but I liked his daddy better.

One of the most enjoyable experiences I have had was a visit to the Rock N' Roll Hall of Fame and Museum in Cleveland, Ohio in the summer of 2006. Van and I went to Cleveland to see the Indians and Tigers play and, in between the two night games, we spent the day at the museum. I was thrilled with the exhibits, particularly one that featured the greatest hits by decade. I listened to nearly all the songs from the 50's and 60's.

OTHER MUSICAL INTERESTS

Over the years, I came to appreciate other forms of music. A university community offers a variety of classical music from student recitals to symphony orchestras and, particularly, in my role as university president, I was expected to attend many of these events. Although I did not grow up listening to classical music and have not studied it, I found many of the pieces beautiful. I like the strings best of all. I once heard a performance by the violinist, Yizak Perlman, which was very moving.

I saw and heard my first opera in Omaha in the mid-70's, a performance by Beverly Sills in "Lucia di Lammermoor." Marlene and I went to several operas there in the Orphrem Theatre, even attending sessions of the Opera Angels (the donor group) to understand the content of the story.

While we were in Akron, I became quite fond of ballet. The university housed the Ohio Ballet Company and we attended their performances, inspired by the beauty and athleticism of the dancers.

OTHER ARTISTIC INTERESTS

An early and continuing interest of my family has been live theatre. When our children were young, Marlene and I would often take them to theatre performances on campus. When they were in school, Amy and Ellen acted in plays and developed an interest sufficient to choose theatre as a major. Wherever we have lived, Marlene and I have patronized the theatre. And we never go to New York without attending a play or two there.

I have seen many of the classics on Broadway, including "The Phantom of the Opera", "Les Miserables", "Chicago", and "42nd Street". Two "non-classic" plays that I really enjoyed were "All Shook Up", based on Elvis' music, and "The Lost Highway", the story of Hank Williams' life. Those plays were seen with BDBB (Big Dave and the Broadway Bombers), a group of guys from Auburn put together by my good friend, David Housel, that has gone to NYC each year for a number of years. But I would have to say that the most meaningful plays that I have seen on Broadway were "Hamlet", starring Ralph Fiennes, and "The Death of a Salesman", with Brian Dennehy in the role of Willie Loman. In both cases, my seats were on the third row which made the experience much more intimate and moving. An even more intimate experience came when I had a seat on stage, as a part of the jury, to see "Inherit the Wind" starring Christopher Plummer and Brian Dennehy.

In a similar fashion, Marlene and I have been regular attendees at the movies, finding that to be excellent entertainment for an afternoon or evening. While we try to see all the films each year that have been nominated for Academy Awards, we also enjoy offbeat independent ones like "The Story of the Weeping Camel". I don't watch television often, except for sporting events—particularly baseball, basketball, and football. Since we did not have a television while I was growing up, I listened to the radio—when it consisted of more than just disk jockeys and talk shows—and loved the old shows like "The Lone Ranger", "Sky King" and "The Green Hornet". But my favorite was "The Shadow". The only television show I can remember getting "hooked" on was "The Fugitive" in the 60's.

Art is another form of entertainment and enlightenment I enjoy. I have gone to almost all of the major art museums in cities like New York, Chicago, Washington, Minneapolis, and Atlanta and in many foreign lands, including the Louvre in Paris. I like the French Impressionists best, among the various schools of art, particularly Monet, Renoir, Degas, Pissarro, and Van Gogh. But I also appreciate painters with a distinctive style like Edward Hopper.

The art that we have collected for our home has often come from artists that we have know personally: Bill Dunlap, a young artist we knew in Boone, North Carolina; Hugh Williams, a distinguished member of the art faculty at Auburn; Sambo Mockbee, an architecture professor at Auburn who established the Rural Studio in Alabama and was also an accomplished artist; Monteigne Mathison, an artist in Auburn; Mose T., an African American artist in Alabama; and Mike Dorsey, the dean of the School of Art at East Carolina University.

Man is capable of expressing great beauty and many other emotions through music, art, dance, and theatre. I am pleased to have had the opportunity to be exposed to these art forms and to have my life enriched in many ways by this experience.

READING

The activity from which I have derived the most cultural enrichment and enjoyment, however, has been reading. I can't remember when I first started reading but two of my teachers in elementary school, observing my intellectual curiosity, gave me books to read. The tiny rural schools that I attended had no library; neither did the community. But I read all the books the teachers gave me, beginning a lifetime of reading.

While in high school, college, and graduate school, my reading list was filled, primarily, by academic assignments. I was one of the few (or it sometimes seemed that way) students who came to class having read the assignments. When combined with all of my extra-curricular activities -- athletics, the fraternity, and other student organizations -- I didn't have much time left for recreational reading, except during vacation periods. When I was a college professor, I read all the time -- just to stay abreast of developments in the subjects I was teaching and the topics on which I was doing research. Likewise, as a university administrator, my desk was constantly covered with reading material -- letters, memos, and reports. Reading for enjoyment came during vacations, which were all too few and too brief.

One of the joys of retirement, then, has been the opportunity to read solely for enrichment and enjoyment. During each year of retirement, I have been averaging 90-100 books a year among a wide range of topics and authors. It is difficult to pick out the "best books" I have ever read, but I have attempted to do that, identifying five. They were read many years ago and the fact that I still remember them well confirms their importance to me. The books are:

Zen and the Art of Motorcycle Maintenance by Robert Pirsig. A journey through one man's thoughts with an incisive analysis of academic life.

North Toward Home by Willie Morris. This is Morris' autobiography, written at age thirty-one. His descriptions of growing up in Mississippi and the "sense of place" that Southerner's have were meaningful to me.

To Kill a Mockingbird by Harper Lee. A remarkable book to have been published in 1960 amidst the civil rights movement. I admired the courage and eloquence of Atticus Finch. While we were living in Alabama, I visited the town of Monroeville, Harper Lee's hometown, and the model for the fictitious town of Maycomb in the novel. A copy of the novel, signed by the author, is a valuable part of our library.

The Summer of '49 by David Halberstam. A great story about baseball during the height of its popularity and in the era when my interest in the sport emerged.

Elmer Gantry by Sinclair Lewis. A novel about the fundamentalist religion I experienced growing up with a deep discussion about religious beliefs and the role of religion in American life.

In retirement, most of my reading has been for enjoyment although a number of serious books have made the list as well. I have discovered mysteries with my favorite authors being Robert B. Parker and James Lee Burke. Parker's novels involve the Boston private eye, Spenser; I have read all of the Spenser series -- about 33 books in all. Burke's novels are set in South Louisiana, West Texas, or Montana and his descriptive prose about people and places is very distinctive.

Other mystery writers that I like include David Baldacci, Lee Child, Harlan Coben, Jeffery Deaver, Robert Ludlum, James Patterson, and Richard North Patterson. And I have read extensively books by the Mississippi trio: William Faulkner, John Grisham, and Willie Morris. I think I have read all of John Grisham's novels, nearly all of Morris' books, and four of Faulkner's novels.

Sprinkled among the mysteries has been a steady supply of baseball books. I enjoy biographies and stories of events that actually occurred. Some of my favorites are: The Boys of Summer by Roger Kahn, Shoeless Joe by W.P. Kinsella, and Three Nights in August by Buzz Bissinger.

One of the benefits of being a university president was the opportunity to meet distinguished guests who came to the campus, including well-known authors. Perhaps the most impressive of this group was James Michener. He came to the University of Nebraska as a "Writer-in-Residence" while I was there and I got to escort him around the Omaha campus while he met with various groups. Michener was very "down-to-earth" and humble about his work, very patiently answering questions from students. This was while he was writing Centennial, a story of the Great Plains. I also met him when I was at Texas A&M and he was in Texas, working on his novel, Texas.

Spending my career on university campuses, I have worked with many authors among the faculty. Most faculty members write academic articles and books that appeal to narrow audiences, but some also author books for general appeal. Included in this latter group are Wayne Flynt, an Auburn professor who wrote the definitive history of Alabama and a prize-winning book, "Poor But Proud"; Ed Harrell, a history professor at Auburn who wrote several biographies, including one on Oral Roberts; James Hansen, the Auburn history professor who authored the authorized biography on Neil Armstrong; George Knepper, an Akron history professor who wrote a highly regarded history of Ohio; Paula Backscheider, an Auburn English professor who was an authority on Defoe; and Elizabeth Neeld, whom I first met at Texas A&M and who has been a good friend thru the years. Elizabeth, an English professor who wrote outstanding books on writing, authored a major book, "Seven Choices", on how to cope with the loss of a spouse.

Among the popular writers that I have met include Mitch Albom, Dave Barry, Rick Bragg, Dennis Covington, Pat Conroy, Rita Dove, James Dickey, William Ferris, Shelby Foote, Paul Hemphill, Robert Inman, David Halberstam, James Hansen, Dan Moldea, Kevin Phillips, James Redfield, Anne Rivers Siddons, Studs Terkel, and Robert James Waller.

The only thing bad about reading is that good books are published much faster than one can read them, not to mention all those that were published long ago that are still waiting to be read. I always have a large stack of books waiting. So many books, so little time!

FOOD

One activity that is only minimally a source of cultural enrichment -- but is certainly a major interest of mine-- is eating. My Momma was a great cook and I grew up on a steady diet of fresh vegetables directly from the garden. My wife, Marlene, is a tremendous cook, also, always willing to try new recipes and never preparing a bad meal.

I have traveled to many countries and have tried almost every kind of food. There are only a few things I do not like, such as liver and strong-tasting fish like anchovies, caviar and salmon. I have eaten in many five-star and other fancy (and expensive) restaurants, but for a good meal, I'd settle for one in a Cracker Barrel restaurant any day.

Once, after returning from a trip to Russia, I described to Marlene the meals we had, complete with a bowl of caviar at each place setting. She was appalled that I would pass up the opportunity to partake of such a delicacy, but its taste does not appeal to me.

Most of the restaurants we prefer, other than Cracker Barrel and another chain, Bonefish Grill, are off-the-beaten path places like the Birchwood Café in Minneapolis, Minnesota; the Norske Nook in Osseo, Wisconsin; the Manitou near Frankfort, Michigan; Café 123 in Opelika, Alabama; the Boone Tavern in Berea, Kentucky; and the West Point Market (also our favorite grocery store) in Akron, Ohio.

My favorite breakfast consists of Uncle Sam cereal or steel-cut oatmeal, with fresh fruit and nuts. An appealing lunch consists of a Subway sandwich or the salad bar at Ruby Tuesday, with dinner being anything Marlene prepares or, if we eat out, spicy-grilled catfish and coleslaw from Cracker Barrel. But I am an "equal-opportunity eater" -- i.e., I eat what is set before me, like almost all kinds of food, and am willing to try new things. I derive a great deal of pleasure from eating, in addition to the sustenance I need for survival.

CHAPTER 17:

INTERNATIONAL TRAVEL – A BROADENING EXPERIENCE

Over the course of my life, I lived in thirteen states, with the longest time being spent in Mississippi (my first 15 years) and Ohio (18 years and counting). In addition, I have visited every state in the U.S.A. except Alaska.

I have enjoyed each place we have lived and particularly value the many good friends we have made in each community. While much is made over regional differences in people, I have found that those differences (even the accents) are insignificant once you get to know the people as individuals.

Travel throughout the United States has always been interesting to me, especially when we get off the interstates and go through small towns and rural areas where people have lived and worked for many years. But, by far, the most enlightening and broadening experience for me has been the opportunity to travel to foreign countries. Having spent my career in institutions of higher education, I have had relationships with many natives of foreign counties since the faculty and students of a major university comprise one of the most diverse cultures in our society as to race, nationality and religion. There is no substitute, however, for visiting a country in person, viewing its landscape and meeting its residents on their home turf, to gain greater understanding of their culture.

It has been my good fortune to visit twenty-five foreign countries and three territories. Some of the visits have been short and pedestrian while others have involved a substantial amount of time and energy. In this chapter, I will discuss my international travels, not in any kind of chronological order but rather focusing on the most significant experience first. By far the most extensive and enriching time was that spent in the far away land of Afghanistan.

AFGHANISTAN

In the summer of 1975, Marlene and I and our three children lived in Afghanistan for three months while I served as a member of a team from the University of Nebraska providing assistance to Kabul University in Afghanistan's capital city, under the auspices of a grant from the U.S. Agency for International Development.

At that time, I knew very little about Afghanistan. What I knew came from a faculty member I had hired at Appalachian State University, Shah Mahmoud, in the early 1970's. The opportunity to visit Afghanistan came through Tom Gouttierre, director of a Center for Afghanistan Studies at the University of Nebraska at Omaha where I was serving as the business school dean. Tom and his wife, Marylu, had been Peace Corps volunteers in Afghanistan and Tom, then, served for several years as director of the Fulbright Program there. He came to UNO to be the director of international affairs and, shortly thereafter, secured a three-year grant from USAID to provide assistance to Kabul University, an assignment that Indiana University had held for many years. The grant called for Nebraska to send a nine-person team (three in engineering, three in agriculture, and three in education) to Kabul to work with the faculties there for three years. The team consisted of professors from both the Lincoln and Omaha campuses of NU and was headed by Richard Gibson, an engineering professor. The grant also provided for a consultant to work with the Kabul University administration in implementing modern management practices. It is for this assignment that I was tapped.

Tom Gouttierre and I were good friends; we played softball together and our families often socialized. So when he asked me to handle the consulting assignment, I was favorably inclined. But there were two important bases I needed to touch. The first was approval from the chancellor and provost of UNO to be absent from the campus for that period of time and to get Larry Trussell, my associate dean in the business school, to assume responsibility for the school in my absence. That base was covered. Secondly, I had told Tom that, if I was going to be in Afghanistan for three months, I wanted to take my family with me. He said that could be arranged and, fortunately, Marlene agreed to come along. By this time, Amy was ten, Ellen was eight, and Van was six and they had become accustomed to the travels and new adventures to which we had subjected them. So everything was set for the journey – this is, everything except getting passports, vaccinations, arranging for a house sitter, and many other tasks associated with traveling half-way around the globe and being gone for three months. I read all the material they gave me on the university and the country, including James Michener's novel, <u>Caravans</u>, in preparing for the assignment.

The flight from Omaha to Kabul took three days. On the first day, we flew to Chicago and, then, to Frankfurt, Germany where we spent the night at a hotel near the airport. Over the next two days, we flew Ariana Afghan Airlines to Kabul with stops in Istanbul, TURKEY and Teheran, IRAN. In both Istanbul and Teheran, we had to vacate the plane and wait at the airport for about an hour before the flight resumed. This allowed the kids to exercise a bit and, in Istanbul, we were able to buy some pistachio nuts freshly roasted in the airport.

On the flight into Kabul, a stark landscape in all directions greeted us. Afghanistan is located in central Asia and is bordered on the west by Iran, on the north by several Soviet republics, on the northeast by China, and on the south and east by Pakistan. The terrain consists of high mountain ranges and plains and there appeared to be hardly any vegetation. I later found out that this was almost true and was told that, over centuries, wild goats that roamed the countryside had eaten all the plants and trees except those that were fenced in.

Kabul, the capital city, had a population of about 500,000 and sat at an altitude of approximately 6,000 feet, creating very pleasant summer temperatures. Afghanistan had operated as a constitutional monarchy for many years under King Mohammed Zahir Shah. But in the year before our trip there, the King's cousin, Mohammed Doud, had taken over the government in a relatively peaceful coup, when the King was out of the country. We traveled all around Kabul and out into the countryside and felt safe doing so.

USAID arranged for us to rent a house, in a nice area of Kabul, from a staff member on "home leave" – i.e. back in the states for the summer. The house, located within a walled compound, came with an automobile (a Volkswagen "bug") and a staff. Khan, the cook, had good command of the English language and was a delightful young man. He lived in the city and purchased local foods each day such as nan (bread baked in clay ovens on the street), and delicious melons grown in the area. Farouk, the "houseboy", was a man who lived in a small building on the property and had the responsibility of cleaning the house. Farouk understood very little English, particularly when you wanted him to perform some task he had not "gotten around to" yet. But they were both good with the kids, which made our time there more enjoyable.

USAID maintained a compound not far away that included a commissary (where Marlene could purchase food and other necessary supplies), a swimming pool (that the kids used regularly), a movie theater that showed films a couple of times a week, and very nice clay tennis courts that I played as often as I could. I also played on the courts at the U.S. Embassy, across town, during a tournament.

My work with the university proved to be very interesting. Kabul University was the only institution of higher education in Afghanistan and over the years had received assistance from several countries (France, Germany, England and the Soviet Union) in addition to the USA. My primary contact became the vice-president of business and finance, a delightful Afghan about my age who had been educated in France (where he married a French woman) and had received a master's degree from Indiana University. He gave me free rein to review all their operations and assigned me an interpreter since almost all the people I would be meeting spoke no English. The vice-president was trilingual, speaking both French and English when needed, but using Dari, the official language for most Afghans, for almost all his business communications. One sect in the country, the Pashtuns, spoke a dialect called Pashtu.

With my interpreter in tow, I visited all the institution's business operations, asking the employees to tell me or show me what they did. We even took a trip to Jalalabad, a city about two hours from Kabul on the road toward the Khyber Pass and Peshawar, Pakistan, where the university operated a medical school and hospital. I found that everything was at a rudimentary level and that an "American model" was of little use to them; I had to understand what they were doing and determine if there were some ways the work could be improved.

I became aware of one of the challenges early in the process when the vice-president assembled all his staff to hear me speak. I took my notes for "Management 101" and condensed them down to an even more elementary level. I explained a basic concept and, then, my assistant interpreted it for the audience. After my opening comments which spanned perhaps two or three sentences, the interpreter spoke for what seemed like five minutes or longer with frequent feedback from the audience. Finally, he turned to me and said that there was no word or phrase in Dari that corresponded to "management". So not only could they not understand management as a concept, there was not even a word to describe it!

On another occasion, I reviewed the accounting or bookkeeping department and had the staff proudly demonstrate an electronic posting machine to me that allowed them to enter accounting transactions on cards representing various accounts. The machine had been purchased for them by Indiana University a few years before. But, by looking further, I found that they posted the same transactions by hand to ledger sheets like before. Obviously, they did not trust the machine to get it right!

One day I sat in the vice-president's office to observe what went on. His office consisted of a large room with his desk in one corner and wooden chairs around the walls. Almost all the chairs were filled and, upon a signal from the vice-president, one of the men got up, paced the center of the floor, and plead his case in an animated fashion. One of the presentations that followed spanned a half-hour or more, with members of the audience interjecting their comments as well. Since the conversation was in Dari, I did not understand it so I asked the vice-president what the issue was. He said that a custodian claimed his broom had been stolen and requested a new broom. The debate was over whether the custodian may have taken the broom himself and whether he should be given a new instrument before the mystery had been solved. It was obvious that even minor issues were being brought to the highest level before decisions were made!

At the end of the summer, I wrote a report for the vice-president suggesting a number of improvements that could be made. But I focused on things I thought they might be willing to implement rather than what the "textbook" said.

There are many experiences that we had that summer that I remember fondly. Two of the most memorable are described below.

The first involved the driver, an Afghan man in his mid 20's, who picked me and several other Nebraska team members up each morning and brought us home after work. One member of our team found out that the driver wanted to marry a girl but that he could not because he didn't have the dowry that her father demanded. So all the riders chipped in to raise the additional funds he needed. As a result we were all invited to the wedding.

The wedding was held at night in a room upstairs over a department store in downtown Kabul. We arrived about 10 pm and found the room filled mostly with Afghan men, a table filled with Afghan food, and a couple of men playing Afghan music. The dancing was done only by the men, either separately or together. The women that were there were in a far corner, dressed in their traditional garments that covered them completely except for a mesh opening through which they were able to see. The groom greeted all the visitors and handled any problems that arose.

Finally, at midnight, the music stopped and the groom assumed a position at one end of the room decorated with flowers. A door opened at the other end of the room and in came the father leading his daughter who was clothed in traditional garb with her face concealed. The bride came to stand by the groom and an Afghan official stepped forward to conduct the ceremony. Only when the ceremony culminated was the bride's veil lifted to reveal her face.

A second event was a three-day trip that Marlene, the kids, and I took, with some other Nebraska team members, out in the Afghan countryside to the villages of Bamiyan and Band-i-Amir. Traveling in Afghanistan at this time was difficult, as there was no railroad and very few paved roads. In fact, the area into which we were traveling had only dirt roads and, often, only trails that were not clearly marked. So for the trip, we rented a Land Rover vehicle and hired a driver who knew the territory.

When the day for our departure arrived, Ellen was very ill and Marlene and I determined she was not able to travel. I asked Marlene, Amy, and Van to go ahead with the group and that I would stay with Ellen, with the possibility of joining them in Bamiyan the next day if Ellen's health improved. Our cook, Khan, told me he knew of an airplane that flew from Kabul to Bamiyan each day and that he would help me get tickets.

By the next morning, Ellen was much better, thanks to some medication I had secured from a nurse at USAID. With Khan's help, we made it to the airfield and boarded a small 10-12 passenger plane. It was filled with Afghan men in their traditional dress – baggy pants, long shirt, and turbans – except for Ellen and me. One man had a cage with two chickens in the seat beside him.

The flight into the Hindu Kush Mountains was awe-inspiring as the plane flew just over the tops of the gigantic red rock formations or sometimes between the mountain peaks on its journey into Bamiyan. Bamiyan is located in a beautiful valley between the mountain ranges. As the plane descended into the valley, I saw no evidence of an airport or runway. That was correct, as the plane settled down into an open field. We were met by the driver of the Land Rover who drove Ellen and me to the inn where our group was staying.

Bamiyan is historically important because it was a great center of Buddhism from the 1st to the 7th century A.D. Thousands of monks lived in cave monasteries in the mountains and they carved two gigantic statues of Buddha (the tallest in the world at 175 feet) into the side of the mountain overlooking the village. Afghanistan was now a Muslin country and the Muslims had carved off the faces of the statues but they were still a magnificent sight. With the help of a guide, we were able to travel through the caves up to a point where we could stand on the head of the Buddha and look across the valley. Wow!

The next day we traveled higher up into the mountains to Band-i-Amir. This small village is surrounded by deep lakes with crystal blue water. Set against brown soil and red rocks, the contrast is striking. I went into a small trading post there. When the merchant heard me speaking English, he went into a back room and brought out a bottle of Coca-Cola that he was polishing. I didn't buy the Coke but I did marvel at the company's distribution system!

On the trip back to Kabul, I got to see the landscape at ground level. I marveled at how little civilization had impacted the people. There was no electricity or running water; the people lived in mud huts surrounded by mud and rock walls to keep wild animals out; and cultivation of land was done with oxen and wooden plow stocks. The people were curious about visitors but seemed to be happy with their lives. We even saw a band of Kochis (nomads) with their camel caravan traveling across the countryside.

By contrast, most of the people living in Kabul were piled on top of one another in dilapidated buildings or huts built up the side of the hills, used a trench next to the street as a toilet, and hauled water from the river in which they washed their clothes and bathed their bodies. Yet, in these impoverished conditions, we found the Afghans to be friendly, extremely hardworking, and very inventive.

I felt dismay a few years later when I learned of the Soviet invasion of Afghanistan that occurred in 1979. We wondered about what happened to the many Afghans we met there and realized that the work my colleagues and I had done at Kabul University was largely nullified. With additional regret I read about how the Taliban assumed greater and greater control, seeming to move the country in a direction away from the progress that had been made. We heard very little about the Taliban while there, although there were often reports that the Mullahs (religious leaders) outside of Kabul were very upset about the "Western ways" adopted by the students at the university, especially the females who shunned their veils and were now wearing makeup and blue jeans. The crowning blow came when the Taliban destroyed the Buddha statues carved into the side of the mountain in Bamiyan.

Overall, the time in Afghanistan was not only educational but enlightening. I admired the Afghan people and always wished they had had the opportunity to use their ingenuity and industry in a more hospitable environment under the kind of leadership that would have capitalized on those talents.

WESTERN EUROPE VIA WASHINGTON, D.C.

During the 1977-78 academic year, I was able to participate in an interesting program called the President's Executive Interchange Program (PEIP) in Washington, D.C. Established by President Nixon, the program brought experienced business executives into the federal government to help install "sound business practices" in its various operations. A counterpart of PEIP placed federal government officials with industrial firms. The assignments in both cases were for one year.

I'm not sure how I found out about the program, but it appealed to me because it would broaden my experience and, perhaps, prepare me for advancement to a university provost or president's position. I was still at the University of Nebraska-Omaha as business school dean and, therefore, talked with the provost and chancellor about applying for PEIP. They were agreeable to a year's leave of absence, should I be selected, with Larry Trussell serving as acting dean in my absence.

Fortunately, I was one of 50 individuals from across the nation who was chosen to participate. Forty-five of the participants came from major U.S. corporations – e.g. General Motors, Xerox, GE, AT&T, IBM, Westinghouse, etc. Five were from higher education – a community college president, a vice-president, and three business school deans. This was the first year that representatives from higher education were included in the program.

Each PEIP participant had a full-time job in one of the federal departments along with a regular series of activities in the nation's capital intended to give each individual a better understanding of how the government operates. Additionally, the program included a two-week trip to Western Europe.

But, first, I had to fly to Washington and interview for my job assignment. They presented about six alternatives including jobs in Defense, Labor, Commerce, and HEW. My first choice was with the Commissioner's office in the Office of Education. At this time, education was a part of the Department of Health, Education and Welfare; several years later, education became a separate department. Fortunately, I got my requested assignment and prepared to report for duty in September 1977.

There were a lot of preparations for the move that would take the family to Washington, D.C. for a year. The PEIP maintained a full-time staff of individuals to assist; so most aspects of the move went smoothly. They helped us locate a four-bedroom house to rent in Fairfax County, Virginia, just south of the Beltway (I-495) and west of the Mt. Vernon Highway in a village called Belle Haven. It was a nice neighborhood with easy access to Alexandria and on into D.C. Ellen and Van attended Hollin Hills Elementary School only a few blocks from our house, while Amy went to William Cullen Bryant Junior High a little further away.

Marlene and I had decided to use this as an educational experience for the whole family and, particularly, for the children. So nearly every weekend we drove off to see the sites in the D.C. area and beyond. We toured the Capital, the White House, the Supreme Court, and all the monuments; traveled down to Mt. Vernon; and visited the Civil War battlefield at Manassas. Then we began to broaden out geographically.

First, we went to Charlottesville to see Thomas Jefferson's home, Monticello; then to Colonial Williamsburg, Jamestown, and Yorktown; to Harper's Ferry to see the John Brown museum; and to Philadelphia to visit Constitution Hall and the Liberty Bell. But the most significant journey was to New York City. We left Union Station in Washington on Friday, traveling by train to Grand Central Station, and staying at the Roosevelt Hotel there. While in the "Big Apple", we tried to see it all – Statue of Liberty, Empire State Building, Central Park, Chinatown. We took a Circle Line cruise around Manhattan Island and went to a performance of "The Wiz" and to another at Radio City Music Hall. But I think the most thrilling stop for the kids was to FAO Swartz, the toy store! We arrived back in Washington Sunday night tired but with lots to talk about.

My assignment at the Office of Education was as special assistant to the Executive Deputy Commissioner, Dr. William Pierce. Dr. Pierce was the number two person in the agency and its chief operating officer. He was a good person to work for as he included me in many of the day-to-day issues as well as gave me a chance to review some projects in depth, such as a center for continuing education for agency employees.

The Commissioner of Education was Dr. Ernest Boyer who had been chancellor of the State University of New York (SUNY) system. I greatly admired Dr. Boyer and enjoyed the opportunities I had to interact with him and to hear him speak. I got to go to high profile events like Congressional hearings "on the hill" but also to work with the bureau chiefs and individuals in the agency who directed programs. Employees at the federal level are generally of two types: political appointees (Schedule C) who hold the top level positions and normally fill those posts for a relative short duration and career employees who are covered under the federal civil service system. The latter group, derided as "bureaucrats" by outsiders, were frequently highly dedicated individuals who kept programs running while the leadership above them changed often.

Our PEIP activities began with a weeklong orientation seminar consisting of speakers from throughout the government representing the various departments and agencies as well as several Senators – Church (Idaho) and Heinz (Pennsylvania) – and Representatives – Udall (Arizona) and McCloskey (California). Then virtually every week there would be a session with someone – a Cabinet Secretary, a Senator or Congressman, a journalist (such as columnist James J. Kilpratrick, <u>Washington Post</u> editor Ben Bradlee, columnist David Broder, and columnist Art Buchwald). Sometimes the sessions would be over lunch, but more often would consist of a meeting of about one hour in which the featured guest would make brief remarks and then respond to questions. Some of the more interesting sessions to me were with Senator Bob Dole; Secretary of HUD Patricia Harris; AFL-CIO President George Meany; Arthur Burns, Chairman of the Federal Reserve System; FBI Director Clarence Kelley, Secretary of Labor Ray Marshall, Senator Ted Kennedy, and Supreme Court Justice William Rehnquist. In addition to the professional sessions, we were able to attend receptions for briefings at the embassies of countries we would be visiting – France and Germany-- as well as Great Britain and Russia.

My biggest regret as to the weekly programs is that we did not get to meet with the President, as is usually the case for each PEIP class. President Carter was in his first year in office when we came to Washington. The PEIP staff scheduled several occasions for us to meet with him but each appointment had to be cancelled because of other matters he had to deal with. I got a chance to meet President Carter many years later but would have loved to have talked with him while he was in the White House.

Washington, D.C. is one of the most "international" cities in the world with representatives from almost every nation living and working there. To be there for a year was an educational experience in itself, but the European trip was clearly the highlight of the year. Spouses were included in this phase of the program; so Marlene was able to go with me. We were fortunate that my brother, Junior, and his wife, Pauline, who were living in Danville, Virginia, were able to come and stay with our kids for the two weeks we were gone.

Our International Study Seminar began on January 21st and was concluded on February 4th, 1978. Our first stop was in Brussels where we were greeted by the Prime Minister of Belgium at a reception at the Royal Palace. Staying at the Palace Hotel, we spent the first full day at the headquarters for the European Common Market (now called the European Union) being briefed on their operations. The second day consisted of briefings at the headquarters of the North Atlantic Treaty Organization (NATO), U.S.'s main military alliance in Europe. That night we had a "night on the town" in Brussels. Marlene and I had dinner at a delightful seafood restaurant or, at least it was delightful to me. Marlene got food poisoning from the mussels she had and was very ill by the time we reached Paris.

On the third day we traveled by train from Brussels to Paris through some of the most beautiful countryside I had seen. We were housed at the Hotel Meurice in Paris for the next four days where we had briefings by various officials in the French government. What I remember most is the number of times the French mentioned the Germans, particularly the threat that a unified Germany would represent. (By contrast, the Germans whom we met with the next week never mentioned the French once!)

Fortunately, through the hotel, I was able to get a French physician to come see Marlene and, with the medication he provided, she began to recover. We had the weekend in Paris to see the sites, including a wonderful museum featuring paintings of the Impressionists. This triggered my life-long interest in this artistic form. We dined at a restaurant along the Champs Elysees where I tried to use the French I had studied in college to order our food only to receive a sneer from the waiter. I also had the opportunity to take a bus trip out to Versailles, the former Royal Palace (Marlene did not feel well enough to do so). It is difficult to describe the splendor of that structure and setting. If this was typical of how the French aristocracy lived, one can more easily understand the motivation for the French Revolution! Our time in Paris was also marked by a lavish dinner hosted by the IBM Corporation.

On Monday, we flew to Bonn, Germany for a briefing by officials at the U.S. Embassy and then transported to the Hotel Bristol. All day Tuesday we attended sessions hosted by representatives of the Federal Republic of Germany (West Germany) and by the German National Chamber of Commerce. On Wednesday, we traveled by bus to Cologne and Duesseldorf and, then, flew to Berlin where we stayed at the Kempinski Hotel.

On Thursday, we had meetings with the U.S. officials in West Berlin, with representatives of the Berlin Senate, and with the Berlin Chamber of Commerce. The evening was highlighted by an opera at a beautiful concert hall in West Berlin. Friday brought a trip to East Berlin. At this time, the Berlin Wall still existed and we had to go through Checkpoint Charlie, after which we were briefed by officials at the U.S. Embassy in East Berlin. The contrast between East and West Berlin was striking; West Berlin was a very modern city, but East Berlin appeared to have changed very little since WWII. But one of the real treasures of East Berlin was the Pergamon Museum which we got to visit. On Saturday, we flew back to Washington via Frankfurt and New York.

I have visited Western Europe on several other occasions but never at such a high level. We each had diplomatic passports which eased our process through customs and the PEIP staff handled all of the travel, housing, and meeting arrangements. A very nice way to see a beautiful region of the world and to interact with leaders in these countries!

EASTERN EUROPE

In the summer of 1990, I received an invitation from an organization called the State Leadership Initiative to participate in a visit to four eastern European countries, along with about 30 other business and education leaders from Ohio. The roster included members of the state legislature, CEO's of companies, chamber of commerce officials, school superintendents, etc.; I was serving as president of the University of Akron at the time. The Berlin

Wall had recently fallen and many of the countries in Eastern Europe were moving toward democracies; our objective was to interact with leaders in those countries.

Our two-week trip took us to Zagreb (which was then part of Yugoslavia, later to become Croatia); Moscow, Russia; Warsaw; Poland; and Budapest, Hungary. At each site we had discussions with government officials and other leaders. The conversations were through interpreters; so they were somewhat laborious. But most enlightening were the questions that they raised.

I remember one session in Warsaw where the Polish leaders were obviously eager to install a democracy and wanted to have it in place by the next year. I remarked to my colleagues later that, while I admired Poland's enthusiasm, I thought that their timetable was somewhat optimistic. After all, we in the USA have had a democracy for over 200 years and we still don't have it right!

In each country, we toured the cities where we were located and often went by bus into the surrounding countryside. In Zagreb, we attended a festival in a large plaza that included music and dance in native costume and went by bus to Ljubljana, Slovenia. In Poland, we were guests at a concert in a beautiful park in Warsaw and traveled by bus to the birthplace of the Polish composer, Chopin. Budapest was, by far, the most vibrant of the cities we visited in terms of the obvious introduction of private enterprise into the economy and the apparent freedom of the people there. We enjoyed sites in both Buda and Pest – on both sides of the beautiful Danube River.

Russia at the time we visited was still a part of the Soviet Union. I admired the beautiful wide boulevards, the ornate governmental buildings, and the awe-inspiring Red Square. But the hotel (build as a dormitory for the Olympics) was falling apart and we had to "bribe" the matron on each floor to get our rooms cleaned each day. In one of our sessions, we met with what was described as "some of Russia's top scientists". In the introductions, I was identified as a university president; after the session, I was approached by several of the scientists who gave me copies of their resumes and indicated they would love to come to the USA.

The visits were enlightening to me; it was good to finally see what was behind the "Iron Curtain" and to sense the desire of the people there for policies that would provide greater freedom and private enterprise.

INDIA

In 1995, while president of Auburn University, Marlene and I had the opportunity to visit India. Dr. Edward Harrell, a Distinguished Professor of History at Auburn, was serving as the director of the American Studies

Research Center in Hyderabad while on a Fulbright Fellowship. He invited me to give the Founder's Day address on the 31st anniversary of the center's establishment and arranged for other activities in the country over a two-week period. While in Hyderabad, I visited with officials at Osmania University and gave the keynote address at an "International Conference on Business Education in the United States and Asia" which was attended by representatives of various business schools throughout the country.

We traveled to New Delhi to visit with the U.S. Ambassador and, then, took a train to Agra to see the Taj Mahal that was indeed spectacular. But it was disappointing to see the deterioration to the structure that was being caused by air pollution. Finally, we flew to Jaipur, perhaps the most colorful and beautiful area that we saw, staying in a hotel that had formerly been a royal palace.

The natives of India that I have met and worked with in the U.S. have been gracious and hard working. This was true of the leaders that we met in India as well. But one can not ignore the abject poverty that is encountered everywhere – the structures in which people live, the beggars that one confronts constantly, and the crowding, particularly in the cities.

THE FAR EAST (JAPAN, KOREA, TAIWAN, AND CHINA)

I have visited Japan on two occasions. The first was in 1990 when president of the University of Akron and also serving as chairman of the Akron Regional Development Board, an economic development agency for the Akron region. The Akron mayor, economic development director, and I flew to Tokyo to attend the International Rubber and Plastics Fair. Bridgestone, a Japanese tire manufacturer, had just purchased the Firestone Tire and Rubber Company, one of Akron's biggest companies; so part of the trip was to meet with top executives of Bridgestone and welcome them to Akron. We, also, rode the "bullet train" from Tokyo to Kobe to visit with another Japanese firm there.

The second trip was to Osaka to attend the annual Southeast U.S.-Japan Association meeting as a delegate from the State of Alabama in 1993 when I was president of Auburn University. This association was established to provide an occasion for the governors and other officials of the southeastern states to meet with Japanese leaders to promote trade and attract investment. In Osaka, as well as Tokyo and Kobe, I was impressed with how clean and well-maintained facilities were and with how efficient the Japanese workers were. But I was also amazed at how expensive goods and services were.

From Osaka, I flew to Seoul, Korea to join some colleagues from Auburn to visit Seoul National University and to explore opportunities for cooperative relationships, particularly, in agriculture. Seoul, like Tokyo, is a very modern, bustling city.

In 1996, I was invited to speak at an Asian-Pacific Conference on Higher Education in Taiwan. Marlene and I flew to Taipei where we attended an Auburn Alumni Club meeting and then visited with several different universities in that metropolitan area. I was overwhelmed by the enthusiasm of the large group of Taiwanese who had attended Auburn and then came back to their home country. We went by train from Taipei to Tainan City on the southern end of the island for the conference at National Cheng Kung University. I was the only speaker from the United States among representatives of a number of Pacific rim countries.

From there, we flew to Hong Kong to visit with Bill and Jayne Mobley, friends from our days at Texas A&M. Bill, who had served as president of A&M, was a visiting professor at Hong Kong University of Science and Technology, a beautiful, totally new campus overlooking the bay. With the Mobleys, we toured many sites in Hong Kong and even took a train to Shenzhen in Mainland China. At the time we were there a decision had been made to bring Hong Kong from its independent status into Mainland China. Hong Kong is a jewel of the Far East, as modern as any city I have seen and seemed to have prospered under the private enterprise economy it enjoyed. The contrast between Hong Kong and Shenzhen was striking, in terms of economic development, but I speculated that, as China allowed private investment to spread into the mainland, that contrast would diminish.

I would say that I was impressed with all the areas I visited in the Far East. The cities were modern and clean with an obvious high level of economic activity. The people were industrious, friendly, and anxious to learn. It is not surprising to me that this part of the world continues to have a high level of economic growth, given these traits as well as the enterprising spirit of the small merchants.

Scandinavia

One of the nice aspects of our time at Auburn was the travel program sponsored by the Alumni Association each year, trips to various exotic locations around the world. The association invited Marlene and me to host one of the trips each year. This made it easier for them to sell spaces on the voyage as there were alums who might be attracted to travel with the President and the First Lady; it was also a good time for us to interact with alums who might be potential donors.

Marlene and I were not able to host a trip every year, as university business conflicted. Once we had agreed to host a two-week tour of Australia and New Zealand, but had to withdraw after the Governor called a special session of the legislature in August to consider the higher education budget. On another occasion, I had to withdraw from a trip to the Bavarian areas of Germany and Austria, with Marlene continuing as hostess, along with our daughter, Ellen. But one of our most memorable trips was to the Scandinavian counties (Finland, Denmark, Norway, and Sweden) in 1996.

The trip was made more enjoyable by the accompaniment of some old friends: Lenwood and Jean Cochran from South Carolina; Sandra Purrington and her sister, Kathy Bowling, from Minnesota; and Auburn alums Mack and Jamie Freeman of Birmingham. Mack, an architect, produced an album of photographs and his original artwork that serves as a memento of this journey.

The first stop in Helsinki, Finland included a visit to the Olympic Stadium and a beautiful Lutheran Church "Built in the Rocks". On another day we drove into the Finish countryside to the home of a renowned Finish architect, Elill Saarinen, and to a monument honoring the Finish composer, Jean Sebeluis. We then flew to Copenhagen, Denmark, seeing the Royal Palace, the Fredericksburg Castle, and the Viking Ship Museum. But I most enjoyed the tour of the countryside, an opportunity to walk the streets of Copenhagen, and a lovely dinner at Tivoli Gardens.

From Copenhagen, we took an overnight ocean voyage to Oslo, Norway, where we toured Vigeland Park with its magnificent sculpture. While in Oslo, Marlene and I joined the Freemans for lunch at a sidewalk café. I was wearing a golf shirt with the Auburn insignia on it. Three young men approached our table, asking if I was from Auburn. I told them I was, whereupon they introduced themselves as swimmers, two of whom were from France visiting their friend in Norway, and indicated they were considering going to Auburn as student-athletes. I quickly told them that I was the president of Auburn and introduced Mark Freeman as the architect who had designed the natatorium there. By the looks on their faces, I knew they were skeptical; so I assured them that Auburn was a great school and that I would tell David Marsh, the swimming coach, that I had met them. When we returned to Auburn, I called coach Marsh to relate the incident to him and learned that the young men had indeed called him and that he had confirmed that I was the Auburn president. As it turned out, the two men from France did come to Auburn, became All-Americans and Olympic swimmers, and helped AU win two national championships.

From Oslo, we traveled by bus across Norway to a little village, Ulvik, located on a beautiful fjord set among magnificent mountains. It was one of the most spectacular places I've ever seen – so serene and peaceful. Then we went by boat and train to Bergen, a medieval town on the east coast that was the home of composer Edvard Grieg and author Henrik Ibsen.

The final stop on our Scandinavian journey was in Stockholm, Sweden. We toured City Hall where the Nobel Prize awards are presented each year and saw the Royal Palace, but the most enjoyable time for me was a trip across the Swedish countryside through the village of Sigtuna to Uppsala, site of one of the oldest universities in the world.

I was enthralled with Norway because of its natural beauty, but there was an ambiance about all the Scandinavian counties – clean, well-ordered, peaceful, serene, safe – that I found very appealing. But we visited in August; perhaps I would feel differently if we were there in January!

SOUTH AMERICA

I had my first visit to South America in 1981 to Brazil. Serving as dean of the college of business administration at Texas A&M at the time, I was invited, along with dean Bob Page of the college of engineering, to come to Brazil to give a series of lectures at universities there. Our host was the president of one of the universities in Rio de Janerio who was interested in establishing a relationship with A&M.

We flew to Rio from Houston and spent several days there, speaking at a different university each day. Bob and I would each speak about trends in our respective areas and then field questions, through an interpreter, from the audience, mostly faculty. But, on our first night there, I got an indication that we were in a different culture.

Our host had told us he would pick us up at our hotel and take us to dinner. Bob and I were, therefore, in the lobby and ready to go by 6:30 pm; hours went by without the host arriving. I went to the snack bar for crackers to tide me over. Finally, about 10:00 pm, our host shows up without any apology for being late. It was nearly 11:00pm when we got to the restaurant; noticing that it was nearly empty, I immediately concluded that we were too late and that it was closing. To my surprise it began to fill up and by midnight was packed. Obviously, the Brazilians ate on a different calendar than we did! So Bob and I learned to pace ourselves for the remainder of the week.

I had heard that the bathers at the beaches in Rio were topless; so we managed to build visits to both Copacabana and Ipanema, the two most famous beaches, into our itinerary. But either our information or our timing was wrong, as we saw only one topless bather.

After our days in Rio de Janerio, we flew over the Amazon to Brazila, the national capital, a new city that had been carved out of the jungle. It was a beautiful place, carefully planned with new buildings and wide green spaces.

The intent, we were told, was to decentralize Brazil's population heavily concentrated along the seashore; but many of the governmental workers continued to live in Rio and flew up to Brazila to work each week, returning to Rio for the weekend. In Brazila we met with the Minister of Education and with the faculty at the University of Brazila.

Brazil is a beautiful country; we saw many captivating sites there. We ate a lot of black beans that seem to come with every meal. And we learned to sleep a little later in the morning, take a nap or rest in the afternoon, and not expect dinner until late at night.

In late 2008 Marlene and I are scheduled to travel to El Salvador to participate in a project of building houses for low-income families under the leadership of the Fuller Center for Housing. Marlene serves on the board of directors of this special ministry attempting to eliminate poverty housing around the world.

ITALY

Each year the School of Architecture at Auburn had its seniors participate in a study-abroad program that introduced them to the most noteworthy architectural achievements in Europe. In the spring of 2000, I was invited to join them for part of that journey.

Marlene and I flew to Venice to join the students as they studied the work of Andrea Palladio. We traveled with the students and the two faculty members, D.K. Ruth and Jack Williams, as they examined many examples of Palladian architecture in both Venice and the surrounding area. Our good friends, Mack and Jamie Freeman, joined us on this venture, with Mack taking a lot of photographs to record our travels. We stayed at the beautiful old Danieli Hotel near St. Mark's Square.

Venice is, without a doubt, the most unusual city I have visited. We flew into Marco Polo airport and then went by boat to our hotel, which looked out on the Grand Canal. In Venice, we saw St. Mark's Square, Doges' Palace, Piozza San Marco, Rialto Bridge, San Giorgio Maggiore Church, and took a ride in a gondola. We also traveled out to the island of Burano.

Some of the most beautiful scenery, however, came during our trips in the Italian countryside to Vicenza (Villa Rotonda, Villa La Rocca Pisani, Villa La Mal Contenta), to Bagnolo (Villa Pisani), and to Treviso (Villa Barboro). But the loveliest site to me was the Village of Bassano along the Brenta River in a valley surrounded by the Dolomite Mountains.

The scenery, the food, and the interaction with the faculty and students in Italy made this trip a truly outstanding experience.

GREECE

One of the most memorable of the trips I took with the Auburn Alumni was to Greece in summer, 2000. It was memorable because of the beauty of that area and because I was accompanied by our daughter, Amy, who was finishing her Ph.D. in English at AU at that time. Marlene was not able to go at the last minute; so fortunately Amy was available to help me co-host the trip. We were also joined by a number of Auburn alums that we knew, including former Trustee, John Denson, and his wife, Rose Ann.

We few to Athens and then went by boat out to the island of Poros where we spent most of the week. The blue waters of the Aegean Sea and the brown and green of the island made for a captivating contrast. Poros was so quiet and peaceful; there were a row of shops and restaurants along the harbor where the boats docked with houses carved into the mountains overlooking the sea.

From Poros, we crossed over to the Peloponnese peninsula and traveled to Epidauros (to see an ancient theatre), to Mycenal (entrance to Kingdom of Agamemnon), to Nauplion (first capital of modern Greece), and to Asklepion at Troizen. Then we took a boat trip out to the Isle of Hydra, a beautiful little island far out in the Aegean.

During our time in Athens, we saw the original Olympic Stadium, toured the Acropolis, and had a farewell dinner at a tavern on the Plaka.

I think it is fair to say that Amy fell in love with Greece, both personally and professionally. She has gone back many times since our trip there to do research or to lead students in study-abroad programs. She and Marlene went to Greece together in 2005 as a mother-daughter adventure that was delightful.

GREAT BRITAIN (ENGLAND AND SCOTLAND)

I have visited England more than any other country. That would seem apropos since this is country from whence my ancestors came. But England was always the place where I felt most comfortable and safe, perhaps because of our common language, and most intellectually stimulated because culture seems to be so highly valued there.

My first visit to England occurred in 1976 when the chancellor of the University of Nebraska at Omaha asked me to go there and to Germany to review academic programs that the university was offering on U.S. Air Force bases in those countries. Because Omaha was the home of the Strategic Air Command, UNO had been invited to provide courses and degree programs on AF bases on Europe. The programs were not doing well and the chancellor wanted to know why.

After completing my assignment of interviewing people on two bases in England and two in Germany, I spent a weekend in London before flying back to Omaha. While there, I took a double-decker tour bus all around the city to see the sights, and went to a performance of "A Little Night Music" at a theatre near Piccadilly Circus.

The most significant trips to England took place in 1998 and 1999. In 1998, I was invited to present a paper at the Third Annual World Congress on Total Quality Management in Sheffield and took that opportunity to bring my entire family with me. We spent a couple of days in London at the beginning and at the end of our trip. In between, I rented a car for the drive to Sheffield, going through Bedfordshire to visit my ancestral home, as described in chapter one. One of the biggest challenges for me was to remember to drive on the left side of the road and to master getting through the "roundabouts" (traffic circles) unscathed. After Sheffield, our kids split up to go see different places. Marlene and I joined our daughter, Ellen, and her husband, Larry, for a driving and walking tour of the Cotswolds area.

In 1999, I was able to go to one of the world's great intellectual centers, Oxford University, to participate in the Oxford Roundtable on Education Policy. The participants included twenty-five university presidents, about equally divided between representatives of the U.S and other countries around the globe. For the week-long program, we were housed in one of Oxford's colleges; each with its own "campus" which usually consisted of housing facilities, a dining hall, meeting rooms, and offices, all surrounded by a wall.

Most of our sessions were held in Rhodes Hall, the building in which the Rhodes Scholars meet while in Oxford. I gave a talk on the "Challenges Facing Higher Education" and led a discussion on that topic. Our meetings each day were quite stimulating. One day we took the afternoon off and traveled out to Blenheim Place, the birthplace of Sir Winston Churchill, a short distance from Oxford.

Each day we usually had some time to wonder around Oxford to soak up the atmosphere. And we had dinner one evening in a college different from the one in which we were staying. To get to Oxford, I had taken a bus from the London Airport which enabled me to see the English countryside. On the return trip, I left myself a night in London to go to the theatre before returning to the U.S.

My other visit to England came in 1994 when Marlene and I hosted an Auburn alumni trip to the Yorkshire area. We flew into Manchester and then went by bus to Leeds and out to the village of Harrogate where we stayed in a lovely hotel there. Each day we would travel out through the beautiful valleys and dales – going up to Whitby on the North Sea and to the historic city of York,

Finally, in 1995, Marlene and I traveled to Scotland where Amy was serving as a visiting professor at Glasgow University. We saw all the sites in Glasgow and, then, traveled by train to Edinburgh to spend a day there. Then I rented a car and we drove up through the Scottish Highlands to the far northwest corner where we crossed over to the Isle of Skye, a ruggedly beautiful land. We stayed in a sheppard's cottage (owned by a colleague of Amy's at Glasgow University), near the village of Dunvegan. During the three days we were there, we traveled all around the island and spent some time in Portree, the capital of the island.

The drive through the Highlands was captivating with its rugged mountain ranges and the scenic valleys. I loved the villages of Glencoe and Fort William, as well as the stark countryside.

NORTH AMERICA

Although the countries that adjoin the United States are, obviously, closer, I have visited these areas infrequently. My first trip to CANADA occurred in 1961 when I drove to Quebec from a camp in Maine where I worked that summer. A few years later, in 1965, I attended the TKE Conclave in Toronto and, subsequently, went back to that city for an academic meeting several years later.

My most significant venture into Canada occurred in 2001 when Marlene and I traveled up to Ontario with our good friends, Gabe and Sandy Campbell, to spend a few days and ended up buying two lots in an area called Goulais Bay along Lake Superior about forty miles north of Sault Ste. Marie. The property is undeveloped at this point and my hope is that it will be a good long-term investment. More recently, we traveled with the Campbells in summer, 2007 to Stratford to see a number of plays at the Stratford Shakespeare Festival.

I spent a week in MEXICO in 1963 while I was a graduate student at the University of Arkansas, traveling to Monterrey, Durango, and Mazatlan. On two occasions, I crossed over the border: once, to Metamoras while vacationing on South Padre Island and second, to Nogalas to see manufacturing plants just over the Arizona line.

In 1967, Marlene and I traveled to the BAHAMAS to attend the TKE Conclave on Grand Bahama Island. This was the meeting at which I was first elected to the TKE Grand Council. In 1982, we flew to BERMUDA to attend a bank directors meeting on this beautiful island. And in 1997, I traveled with the Auburn basketball team to SAN JUAN, PUERTO RICO to see them compete in the San Juan shoot-out, an eight-team tournament. This was exciting as Auburn won the tournament.

AFRICA

In 2008, I attended a World Congress on Civic Education in Morocco on the northern coast of Africa. The sessions were held in Casablanca and Ifrane. We also made side trips to Fez and to Rabat. I represented the Kettering Foundation and made a presentation during the meetings. This was my first time on the African continent.

REFLECTIONS

Growing up as a kid in rural Mississippi and never traveling further north than Memphis until I was as senior in high school, I would never have imagined that I would have the opportunities to travel all over the world. I am grateful to have seen the places that I have visited and still marvel at the natural beauty that exists around the world. The two areas that captivated me the most were the Greek Isles and Norway, although I have found beauty wherever we went.

I believe that there are wonderful people all over the globe, individuals who are intelligent, industrious, and caring. It is a shame that our different cultural values, different religious belief systems, and, perhaps, our different languages serve as barriers to our ability to achieve peaceful coexistence. But the enormous disparity among countries and regions in the distribution of wealth may be the biggest impediment to achieving that goal.

CHAPTER 18:
MY SPIRITUAL JOURNEY

No story of an individual's life would be complete without some discussion of religious beliefs and values. Religion has been one of the most significant (perhaps the most significant) influences on man's attitudes and behavior throughout his lifetime. For the most part, religious beliefs have had a definite positive effect, being the primary source for formation of moral principles and codes of conduct that have enabled the human race to coexist and advance. However, religious beliefs (or, more correctly, the intolerance for differences in such beliefs) have largely been responsible for tremendous destruction of human life and property over man's history.

My own religious journey has been, perhaps, an unusual one. It has been affected deeply by the religious beliefs and values of my parents but also informed by a lifetime in higher education, a culture that values critical analysis and embraces a wide diversity of beliefs. One of the issues that has tended to provoke controversy in the academy is the attempt to reconcile science and religion. That has been an issue that I have dealt with often over my career.

Science bases conclusions on evidence or proof; hence, experiments are often replicated to insure that the results are consistent and many studies conducted before agreement is reached. Religion, on the other hand, is based on faith in a set of beliefs that arise from one's feelings. Hence, religious believers are called the "faith community" and religious denominations "faiths". But it is important to acknowledge that a lot of things that are important to man-- like love, hope, and loyalty—are also founded primarily on faith.

A brief overview of human history would reveal that the need for religion or faith emerged as human beings developed the ability to think abstractly and began to wonder about those things in their environment they could not understand or control – e.g. the sun, moon, wind, fire, etc. These objects or elements became man's first "Gods", to be worshipped in order to get favorable treatment. In later stages of man's development, the Greeks formalized this polytheistic (i.e. many Gods) concept with Gods or Goddesses being established for almost every occasion or condition. Abraham is credited with originating the belief in one God and it is from him that the three major monotheistic religions – Judaism, Christianity, and Islam – evolved. Each of these religions recognizes its own prophets or messengers from God whose teachings form the basis of its beliefs. But while these three major religions recognize the same God, they are composed of many different groups, sects, or denominations with varying patterns of worship and doctrine.

My Pentecostal Roots

Since my Daddy was a Pentecostal preacher, my world from birth to school was totally defined by the church. I was there for every service and was significantly affected by the fervent beliefs and demonstrative behavior by all those around me. Religion was the central element in the lives of my parents and in the lives of all those that I knew. They practiced their beliefs not only in the church but also in all aspects of their lives. There was an authenticity to their beliefs that was unquestionable.

One of my favorite memories is of the Bassett family that lived across the road from the Rocky Hill Church of God in rural Mississippi that Daddy pastored during my pre-teen years. Brother Oscar and Sister Nellie had twelve kids and operated what could best be described as a subsistence farm. They grew practically all the food they needed and would perhaps be able to sell a few bales of cotton each year. The Bassetts were at church for every service, with Brother Oscar always in his same seat, wearing his blue overalls, freshly washed before each Sunday. He loved to testify about how good the Lord was to him and would often begin speaking in tongues before he was finished. During the week, I could hear Brother Oscar praying and praising the Lord as he worked in the fields. The Bassetts were good examples of the sort of people with whom I grew up.

Daddy was a good preacher, presenting a message of hope, trust in God, living a life as taught to us by Jesus, and seeking forgiveness. The reward for such a life was Heaven, admittedly a much nicer place than members of the congregation were currently experiencing. I fully embraced this set of beliefs.

My first encounter with religious prejudice came during my first year at school. Up until this time, virtually all the people I knew were in the Church of God congregation. On the playground at school, I was involved in a game and won the contest. In retaliation, my opponent called me a "Holy Roller". I didn't think much of it until the other boys standing around started laughing. Realizing I was a subject of ridicule, I ran away. That night I asked Daddy "what is a Holy Roller"? He wanted to know where I heard that term and I told him. He said, then, that some people in the Pentecostal churches, when overcome by the Holy Spirit, would faint and lay on the floor. I admitted that I have witnessed that but that I didn't see them rolling around. He laughed and said that "Holy Roller" was just a term that some people used to make fun of Pentecostals and that I should not let it bother me.

As I grew up and became more observant of my environment, I found that there were other churches with different congregations and that these churches operated in various levels of social status. There weren't any Catholic churches in the rural communities where I grew up, although what I read about them sounded exotic. Additionally, I'm not sure that I even knew Judaism was a religion; the only Jews I had heard of was a family who owned the jewelry store and I thought Jews were a racial or ethnic group. At the top of the heap in prestige reigned the Baptists and the Methodists. The Assembly of God occupied the same strata as the Church of God and below us resided the independent "Pentecostal Holiness" congregations suspected of occasionally handling live snakes to prove their faith in God. Even at a young age, I wondered: why should one church be better than another if Jesus said that God loves us all and that we are equal in his eyes?

Another component of my religious education came from the traveling evangelists who came to the church to preach revivals each year, usually toward the end of summer. The evangelists always seemed to be colorful and flamboyant, usually playing an instrument and singing, and would stalk the church as they preached. Almost always they would pack the church, as people came both for the message and the "show". The message usually focused on "Hellfire and Brimstone", making everyone want to avoid such an awful place. As a result, the altar typically filled during the altar call at the end of the service. Some of these converts would join the church but others seemed to disappear until the next revival.

As a young boy hearing these evangelists, I became aware that I did not particularly like the alternatives being offered. I certainly didn't want to go to Hell; living in Mississippi in July and August without air conditioning was about as hot as I could stand! But, at the same time, I didn't find Heaven that appealing. Who would want to live in a place where the streets were paved with gold, they served only milk and honey, and, as far as I could tell, they didn't even play baseball there! But fear won out and I adopted a strategy of avoiding Hell by shunning sin wherever possible.

During this period, I went to the altar, prayed to God to save me and felt a satisfying warmth and peacefulness come over me. I never felt moved to speak in tongues that the Church of God believed was evidence of being filled with the Holy Ghost. But that did not particularly bother me; what mattered to me was being "saved" and not going to Hell. Typical of boys my age, I was often tempted by sin (or at least impure thoughts!) and had to return to the altar often to seek forgiveness and remain in the saved category. As I grew older and became aware of other religious practices, I came to admire the Catholic Church for the manner in which it institutionalized this process through confession, allowing its members a way to regularly and privately confess their sins and obtain forgiveness.

My favorite memories of an evangelist are of Sister Thelma Bentley who preached revivals at the Goodwill Church of God in the Mississippi Delta, a church Daddy pastured during my teenage years. She was a novelty in that women were not allowed in the pulpits of many churches in those days. Furthermore, she looked and sounded like Loretta Lynn (before Loretta Lynn came along). She played the guitar and sang and was a powerful speaker. Many of the men would bring their wives to church but would stay outside, hunkering down around an old oak tree, talking and chewing tobacco. But the allure of seeing and hearing Sister Bentley would finally get the best of them. They would sneak into church at the last minute, occupying the last row. When Sister Bentley began to preach, she would spellbind the audience and, when the altar call came, she would head straight for the back row. Some of the men would actually leap up and run out of the church but she led many others straight to the altar. For most of them, this process would be repeated at the next revival.

As I was growing up, when others learned that my dad was a minister, they would refer to me as a P.K. – preacher's kid. The expectations seemed to be that PK's fell into two categories: a) "hell raisers" who rebelled against their strict upbringing and were always getting into trouble or (b) "goody two shoes" who would never do anything wrong. But I was neither. I had too much respect for my parents to do anything that would bring them embarrassment. So all the years that I was at home, I attended church regularly and participated in activities there and did not smoke or drink. The Church of God believed that its members should not engage in "worldly things" like smoking, drinking, dancing and going to movies, although I think those standards were less strict as I was growing up, compared to the times when my older brothers came along.

In high school, I occasionally went to a movie with friends and even attended the senior prom, my first big dance. But my biggest "transgression", however, was in sports. As described earlier, I developed a real passion for baseball and began to play the sport in junior high school. Daddy never objected to me doing so; if he caught a lot of grief from some church members for allowing me this discretion, he never told me. I learned later from my older brothers that Daddy had been quite a good baseball pitcher in his younger days, so he may have been able to better understand my love for the game. In my high school days, sports filled my time, not only baseball but also football and basketball. The compromise we made was that, while my parents didn't feel they could come to see me play, they did not prevent me from doing so.

As a young boy I often told people that I wanted to be a preacher like my Daddy because his position seemed to be the most important one in the world I knew. As I grew older and advanced through school, I began to see other possibilities for me and no longer expressed that desire. While I know that Daddy would have been delighted to see me follow him in that profession, he never pressured me in that direction. In fact, he never even pushed me to join the church; so I never became a member of the Church of God. Maybe he was wary of what occurred years earlier when my older brothers, Junior and Clyde, were dropped from the church rolls because they played basketball and he didn't want to repeat that experience with me.

For whatever reasons, Daddy let me make up my own mind about my religious beliefs and practices. I have an enormous respect for him in allowing me to do so. As early as I can remember, I began to think for myself about what I was taught and what I observed. I loved my parents and had great admiration for the people I grew up with in the Church of God, the sincerity of their beliefs and their diligence in practicing those beliefs in their daily lives. This experience gave me an appreciation and respect for the religious values that others hold sincerely.

LEAVING HOME

When I left home to go away to college, my participation in church changed dramatically. During the whole time I was in both undergraduate and graduate school, I did not join a church nor attend any church on a regular basis. Of course, when I went home on a vacation break, I always went to church with Momma and Daddy. But at school I used the Sunday mornings to read or to study. There were a couple of reasons for this behavior. The first is that when I did go to church, usually a Baptist or Methodist, after a classmate invited me to do so, I found the services exceedingly boring. They were not at all lively like those in the Church of God and the ministers did not compare in terms of holding one's interest, so I rarely returned. Secondly, when anyone asked about my religion and were told my father was a Church of God minister, they frequently displayed a reaction that I would describe as "backing off" as though such an affiliation was second-class. So I usually just remained quiet about my religious experience unless pressed on the issue. I did not "reject" religion during this period; to the contrary, I frequently thought about what I experienced growing up as well as all the new ideas I was learning in school. I had many conversations with myself as to how all of this could be reconciled.

THE EARLY YEARS OF MARRIAGE

During the year I worked for TKE following graduate school, I met Marlene and we were married. She was raised as a Baptist and we were married in her church in Scottsburg, Indiana. But over the first seven years of our life together, we did not join a church. With three children being born during that time, there was always plenty to do to take care of them. Additionally, I was fully absorbed in the early years of my academic career.

But Marlene and I both felt strongly that we wanted our children to have the experience of growing up in a church and wanted them to learn what Jesus taught during his ministry. And I think we were ready to return to church ourselves. The first step back was a tentative one into a Unitarian Fellowship in Boone, North Carolina that met in public facilities. We enjoyed the interaction with individuals we knew, almost all of whom were fellow faculty members at Appalachian State, on issues of broad moral dimensions.

When we moved to Omaha, we joined our first "real church", affiliating with a large Congregational church near downtown. Close friends, particularly Ron and Cara Beer, who were members there, drew us to the church and the minister, Myrt Rympf, proved to be an excellent pastor. We enjoyed the services and felt that the kids benefited from the youth program. In Texas, we joined a Presbyterian church for many of the same reasons. We liked Bob Leslie, the pastor, and had many friends who were members there. I even served for a term as a member of the session, the governing body of the church.

A MATURING OF FAITH

The most significant stop for me on my religious journey was in Akron as a member of the First Congregational Church. The Pastor was Gabe Campbell, a well-educated (both Doctor of Divinity and Ph.D. degrees) individual who was a powerful thinker and speaker. He had the ability to meld the intellectual and the spiritual aspects of life in a way that many things made sense to me for the first time. I came to understand that our lives have three dimensions: the physical (as represented by our body that will at some point die), the intellectual (as represented by our mind that will cease to function when the body dies), and the spiritual (as represented by our soul or spirit that will not die). It is through the soul or the spirit that we attain eternal life.

During the years we lived in Auburn, Marlene and I were active members of a large United Methodist Church near the campus. The pastor, George Mathison, was part of a ministerial family that included his brother and his father. George's sermons were well organized and appealed to an audience that included substantial numbers of university students and faculty. He invited me to preach on several occasions and I accepted the challenge to convey my spiritual thoughts and understanding to the congregation.

In Greenville, North Carolina, we attended a Methodist church there but did not join. During the year we owned a condo in Vero Beach, Florida, we became associate members at a large United Church of Christ, pastored by Bobby Baggott, whose father was a Baptist minister in Auburn. And in retirement, we affiliated with a Presbyterian church in Cincinnati in which our daughter, Ellen, was a member. Marlene became a member of the Board of Deacons and I was appointed to the Session. We enjoy our association with the Pastor, Susan Quinn Bryan, and the congregation that values highly peace and justice.

By the journey through a number of protestant denominations, I came to appreciate the value of a church as a place where one can come to better understand the spiritual dimensions of one's life, can clarify and reinforce one's beliefs through discussion with others and through the rituals of the worship experience, and can practice one's beliefs though various programs the church operates in the community. The differences in the doctrines of the denominations were of little concern to me.

ARRIVING AT A BELIEF

Over the course of my lifetime I have worshipped in almost every major Protestant denomination, as well as attended services in both Catholic churches and Jewish synagogues. Additionally, I have had close friends who were Hindu and Muslim, as well as others who held secular or agnostic views. Extensive reading about religion has also informed my opinions. In the final analysis, I see so many commonalties in the core beliefs that people possess and that shape their conception of God or a higher power. The dysfunction and conflict that arises in our society over religion seems to emerge from the extremists in each religion who not only adopt rigid positions but are inclined to persecute or even hurt others who possess different views and, furthermore, feel that God "authorizes" them to do so. What sort of God would encourage or even condone such behavior?

Above all, I believe that religious beliefs are a matter of individual choice. Whether arrived at by accepting what one has been taught without question or through years of dedicated study, such beliefs – when honestly and sincerely derived – should be respected. Correspondingly, individuals ought to respect the right of others to hold beliefs that are different from theirs. Religion should definitely not be a function of the state. The United States was formed on a principle of freedom of religion; any nation that would impose one set of beliefs on its citizens is inconsistent with that concept.

The beliefs that emerge from my experience and make the most sense to me are described below:

1. I believe that God exists. He is not an object or a being but is a Spirit – a Holy Spirit – with whom our souls or spirits can communicate. God is Love, Compassion, and Concern for others, particularly those who are less fortunate – feelings that emerge when we let the Holy Spirit into our lives.

2. I believe that, when our body dies and our minds cease to function, our soul or spirit survives and that thru this spirit we achieve eternal life.

3. I believe that Heaven and Hell are not physical places but spiritual states to which our soul travels. If love, compassion, and good works have dominated our lives, our souls will be surrounded by the love of others we have helped – a place of peace (Heaven). If our lives have been characterized by hate, greed, and disregard for others, our souls will be confronted with the evil that we emitted – a state of eternal torment (Hell).

4. I believe that the process of repentance or confession is available to seek forgiveness of sins or transgressions and must be sought to repair the damage to one's soul and to correct or compensate for the hurt that one has caused.

5. I believe that there are multiple avenues via which one's soul can communicate with the Holy Spirit and find the way that leads to peace and understanding. No one religion or denomination has the only answer to this eternal question.

In arriving at these conclusions, I have attempted to use both my mind and my heart, to consider what I know and what I feel, to reach reconciliation – a belief in which I can have faith. It might seem as though I have ventured far from my roots but, to the contrary, I value deeply that experience and have great respect for those who hold such beliefs and try to apply those values on a daily basis.

CHAPTER 19:
EVERYONE NEEDS A HERO OR TWO

I believe that all of us need heroes in our lives. They provide an example – i.e. a role model – of the sort of person we would like to be. In doing so, they can provide the inspiration and motivation for us to strive to reach that goal, putting forth the effort and making the sacrifices that are often necessary to achieve our objectives.

As I was growing up, I didn't have the kind of heroes that many boys my age worshiped – e.g. cowboys or fantasy figures like Superman. That may have been because my parents never owned a television until I was in graduate school; I attended my first movie while in high school and was not permitted to bring comic books into the house. When I began to follow sports, particularly baseball, I had my favorite players but only one rose to heroic status. My only venture into "fantasy land" came through the radio. I liked to listen to programs like "The Long Ranger", "Sky King", and "The Shadow" but didn't claim any of them as heroes.

Over the course of my career, I had the opportunity to meet many "Famous People" – e.g. political leaders (three U.S. Presidents, many Senators and Congressmen, Governors, State Legislators, Mayors, etc.), corporate CEO's, outstanding athletes and coaches, authors, entertainers, and individuals who excelled in virtually every occupation. I admired many of them for their achievements. Often I got to work with these individuals and to know them personally.

But all of my heroes are individuals with whom I have had a long-term personal relationship. Many of them are "famous" but they were not selected just for their accomplishments. Instead, they were chosen because their lives and the example they set touched me in special ways.

I have selected a total of sixteen individuals (the Sweet Sixteen) who are discussed in this chapter. The first five had a significant impact on me as a young boy and helped shape the kind of person I became. The others are men and women that I met as adults and came to admire for various reasons.

MOSE LEE MUSE – MY DADDY

Ideally, every boy's first and most important hero should be his dad. That was certainly the case with me, although I don't remember thinking of him as a hero at the time. Daddy was a very unusual man. I have described him in considerable detail in Chapter Two and a reading of that chapter will reveal what a powerful example he set for me.

Unlike many boys today whose fathers work long hours away from home, Daddy always seemed to be around while I was growing up. Because he was a minister, he prepared his sermons and met with visitors there in the parsonage – our house. And he would often take me with him when he went to visit members of the church or to public places.

One of the first things I remember about Daddy is the enormous respect that people had for him. Wherever we went, everyone knew "Brother Muse" or "Preacher Muse", as he was called. He was the person to whom almost everyone in the community went for guidance and support in times of personal crisis. Since the church did not have an office for him, Daddy would meet with these individuals in our living room. I often sat in on the discussions or, even if I was in another room, I could overhear the conversation. Daddy was a very good listener. After hearing the person's story, he rarely told them what to do. Instead, he would pray with them and ask God to provide guidance as they dealt with their problems.

Daddy was a good preacher, although not necessarily eloquent. His messages came from the heart. But what was most influential with me was that he practiced what he preached. I never saw any hint of hypocrisy in him. People mattered most to him, not money or social position. None of the churches he pastored provided enough income to fully support the family; therefore, he often worked at odd jobs to make ends meet. But he would always share whatever he had – food, clothing, and his time – with those who needed it, particularly the poor and the downtrodden.

Daddy wanted me to become a minister and that would have been a fulfillment of his dream. But he never pressured me in that direction. Instead he showed me by his example the type of man he was and let me make up my own mind as to what I wanted to do with my life. If he was disappointed in my decision, he never let it show. Instead he always seemed to be proud of me and what I accomplished.

As I grew older, I appreciated even more Daddy's willingness to let me "make up my own mind". From a very early age, I was able to think independently and draw my own conclusions. When I developed a love for baseball and began to play this sport and others, Daddy let me do so, even though I am sure there were members of the church who complained about my involvement in such things. As an adult, I learned from Clyde that he and Junior, while in the ninth grade, had started playing basketball and had joined the Boy Scouts. Some deacons in Daddy's church pushed through a motion to "turn them out" (drop them as members) of the church for being involved in "wild and wooly (worldly) things", perhaps as a move to provoke Daddy. The church minutes actually included the word "wooly", rather than worldly, something that Clyde and Junior often joked about later. But Daddy never quit or backed down; instead he supported his sons all the way and did not let this impede his ministry.

Daddy was a very powerful role model for me in several respects. First, he let his actions speak for themselves. For a person who spoke publicly every week, he was very quiet at home. He rarely ever talked about himself. Secondly, he was able to elicit great respect from others. They looked up to him and trusted him, not just because he was a minister, but also because he would do what was right and was a man of his word. Thirdly, he had a big heart; he loved others, practicing the message that Jesus taught to his disciples and followers.

MARY ELIZABETH MUSE – MY MOMMA

Momma was totally devoted to her family, the church, and, particularly, to Daddy. She worked hard every day but was at church every time the doors were open. I don't remember ever hearing her complain or hearing her and Daddy have a cross word. She supported whatever he wanted to do.

Although Daddy was home most of the time, Momma supervised and monitored my behavior as I was growing up. But, unlike Daddy, she never hesitated to tell me what to do! Her instructions were always couched in terms of what a "good boy" would do – e.g. good boys go to church, good boys always tell the truth, good boys do their homework, etc. The reward was that, if you were a good boy, you would be "somebody" some day. She always complimented and praised me on the "good work" I had done, whether it was bringing home a good report card or doing my chores on time.

I am confident that many of my achievements, particularly those early in life, can be traced to the positive reinforcements that Momma gave me. And she provided a splendid example of what it means to be loyal to the people and things that you love.

Vernon Clyde Muse – My Brother

I loved all of my brothers and I'm sure they loved me. While growing up, as well as during adulthood, I always enjoyed the times when I could be with them, hearing of the things in which they had been involved. But, as the youngest in the family, nearly all of them were out of school, married, and had families of their own by the time I was in elementary school. Clyde was the closest to me in age, although he was nearly ten years my senior.

Clyde became my most powerful role model, not only because he was closest in age, but also because he was an outstanding athlete and, later, a coach, and he was the first member of our family to go to college and get a degree. As a young boy, I also wanted to be an outstanding athlete and even thought seriously of becoming a coach. And, without Clyde's example, I may not have gone to college. Momma and Daddy did not discourage me from thinking about college, but they did not encourage me either, perhaps because they knew they could not afford to send me. But, all the time, I kept thinking that "if Clyde could do it, so could I".

Clyde always had the uncanny ability to make whomever he was talking with feel like they were the important person in the universe. This was particularly true for young boys like myself. When I knew Clyde was coming home from college or, even after he was married and coming for a visit, I waited on the front porch or near the front door in order to be the first one to greet him, usually with a basketball in my hands and/or a baseball glove by my side. Clyde would always take the time to talk with me and would usually show me how to do something with the basketball. Those few minutes would "make my day" or even the next week or month, as I would practice what he had taught me, ready to demonstrate what I had learned during his next visit.

As I progressed through school, and, later, as I pursued a career in higher education, my visits with Clyde were among my most treasured moments as we discussed the issues we were confronting in our jobs. Clyde remained in Mississippi and became one of the most influential and highly respected individuals in that state. He has been and continues to be a very positive role model not only for me but also for all those who know him.

Clyde has served as president of Hinds Community College, developing it into not only the largest in the state, but one of the most respected in the nation for over 25 years. But, perhaps, his most challenging moment came as Superintendent of Schools in Hinds County when all Mississippi public schools were under a federal mandate to integrate. He led the school system through a peaceful integration and has always been a strong proponent for a quality education for everyone.

Ms. Mary McBeth and Ms. Ruby Germany – My Teachers

I have had many great teachers over my years in school, but none more influential than my first two – Ms. Mary McBeth, my first grade teacher, and Ms. Ruby Germany, who taught me in the third grade. In fact, I made so much progress under Ms. McBeth that I skipped second grade.

Because of the personal attention and encouragement they provided, I not only learned fast but also acquired a lifelong love for learning that has never been quenched. They were both teachers in an elementary school called Dixie that I attended in rural Neshoba County, Mississippi. The school had very few resources and I doubt if either of them were college graduates, but they knew how to light the flame for learning.

I don't remember reading at home before going to school, nor do I recall any children's books in our house. But Ms. McBeth taught me to read and, then, both she and Ms. Germany would continually provide me with books. And they always made me feel special when I achieved the goals they set for me.

Like many students, I imagine, I never went back and expressed my appreciation to Ms. McBeth and Ms. Germany for the foundation and springboard they provided for me. But I hope they understood that the guidance they provided was a major factor in my success.

The remaining individuals on my "Heroes List" are discussed in alphabetical order, as there is no other sensible way to rank them. The difficulty I encountered in constructing the list was not in coming up with people, but in limiting it to a reasonable number. I have been fortunate to know many individuals with heroic qualities and I could have included many others.

Gabe Campbell

I first met Gabe Campbell when we moved to Akron, Ohio in 1984. At that time, Gabe was senior pastor of the First Congregational Church, located adjacent to the University of Akron campus where I had just been appointed president. Marlene and I had been Presbyterians in Texas; so it was assumed we would join the Presbyterian Church in Akron. But after we met Gabe and his wife, Sandy, those plans were discarded and we became active members of First Congregational.

Gabe grew up in Greenville, Ohio and attended Ohio State University, earning a bachelor's degree in political science. While enrolled in law school, however, he met Roy Burkhart, the senior minister at a large community church in Columbus, Ohio, an encounter that would change his life dramatically. Gabe decided he wanted to become a minister and transferred to the divinity school at Vanderbilt. While completing his Divinity degree, he served as interim pastor of a small church in Smartt Station, Tennessee, an experience that would supply many stories he would later use in his sermons.

After graduation, Gabe became a youth minister at a Congregational Church in Greenwich, Connecticut, eventually moving up to become senior pastor of the First Congregational Church in Stamford, Ct.. While there he enrolled in the doctoral program at New York University and earned a Ph.D. in neuro-biological science. Gabe was very interested in how the brain works, particularly the left brain-right brain phenomenon.

He was recruited to become the senior pastor in Akron of an old historic church that had earlier had as its pastor, Lloyd C. Douglas, a famous novelist who wrote <u>Magnificent Obsession</u> and many other books. Gabe and Sandy had come to Akron only a year before we arrived.

Gabe is the first minister that I had known who integrated and exemplified the spiritual and intellectual dimensions of religion in a very meaningful way. His sermons were interesting and thought provoking, the kind that would cause one to think about them days later. He helped me understand that it is through the spirit that we can attain eternal life. Gabe's sermons were sometimes unsettling for those who wanted to maintain the status quo or those who saw the church as something to control rather than a way to contribute. He, on many occasions, exhibited both moral and mental courage in expressing and acting upon his beliefs.

Gabe and Sandy have been great friends to Marlene and me over the years. Some of the most wonderful times together have been at their cottage on Crystal Lake in Northern Michigan where we have had the opportunity to relax and talk.

LENWOOD COCHRAN

My relationship with Lenwood Cochran goes back to 1961 when I was a graduate student at the University of Arkansas and assisting a group of young men in their efforts to become a chapter of Tau Kappa Epsilon. Lenwood was a TKE national officer and came to inspect the group. He and I became good friends, with his friendship, guidance, and example impelling me to become a national officer in later years.

Lenwood grew up in Greenville, South Carolina, and graduated from Furman University where he became a Teke. He joined Steel Heddle Corporation and rose to an executive position. He and his wife, Jean, settled in Greenville where they still live. He has been a strong supporter of Furman, having served as president of its alumni association.

What Lenwood exemplified in many ways was his loyalty to TKE fraternity. He practiced its motto of "the fraternity for life". After serving as a member of the Grand Council and as Grand Prytanis (international president), he was chairman of the nominations committee to screen candidates for the Grand Council and as a board member of the TKE Educational Foundation. One of my great memories is serving as a member of the Grand Council while Lenwood was Grand Prytanis. Without the great example that Lenwood set, I might not have strived to reach the leadership positions in the fraternity that I did.

Lenwood and Jean have been wonderful friends over the years. We have enjoyed our times together at TKE Conclaves, watching baseball games during spring training in Florida, having them as guests in our home, and visiting with them in Greenville.

EMORY CUNNINGHAM

Emory Cunningham grew up in the little town of Kansas, Alabama, and attended Auburn University, earning a degree in agriculture. After graduation, he joined Progressive Farmer magazine and rose through the ranks to become its president. He then formed Southern Progress Corporation and launched a very important new magazine, Southern Living. He headed that corporation until it merged with Time, Inc.

Emory was a member of the Board of Trustees at Auburn when I went there. He was a highly effective trustee, coming to the meetings well prepared and not being afraid to voice his opinion, even when he was in the minority. Because of his corporate experience, Emory understood that the proper role of the board was to set policy and to provide oversight. The time that he served as president pro tem of the board was the most gratifying time for me as president, with excellent progress being made with a minimum of turmoil.

What I admired most about Emory was his integrity and selflessness. He was unusually kind and always thoughtful of others. His objective was always to find the right solution, not necessarily the one that best served his interests. Emory died in 2000 at age 78, shortly after his service on the Auburn board was completed. His death was a great personal loss for me and I still miss him.

WAYNE FLYNT

I have worked with many outstanding faculty members during my career – some who were great teachers, others who were distinguished researchers, and others who worked effectively to reach audiences beyond the campus – but few exhibited all those skills more successfully than Wayne Flynt.

Wayne grew up in Alabama, earning a bachelor's degree from Samford University and, later, receiving his M.S. and Ph.D. degrees from Florida State University. After teaching at Samford for several years, he came to Auburn and served as Chairman of the Department of History for eight years. Wayne was a highly regarded faculty leader, being elected chair of the Faculty Senate. By the time I first met Dr. Flynt, he had published Poor But Proud, a book about Alabama's poor whites that won several prestigious awards, and had been named a Distinguished Professor.

Although Wayne had many publications and was recognized as an authority on both Alabama and Southern history, I most admired him for his willingness to carry his message into the community and to speak out on issues of importance even those that were controversial. One such incident occurred shortly after I arrived at Auburn.

A statewide group had been organized to try to bring about tax reform that required amending the state constitution. Alabama's property tax rates were the lowest in the nation, considerably below Mississippi who was in 49th place. Since property taxes were the primary source for funding public schools, there was little mystery as to why Alabama's schools were so poorly funded. Wayne spoke to many community groups, citing data as to Alabama's comparative standing and the unsuccessful record of tax reform in the past. He was asked why previous efforts were not effective and he replied that the Alabama Farmers Federation, a powerful state lobby, had worked hard to defeat any measures to raise property taxes. This was hardly a revelation to anyone who followed Alabama politics but was something few were willing to state publicly.

The Farmer's Federation responded quickly and publicly, calling for Dr. Flynt to be fired. I never considered doing that because, first, Dr. Flynt had tenure and, second, because he had the courage to use the protection that tenure provides. The CEO of the federation then threatened to withdraw their funding to Auburn. After researching the funding they provided, I informed the CEO that, if they did so, they would be hurting themselves since their only funding was for scholarships for students in agriculture. Cooler heads soon prevailed and our discussions eventually led to a $5 million contribution to construct a building on the Auburn campus. But, I'm sorry to say, the effort at tax reform still did not prevail.

Dr. Flynt is now retired from Auburn but is still writing, still speaking out, and working diligently for the Alabama Poverty Project, an effort that he has led for many years to provide support for the poorest of the poor.

MILLARD FULLER

Millard Fuller is the most inspirational person I have known – inspirational in what he says but, most importantly, in how he has lived his life. Millard grew up in Lanett, Alabama, in a family of modest means. He attended Auburn University and, after graduation, went to law school at the University of Alabama.

While in law school, he partnered with a fellow student to launch several entrepreneurial ventures, mostly mail-order sales and rental property. They continued and expanded these ventures after graduation, becoming so successful that Millard was a millionaire by age 29, quite a feat in the early 1960's. But in doing so he nearly lost his marriage to a lovely girl, Linda, he had met in Tuscaloosa.

Linda left Millard and went to New York, contemplating a divorce. He pursued her and, after a tearful session, they decided to sell all their possessions, give the money to the poor, and seek a life of Christian service. The couple first joined a small Christian community in southwest Georgia called Koinonia Farm. After a brief stay, they left to engage in other Christian enterprises for a couple of years before returning to Koinonia. A project of house building for the poor was launched called Partnership Housing. Millard worked closely with Clarence Jordan who founded Koinonia with his wife, Florence, in 1942.

While the first house was under construction, Jordon died suddenly of a heart attack. But Millard continued the work, steadily expanding it over the next four years. Then Millard, Linda, and their four young children went to Africa to serve as missionaries. Upon returning to America, they returned to Koinonia and, in September of 1976, convened a small group of friends with whom they organized and incorporated Habitat for Humanity. Millard had come to believe that one of the most basic needs of every human being was a decent place to live and his travels had shown him that a significant percentage of the world's population did not have that.

The idea for Habitat for Humanity was relatively simple: Each recipient of a house had to invest their own "sweat equity" by working on their house and/or houses of others and had to repay the costs incurred which would be used to help another poor person get a house. The costs were relatively modest, since most labor and many materials were donated and no interest was charged on the mortgage. Over the course of the next 29 years, Millard

---

and Linda developed Habitat for Humanity into a worldwide ministry, operating in 100 countries and providing decent housing for over 1,000,000 people, while recruiting many well-known volunteers such as former President Jimmy Carter. They established the headquarters for Habitat in Americus, Georgia.

I first met Millard when I was president of the University of Akron. The Akron Habitat affiliate with which Marlene was working invited him to Akron and a group of students at UA were interested in forming a student chapter. Marlene and I invited him to stay with us at the President's House. We were very impressed with his ministry and with him. Marlene's work with Habitat continued during our years at Auburn, serving as president of that affiliate. We invited Millard and Linda to visit with us on several occasions in Auburn, including for the presentation of the President's Award for Excellence to Millard for his achievements.

In 2005, though, Marlene and I were startled to learn that the Habitat board had dismissed Millard and Linda on trumped up charges that were never proven. A segment of the board that saw Habitat more as a business than a ministry had gained control and pushed through this action, without any compensation or consideration for Millard. Not a very Christian thing to do! Millard had never paid himself very much as the full time CEO of Habitat, earning only $79,000 annually at the highest, choosing instead to plow all money possible into building houses.

So, at age 70, after giving his life to building an organization, he was kicked out. Most folks at that point would have given up; but not Millard and Linda! Instead they formed a new organization, the Fuller Center for Housing, to continue their ministry. Marlene was invited to serve on the Fuller Center board; we have enjoyed attending these meetings and have been overjoyed at the growth in funding and projects that have occurred. The Fuller Center supplements the work of Habitat in pursing the never-ending goal of providing decent housing for the poor around the world.

JAMES RAY JONES

I have known James Ray Jones since we were babies or, at least, I am told that we played together as babies. James' mother, Lula Belle, lived with my parents from the time she was about fifteen until she married and was considered a part of our family. My first real relationship with James occurred, though, when we moved back to a rural area near Marks, Mississippi as I was entering the ninth grade.

For the two years we lived in the Locke Station community, James and I were best buddies. He played ball and hung out together, doing whatever teenage boys do in a rural area. When we moved to Delhi, Louisiana as I entered the eleventh grade, James came to visit me on one occasion and we had a great time together. But, then, we lost touch with each other as our lives went in separate directions. It was not until many years later that I learned about the challenges James had faced.

After graduating from Marks High School, James joined the U.S. Navy; he didn't have the option of going to college, as his folks could not afford that. But James' high school sweetheart went to Ole Miss so that when James came home after four years in the Navy, she was graduating from college. But she was, then, killed in what was apparently an accidental shooting in her apartment. Brokenhearted, James went to Joliet, Illinois where his dad worked in a steel mill and where his family had recently moved. He found a job with the Caterpillar Corporation.

James began to hang around the bars in Joliet, eventually meeting a woman there whom he married. They settled down near Joliet to live and eventually had four boys. But the marriage began to come apart as James discovered that his wife was an alcoholic and later that she was into hard drugs. He filed for divorce and got custody of the children.

For the next ten years, James raised the boys as a single parent. In the meantime, the Caterpillar Corporation for whom he had worked for twenty years, asked him to transfer to their plant in Memphis. He readily agreed since this took him back to the region where he had grown up and to where his sister lived. In addition, his mother and dad had moved to north Mississippi after his dad retired. But within a year after he accepted that assignment, Caterpillar closed their plant in Memphis, leaving James without a job. He eventually found another job with Alice Chalmers, another tractor company, and worked for them for ten years.

James' fortunes began to improve when he met Carol. She had also had a disastrous first marriage. They have had a wonderful marriage, living in Olive Branch, Mississippi, an apt name for a town where two wounded hearts came together. James continues to care for his youngest child who has a learning disability and took care of his mother until her death in 2006.

James does not have the "pedigree" that some others on this list have. But he has had the determination to survive and to succeed in spite of obstacles that would have made many others give up. I know where he came from and I admire his courage and fortitude to keep going. He is a good man.

GEORGE KELL

George Kell was my first boyhood idol as the star player on the baseball team I adopted at age eleven and still root for today. He was an outstanding hitter for the Detroit Tigers, winning the American League batting championship in 1949, and always seemed to come through in the clutch. And he was one of the best fielding third basemen in the league. As I was learning to play baseball, I would throw the ball against the wall for hours, imaging myself as George Kell fielding grounders at the hot corner.

I was aware that George had been inducted into the Baseball Hall of Fame, the highest honor possible, and that he had served many years (38 to be exact) as a broadcaster for the Tigers. But it was not until I read his autobiography in 1998 that I learned his full life story.

Throughout his distinguished career, George had maintained a home in Swifton, the small town in northeast Arkansas where he was born and grew up. He was a leader in the church in which he was raised and helped the nearby town of Newport build a baseball park that is named for him. And he served for ten years on the Arkansas Highway Commission.

After reading the book, I wrote George a letter, telling him how much I admired him as a player and was impressed with his life afterwards. Never expecting a response, I was surprised to receive a package from George in a week or so that contained a long letter from him, an autographed copy of the book, the book on tape, and other memorabilia. This began a correspondence that still continues today.

I have visited with George on three different occasions. The first was before an Auburn-Arkansas football game where we met at a restaurant in Little Rock. We talked until the place was ready to close. Twice I have gone to Swifton to talk with George in his home, once after he had been involved in a severe automobile accident.

I suspect it is unusual for someone to encounter his boyhood idol late in life and find him to be everything he hoped he would be. That was certainly the case with George. He is humble and gracious, giving back to the community that raised him. Many of our famous athletes never amount to much after they leave the "field of glory". But George has never quit growing and contributing.

PAUL MARTIN

I first met Paul Martin when I was president of the University of Akron. Paul was a graduate of the university and a very successful automobile dealer in northeast Ohio. I asked him to chair the university's capital campaign and he agreed to do so. It is though that effort that we became close friends. We raised over $50 million in the campaign; the institution's only previous effort had yielded $10 million.

Paul was very generous to the university, providing funds for a beautiful fountain in the middle of the campus, for an entrance gateway, and for the renovation of the University Club (now called the Martin Center). And he was very loyal to his fraternity, Phi Delta Theta, donating dollars for their housing renovations. When Paul's wife, Dorothy Garrett Martin died, he established an endowment through her sorority, Delta Gamma, to fund a lecture series at Akron and several other universities to bring distinguished speakers to the campus.

I admire Paul for his success as a businessman but, mainly, for his loyalty and generosity to his university, his fraternity, and to his wife. At age 92, Paul is still going strong. He has turned the automobile business over to his son, Fred, but still remains active supporting those institutions, organizations, and individuals that have helped him along the way.

ELIZABETH HARPER NEELD

Elizabeth Harper grew up around the mountains of east Tennessee where her daddy was a Church of God minister. She attended Lee College, the Church of God institution, in Cleveland, Tennessee and then the University of Chattanooga (a private university that is now part of the University of Tennessee system and known as the University of Tennessee at Chattanooga) where she earned her B.S. and M.Ed. She then received her Ph.D. degree in English from the University of Tennessee in Knoxville. She developed a distinguished academic career, serving for a time as Director of English Programs with the Modern Language Association in New York City. She married Greg Cowan, another English scholar, and together they wrote one of the leading textbooks in English composition.

Elizabeth and Greg joined the English faculty at Texas A&M University, but three years after moving to A&M Greg died suddenly while jogging. Cause of death was a congenital heart defect so small the coroner said it would have never been detected. I am sure this was a terrible shock to Elizabeth both personally and professionally. Ten years after Greg's death, Elizabeth published a book entitled, Seven Choices: Finding Daylight After Loss Shatters Your World that is now in its fourth edition and that has been a tremendous solace to others who have experienced similar loss. Seven Choices was the book chosen by the American Red Cross to distribute after 9/11; and Elizabeth and the book have been the subject of two public television hour-long documentaries.

The first time I met Elizabeth was when I was Dean of the Business School at A&M, shortly after Greg had died. Elizabeth had been tapped by President Chuck Sampson to serve as one of his executive assistants and, since my work often brought me to the president's office, I began to get to know her. Through our conversations, I learned about her Church of God background. She was the first individual whom I had met in academia with a religious background parallel to mine. We became very good friends and I always treasured the opportunities we had to visit.

Elizabeth met Jerele Neeld, who was from New Mexico, in Houston. Jerele, a graduate of Texas A&M, later was employed in the psychology department of the university, where he and Elizabeth got to know each other. Several years later they were married. Jerele's career took the two of them first to Houston and then to Austin and later London, England, as he advanced in his career in the technology world. At the same time, Elizabeth continued her work as a scholar, authoring or editing a total of twenty-one books. She also serves as a corporate consultant and teaches spiritual seminars and retreats.

I admire Elizabeth for how she has handled the adversity in her life. She always has a positive attitude and a strong faith that she will prevail. And she has and does. Furthermore, she has helped thousands of others thru her writing and her seminars to cope with the challenges in their lives.

JIMMY TAYLOR

Jimmy Taylor and I first met in the summer of 1961 when we both were counselors at Camp Takajo in Maine. Jimmy at that time was a student at Mississippi State and was the camp basketball instructor; I was a student at the University of Arkansas and was Takajo's baseball instructor. As the only two guys at the camp with southern accents, we became close friends.

Our paths did not cross again until Marlene and I moved to Alabama in 1992. After graduation from MSU where he was an All-SEC performer in track, Jimmy became a highly successful basketball coach at a high school in the Birmingham area. He then advanced to become the head basketball coach at the University of South Alabama where he had an outstanding record. His next step was as color commentator on the Auburn basketball network. Along the way, Jimmy and some other investors bought a bank in a small town in Alabama.

Admitting that he did not know the first thing about banking, Jimmy knew that he had to hire someone who did. Jimmy did what he did best, which was to make friends and to learn how to evaluate opportunities. By the time Jimmy and I reconnected, he had bought several other banks and was in the process of establishing a bank holding company, Alabama National BanCorporation. He invited me to serve on the bank's board of directors and that experience was a very enjoyable one for me.

I served on the Alabama National board until we effected a merger with National Bank of Commerce in Birmingham. As a part of that settlement, Jimmy agreed to leave the bank and not start another bank for a year and I became a director of SouthTrust bank. Approximately one year later, Jimmy started a new bank, The Bank of Birmingham, and expanded this new bank by buying banks in Alabama and Florida, growing it into a major holding company before retiring in 2006.

I don't think I have known anyone who enjoys life and other people as much as Jimmy. He has a knack for making everything fun, including work. He became very skilled at making money and enjoyed the money he made. In retirement, Jimmy has become the primary caregiver to his wife, Martha, who has been fighting a battle with cancer. But he has approached this task with the same enthusiasm he has brought to everything else in life.

For a skinny kid who grew up in Fayette, a small town in northwest Alabama, Jimmy has come a long way. But he is still the same kid that I met in the backwoods of Maine many years ago.

JAMES VOSS

James Voss has gone further in this universe than anyone else I know. As a NASA astronaut, he has flown five missions in space, including one six-month stay at the space station. But I always found him to be a very "down to earth" guy.

Jim grew up in Opelika, Alabama and earned a degree from Auburn in aeronautical engineering. He joined NASA after graduation and became one of six astronauts who had degrees from Auburn. I was with Jim on several occasions when he visited the campus and was always impressed with how he addressed audiences, making them feel comfortable with a very technical subject. I invited him back to visit with small groups of students and he was always very effective in those interactions.

I admired Jim for his significant career achievements but also for his low-key, non-pretentious attitude. Out of his space suit, one would have never guessed he was an astronaut. Jim was also very supportive of the work of his wife, Susan, who has a Ph.D. and is manager of one of the NASA programs.

On two of Jim's space trips, he took pictures of our two oldest grandchildren, Henry and Madelyn, with him and brought them back as a memento for us. This is something that the grandchildren will treasure as they get older. One of the thrills that Marlene and I enjoyed was a trip to Cape Kennedy to see one of the space launches that included Jim.

"HONORABLE MENTIONS"

There are many additional individuals I could include on my "Heroes List", as I have been very fortunate to know many people that I admire for their professional achievements and personal qualities. And there are four others who did not qualify for the list because I did not know them personally but who deserve to be mentioned because they had a significant impact on me.

The first two are individuals that I met but did not know well. The first is RONALD REAGAN. I met Reagan on two occasions, one before he became President and once while he was in office. But I had felt close to him for many years because he was a Teke; in fact, he was always listed as one of the fraternity's most famous alums. Unlike many other celebrity alums, Reagan was supportive of the fraternity throughout his career. He would visit the Teke chapter when he was on a campus and narrated a film that TKE used in recruiting new members for many years. When I was elected as international president of the fraternity, I contacted him about serving as chairman of a Grand Prytanis Advisory Committee. He agreed and came to Indianapolis for our first meeting. Then, while he was in the White House, he invited me and several other members of the fraternity to join him for lunch. I admired President Reagan for his gracious style, his eloquence in speaking, and, above all, his loyalty to his fraternity.

The second is WARREN BUFFETT. During the time that I was dean of the business school at the University of Nebraska at Omaha, Warren lived a couple of blocks from the campus in a nice, but non-pretentious house. As he was developing his strategy for investments, he would walk up to the university library to do his research. By the 1970's, he was already a successful investor but few expected him to one day be one of the richest men in the world.

Although I saw Warren on several occasions, I had only one extended conversation with him. We were building a new business school building at UNO and I approached him about a major gift to name the building for his father-in-law who had been a dean at the university. My efforts were unsuccessful but he was very gracious in declining. I always regretted that I did not approach him in a different way.

Over the years I have admired Mr. Buffett for his intelligent investing and his ability to make money, but, even more importantly, for his willingness to use his accumulated wealth to help others. His substantial gift to the Gates Foundation will have a significant impact worldwide.

I never met the other two individuals I will mention, although that would have been a great thrill for me. They were both fellow Mississippians who grew up during the same era and had unusual talents. ELVIS PRESLEY came from a poor family and attended a fundamentalist church. I followed his life and career closely, loved all of his music, and even saw all of his movies. In many ways, I identified with Elvis, growing sideburns to look like him, and performing his songs both in the shower and on the stage. His music resonated with me like no others did. It was great to see Elvis perform in person once in Las Vegas, but I would have loved to have met him and talked with him. I have often regretted missing out on the one time I could have been with him, when he was initiated as a member of TKE.

WILLIE MORRIS grew up in Yazoo City and became one of the most significant writers of the twentieth century. I had never heard of Willie until I read his autobiography, <u>North Toward Home</u>, which was written when he was 33. His writing touched my heart in ways few others have. He seemed to understand Mississippi and the times during which we grew up better than anyone else. I have read all the books that Willie authored as well as a biography of him, <u>In Search of Willie</u> Morris, by Larry King. I wrote him a letter once (but got no response) and tried unsuccessfully to arrange for him to come to the University of Akron to speak while I was there. But this was during a period when he was depressed and troubled, following his dismissal as editor of <u>Harper's</u> Magazine at an early age.

Both ELVIS and WILLIE had unique talents but lived troubled lives during significant periods of their careers. I wish that I had known them somewhere along the way or have had a few moments to spend with them.

The people that I admire – my heroes – are most often individuals who came from modest beginnings, rather than privileged backgrounds. They worked hard and used their talents to achieve a level of success, but remained humble, not ego-centered, and were appreciative of and loyal to their roots. They tend to have faced adversity and challenges in their lives but have had the determination and courage to persevere. I consider it an honor to have known them.

CHAPTER 20:
REFLECTIONS AND CONCLUSIONS

Have I been successful in my career? Has my life been one of meaning and substance? Is life a "random walk" or is it guided by a higher power? Can one's life be informed by the knowledge and insights gained by those who precede us? Such questions are important and likely arise at some point in one's life, particularly near the end of life's journey.

One of my favorite books is Robert Pirsig's <u>Zen and the Art of Motorcycle Maintenance</u>. The story is built around a cross-country motorcycle trip that the main character takes with his young son. As he sits on the cycle for long periods of time, he thinks about life in all its various dimensions and has a conversation with himself that he calls a "Chautauqua of the Mind". Riding motorcycles was not my thing, but I have had many such "inner conversations" as I have pondered what I have seen and heard. In fact, I have "talked to myself" as far back as I can remember.

Perhaps everyone has a similar experience. But, in my case, I didn't have anyone else to talk to. My older brothers were ten years or more ahead of me and busy with their activities and my family moved so frequently that I had very few close friends growing up. So I had conversations with myself and became skilled as a listener and observer. Rarely did I feel the need to share my conclusions with others.

These skills served me well as I was always a "good student" in school, paying attention in class and following the instructions given. If called upon, I could provide a good answer but rarely felt the compulsion to raise my hand. As I advanced to college, graduate school, and into an academic career, I was constantly confronted with the same challenge – i.e. how to move into a new environment where I was unknown and establish relationships and a position of importance. I had to learn how to communicate my views and ideas clearly and to hone interpersonal skills, but my inner conversations were always the foundations for my actions.

THE PURSUIT OF A CAREER

No one, not even my Momma, would have predicted or even imagined the heights to which I rose in my career. Momma always told me I could be "somebody", but I doubt if she had a university presidency in mind. But Momma's aspirations for me were always influential. My translation of her advice was that I should strive to be someone of importance in the organizations in which I worked and in the communities where I lived. I think that I achieved that goal.

My earliest ambitions were to be a preacher like my Daddy; then to be a major league baseball player; then to be a coach like by brother, Clyde. When I finally selected a major in college, my choice was highly influenced by the need to get a job. A career in accounting or business seemed to offer the best possibilities of achieving that goal. I enjoyed the courses that I took but, to a great degree, I liked all the courses that I studied. It was not until I was in graduate school that I began to think about an academic career and largely because I loved the ambience and intellectual excitement of a university campus. Then the opportunities for administrative leadership began to emerge – department head at age 27, dean at 31, and president at 45 – without any grand design. Success at each level produced both the opportunity and desire to advance to the next plateau.

I had the good fortune to be able to practice throughout my career what I had studied in school – not only studied, but also taught and researched. As early as I can remember, I was intrigued by questions such as these: What does it take to make an organization successful? How do you get people to work together toward a common goal? In many respects, I think I learned as much from my personal experiences as a member of athletic teams and as a leader in my fraternity and in other organizations as I did from the textbooks I read. But, throughout my career, an abiding interest in management and leadership prevailed.

Much of the early literature in the field tried to distinguish between management and leadership, but I found that exercise non-fruitful, as the skills are so interrelated. A manager has to have leadership ability to get others to work together and a leader needs managerial skills to insure that the goals are appropriate and that resources are efficiently utilized. One without the other is likely to produce ineffective results.

Over time, I came to conclude that someone desiring to lead an organization needed to develop or possess four basic skills. In speeches to student groups and other audiences, I would often build my presentation around this idea. The skills or characteristics are:

1. The ability to think or analyze. The whole educational process is one that focuses on making appropriate judgments and drawing correct conclusions from information available. A manager has to be able to define problems, evaluate alternative solutions, and chart courses of action leading to desired ends. All of this involves thinking and thinking clearly.

2. The ability to communicate. The most brilliant ideas are worthless unless they can be communicated clearly and persuasively to others. The ability to express one's thoughts and ideas in writing, orally, and/or through some other medium is critical to a manager. Listening is an important part of communication.

3. The ability to relate to others – i.e. interpersonal skills. A successful leader and manager is able to engender trust and confidence from others by helping them believe they can achieve their goals by making the organization successful.

4. The ability to be there when needed – i.e. the physical and intellectual energy to be "on top of things". Woody Allen reportedly once said that "90% (or some such high percentage) of life is just showing up", being there physically and mentally when one's input is critical.

Over the course of my career as a manager, I tried to develop and to hone these skills but never felt that I perfected them. There was always room for improvement. For example, while I had to engage in public speaking often, particularly as a university president, I never felt that I was able to achieve the dynamic, spellbinding qualities that I sometimes observed in others.

While developing these skills, I began to formulate a managerial style that emanated both from my study and from my experience. One critical insight came from a seminar that I attended at Tau Kappa Epsilon headquarters. The fraternity had brought in a guest speaker named Sonny Davis to talk to the national officers and executive staff. Davis' theme was that "people support what they help create" – i.e. if you want people to work toward the goals of an organization, you need to involve them in the process of formulating those goals. I never forgot that lesson and attempted to use this strategy in every organizational setting where I worked. This approach was also very appropriate in an academic environment where consultation is highly valued. Consultation became an integral component of my style.

I came to realize the importance of listening. By the time I assumed managerial responsibilities, my listening skills had already been substantially developed and were put to good use. As a dean and a president, I found that many of the people who came to see me wanted foremost to be heard – to share their ideas or complaints. All I had to do was listen and, perhaps, ask a question or two. But they left with a feeling that their "voice" mattered and their input valued. And it did. Not only did listening help engender a feeling of inclusion in the organization but, as Yogi Berra or someone once said, "you hear a lot by listening".

The management strategy that I developed and practiced at every level of the university – from department head to president – was relatively simple. I felt that it was very important that the organization have a set of goals that were understood and supported. So I spent a lot of time at the beginning listening to individuals within the organization, learning about their needs and frustrations and what they wanted the organization to do or become. With this extensive input, I was able to articulate goals that were consistent with the desires and ambitions of the individuals in the organization. To test this assumption, the goals were shared with everyone for discussion and possible modification before being finalized.

One of the constant criticisms that I encountered from trustees, who were business executives, as well as others from outside the university, was the length of time it took to develop a plan or formulate a solution to a problem area. They seemed to have little appreciation for the value of consultation. But, within the university, efforts to secure input before a decision was made were expected. Faculty often were anxious to provide their ideas and suggestions. Some had unrealistic expectations, but having the opportunity to share their insights and participate in the process was a key factor in securing their support for the solution desired.

The second major piece of the strategy was to select the best person available for each job and to treat them like I wanted to be treated. I always responded best to a coach or supervisor who was clear about what he/she wanted accomplished, gave me the freedom to do the job as I felt was best, and provided encouragement and positive reinforcement when my performance met expectations. I did not react positively when goals or expectations were unclear or non-existent, when someone was constantly "looking over my shoulder", and when every perceived mistake was criticized and/or achievements ignored. So, in addition to organizational goals, I would ask each person who reported to me, particularly those with managerial responsibilities, to formulate objectives as to what they believed could be accomplished over a specified period. Those objectives, then, became the focus of our periodic discussions, with progress toward those objectives being the basis for the evaluation of performance. I offered praise when objectives were accomplished and tried to deal with shortcomings in private conversations. I let people do their jobs as they thought best, looking at results rather than process. Only when results fell well short of expectations did I probe into the way the work was done.

This approach or strategy did not work with everyone but the overwhelming majority of the individuals who reported to me at every level responded positively and every organization made impressive progress. And my relationship with those with whom I worked was typically strong and personal. The organizational achievements made and the positive relationships established with others, I believe, accounted for my rapid ascendancy up the ladder in higher education. There were always a few employees who took advantage of the freedom provided and did not meet expectations, leading to their reassignment or dismissal. And there were a few "mistakes" that I made in the hiring process, as individuals did not fulfill the promise they represented. But, overall, I am very pleased with the success that was achieved at every level and at every institution where I was employed.

I was fortunate that, in almost every case where I had managerial responsibilities within universities, I had a supervisor or supervisors who treated me like I wanted to be treated. They were clear about the goals of the institution and/or their expectations for the unit that I headed, gave me the freedom to do the job "my way", and were quick to provide praise when achievements occurred. As a result, I worked even harder to move the organization forward. I benefited particularly from guidance provided by mentors and supervisors like Harry Evarts at Ohio University, Herb Wey and Paul Sanders at Appalachian State, Ron Roskens at the University of Nebraska at Omaha, Art Hanson at Texas A&M, John Steinhauer and Ben Ammons at the University of Akron and Emory Cunningham at Auburn.

In my last two assignments, the situation was very difficult. At Auburn, the trustees as a group never made clear what their vision for the university was and even hampered my efforts to put a carefully conceived strategic plan in place. And, although some individual trustees were quick to praise my achievements, there was never any recognition by the board of the significant success that the university had under my leadership. These conditions, plus the frequent interference by individual trustees in the work of the university, made the job extremely frustrating. The environment at ECU was different but produced similar anxieties. In both cases, I could have elected to "go with the flow" – i.e. not have been as proactive and aggressive as I was in pursuing the goals that I had for the university – and, perhaps, reduced the conflicts that arose. But that was not the sort of leader I had been or wanted to become.

Hiring the right individuals, particularly those at managerial levels, was always a challenging task in higher education. Almost always a search committee was employed to screen and nominate candidates for consideration, with the committees becoming larger and more diverse at higher levels of administration to insure that all constituencies were represented. This process, while deemed to be necessary, had several weaknesses. First, very few of the search committee members had ever performed the job for which they were selecting candidates and, therefore, would often not know what characteristics to value. Secondly, credentials of candidates were typically over-valued. For example, a degree from or work experience at a prestigious university would often vault an individual to the top of the list. And committees sometimes had to be reminded that they were recommending finalists for consideration, not making the hiring decision; without such reminders, they would recommend the candidate they liked best, leaving the decision maker with the awkward situation of "going against" the committee's recommendation if someone else was chosen.

An example from a university that I served as business school dean might illustrate some of these factors. I was appointed to a search committee for a new dean of fine arts, being the only dean on the committee. The rest of the committee was composed of faculty from various units in that college, plus representatives from the arts community in the city. As we began to evaluate candidates for the position, I emphasized the importance of managerial experience, citing what was expected of deans within the university. Each time I raised this point, a brief silence would ensue accompanied by blank stares; then the committee would go back to discussing where the candidates went to school and what their artistic achievements had been. As a result, the final list was heavily weighted toward individuals with "stature" in their field of artistic performance and the person eventually hired was widely applauded by the fine arts faculty and arts community for these achievements. This period of euphoria lasted nearly a year; by then, however, the faculty were complaining about things that had been done or not done that were critical to their work. Eventually, the dean was moved to a faculty position and the process began anew.

Over the years in higher education, I came to realize that the academic divisions of the university rarely valued managerial expertise. Individuals were frequently selected for positions, even those with major leadership expectations, on the basis of their credentials and academic achievements. As a result, some would be quickly overcome by the managerial responsibilities and fall short of what was needed. Others, fortunately, were able to learn quickly on-the-job and perform at acceptable levels. But the focus on managerial skills was rarely the central concern.

There was, also, a frequently expressed bias against operating "like a business". Surprisingly enough, that sentiment sometimes even arose in the business school – by faculty who were teaching good business practices! Although I firmly believed that managerial practices that worked in business could and should be applied in universities as well as other organizations, I learned over time to avoid the use of business terms whenever possible. So my practice of management could be considered somewhat "subversive" – listening carefully to what people wanted, fashioning a set of goals they could accept as their own, involving them in the planning process, and recognizing and rewarding performance – moving the organization forward in a way that it seemed like it was not being managed.

As I look back over my career, I am proud of what I accomplished at every level, especially in the situations where the challenges were so significant. I think Momma, if she were alive today, would be proud of me and agree that I had become "somebody". But, I have to admit that Momma would be proud of me even if I had been a chicken farmer, as long as I was the best chicken farmer around!

The regrets that I have are the ways in which my tenure at Auburn and ECU ended. At Auburn, I could have resigned as president and moved to a faculty position, simply fading into the background. But I was too hurt by the way the trustees treated me after leading the university successfully, under very trying circumstances, to do that. The actions taken by the trustees, after I had accepted the job at ECU, were unwarranted and ill advised, resulting in much turmoil and difficulties for the university. Throughout the process, my spirits were sustained by a tremendous outpouring of affection and appreciation from every segment of the university, except the trustees.

At ECU, I still do not fully understand all the factors that were at play. The actions taken by President Broad were unexpected and, in my opinion, unnecessary. But, at that point, I was too weary and too disgusted to fight any longer. I know that at Auburn and ECU, as well as every other place I served, I worked long and hard to make the organizations stronger and more successful. And I am proud of what was accomplished in every job. That sense of inner satisfaction and the preponderance of positive experiences and wonderful memories from every location help salve the few disappointments that occurred.

As I have reflected on my career, there have been some inevitable "what ifs" – i.e. what if I have made different decisions at various points. For instance,

I have sometimes wondered what if I had stayed with my initial training and gone into business rather than higher education. Given my managerial skills, I'm confident that I would have done well, perhaps risen to a CEO position, and would have earned a lot more money than I did in higher education. But, amazingly, I do not regret that decision, as I believe the personal satisfaction I got out of the work that I did surpasses any difference in financial rewards.

I have also wondered whether it would have been better to stay in one location, rather than changing jobs as often as I did. And, certainly, my family might have benefited from such stability. Interestingly, I was recruited for each new job I took and, with the exception of Auburn, moved more for the opportunities and career advancement that the new job offered, rather than dissatisfaction with the job I was in. I suspect I may have "inherited" some wanderlust from my father or at least came to welcome frequent moves from my experience growing up. In any case, I found moving into a new environment with new challenges exciting and may have become bored after too long in one location. In fact, I stayed at Auburn (nearly ten years) longer than any other location and have often wondered if I would have been wiser to accept one of the opportunities I had to leave, rather than sticking it out. That probably would have allowed me to have a smoother transition to retirement.

But the career was what it was – one of great satisfaction and considerable achievement. The "what was" greatly exceeded the "what ifs".

A LIFE WELL LIVED

My life has been long, happy, and productive. I was fortunate to have two wonderful parents and a happy childhood. I had excellent teachers who motivated me to learn and, because of my educational achievements, earned scholarships that allowed me to finance my education throughout undergraduate and graduate school. I took advantage of the opportunities I had and enjoyed a fulfilling and enjoyable career.

Of greatest concern and value to me has been my family – a marvelous wife, three intelligent and caring children, and, now, four wonderful grandchildren. To love and be loved by one's family is the greatest of gifts. I hope that I will have an even longer life so that I can interact with my family members and watch them grow with their lives and their careers.

My relationships with other people have always been important to me. I have tried to treat people as I wanted to be treated and have valued people regardless of their position in life. I think these values and attitudes emanated from my humble beginnings and from my religious upbringing. Arrogance and self-importance are qualities that I do not respect in others and have attempted to avoid in myself. I am pleased that almost all of the people who worked for me in every location viewed me as a "real person".

I am particularly proud of the attitudes I possess and the actions I have taken in my life concerning race relations, particularly recognizing the environment in which I was raised and the time during which I grew up – rural Mississippi in the 40's and 50's. The lack of prejudice that I witnessed as a young boy was highly influenced by a father who believed and preached that we are all equal in the eyes of God and a home environment where feelings of prejudice were not expressed. I had frequent interactions with black members of the community as we picked cotton together, particularly during the times we lived in the Mississippi Delta.I accepted the fact that there were separate schools and churches for blacks and whites because that was "the way things were".

When the Civil Rights movement began to unfold in the late 50's and 60's, I was initially convinced that the unrest was a result of "outside agitators" from the North stirring up the blacks. That was the position that I heard expressed by almost every leader in the South. It was not until I was in college that I fully understood that blacks did not have the same opportunities as whites. While I did not join any protest marches or any such events, I did resolve to treat everyone fairly and equally when I had the opportunity to do so. Over the course of my career, I hired and promoted many blacks and other people of color and tried never to discriminate against anyone on the basis of characteristics over which they had no control. I am also particularly pleased with the number of females that I hired into managerial positions and supported in their career advancements.

I often heard it said that whites in the South accepted blacks as individuals but discriminated against them as a group, while whites in the North accepted blacks as a group but discriminated against them individually, largely through housing patterns and private facilities where wealth was the basis for access and acceptance. My experience would be somewhat consistent with that observation, but neither alternative is acceptable. Hopefully, one day all people will be equal not only in the eyes of God but in the eyes and actions of their fellow human beings.

I have also been able to observe the interactions between money, power and politics throughout my life, knowing and working with people of considerable wealth, those with power and those in political positions.

As a young boy, I heard a preacher talk about "money as the root of all evil". I was troubled by that admonition, as I felt having a few nickels in my pocket was very desirable, enabling me to buy a soda pop or a candy bar occasionally. I approached Daddy about my concern. He laughed, as he usually did before responding, telling me that the other preacher had it wrong. The Bible said, Daddy explained, that the <u>love</u> of money was the root of all evil, not money itself. He said that money was necessary to support a family and to buy those things that one needed to have a comfortable life. But, he added, if people love money more than anything else, they will do anything to get it and keep it, including hurting other people.

It was my observation that money meant very little to my father. He struggled all his life to support his family, but we had a wonderful life. I have certainly earned a lot more money than Daddy ever did, a result of being able to acquire a good education and a willingness to take advantage of opportunities received. But I always considered my salary more a barometer of my importance in the organization than a means to accumulate wealth. I was interested in whether my compensation compared with peers performing similar roles and, of course, whether it allowed me to support my family. Fortunately, I was able to do that and, through savings and investments, prepared for a comfortable retirement.

What I learned over my lifetime was that it was power, rather than money itself, that was the corrupting influence. I have known many wonderful people with significant wealth; in fact, I spent much of my time as a university president visiting with wealthy individuals, cultivating them for major gifts to the university. Many of these people felt lucky to be wealthy and gave away significant amounts of money to schools or charitable organizations to assist those who were less fortunate. The evils tended to come from those who used money to gain power over resources and over others. The acquisition of power – and, in the process, money – often is an unsatisfying goal because there always seems to be someone who has more of it. This then motivates one to strive for more, often hurting and abusing others to achieve that goal. A certain amount of power is a necessary asset that a leader must have to get people to work together and to achieve other worthwhile ends. But, as Lord Acton said, "power corrupts and absolute power corrupts absolutely."

One of the areas where I have seen the corrupting influence of money and power has been in politics. I have always been interested in politics or, more accurately, public affairs. I can't remember when I have not voted and, wherever we lived, I tried to become acquainted with the elected leaders and to understand the issues facing the community. As a university president, I worked with local, state, and national leaders on a regular basis. During the time I grew up in the South, everyone was a Democrat; Republicans were those who lived up North and had a lot of money! Although raised as a Democrat, I have always voted for the candidate I felt was best qualified and have worked with leaders in both parties.

Many decades ago it seemed to me that elected leaders were frequently "public servants" who tried to represent all the people. That has changed over time primarily because of the increasing cost to get elected, particularly at the statewide or national level. As a result, a politician has to raise monies from organizations and individuals of wealth. This creates a dependency relationship in which the major contributors gain greater access and influence over the public policies that are adopted. Therefore, the politician represents those who got him/her elected (and on whom he/she will depend for re-election) rather than all the people. This is a dangerous trend for our democratic form of government.

WHERE ARE YOU FROM?

Throughout my life, I have been asked the question: Where are you from? Anyone who has grown up in the South will recognize that question as the first one asked of a newcomer in that region of the country. Southerners, as Willie Morris so eloquently described in his book, <u>North Toward Home</u>, have a passionate "sense of place". Families often have deep roots in a particular location with several generations growing up in the same town, sometimes even in the same house. Where one is from (or a more personal inquiry of "who is your family?" or an even more personal query of "who is your daddy?") helps define one's station and status. A much higher percentage of residents in the Deep South, as compared to other regions of the country, have not lived outside the state or even traveled beyond its boundaries. By contrast, the most frequently asked question in other regions of the country is said to be "what do you do?" signaling that one's occupation or position is most important there.

When asked where I was from, I most often responded by naming the place where I was currently living. That answer changed a lot over time, as I moved my family to many different locations in the South and Midwest. But, increasingly, as I have gotten older, I have identified my roots in Mississippi. Even though I have not lived in that state since age fifteen, Mississippi still feels like "home", the place I am from. I enjoy the annual Muse family reunion in Mississippi every year, seeing those who have meant so much to me and being back in the places where I grew up.

WHAT ARE THE MOST IMPORTANT THINGS IN LIFE?

Well, if money, power and influence are not the most important things in life, what is? A few years ago, one of my children gave me as a Christmas gift a set of CD's entitled "This I Believe", taken from a National Public Radio program of the same name. It consisted of the testimonies of many individuals – both well-known people and just common folk – as to what they thought were the most important things in life. I was fascinated by these statements and, as a result, was motivated to write my own response:

The most important things in life, I believe, are:

1.   <u>A belief in God</u>. Such a belief provides one with a set of principles by which to live his life, as well as a promise of a reward at the end of one's life for adhering to those principles. Letting the Holy Spirit into one's life produces a peacefulness and concern for others that gives life meaning and purpose.

2.   <u>The Love of a Family</u>. A family is a place where one is loved and cared for and where those feelings can be returned. A family does not have to be just a "mother, father, child" combination but can be composed of grandparents, aunts or uncles, foster parents or individuals of the same or different genders. The important ingredient is the love that is shared.

3.   <u>The Desire to Learn</u>. The desire to learn is important, not only to the individual who has the opportunity to develop his/her intellectual talents and use them in productive ways, but also to our society in general. The wisdom that is the product of what past generations have learned from their experiences becomes the foundation for the following generation to build upon, expanding the body of knowledge and how it can be applied.

4.   <u>The Compassion to Serve</u>. As humans, it is important that we have concern for others and be willing to respond to those needs in ways that are meaningful and relevant to us. The central message of Jesus was to love our neighbor and to have compassion for those who are less fortunate. Unless those feelings are present in our lives and in our society, greed and callousness will come to dominate our relationships with others.

I have tried to live my life in a way that these values and beliefs were given centrality. My belief in God has undergone many stages of development but remains strong. The love of my family has always been important. The desire to learn has defined my whole career, enabling me to advance in knowledge and to help others do likewise. And the compassion to serve has been a continuing quest.

Wherever we have lived, I have been involved in the community in a variety of capacities and organizations – Chambers of Commerce, United Way, Salvation Army, etc. I have been a member of Rotary Clubs in seven different cities. Marlene has been even more involved in various locations in organizations like Habitat for Humanity and Boys and Girls Club and presently serves on the board of the Fuller Center for Housing, established by the founders of Habitat for Humanity. Together we have and continue to contribute to many national and local causes that serve human needs.

My brother, Clyde, and I have frequently talked about how Daddy wanted each of us to follow him into the ministry. We each chose, instead, the field of education. I don't feel that there is any function in our society that is more important than education. Helping individuals acquire the knowledge and skills they need to have a productive career and the insights that can lead to a life of meaning and purpose is without equal in its importance to those individuals and to society at large. I believe that both Clyde and I, while not following in his footsteps, have fulfilled Daddy's dream of a life of service to others.

These remarks are written not to advocate a particular path that one should travel. Each person has to find his/her own way. But each of us needs to listen to those who precede us and consider what they have learned in order to better prepare for the journey that lies ahead.

LaVergne, TN USA
31 March 2010
177664LV00002B/11/P